Understanding Media Economics

D1627834

Understanding Media Economics

Second Edition

Gillian Doyle

Los Angeles | London | New Delhi
Singapore | Washington DC

Los Angeles | London | New Delhi
Singapore | Washington DC

SAGE Publications Ltd
1 Oliver's Yard
55 City Road
London EC1Y 1SP

SAGE Publications Inc.
2455 Teller Road
Thousand Oaks, California 91320

SAGE Publications India Pvt Ltd
B 1/I 1 Mohan Cooperative Industrial Area
Mathura Road
New Delhi 110 044

SAGE Publications Asia-Pacific Pte Ltd
3 Church Street
#10-04 Samsung Hub
Singapore 049483

Editor: Mila Steele
Editorial assistant: James Piper
Production editor: Imogen Roome
Copyeditor: Rose James
Proofreader: Sharika Sharma
Marketing manager: Michael Ainsley
Cover design: Jennifer Crisp
Typeset by: C&M Digitals (P) Ltd, Chennai, India
Printed in Great Britain by MPG Printgroup, UK

Library of Congress Control Number: 2012949459

British Library Cataloguing in Publication data

A catalogue record for this book is available from
the British Library

MIX
Paper from
responsible sources
FSC
www.fsc.org   FSC® C018575

ISBN 978-1-4129-3076-5
ISBN 978-1-4129-3077-2 (pbk)

To Jenny and Finn

Contents

Illustrations

FIGURES

TABLES

Preface

Despite the traditional predominance of sociology and political science within studies of media and communications, interest in economic aspects of media has grown enormously over recent years. One important factor underlining the relevance of economics has been the so-called digital revolution and its effect in reshaping businesses and provision across the media while, at the same time, presenting new challenges for policy-makers. Digitization has helped propel economic questions – for example, related to the impact of convergence, exploitation of digital rights, support for content production, globalized competition and international trade – ever more firmly onto the agenda of mainstream studies of media and communications.

As the application of economic theories and concepts to all aspects of media has grown in popularity and status over recent years, so too has the need for suitable texts to support learning and teaching in this area. This was the inspiration behind the first edition of *Understanding Media Economics* published in 2002. However, the decade which has elapsed since then has been a time of considerable change and, to some extent, of upheaval for media industries and markets. New technologies, changing consumption behaviours and greater competition have impacted significantly on the organization and economics of media and this has created a need for a fresh analytical approach to questions and themes that, in the digital era, are essential to an understanding of the economics of the contemporary media industries.

In line with the rapidly evolving digital media landscape, this second and fully revised edition of *Understanding Media Economics* moves beyond the convention of a sector-specific approach to analysis of media economics, and instead offers a framework focused on key themes and imperatives that, in the twenty-first century, are central to a grasp of how economic forces impact on the operation of media industries. It explores a series of topics of relevance to the economics of media – such as innovation, digital multi-platform developments, economics of networks, the impact of two-way connectivity on market demand, risk-spreading strategies, copyright, corporate expansion, advertising – whose resonance frequently extends beyond individual sectors and across the industry as a whole. The general aim is to open up to non-specialists in economics the many fascinating economic traits and pressing industrial policy questions surrounding media industries and markets in the digital era.

Thanks are due to the numerous students who have undertaken my courses in media economics at the University of Glasgow, the University of Oslo and elsewhere, and to a range of leading industry speakers and interviewees whose generous engagement has helped shape and enrich the approach taken in preparing this book. I should also like to express thanks to my colleague Professor Philip Schlesinger for wisdom and support over many years. Thanks too to Julia Hall at Sage who commissioned the first edition of the book, and to Mila Steele who has been a tremendous support in enabling production of this second edition.

1

Introduction

The study of communications and of media has traditionally been dominated by non-economic disciplines. Analysis of dominant representations in the media, for example, provides a means of understanding the societies in which we live and our value systems. But economics is also a valuable subject area for media scholars. Most of the decisions taken by those who run media organizations are, to a greater or lesser extent, influenced by resource and financial issues. So economics, as a discipline, is highly relevant to understanding how media firms and industries operate.

This book provides an introduction to some of the main economic concepts and issues affecting the media. It is designed for readers who are not specialists in economics but who want to acquire the tools needed to unravel some of the more interesting economic features and pressing industrial policy questions surrounding media firms and markets. No prior knowledge of economics is assumed.

The first three chapters explain a number of broad and fundamental concepts relevant to the study of economics as it affects the media. This opening chapter introduces you to firms and markets and examines the distinctive economic characteristics of media. Chapter 2 examines the organization of media industries and how firms are adjusting to the immense changes brought on by digitization and convergence. Chapter 3 focuses on the relationship between the distinctive economic characteristics of media, changing market conditions and the corporate strategies that are commonly deployed by media firms.

These initial chapters are followed by six others, each of which explores dimensions of supplying media that are of special importance to understanding the economics of media, e.g. consumer behaviour and market demand, networks and network effects, content production and risk-spreading strategies, copyright and the role of advertising in two-sided media markets. These six chapters establish a framework within which, for each theme, two or three of the main economic concepts or questions that are commonly associated with or best exemplified by that topic may be examined more closely. So, the structure of the book enables a series of economic themes and questions relevant to the media to be gradually and progressively opened up and explored. The final chapter of the book examines the increasingly important role media economics can play in informing public policy questions.

After studying this opening chapter, you should be able to:

- identify the kinds of questions that media economics seeks to address;
- explain what a firm is and its motivations;
- describe the different types of competitive market structures which exist;
- understand what is special about the economics of the media;
- identify and explain some of the key economic characteristics of the media.

WHAT IS MEDIA ECONOMICS ABOUT?

Media economics seeks to combine the study of economics with the study of media. It is concerned with the changing economic forces that direct and constrain the choices of managers, practitioners and other decision-makers across the media. The economic concepts and issues introduced in the course of this book provide a basis for developing your understanding of the way in which media businesses operate and are managed.

Some attempts have been made to formalize a definition of media economics. Economics has been described as 'the study of how people make choices to cope with scarcity' (Parkin, Powell and Matthews, 2008: 4). Scarcity is a familiar concept for most, and we are all economists to the extent that we have to decide how to make the best of our limited incomes or resources. According to Robert Picard, media economics 'is concerned with how media operators meet the informational and entertainment wants and needs of audiences, advertisers and society with available resources' (1989: 7). It is about applying economic theory 'to explain the workings of media industries and firms' (Picard, 2006: 15). Albarran likewise describes media economics as involving the application of economic ideas and principles to study 'macroeconomic and microeconomic aspects of mass media companies and industries' (2004: 291).

Media economics, then, is concerned with a range of issues including international trade, business strategy, segmentation, risk-spreading, exploitation of rights, pricing policies, evolution of advertising markets, competition and industrial concentration as they affect the media firms and industries. These themes are explored in the chapters of this book. The predominant focus is 'microeconomic' (i.e. to do with specific individual markets or firms), but some of the questions addressed also have a macroeconomic dimension.

MACROECONOMICS AND MICROECONOMICS

The distinction between macro-and microeconomics is about whether that which is being studied involves either large groups and broad economic aggregates or small well-defined groups and individual firms and sectors. Macroeconomics is concerned with very broad economic aggregates and averages, such as total output, total employment, national income, the general price level and the rate of growth of the economy as a whole. These sorts of aggregates are arrived at by summing up the activities carried out in all individual markets and by summarizing the collective behaviour of all individuals.

One of the most commonly used measures of a nation's overall level of economic activity is called its gross domestic product (GDP). A country's GDP represents the sum of the value of all goods and services produced within the economy over a particular period, usually a year. Media goods and services represent a small but growing proportion of total economic activity in developed countries and in the UK, for example, they account for some 3–5 per cent of GDP. Many sectors of the media (e.g. television production, publishing) count as 'creative' industries which are regarded as especially important in driving growth in the wider economy (Andari et al., 2007).

In the UK, the long-term trend in GDP since the Second World War has generally been upwards and this, in turn, has facilitated a substantial increase in living standards. Within this overall growth trend, a second feature of movements in GDP has been short-term fluctuations around the trend. Rather than growing at a steady and consistent pace, economies tend to move in a series of irregular up and down 'business cycles' which are characterized by five phases: growth, peak, recession, trough and recovery.

The overall performance of the economy has important implications for the business performance and prospects of firms in all sectors, including media. Indeed, the fortunes of most media firms are highly sensitive to the ups and downs of the economy as a whole. As will be discussed below, many media firms rely on advertising as a primary source of income. Despite recent divergences, analysis of long-term trends in advertising suggest a strong association between the performance of the economy as a whole and levels of advertising activity. Revenues for media firms from direct expenditure by consumers are also clearly dependent on broader economic aggregates such as levels of disposable income and consumer confidence.

In theory, public policies towards the economy (monetary, fiscal etc.), and policies to promote or restrain growth or social welfare may have an affect on the economic environment in which media firms and industries operate. For example, government control over the supply of money and over interest rates provides a means of influencing levels of investment and economic activity in general (Baumol and Blinder, 2011). However, it may be argued that the power of state authorities to exert such influence is waning. 'Globalization' means that it is increasingly difficult for open economies to predicate monetary and other economic policies on domestic considerations alone.

Whereas macroeconomics is about forces that affect the economy as a whole, microeconomics is concerned with the analysis of individual markets, products and firms. An economy is a mechanism that determines 'what, how and for whom goods and services get produced' (Parkin, Powell and Matthews, 2008: 6). These decisions are taken by three types of economic actors – consumers, firms and governments – and are co-ordinated in what are called 'markets'. Economics relies on certain assumptions about how these actors make their choices.

Each consumer, for example, is seen as having unlimited wants and limited resources. It is assumed that all consumers seek to maximize their total 'utility' or satisfaction. 'Marginal' utility represents the change in satisfaction resulting from consuming a little more or a little less of a given product. The law of diminishing marginal utility suggests that the more of a given product that an individual consumes, the less satisfaction they will derive from successive units of the product. The example used by Lipsey and Chrystal to illustrate this principle shows that, everything else being equal, the more films a consumer attends each month, the more satisfaction they get. However, the marginal utility of each additional film per month is less than that of the previous one – i.e. marginal utility declines as quantity consumed rises (1995: 128–9).

THE FIRM IN ECONOMIC THEORY

In economics, production is an activity that involves conversion of resources or inputs (e.g. raw materials, ideas, knowledge) into outputs (goods and services). 'Firms' are establishments where production is carried out and industries consist of a number of firms producing a commodity for the same market. The concept of a media firm spans a variety of different types of business organizations; from the online fanzine publisher to the vast television corporation, and from single proprietorship to major transnational stock exchange listed companies. What all media firms have in common is that they are involved somehow in producing, packaging or distributing media content.

All media firms are not, however, commercial organizations. Most countries have a state-owned broadcasting entity which takes the form of a public corporation and which is dedicated to 'public service' television and radio broadcasting. Many public service broadcasters (PSBs) rely on public funding (e.g. grants) but some depend, in part or in whole, on revenues derived from commercial activities such as sale of airtime to advertisers. Even when they compete for revenues from commercial sources, PSBs are usually distinguished from commercial firms by the fact that their primary goal is to provide a universally available public broadcasting service rather than to make profits.

By contrast, it is assumed that a commercial firm's every decision is taken in order to maximize its profits. The assumption that all firms seek to maximize profits is central to the neoclassical theory of the firm. It allows economists to predict the behaviour of firms by studying the effect that each of the choices available to it would have on its profits.

However, there are two commonly cited criticisms of the traditional theory of the firm, and both are relevant to media. The first suggests that it is too crude and simplistic to assume that businesses are motivated purely by pursuit of profits. The case for profit maximization on the part of business owners is thought to be self-evident but, in fact, some are undoubtedly motivated by alternative goals. These range from straightforward philanthropy to the desire for specific benefits associated with owning certain types of businesses. An alternative motivation – especially in the case of media firms – might well be the pursuit of public and political influence.

A second criticism is that the theory assumes that all firms will behave in the same way, irrespective of their size and organizational structure. In reality, a firm's institutional structure may have an important bearing on its priorities. Rupert Murdoch's involvement in the running of News Corporation shows how some media firms are closely managed by their owners. The dominant form of industrial organization these days is the public limited company (or plc) under which, more typically, the day-to-day running of the firm is carried out not by the owners (or shareholders) but by managers.

When ownership and control of an organization are separate, its managers may decide to pursue goals other than maximising profits and returns to shareholders. This conflict of interest is referred to as a type of 'principal–agent' problem. The managers appointed to run a media firm (agents) may not always act in the manner desired by shareholders (principals) but might, instead, have their own agendas to pursue. When the agent's goal is allowed to predominate then pursuit of profits may be superceded by, for example, a desire to maximize sales revenue or the firm's growth.

There are good grounds for questioning how well the broad assumptions of conventional economic theory apply in practice to the behaviour of media firms. Even so, to the extent that economic actors (firms and households) make their decisions in a 'rational' manner and in pursuit of what are assumed to be their own individual goals (of, respectively, profit and utility maximization), there is clearly an important role for government to play in creating a regulatory environment within which these individual goals are not achieved at the expense of societal welfare (Owers, Carveth and Alexander, 2002: 17). The issue of supplying violent media content provides an example of an economic activity that maximizes the goal attainment of individual economic units (i.e. it contributes to the success and profitability of film and television programme-makers) but, arguably, may detract from overall social welfare (ibid.).

A firm's profits are the difference between its revenues and costs. Costs in economic theory refer to all 'opportunity costs', a concept that involves recognizing whatever benefit must be foregone or sacrificed when choosing to use a resource in one particular way rather than another. The opportunity cost of the inputs used to produce something is the value of the goods and services that otherwise could have obtained from those same inputs if they were put to their next-best alternative use (Allen et al., 2005: 326). So, as well as assigning costs to purchased or hired inputs, an 'imputed' cost must also be calculated for and assigned to any factors of production owned by the firm, especially the firm's own capital.

The concept of opportunity cost is important in economics. Our resources can be used in many different ways to produce different outcomes but, essentially, they are finite. All of the land, labour and capital that is available to us will be relatively more efficient in some activities rather than others. Opportunity cost is inevitable and requires firms to make trade-offs. The most productive outcome will be achieved when every worker, piece of land and item of capital equipment is allocated to the task that suits it best (i.e. the one that results in the most productive outcome).

For example, if we want more new and inventive media-related software apps and fewer computer games, we might switch some of the creative, marketing and administrative personnel and the computing and IT expertise and equipment, etc. involved in producing computer games into publishing apps instead. However, because game inventors may be less good at creating apps than dedicated apps inventors, the quantity of marketable apps produced is likely to increase by a relatively small amount while the quantity of computer games produced falls considerably. Similarly, app inventors can be reassigned to the task of producing online computer games but, because they are not as good at this activity as the people who currently make games, there will be an opportunity cost in terms of lost output. The opportunity cost of switching resources from computer games to app creation (or from apps to games) can be calculated as the number of games that must be given up in order to produce more apps (or vice versa).

In order to maximize profits, firms need to decide which overall rate of output would be most profitable (e.g. whether to produce 100,000 or 200,000 copies of a periodical). To do so, they need to know exactly what costs and revenues might be associated with different levels of output. The so-called 'production function' describes the relationship between input costs and different levels of output. Changes in relative factor prices (of labour, capital equipment, etc.) will cause a replacement of factors that have become relatively more expensive by cheaper ones. For example, the introduction of computing and desktop publishing technologies in the 1980s and 1990s reduced capital equipment costs and allowed a reduction in costly labour inputs associated with production such as typesetting etc., thus enabling a reorganization within print publishing industries. Another example of factor substitution, this time in the audiovisual sector, was the switch towards production of animated movies in response to a period a 'escalating salaries' among movie stars in the early twenty-first century (Hoskins, McFayden and Finn, 2004: 92).

'Marginal product' is the change in total product (or the total amount produced by the firm) that results from adding a little bit more or a little less of a variable input to a fixed input. The law of diminishing returns suggests that if extra quantities of a variable factor (e.g. freelance technicians) are applied to a given quantity of a fixed factor (e.g. plant and equipment), the marginal and average product of the variable factor will eventually decrease. Hoskins, McFayden and Finn offer the example of a small company that produces DVDs (the 'output') using a machine designed to be operated by three people (whose labour represents the 'input'). Productivity increases as the number of people operating the machine increases from one to three. Thereafter, however, the onset of diminishing returns occurs because, as more personnel are added and the use of production equipment has to be shared, the efficiency and productivity of each machine operator begins to reduce (2004: 87).

However, contrary to what is implied by the law of diminishing returns, many media firms tend to enjoy increasing rather than diminishing marginal returns as their output (or, rather, consumption of it) increases. The explanation for increasing returns to scale in the media industry lies in the nature of the product and how it is consumed. The value of media content lies not in the paper that it is printed on or the ink or videotape that conveys its text or images but in the meanings, messages or stories that it has to offer – its intellectual property. This is an intangible and costs virtually no more to reproduce in large than in small quantities. The cost of producing a television programme or a film is not affected by the number of people who watch it. So, for media firms, the relationship between input costs and different levels of output tends to be skewed positively by the availability of increasing returns to scale.

COMPETITIVE MARKET STRUCTURES

As discussed above, the production function describes how costs vary at different levels of output. Firms that wish to maximize profits are not only concerned with costs but also need to know what revenues are associated with different levels of output. To a large extent, this depends on what sort of competitive market structure a firm finds itself operating in.

Economic theory offers us a model for analysing the different sorts of structures a market can have and the degree of competition between firms in that market. The competitive market structures within which media operate will have an important bearing on how efficiently media firms organize their resources and business affairs. The main theoretical market structures are perfect and imperfect competition (i.e. monopolistic competition and oligopoly) and monopoly. The distinction between these structures is largely dictated by the number of rival producers or sellers in a given market. This is important because it is an indication of the 'market power' that individual firms possess and their ability to control and influence the economic operations in that market (e.g. to set prices). The less market power that individual firms have, the more competitive the market structure in which they operate.

The structure of a market depends not only on the number of rival sellers that exist but on a variety of other factors, including differences in their product, the number of buyers that are present and barriers to the entry of new competitors. Perfect competition and monopoly are at opposite extremes. In perfect competition, markets are highly competitive and open, and each firm has zero market power. In monopoly, a single firm has absolute control over the market. Most firms tend to operate in some intermediate market structure rather than at the extremes.

Perfect competition exists when there are many sellers of a good or service that is homogeneous (i.e. exactly the same or not differentiated) and no firm(s) dominate(s) the market. In such a situation economic forces operate freely. Each firm is assumed to be a price-taker and the industry is characterized by freedom of entry and exit. So, under perfect competition, no barriers to entry exist – i.e. there are no obstacles (e.g. lack of available spectrum, or high initial capital costs) to prevent new rivals from entering the market if they wish. Monopoly, at the other extreme, involves just one seller, no competition whatsoever and (usually) high entry barriers.

It is very rare to find an example of perfect competition in the real world. Most industries, including the media, sell 'differentiated' products, i.e. products that are similar enough to constitute a single group (e.g. books) but are sufficiently different for consumers to distinguish one from another. In other words, they may be close substitutes but are not exact substitutes, as would be the case in perfect competition. Monopolistic competition exists when there are a number of sellers of similar goods or services, but the products are differentiated and each product is available only from the firm that produces it. Firms thus have some control over their prices.

If there are only a few sellers in a market but some competition exists for their products, either homogeneous or differentiated, the market structure is described as oligopoly. How few is 'a few'? The most usual method of measuring the degree of oligopoly in a market is by applying a 'concentration ratio'. These measures show the proportion of, say, output or employment or revenue accounted for by the top four or top eight firms in the sector. Another measure of market concentration is the Herfindahl–Hirschman Index (HHI) which measures the percentage market share of all firms in an industry to provide a rough guide as to levels of competition (Fisher, Prentice and

Waschik, 2010: 175–6). In the media sector, concentration levels can be calculated on the basis of audience shares (as defined by ratings or readership figures). According to Lipsey and Chrystal, in an oligopoly 'each firm has enough market power to prevent it from being a price-taker, but each firm is subject to enough inter-firm rivalry to prevent it from considering the market demand curve as its own' (2007: 188). So, in an oligopoly situation, firms have a greater degree of control over the market than in a monopolistic competition.

Oligopoly is the most common type of market structure in which media firms operate. Chapter 3 addresses the question of why it is that so many sectors of the media are dominated by a few large firms. In many cases, the answer is to be found in falling costs due to the economies of large-scale production. Economies of scale are prevalent in the media because the industry is characterized by high initial production costs and low marginal reproduction and distribution costs. Economies of scope – economies achieved through multi-product production – are also commonly characteristic of media enterprises. So, there are major advantages of large size for firms that operate in the media industry.

The theory of imperfect competition says that cost advantages associated with size will dictate that an industry be an oligopoly unless some form of market intervention or government regulation prevents the firms from growing to their most efficient size. If no such intervention takes place, existing firms in the industry may create barriers to entry where natural ones do not exist so that the industry will be dominated by a handful of large firms only because they are successful in preventing the entry of new firms. But substantial economies of scale in any industry will, in themselves, act as a natural barrier to entry in that any new firms will usually be smaller than established firms and so will be at a cost disadvantage.

MARKET STRUCTURE AND BEHAVIOUR

The expectation that the behaviour or conduct of firms may be determined by the market structures within which they operate is formalized in what is called the structure–conduct–performance (SCP) paradigm first propounded by Joe Bain (1951). The SCP paradigm suggests that market structure (i.e. the number of firms, barriers to entry, etc.) will determine how the firms in an industry behave (e.g. their policies on pricing and advertising) and this conduct will, in turn, determine the performance of the industry in question – i.e. its productive efficiency (Moschandreas, 2000: 7). This model implies that the fewer firms in a market, the greater the likelihood of collusion, anti-competitive strategies and other inefficiencies.

While empirical studies often demonstrate some sort of link between structure and performance, the SCP approach is recognized as having limitations because there is 'simultaneity in relationships' between structure, conduct and performance (ibid.; Martin, 2002). Recent theoretical work suggests that firms in monopoly and oligopoly are not always prone to inefficient behaviour and that contextual factors other than competitive market structure will have a bearing on the performance of firms (Tremblay, 2012: 85). Most notably, the theory of market contestability, as developed by US economists William Baumol, John Panzar and Robert D. Willig, suggests that the very fact that a market is potentially open to a new entrant will serve to contain the behaviour of monopolists – i.e. market contestability prevents the exploitation of market power to restrict output and to raise prices (Lipsey and Chrystal, 2007: 198).

Game theoretic approaches, which have become more popular in mainstream economics, place emphasis on how the performance of firms can be determined by their own decisions and their interactions with other market players. Game theory modelling involves building and testing assumptions about how firms will behave in strategic interactions so as to maximize their own self-interest (Allen et al., 2005: 570). The formalities of mathematical game theory have only sparingly being adopted (mostly in relation to modelling programming strategies) as a guiding framework for the analyses of media (Wildman, 2006: 85). However, interdependence between firms is a recognized aspect of oligopoly markets – the prevalent market structure for media. Given that 'the behaviour of oligopolists can be seen as akin to that of a strategic game' (Moschandreas, 2000: 169), it is not surprising that many studies of economics of media, while drawing the traditional frameworks of industrial organization, also involve some conjectural analysis in relation to the behaviour and responses of rivals. How media firms behave, in practice, under different market structures and circumstances is a concern for many media economists (Picard, 2006; Wildman, 2006; Wirth and Bloch, 1995) and will be a subject of interest throughout this book.

WHAT IS SO SPECIAL ABOUT ECONOMICS OF THE MEDIA?

Because media and other 'cultural' output have special qualities not shared by other products and services, the application of economic theory and economic perspectives in the context of media present a variety of challenges. Media output seems to defy the very premise on which the laws of economics are based – scarcity. However much a film, a song or a news story is consumed, it does not get used up.

Economics seeks to promote 'efficiency' in the allocation of resources. The notion of economic efficiency is inextricably tied up with objectives, but the objectives of media organizations tend to vary widely. Many media organizations comply with the classical theory of the firm and, like commercial entities in any other industry, are primarily geared towards maximizing profits and satisfying shareholders. A good number, however, appear to be driven by alternative motives. For those who operate in the public service sector, quality of output and other 'public service'-type objectives form an end in themselves. Some broadcasting firms find themselves between the market and the non-market sector – appearing to fulfil one set of objectives for an industry regulator and another set for shareholders. Because objectives are hazy, the application of any all-embracing model based in conventional economic theory is difficult.

In free-market economies, most decisions concerning resource allocation are made through the price system. The relationship between price and resource allocation in the media is somewhat unusual, particularly in broadcasting where, notwithstanding growth in subscription-based television services, it remains the case that many of the services consumers receive do not involve a direct payment from the viewer. Without price as a direct link between consumers and producers, there is a failure in the usual means of registering consumer preferences with suppliers.

In terms of economics, production methods are said to be inefficient if it would be possible to produce more of at least one commodity – without simultaneously producing less of another – by merely reallocating resources. However, when it comes to the production of media output, this approach begins to look inadequate. For example, it might well be possible for a television company to redistribute its resources so as to produce more hours of programming output or bigger audiences for the same cost as before. But if, at the same time, this were to narrow the diversity of media output, could it be said to be a more efficient use of resources?

These questions about the efficiency of production and allocation belong to the branch of economic theory called welfare economics. Much of the work that has been carried out in the UK in relation to broadcasting economics and associated public policy issues – most notably by Alan Peacock and, more recently, by Gavyn Davies and others – belongs to this area. Implicit in this approach is the assumption that a social welfare function (i.e. a functional relation showing the maximum welfare that can be generated by alternative resource decisions) can be defined for society as a whole. Within such a conceptual framework, media economics can play a role in showing how to minimize the welfare loss associated with any policy choices surrounding media provision.

KEY ECONOMIC CHARACTERISTICS OF THE MEDIA

A good way of getting to grips with what is special about media economics is to consider the characteristics of media that distinguish it from other areas of economic activity. One such feature is that media firms often operate in what Picard has called 'dual product' markets (1989: 17–19) or what can be understood as 'two-sided markets' – two-sided in the sense that media firms simultaneously produce two different commodities which, in turn, can be sold to separate and distinct user groups (Rochet and Tirole, 2003). The two different outputs that media firms generate are, first, content (i.e. television programmes, newspaper copy, magazine articles, etc.) and, second, audiences. The entertainment or news content that listeners, viewers or readers 'consume' constitutes one saleable form of output. The audiences that have been attracted by this content constitute a second valuable output, insofar as access to audiences can be packaged, priced and sold to advertisers.

Audiences are the main currency for many media companies, because these provide advertising revenue which, as later chapters will discuss, is a primary source of income for commercial television and radio broadcasters, online media service providers and newspapers and magazine publishers. Even non-profit-seeking media organizations are concerned with audiences. Public service broadcasters, for example, must pay close attention to their ratings and the demographic profile of their audience because the audience utility or satisfaction they can demonstrate is normally central to negotiations surrounding what level of funding, whether public or otherwise, is made available to them.

The other type of media output – i.e. content – exhibits a number of interesting and unusual features, as have been noted by, for example, Blumler and Nossiter (1991) and Collins, Garnham and Locksley (1988: 7–10). Media content is generally classified as a 'cultural' good. Feature films, television broadcasts, books and music are not merely commercial products but may also be appreciated for the ways they enrich our cultural environment. Many cultural goods share the quality that their value for consumers is symbolic and tied up with the information or messages they convey, rather than with the material carrier of that information (i.e. the radio spectrum, the digital file and so on). Messages and meanings are, of course, intangible and, to that extent, do not get used up. So, like other information goods, media content is not 'consumable' in the purest sense of this term (Albarran, 2002: 28; Withers, 2006: 5)

It is sometimes difficult to define what constitutes a unit of media content. This could describe, for example, a story, an article, a television programme, an entire newspaper or a radio channel. One way or another, the essential quality that audiences get value from is meanings, which are not, in themselves, material objects. Because the value of media content is generally to do with attributes that are immaterial, it does not get used up or destroyed in the act of consumption. If one person watches a television broadcast, it doesn't diminish someone else's opportunity of viewing it. Because it is not used up as it is consumed, the same content can be supplied over and over again to additional consumers.

So, television and radio broadcasts exhibit one of the key features of being a 'public good'. Other cultural goods such as works of art also qualify as public goods because the act of consumption by one individual does not reduce its supply to others. Public goods contrast with normal or private goods in that private goods (e.g. a loaf of bread, jar of honey or pint of Guinness) *will* get used up as they are consumed. As soon as one person consumes a loaf of bread, it will no longer be available to anyone else. So, a loaf of bread can only be sold once. But when an idea or a story is sold, the seller still possesses it and can sell it over and over again.

The consumption of private goods uses up scarce resources and therefore needs to be rationed (usually by the market and by prices). Public goods do not comply with this logic. The initial cost involved in creating a public good may be high but then the marginal costs associated with supplying an extra unit of it are next to zero. The marginal cost involved in conveying a television or radio programme service to an extra viewer or listener within one's transmission reach is typically zero, at least for terrestrial broadcasters. Likewise, the marginal cost of providing an online media content service to one additional Internet user is negligible. Although producing a new book, music recording or feature film typically involves a heavy investment of 'sunk costs' (Van Kranenburg and Hogenbirk, 2006: 334), it then costs relatively little and sometimes nothing to reproduce and supply it to extra customers. So, increasing marginal returns will be enjoyed as the audience for any given media product expands.

Conversely, there are relatively few savings available for media firms when audiences contract. In most other industries, producers can vary some of their costs up and down in response to how much of their product is being sold (e.g. they can cut back on purchases of raw materials if demand slows down). For broadcasters, however, the cost of putting together and transmitting a programme service of given performance characteristics is fixed, irrespective of how many viewers tune in or fail to tune in. The same is true for Web-based media suppliers – lack of uptake will not affect the costs necessitated in producing a site and its content. Similarly, few savings can be made by newspaper and other print media publishers when circulations fail to live up to expectations (albeit that, unlike in broadcasting and electronic publishing, marginal print and distribution costs can be significant).

The presence of risk counts as another distinctive feature of media and other creative industries (Caves, 2000). Creating the initial copy of a television programme or another media product is often very expensive but, at the same time, the media industry is characterized by high levels of uncertainty about demand – which content properties will make a 'hit' with popular taste and which will not. The need for strategies to counteract risk, which often exert a significant influence over how media organize themselves and their activities, is another theme that will be explored in the later chapters of this book.

ECONOMIES OF SCALE

Economies of scale, then, are a highly prevalent feature of the media industry. They will be mentioned and discussed frequently throughout this book, so it is worth clarifying what is meant by the term. Economies of scale are said to exist in any industry where marginal costs are lower than average costs. When the cost of providing an extra unit of a good falls as the scale of output expands, then economies of scale are present. This is summarized by the function coefficient (FC) which measures the average cost (AC) to marginal cost (MC):

$$FC = \frac{AC}{MC}$$

Many industries experience economies of scale, especially those engaged in manufacturing (e.g. of cars) where larger production runs and automated assembly line techniques lead to ever lower average production costs. A variety of reasons may explain why economies of scale are present. For example, sometimes it is because large firms can achieve better (bulk) discounts on required inputs than smaller firms can. Often, economies of scale are to do with the benefits of specialization and division of labour that are possible within large firms.

Economies of scale exist in the media because of the public good attributes of the industry's product. For media firms, marginal costs (MC) refer to the cost of supplying a product or service to one extra consumer. Average costs (AC) are the total costs involved in providing the product or service, divided by its audience – i.e. the total number of users who watch, read, listen to or otherwise consume it. In most sectors of the media, marginal costs tend to be low and, in some cases, they are zero. Marginal costs are virtually always lower than average costs. Consequently, as more viewers tune in or more users visit a content service website or more readers purchase a copy of a magazine, the average costs to the firm of supplying that commodity will be lowered. If average production costs go down as the scale of consumption of the firm's output increases, then economies of scale and higher profits will be enjoyed.

ECONOMIES OF SCOPE

Economies of scope are also to do with making savings and gaining efficiencies as more of a firm's output is consumed. In this case, however, savings are created by offering variations in the character or scope of the firm's output. Economies of scope – economies achieved through multi-product production – are commonly characteristic of media enterprises and, again, this is to do with the public good nature of media output.

Economies of scope refer to the savings and cost-efficiencies made possible 'by simultaneous production of many products by one firm' (Baumol and Blinder, 2011: 267). Such economies will be present if large-scale multi-product production and distribution enables a firm to supply goods more cheaply than would be the case were each good being supplied separately by individual firms. Economies of scope arise when there are some shared overheads, or other efficiency gains available that make it more cost-effective for two or more related products to be produced and sold jointly, rather than separately. Savings may arise, for example, if specialist inputs gathered for one product can be reused in another.

Economies of scope are common within the media because the nature of media output is such that it is possible for a product created for one market to be reformatted and sold through another. For example, an interview with a politician which is recorded for broadcast within a documentary might also be edited for inclusion within other news programmes, either on television or, indeed, on radio. The same television content can be repackaged into more than one product. And the reformatting of a product intended for one audience into another 'new' product suitable for a different audience creates economies of scope.

Assuming economies of scope are present, the benefits available through a reduction in costs (C) for a multi-product firm producing, say, good A and good B can be described by the following mathematical equation:

$$C (A,B) < C(0,A) + C(B,0)$$

Whenever economies of scope are available to be exploited, diversification will be an economically efficient strategy because 'the total cost of the diversified firm is low compared with a group of single-product firms producing the same output' (Moschandreas, 2000: 102). Strategies of diversification are increasingly common among media firms and this reflects the availability of economies of scope which, thanks to digitization, have become even more widespread. Economies of scope and scale are important characteristics of the economics of media and these concepts will be developed and exemplified in later chapters.

CHANGING TECHNOLOGY

Media industries are heavily reliant on technology and as such are regularly affected by new advances in how media may be produced or distributed. Each major evolutionary step – from the invention of the printing press, to the arrival of broadcasting, to the spread of the Internet – has brought both upheaval and opportunity for market incumbents. Thus, media firms are no strangers to the so-called 'gales of creative destruction' discussed further in Chapter 2.

Digitization has unquestionably had a transformative impact on media industries and markets. The spread of digital distribution methods has both increased the volume of media content offerings in circulation and fragmented audiences, thus shifting the emphasis of scarcity within the media supply chain away from content and delivery and towards capturing audience attention. As digital convergence and growth of the Internet have eroded traditional boundaries and reshaped media markets and modes of consumption, the advent of greater competition, the necessity for organizational adjustment and the unraveling of conventional revenue strategies have posed new challenges for media suppliers. At the same time, the transition to digital delivery platforms has brought with it a host of commercial and creative possibilities.

Content producers have also been profoundly affected by recent technological change. Digitization has affected production costs and facilitated the introduction of automated content management systems which enable more efficient exploitation and management of content assets. But it has also introduced new hazards, including the greater threat of intermediation, i.e. lifting and reassembling of online content, and other 'free rider' problems.

Throughout this book, great emphasis is placed on understanding the economic significance of digital developments. However, it is worth bearing in mind that, despite changing technology and widening market access, many aspects of the economics of content provision – e.g. the public good characteristics of media content and the prevalence of economies of scale and scope – remain unchanged. The business of supplying media is and always has been centred around conveying stories and messages to consumers – enabling a connection between content and audience and generating an economic return from this activity. While the struggle to discover how to make the most of advances in technology is a perpetual challenge in the media, it is evident that the structure of markets and the interactions and behaviours of organizations in this industry are frequently guided by a distinctive and core set of economic fundamentals and principles with which this book aims to familiarize you.

2

Convergence and Multi-platform

Digitization and convergence have had a significant and ongoing impact on production, distribution and consumption of media over recent years. This chapter explores how these developments have altered resource usage within media firms and reshaped the economic organization of media industries with, on account of convergence, much greater emphasis now on multi-platform approaches at all stages in the process of producing and supplying media. The chapter introduces concepts of market structure, market boundaries and barriers to entry. It introduces the vertical supply chain and examines how digitization is affecting interdependencies, competition and growth. It also considers the relationship between technological change and innovation.

After studying this chapter, you should be able to:

- appreciate what is meant by the vertical supply chain;
- discuss the implications for media firms and markets of convergence and globalization;
- understand the concept of 'creative destruction' and how technological change, innovation and economic growth are interrelated;
- assess multi-platform strategies as a response to digital convergence.

THE VERTICAL SUPPLY CHAIN

In order to analyse an industry, one approach used by economists is to carry out a vertical deconstruction or disaggregation. The production of any good or service usually involves several stages that are technically separable. Vertical deconstruction means breaking the industry's activities up into a number of different functions or stages so that each activity can be studied more closely. The concept of a vertical supply chain was pioneered by management theorist Michael Porter (1985), who suggested that the activities of an industry are ordered in a sequence which starts 'upstream' at the early stages in the production process, works its way through succeeding or 'downstream' stages where the product is processed and refined, and finishes up as it is supplied or sold to the customer.

This framework provides a useful starting point for analysing the media. For media industries, it is possible to identify a number of broad stages in the vertical supply chain which connects producers with consumers. These include, first, the business of creating media content (e.g. gathering news stories, or making television or radio programmes or Web content). Second, media content has to be assembled into a product (e.g. a newspaper or television service). Third, the finished product must be distributed or sold to consumers.

The concept of a vertical supply chain or 'value chain' assumes an orderly sequence of links from production through to assembly and processing and then onward to the eventual interface with consumers with, at each stage, value being added. In practice, the creation of value within the media industry is a somewhat more dispersed and complex activity. With the spread of digital technology and the growth of the Internet, it is notable that many consumers have themselves become prodigious makers and publishers of content. The increasing involvement of consumers in upstream activities is indicative of how the conventional conception of a vertical supply chain struggles to do full justice to the complexity of the media industry. In addition, many media firms operate in markets that are two-sided so that, in addition to supplying content, the sale of audience attention to advertisers represents an integral aspect of their business model.

Nonetheless, the media industry is essentially about supplying content to consumers. Albeit that many operate in markets which are two-sided, the core defining activity of any media firm is its involvement in supplying media content. The general aim is to make intellectual property, package it and maximize revenues by selling it as many times as

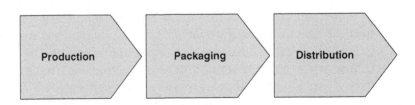

Figure 2.1 A simplified vertical supply chain for media

is feasible to the widest possible audience and at the highest possible price. To that extent, the vertical supply chain provides a useful analytical framework.

The first stage in this process is usually 'production'. Typically, the creation of media content is carried out by film-makers, writers, journalists, musicians, television and radio production companies. Thanks to the rise of the Internet, content which is co-created with or made entirely by users has come to feature more prominently as an aspect of production. Producers may sometimes supply content directly to consumers (e.g. by publishing on a website) but often their output (e.g. television programmes) created takes the form of inputs for a succeeding 'packaging' stage. This is when content is collected together and assembled into a marketable media product or service and it is carried out by, for example, television networks, online aggregators and magazine or newspaper publishers. Finally, there is 'distribution', which involves delivering a media product to its final destination – the audience.

Distribution of media output takes place in several different ways and, for some products, is quite a complex phase. In the twenty-first century, the distribution phase has become progressively more oriented towards digital platforms and mobile devices as media consumption habits have changed in favour of these outlets. Television and radio services are still transmitted over the airwaves and conveyed via broadband communication infrastructures. For pay-television the distribution stage involves encryption and subscriber management activities as well as transmission of signals. Newspapers and periodicals are still conveyed to the consumer via newsagents, or they may be delivered directly to the home or to places of employment on a subscription basis. However, for most if not all forms of media content, electronic distribution over the Internet is important and many media organizations have come to regard distribution as a multi-platform activity – i.e. involving multiple digital delivery platforms and formats.

All of the stages in the vertical supply chain for media are inter-dependent. For example, media content has no value unless it is distributed to an audience and, likewise, distribution infrastructures and outlets or portable devices for consuming media have little or no value without content to disseminate. No single stage is more important than another but all are interrelated. So, the performance of every firm involved in the supply chain will be threatened if a 'bottleneck' develops – i.e. if one player manages to monopolize any single stage in the chain. If, for example, one company gains control over all the substitute inputs at an upstream stage, or all of the facilities required for distribution or for interfacing with consumers, then rivals will be put at a considerable disadvantage and consumers are also likely to suffer.

The interdependent relation between different phases in the supply chain has important implications for what sort of competitive and corporate strategies media firms will choose to pursue. The desire for more control over the market environment may act as an incentive for firms to diversify into additional upstream or downstream phases. Vertical integration refers to the extent to which related activities up and down the supply chain are integrated or are carried out jointly by vertically integrated firms whose activities span across two or more stages in the supply process. Media firms may expand their operations vertically either by investing new resources or by acquiring other firms that are already established in succeeding or preceding stages in the supply chain.

CHANGING MARKET STRUCTURES AND BOUNDARIES

Economics provides a theoretical framework for analysing markets based on the clearly defined structures of perfect competition, monopolistic competition, oligopoly and monopoly. In practice, many media firms – especially broadcasters – have historically tended to operate in markets where levels of competition have been strongly influenced by technological factors (e.g. spectrum scarcity) or by state regulations (e.g. broadcasting license requirements) or by both. Up until the 1980s and 1990s, these factors have held back competition. In addition, the traditional tendency for media organizations to operate in quite specific geographic markets, and to be closely linked to those markets by their product content and the advertising services they provide within those markets, has curtailed levels of domestic and international competition in some, though not all, mass-media products and services.

Things have changed however, mostly because of advances in technology which have had a truly transformative affect in eroding barriers to entry to media markets. The Internet has dramatically reduced entry costs for anyone seeking the means to publish media content (Flew, 2009; Shirky, 2010). This has resulted in a proliferation of Web-delivered media services, a number of which have become immensely popular, e.g. the Netflix subscription-based online video streaming service, or YouTube which is based around distribution of user-generated or other zero-cost content.

Even before the arrival of the Internet, changes in production methods in the print industries – a general shift from the old labour and capital-intensive 'hot metal' to cold metal printing technologies around the 1980s – had already served to reduce some of the high production costs which used to impede industry entry into print publishing. In broadcasting, a steady expansion in the means of delivery over recent decades (via cable and satellite and, more recently, through digital and Internet-based delivery) has effectively swept aside earlier constraints over distribution imposed by scarcity of spectrum. Thus, broadcasting markets have opened up to new service providers (Brown, 1999: 17; Lotz, 2007). In television and feature film production, lower capital costs for digital equipment have reduced technology-based entry barriers. Across the media and at all stages in the supply chain, technological advances have lowered entry barriers and introduced more competition.

But just as new technologies and liberalizing legislation have done away with some of the conventional entry barriers affecting media markets, one or two other new barriers seem to have sprung up in their place. Greater abundance in distribution has placed more emphasis on the fight for audience attention (Aris and Bughin, 2009: 21) and on the importance of control over key access points to content. Expansion in digital distribution avenues has introduced new stages and additional functions along the supply chain for media, some of which are highly prone to monopolization. For example, search engines have become an indispensable tool to enable consumers to navigate towards whatever digital content they are interested in. It is fair to argue that 'Google wields tremendous power to make or break businesses on the web … it can bring a flood of traffic … or cast them into the online equivalent of Siberia' (Waters, 2010: 22). Search engines occupy a crucial position, but because the activities they carry out are characterized by economies of scale and network effects the sector is naturally susceptible to monopolization (Schulz, Held and Laudien, 2005; van Eijk, 2009).

The term 'gateway monopolist' is used to describe firms that gain control over some vital stage in the supply chain or gateway between media content and audiences. When individual firms gain control over a gateway that all media suppliers need in order to reach audiences then effectively they become 'gatekeepers' with power to decide who may or may not be allowed market access. Gateway monopolies can occur both in upstream stages (e.g. through monopolized control over particular forms of content) and downstream (e.g. through ownership of dominant navigation systems or some other essential interface with consumers). For example, as mobile devices have grown in popularity in the twenty-first century, their importance as a conduit between content publishers and digital subscribers is such that gatekeeping powers will accrue to the manufacturers of any exceptionally dominant market-leading devices. If left unrestrained by regulators, such gateway monopolists clearly threaten to create new entry barriers in the media sector.

More generally, the traditional boundaries surrounding media markets have been eroded. One of the key drivers for this has been globalization – a process affecting many areas of economic activity and not least media and communications. The term globalization has been around since the 1980s and can have different meanings but, in an economic context, is usually taken to refer to the gradual whittling away of national boundaries through removal of legal or logistical impediments to transnational trade in goods and services. For social theorists, globalization refers to processes of transnationalization of cultural phenomena. In an economic sense, globalization is about erosion of the boundaries around national economies because of, for example, more trade agreements, greater mobility of capital, increased international inward investment and new technologies.

The Internet – a borderless communications infrastructure – has been a crucial vector of change. The rapid growth and development of this infrastructure which seamlessly conveys not only communications but digital content of all sorts across transnational boundaries has reshaped the competitive environment for all media businesses. The transnational integration of markets that were previously just national markets through, for example, the European Union and the North American Free Trade Agreement (NAFTA), has accelerated the emergence of a more globalized media environment. Many media products – newspapers, television channels, radio services – remain strongly orientated towards specific national and local markets through their relationships with audiences and constituencies of advertisers. Nonetheless, globalization has diminished geographical market boundaries and encouraged commercial and even non-commercial media organizations such as the British Broadcasting Corporation (BBC) to become much more outward-looking in their approach.

It is not just geographical market boundaries that have diminished over recent years but also, to some extent, the boundaries between different sorts of media and communications products and services have also become blurred (Hoskins, McFayden and Finn, 2004; Picard, 2002). The boundaries which used to surround and distinguish one specific market from another (e.g. newspapers, television, telecommunications) are less clearly delineated now than in the past. At the root of this aspect of transformation in market structures and competition is digital convergence.

DIGITAL CONVERGENCE

The term 'convergence' has been used in many different ways. According to Jenkins, it 'manages to describe technological, industrial, cultural and social changes depending on who's speaking and what they are talking about' (2006: 3). For many years, a mismatch between levels of hype and of ground-level progress resulted in scepticism and warnings against allowing media business strategies to be driven by the 'myth' of convergence (Noll, 2003). However, spurred on by growth of the Internet and rapid uptake of mobile devices, digital convergence has become very much a reality in the twenty-first century.

Convergence stems from a migration towards common digital technologies right across the communications industry and in all stages of production and distribution of media content. The term refers to the coming together, on account of shared use of digital technologies, of sectors and product markets that were previously seen as distinct and separate. Thanks to the use of common technologies to capture, tag, store, manipulate, package and deliver digital information (including all types of media content), media output can more readily be repackaged for dissemination in alternative formats. For example, images, text and/or video gathered for a profile of a celebrity or of a contemporary music star, once reduced to digits, can very easily be retrieved, reassembled and delivered in a number of different formats and guises. Thus digitization and convergence are weakening some of the market boundaries that used to separate different media products.

The use of common digital technologies has spurred on the development of new forms of content (combining video with text, for example, and involving interactivity and multiple layers) and of converged devices (such as mobile phone/media players). The transition towards digital platforms – the Internet being the principal example – means that content of all kinds can circulate and be delivered to audiences across numerous settings (e.g. television over mobile or radio via Digital Terrestrial Television (DTT) or the Internet). The experience of the UK is typical of developed economies in that, as demonstrated by Figure 2.2, the number of households and individuals with high-speed access to the Internet through broadband cable infrastructures and Web-connected mobile devices has grown rapidly in recent years.

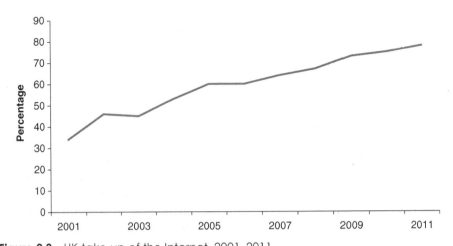

Figure 2.2 UK take-up of the Internet, 2001–2011
Source: Ofcom Tracker Data from Ofcom CMR (Ofcom, 2011a: 205)

Convergence has affected not only content and delivery but also the operational and corporate strategies of media and communications organizations (Küng, Picard and Towse, 2008). By inducing greater overlap between the activities of broadcasting, communications and computing, it has gradually drawn these sectors more closely together. Convergence has intensified competition: it has also been an especially powerful driver of strategic change in recent years (Chan-Olmsted and Chang, 2003; García Avilés and Carvajal, 2008). For many media suppliers, a major part of the response to convergence has been to adopt a more multi-platform approach towards distribution of their wares in the hope that this strategy will shelter them from what Austrian economist Joseph Schumpeter termed 'the gales of creative destruction' (1942).

TECHNOLOGICAL CHANGE, INNOVATION AND CREATIVE DESTRUCTION

More so than in many other industries, technology is at the heart of the media business. As a result, media firms that want to survive must be constantly vigilant for technological advances that may affect one or other aspect of production, distribution or consumption of their output. Economic success in the media industry is naturally dependent on the ability to adjust to and capitalize on technological advances.

Schumpeter coined the phrase 'creative destruction' to describe the process whereby technologies change and new innovations emerge that force existing businesses either to adapt or die out (McCraw, 2007). As entrepreneurs innovate, this brings opportunities and growth but it also results in existing products and services losing ground, so the value of large dominant incumbent firms who fail to transform in response to technological change will be eroded and eventually destroyed.

Schumpeter's view was that processes of innovation, economic advancement and the demise of existing businesses are all inextricably intertwined with one another. As entrepreneurs spot and seize upon opportunities created by advances in technology to gain profit, this fuels a continuous and ongoing process of creative destruction which, in turn, brings economic growth. Schumpeter's work provided the inspiration for development of the field of so-called evolutionary economics which argues that capacity for innovation offers a vital source of advantage to firms as they seek to compete with each other (Metcalfe, 1998:17).

Schumpeter's notion that the phenomenon of constant restructuring and replacement of old products and businesses by new ones is central to economic growth has been well supported in many earlier economic surveys and studies (Aghion and Howitt, 1992; Caballero, 2006). This conceptual approach appears to have a strong resonance in the context of recent developments affecting media and cultural industries, whereby advances in technology have brought not only opportunity for new entrants but also significant upheaval for market incumbents. One example relates to the music sector, where vinyl records were replaced by cassette tapes which, in turn, were replaced by CDs which are now being usurped by MP3 digital files. Each successive innovation has brought success and growth for some players and destruction for others who have been unable to adapt.

Many areas of media content production and distribution and especially print publishing also appear to be caught up in the gales of creative destruction. In the newspaper industry, innovative new products such as the *Huffington Post* have rapidly achieved popularity and success while among conventional titles numerous closures have taken place, largely as a result of technological advances and altered consumption and advertising patterns (Patterson, 2007; Slattery, 2009). In magazine publishing too, many businesses and titles are struggling to innovate in the face of threatened extinction (Luft, 2009). Digital convergence and growth of the Internet have provided extensive opportunities for innovation – thus acting as a 'creative' force – but also, as evidenced by recent closures among newspapers, these developments have engendered difficulty and even demise for some market incumbents.

Schumpeter's view was not only that creative destruction is an inherent feature of capitalist societies but also that it is a beneficial one (1942). In a similar vein, Schumpeter and other economists (such as Friedrich Hayek and Lionel Robbins) have argued that recessions serve the useful purpose of encouraging a reallocation of resources away from less productive activities (as reflected in higher company liquidations) and towards what are ultimately more productive economic activities. Thus in periods of technological change and of recession, such as were experienced by media companies in 2009–10, the combined forces of liquidationism plus creative destruction are apt to speed the pace at which slow adaptors get weeded out.

It is possible to draw a distinction between creative destruction – a process that is potentially helpful to the economy – and the possibility of 'destructive' destruction. The latter alludes to a phase in which businesses are eradicated but without any positive benefits being created. If the innovation that allows a firm to displace market incumbents is based on practices or activities that are not conducive to the wider economic or public good – if, say, it involves pollution – then what appears to be creative destruction may, in fact, turn out to be something else. Getting the diagnosis right is important from the point of view of ensuring an effective and appropriate policy stance.

Digital convergence is associated with countless claimed gains for citizens and consumers related to the arrival of innovative services, more flexibility and control over how and when to access media plus greater opportunities for participation. However, the more negative impact of digitization and the Internet on the ability of content suppliers to derive revenues from their intellectual property has prompted concerns in some quarters about whether changes sweeping across content provision industries amount to creative destruction or 'just plain destruction' (Liebowitz, 2006: 1). The fact that online service providers such as Google and YouTube, who may not have borne any of the investment costs involved in making content, will nonetheless often find themselves well-placed to siphon off audiences and revenues poses an obvious threat to broadcasters and other professional creators and suppliers of media content worldwide.

Opinions differ as to whether digital convergence and the Internet count as revolutionary and disruptive rather than just evolutionary technological changes, but it is widely accepted that significant technology transitions such as these are 'always highly problematic for incumbent players' (Küng, Picard and Towse, 2008: 33). Even so, firms across many sectors have historically survived processes of creative destruction and, in the media sector, the challenge of adapting to technological change is certainly nothing new (Carlaw et al., 2006). If, as some have argued, most media incumbents can be expected to survive (Cole, 2008), this requires that operational and corporate strategies must be adapted successfully to the era of convergence.

MULTI-PLATFORM

Across the media, many firms have responded to digital convergence by adopting a multi-platform strategy in relation both to production and to exploitation of their content assets. In response to a progressive blurring of market boundaries, many have migrated to an approach in which the aim is to supply and exploit content across multiple platforms and formats, including digital, rather than just one (Doyle, 2010a). The strategies of newspaper and magazine publishers are increasingly reliant on building online subscriptions. Many if not most television companies have embraced multiple and cross-platform distribution as a vital means of retaining and building audiences in the face of vastly increased competition. In the UK for example, virtually all speak of having a multi-platform or '360-degree' approach to content acquisition and distribution (Parker, 2007; Strange, 2011). A 360-degree approach means that from the earliest stages at which a new content property is considered, thought is given to what potential exists for that property to be distributed and exploited across *multiple* delivery platforms (including online and mobile) rather than just one.

The view that the business of supplying content should be seen as a multi-platform rather than a single platform activity has been embraced by most sizeable media companies and, in the television industry, by public service providers and commercial players alike. In the UK, the most prominent providers of PSB are the BBC and also advertiser-funded Channel 4. Channel 4's chief executive summarized the shifting landscape as follows: 'Broadcast television is no longer the funnel through which entertainment and information are channelled to millions of waiting consumers in a one-way flow' (Duncan, 2006: 21). An expanding range of delivery platforms and the growing popularity of the Internet have undermined the long-established position of television broadcasters as 'overseer in the great treasure house of content' (ibid.). The ways in which digital developments and fragmentation have changed relationships with audiences and introduced new expectations was summarized by a senior executive at BBC Scotland:

> Across all media, everyone now has multi-platform approaches to content. That is driven by the market – by audiences. Audiences are determining what *they* want and how they want the material.[1]

---

[1] Small: interviewed in Glasgow in 2009.

The move to multi-platform involves adjustment in the nature of an organization's ethos as well as its activity. At the BBC, Director-General Mark Thompson framed a major strategic restructuring of the corporation's activities around the new imperative that '[f]rom now on, wherever possible, we need to think cross-platform' (Thompson, 2006: 12). In the commercial sector too many broadcasters have consciously overhauled their organizational cultures so as to execute strategies that capitalize on a multi-platform approach more effectively. Perceptions about what the business of supplying content is about have changed fundamentally, according to the Head of Digital at MTV Networks UK:

> The future of media companies isn't just in making movies, broadcasting TV and making TV. It also is making console games like *Rock Band* ... and games online ... and virtual worlds, which have millions of people communicating with each other within our brand but has got nothing to do with TV ... MTV in the UK is a completely 360-degree media owner ... We're *not* a broadcaster; that's just part of what we do. We make programmes, we own brands and we media-cast [across] multi-platforms.[2]

As a great many recent studies indicate, the urge to invest in development of multimedia and online businesses is widely evident across the media industry and on an international basis (Friedrichsen and Mühl-Benninhaus, 2012; Krone and Grueblbauer, 2012; Medina and Prario, 2012; Nieminen, Koikkalainen and Karppinen, 2012; Vatanova, Makeenko and Vyrkovsky, 2012). Greater investment is reflected, for example, by a progressive increase over time in the number of media employees devoted to such activities. Empirical research focused on the UK television industry has shown how 'the sector is responding to technological advances through attrition and disappearance of jobs in some areas while, in functions related to the Internet and digital or future media, the flow of new jobs has increased markedly' (Doyle, 2010b: 253).

In theory, the impetus to adopt a multi-platform approach towards supplying content seems to make a great deal of economic sense, because it capitalizes on the public good characteristics of media content discussed in Chapter 1. It allows fuller and more thorough exploitation of intellectual property assets across additional outlets at what may be a relatively low marginal cost. Repurposing and recycling of content is

---

[2] O' Ferrall: interviewed in London in 2009.

by no means new and has long contributed towards the profitability of major media conglomerates (Caldwell, 2006; Murray, 2005; Vukanovic, 2009). In practice, however, the effect of a multi-platform approach on profits is not straightforward because the level of ambition involved in such a strategy can vary widely from one organization to another, with differing implications for costs and hence profits both in the short and long term.

While adoption of a multi-platform approach is widespread among media firms, what this actually means in terms of the sort of content being supplied, the combination of delivery platforms being used, the sorts of opportunities being pursued and the level of investment and experimentation involved varies widely (Anderson, 2006; Bennett and Strange, 2011; Johnson, 2007; Krone and Grueblbauer, 2012; Medina and Prario, 2012; Pardo, Guerrero and Diego, 2012; Roscoe, 2004). For some, the essence of the strategy appears to be low-cost reuse of existing content. For others, dispersal of content across multiple platforms involves significant investment in creation of multiple texts and ancillary materials to enhance the suitability of content for different modes of delivery. Whereas the economics of supplying media will be enhanced where multi-platform distribution enables firms to derive further value from their content properties and to reap economies of scale and scope, it remains possible that, in a world of fragmenting audiences, the additional costs involved in deploying such a strategy effectively will not be matched by marginal revenues, at least in the short term (Doyle, 2010a: 9–14).

Irrespective of how costly it may be, the need to innovate and to adapt in response to technological change is widely recognized as essential to the survival and competitive success of firms operating in free-market economies (Baumol, 2002). For media firms, adaptation that accords with emerging patterns of audience and advertiser behaviour which digital convergence has brought about is vital (Gershon, 2012). The experience of UK-based broadcasters suggests that adjustment and innovation based around switching to a multi-platform approach is generally based on the promise of advantages in two main areas. One relates to providing more and improved access to content, the other to new forms of audience engagement.

With regard to the former, a key incentive for broadcasters or indeed newspaper and magazine publishers to adapt their strategies to make sure that delivery via the Internet and other digital outlets will, in future, play a much greater role, is the potential for fuller exploitation of content assets. In the television industry, the rapid growth in popularity of online television services such as, in the UK, the BBC iPlayer catch-up service or, in the US, the Hulu on-demand video streaming service owned by NBC, Fox and Disney provide good examples of how a multi-platform approach can generate additional audience value. Recycling and 'windowing' of content across additional audience segments, although by no means a new practice, makes very good economic sense.

A second area where digitization and multi-platform distribution provide opportunity for innovation and improved efficiency relates to the unprecedented ways that new technology allows suppliers to get to know their audiences and to match content more closely to their needs and desires (Caldwell, 2003; Doyle, 2010a; Shapiro and Varian, 1999). Because of improved signalling of audience preferences (via the digital return path), the ability of content suppliers to trace, analyse, monitor and cater more effectively to shifting and specific tastes and interests among audiences has increased vastly. In addition, as is discussed further in Chapter 4, because of the 'lean forward' rather than 'lean back' character of digital media consumption, a much more intensive relationship with audiences can be constructed and this represents a source of both creative and commercial opportunities.

A NEW CORNUCOPIA?

Adoption of a multi-platform approach is widespread among media firms and is motivated partly by the desire to exploit content more effectively and to harness the advantages of digital two-way connectivity. However, the re-envisaging of corporate missions in a more platform-neutral way also reflects a widespread recognition that major changes in consumption patterns and in the appetites of (especially younger) audiences have taken place. At the same time as offering opportunities to innovate, these changes threaten to simply leave behind those media organizations who fail to adapt.

To what extent has multi-platform distribution *improved* allocative efficiency within processes of supplying media content? This approach to distribution has engendered a vast increase in opportunities for consumption and engagement with content. On account of multi-platform dissemination the volume of outputs and the supply of opportunities to consume media content have ballooned, reflecting wider cross-platform access to media content and tendencies to create and supply multiple versions of narratives out of individual stories and content properties and brands. Digitization has removed constraints over distribution capacity and made reversioning of content easier and, as a result, dissemination across additional platforms and especially the Internet is now fairly common as a strategy.

However, whereas volumes of output have grown and opportunities to access it have multiplied, whether this has brought about an improved experience for audiences is open to question. Because the construction of attractive multi-platform content propositions can be expensive and because some forms of media content are inherently much better suited towards diversified distribution than others, the widespread adoption of a multi-platform approach is inevitably contributing to the ascendance of some forms of content at the expense of others (Johnson, 2007; Murray, 2005: 431). The problem is that – particularly at a time when budgets are constrained – multi-platform strategies can encourage more recycling of content across platforms and a greater reliance on safe and popular themes and brands that achieve high visibility and impact (Doyle, 2010a). To the extent that widespread adoption of multi-platform strategies results in a tendency towards narrowing of diversity or degradation in content quality, it might well be argued that this outcome detracts from rather than improves efficiency.

This underlines the more general point made earlier that, where media and other cultural industries are concerned, judgements about economic efficiency are inherently complex. On account of the socio-cultural dimensions of supplying media, any complete assessment of the economic merits of one set of arrangements for provision versus another calls for some consideration of whatever welfare impacts those differing arrangements would give rise to.

3

Corporate Growth and Concentration Strategies

Media industries have long been characterized by concentrations of ownership and by the presence of organizations whose activities span both numerous sectors of the media and transnational boundaries. The spread of digital technology, although transforming the competitive landscape, has served to accentuate some of the advantages of scale and of cross-sectoral ownership which accrue to large media firms. This chapter reviews the special economic features of media output, focusing particularly on the significance of its public good characteristics and on economies of scale and scope, and examines the relationship between such economic characteristics and the corporate configurations adopted by media firms. Thus the main economic advantages and implications associated with strategies of vertical, horizontal, conglomerate and international expansion in the media will be explored.

After studying this chapter, you should be able to:

- distinguish between strategies of vertical, horizontal and diagonal growth;
- explain the principal motivations behind media and cross-media expansion;
- understand the impetus towards transnational growth strategies;
- analyse the economic advantages and disadvantages associated with concentrated media ownership.

STRATEGIC RESPONSES TO DIGITIZATION

The media landscape has evolved rapidly since the early 1990s when, in the US, the 'information super-highway' was first talked about by then vice president Al Gore and, at the same time, the concept of the 'information society' was first advanced by European policy-makers. Growth of the Internet has done much to usher into reality these differing visions of an era in which citizen-consumers can easily connect with each other and with a rich array of media and communication offerings via high-capacity distribution infrastructures and through smart devices. Alongside the spread of digital technologies and of the Internet in the first decade of the twenty-first century, the whittling away of traditional sectoral and product market boundaries plus rapid uptake of Web-connected mobile devices have resulted in numerous forms of conjunction, overlap and convergence affecting firms involved in all stages of media, communications and computing provision.

Media firms have naturally adapted their business and corporate strategies in the face of these changes. As traditional market boundaries and barriers have blurred and some have faded away, increased competition among organizations has been characterized by a steady increase in the number of perceived distributive outlets (or 'windows') which are available to media suppliers.

The logic of exploiting economies of scale creates an incentive to expand product sales into secondary external or overseas markets. As market structures have been freed up and have become more competitive and international in outlook, the opportunities to exploit economies of scale and economies of scope have increased. Globalization and convergence have created additional possibilities and incentives to repackage or to 'repurpose' media content into as many different formats as is technically and commercially feasible (book, magazine serializations, online content, television programmes and formats, podcast, DVD, etc.), and to sell that product through as many distribution channels or windows in as many geographic markets and to as many paying consumers as possible.

At the same time as creating opportunities to reap additional economies of scale, the spread of digital delivery platforms and, in particular, growth of the Internet has established a market space for media content whose defining characteristics are different from those of the analogue era. One key difference is that the two-way interactivity facilitated by digital platforms has contributed to a rebalancing of powers between suppliers and consumers in favour of the latter – the 'one-to-many' model of media provision which historically placed suppliers in complete control of what is made available has been usurped, at least partially, by the introduction of alternative and more user-driven modes of interface across digital platforms. Another change is that the Internet has established what Anderson (2006) has termed an 'extended' marketplace with additional and lengthier opportunities to sell content of the less popular variety, thus improving the potential for development and exploitation of specialist market niches.

The media industry's response to these developments has been marked. Notwithstanding the periodic constraining effects of economic recession, media firms have been energetic participants in corporate activity through takeovers, mergers and other strategic deals and alliances (PwC, 2012). Traditional media firms have been keen to acquire partners with digital capabilities and, more broadly, convergence has steadily drawn players from media, telecommunications and IT sectors more fully into each other's territories. Many are now suppliers of both media and communication services, especially the so-called 'triple play' of telephone, Internet plus television. Providers of high-capacity communication infrastructures have become increasingly interested in media content businesses (and vice versa) and in the commercial possibilities surrounding provision of multimedia, social networking and other interactive digital services in addition to conventional television and telephony. Because of the potential for economies of scale and scope, the greater the number of products and services that can be delivered to consumers via the same communications infrastructures, the better the economics of each service.

Convergence and globalization have increased trends towards concentrated media and cross-media ownership, with the growth of integrated conglomerates (e.g. News Corporation, Time Warner/AOL, Pearson, Bertelsmann) whose activities span several areas of the industry. This makes sense. Highly concentrated firms who can spread production costs across wider product and geographic markets will, of course, benefit from natural economies of scale in the media (Hoskins, McFayden and Finn, 1997: 22). Expansion is, of course, always accompanied by risk. As highlighted by Sánchez-Tabernero and Carvajal, the financial and managerial challenges associated with enlargement can and do sometimes cause serious problems for media firms who, in the process of enlargement, lose their focus and momentum (2002: 84–7). Nonetheless, enlarged, diversified and vertically integrated groups appear well-suited to exploit technological and other market changes sweeping across the media and communications industries.

At least three major strategies of corporate growth can be identified and distinguished: horizontal, vertical and diagonal expansion. A 'horizontal' merger occurs when two firms at the same stage in the supply chain or who are engaged in the same activity as each other combine forces. Horizontal expansion is a common strategy in many sectors and it allows firms to expand their market share and, usually, to rationalize resources and gain economies of scale. Companies that do business in the same area can benefit from joining forces in a number of ways including, for example, by applying common managerial techniques or through greater opportunities for specialization of labour as the firm gets larger. In the media industry, the prevalence of economies of scale makes horizontal expansion a very attractive strategy.

Vertical growth involves expanding either 'forward' into succeeding stages or 'backward' into preceding stages in the supply chain. Vertically integrated media firms may have activities that span from creation of media output (which brings ownership of copyright) through to distribution or retail of that output in various guises. Vertical expansion generally results in reduced transaction costs for the enlarged firm. Another benefit, which may be of great significance for media players, is that vertical integration gives firms some control over their operating environment and can help them to avoid losing market access in important upstream or downstream phases.

Diagonal or 'conglomerate' expansion occurs when firms diversify into new business areas. For example, a merger between a telecommunications operator and a television company might generate efficiency gains because both sorts of services – audiovisual and telephony – are distributed jointly across the same communications infrastructure. Newspaper publishers may expand diagonally into television broadcasting or radio companies may diversify into magazine publishing. A myriad of possibilities exists for diagonal expansion across media and related industries. Such strategies often create economic gains and synergies, but not necessarily so. One possible benefit is that it helps to spread risk. Large diversified media firms are, to some extent at least, cushioned against any damaging movements that may affect any single one of the sectors in which they are involved. More importantly perhaps, the widespread availability of economies of scale and scope means that many media firms stand to benefit from strategies of diagonal expansion.

In addition, many media firms have become what are called multinationals – i.e. corporations with a presence in many countries and (in some cases) an increasingly decentralized management structure. Globalization has encouraged media operators to look beyond the local or home market as a way of expanding their consumer base horizontally and of extending their economies of scale. For example, UK media conglomerate EMAP plc acquired several magazine publishing operations in France in the mid-1990s and gradually became the second largest player in that market. But in 2007 EMAP's consumer magazine and radio activities were taken over by German publishing giant Bauer which, in turn, was keen to extend its international operations through acquisitions. A number of Scandinavian and German publishers such as Sanoma and Axel Springer expanded their operations into central and eastern Europe in the early years of the twenty-first century. Examples of deals involving transnational expansion abound across the media. US group Viacom, the parent company of Paramount Pictures, has achieved a market presence in a vast number of international territories through its high-profile television subsidiary MTV.

The basic rationale behind all such strategies of enlargement is usually to try to use common resources more fully. Diversified and large-scale media organizations are clearly in the best position to exploit common resources across different product and geographic markets. This is not to deny the potentially numerous difficulties and challenges associated with the management of enlarged and multi-faceted enterprises (Sánchez-Tabernero and Carvajal, 2002: 84–7). In terms of profits performance, the financial pitfalls and managerial complexities associated with expansion and diversification may sometimes outweigh any economies of scale and scope (Kolo and Vogt, 2003), at least in the short term. Even so, large, diversified and transnational entities are at least potentially better able to reap the economies of scale and scope which are naturally present in the media industry and which, thanks to globalization and convergence, have become even more pronounced.

This points towards what Demers calls the 'paradox of capitalism' – that increased global competition results in *less* competition over the long run (Demers, 1999: 48). Even with a loosening up of national markets and fewer technological barriers to protect media incumbents from new competitors, the trend that exists in the media – of increased concentration of ownership and power into the hands of a few very large transnational corporations – clearly reflects the overwhelming advantages that accrue to large-scale firms.

MANAGERIAL THEORIES

Although recent market changes combined with the public-good characteristics of media provide a compelling economic account as to why profit-maximizing media firms would seek to build empires, it is worth noting that propensities towards expansion may be motivated by alternative factors that have little to do with economics or profit maximization. This is true of all sectors of industry – the desire to build empires may reflect personal or managerial agendas – but it is obviously a particularly relevant consideration in the context of media, where control over the main channels for public communication is accompanied by significant political and cultural influence.

Managerial theorists have tended to highlight the role played by the personal interests of managers as a key driver behind growth strategies in general. Robin Marris, Oliver Williamson and others have argued that growth is the main strategic objective for many firms not because of profit maximization but because enlargement will bring a variety of personal benefits for the senior managers of firms that are growing (Griffiths and Wall, 2007: 80).

Most firms these days take the form of a public limited company (or plc) and are run by managers rather than by owners (or shareholders). Ownership and control of the firm are therefore separate and, because managers who are employed have different objectives from shareholders, a divergence from profit maximization becomes possible.

> Principal–agent analysis shows that, when employees [i.e. managers] have some range of discretion, their self-interested behaviour will make profits lower than in a 'perfect', frictionless world in which principals … [in this case, media shareholders] … act as their own agents [in this case, media managers] (Lipsey and Chrystal, 2007: 242).

Managers are, of course, concerned with keeping up profits, but they also have their own personal concerns. Marris – an influential management theorist – suggested that a principal aim for managers is to try to expand the firms they are running, at all costs, and irrespective of whether it would make the firm more efficient or more profitable (Moschandreas, 2000: 206–7). The suggestion by Marris, Williamson and other managerial theorists is that growth of the firm is the main objective because this raises managerial utility 'by bringing higher salaries, power, status, and job security' (Griffiths and Wall, 2007: 80).

So the reasons why managers try to expand the firm might be because, first, salary levels for senior management are quite closely linked to the scale of a firm's activities. For example, the chief executive of British Telecommunications (BT) earns more than the chief executive of Guardian Media Group or of Scottish Television plc. It is also the case that fast-growing rather than static firms will give higher remuneration to managers. Second, as a firm grows, its senior managers become powerful captains of industry and are often invited to join prestigious industry bodies, such as the Confederation of British Industry (CBI). Being the senior manager of a large media firm is clearly a powerful and politically influential role.

Another reason why managers try to build empires may be because it makes it more difficult for their firm to be taken over by a predator. Senior managers usually want to avoid takeover and the risk of replacement by a new management team. By expanding – e.g. through acquisition of several smaller companies – a firm makes itself a more expensive and difficult target for takeover. The less prone a firm is to takeover, the greater the job security for its senior managers.

Looking at ownership strategies specifically in the context of media, Sánchez-Tabernero and Carvajal have pointed towards a range of not only economic but also non-economic factors which fuel an 'obsession' with enlargement and with increasing company size, for example, political and psychological motives or pressure from investors (2002: 83). To the extent that strategies of enlargement are simply a response to prevailing pressures or are founded on personal or political motives, little positive impact can be expected in terms of the economic strength and performance of the firms in question. As Picard has argued, '[l]argeness produces both advantages and disadvantages and is not the answer to all the pressures and issues that companies face' (2002: 191). Expansion is by no means an assured route to increased profits and, indeed, earlier research into corporate activity in the media industry has uncovered instances where strategies of growth and diversification, although accounted for explicitly in terms of available cross-synergies and economic benefits, have in practice yielded little or no meaningful efficiency gains or other opportunities for improved use of resources (Doyle, 2002: 115–16).

Most scholars of industrial economics accept that managers have some element of discretion to pursue goals other than profit maximization, and that managerial agendas can sometimes help explain corporate behaviour. Even so, expansion on the part of firms – including media firms – may often be explained by the presence of convincing strategic motives that will contribute over time to the security and profitability of the organization (Griffiths and Wall, 2007: 81).

The remaining sections of this chapter draw on examples of what sorts of benefits and advantages accrue in practice as media firms expand.

HORIZONTAL EXPANSION

In general, horizontal expansion – i.e. expansion in a firm's market share, either through internal growth or by acquisition of another firm with a similar product – may be motivated by the profit-maximizing firm's desire for greater market power (e.g. the ability to exercise some control over price) or by efficiency gains. The net impact of expansion on market performance and, ultimately, on societal welfare generally depends on the trade-off between these two possible outcomes. Whereas the achievement of efficiency gains (i.e. an improved use of resources) may be seen as serving the public interest, the accumulation of market power and market dominance may lead to behaviour and practices which run contrary to the public interest.

Looking first at the potential impact on efficiency, horizontal mergers or acquisitions (or, indeed, organic growth) in the media sector which result in an enlarged market share for, say, a television company, a radio broadcaster, an online content service or a newspaper publisher are liable to result in improved efficiency because of the general availability of economies of scale, i.e. where marginal costs are less than average costs as output expands. The desire to capitalize on economies of scale is the classic incentive underlying horizontal growth strategies in general (Griffiths and Wall, 2007: 79) and, in media industries, is an obvious motivating factor.

Naturally, factors other than size are likely to a have a strong bearing on the financial performance of individual media companies, for example, variations in managerial efficiency or niche product positions. Even so, some earlier empirical research work has found evidence of a positive correlation between size (in terms of market share) and profits performance for media companies with, for example, large television broadcasters generating higher profit margins than small ones (Doyle, 2000). Such a correlation is not entirely surprising. As many writers have noted, extensive product-specific economies of scale exist in the broadcasting industry because, once a delivery infrastructure is in place, the marginal costs of providing the service to an additional viewer (within one's transmission area or 'footprint') are zero or extremely low (Cave, 1989: 11–12). The overhead costs associated with providing a given service tend to be equal, regardless of audience size and so, *ceteris paribus*, economies of scale arise, as larger audiences are translated into more revenue.

Economies of scale are present in virtually all sectors of the media (Hoskins, McFadyen and Finn, 2004: 97). In newspaper or magazine publishing, for example, the marginal costs involved in selling one additional copy of the same edition of a product are relatively low, so product-specific economies of scale will arise as circulations expand. The widespread availability of economies of scale in the media industry is generally associated with low replication costs for media output.

Initial production costs (i.e. the cost of creating the first or master copy) may be high but then very few marginal costs are incurred as the product is replicated and distributed or sold over and over again to ever greater numbers of consumers. However, even within the expensive initial content production phase, economies of scale may be present. Firms engaged in content production may find that marginal costs (say, the cost of creating one additional hour of a television drama) are lower than average costs (total production costs divided by the number of hours of drama already produced) as output expands.

As the output of a television production company increases, the firm may derive economies of scale on fixed overheads by, for example, making better use of capital equipment (cameras, post-production facilities, etc.) or salaried personnel. Horizontal expansion may be motivated by the desire to increase the use of underutilized resources. Media companies that expand horizontally and increase their output may also enjoy productivity gains because of the opportunity for specialization of tasks as the firm grows larger. The realization of economies of scale may, arguably, facilitate higher levels of gross investment and speedier adoption of new technologies on the part of large media firms. For example, research in Norway has found that titles which are part of large newspaper groups are more inclined to innovate than smaller independent papers (Krumsvik, Skogerbø and Storsul, 2012). And faster-growing media firms may be able to attract better-quality personnel.

When a media firm expands horizontally, an important potential efficiency gain is the opportunity to share the use of specialized resources or expertise across more than one product. Any savings made in this way represent economies of scope. Efficiency gains will arise, for example, if specialist content gathered for one media product can be reused in another. So, economies of scope as well as economies of scale may co-exist for broadcasters who operate more than one programme service and the more homogeneity possible between both services, the greater the economies of scope. Broadcasting networks, which are discussed in Chapter 4, are based around the logic of exploiting such advantages.

As a broadcaster expands horizontally and increases the number of services it is delivering, opportunities will arise to combine back-office activities (e.g. finance and administration) as well as specialist support functions such as airtime sales or secondary programme sales. The availability of all such cost-efficiencies provides the obvious motive behind many corporate deals whereby one radio or television company acquires another or several others. A good example of this is the series of mergers and acquisitions in the UK television sector

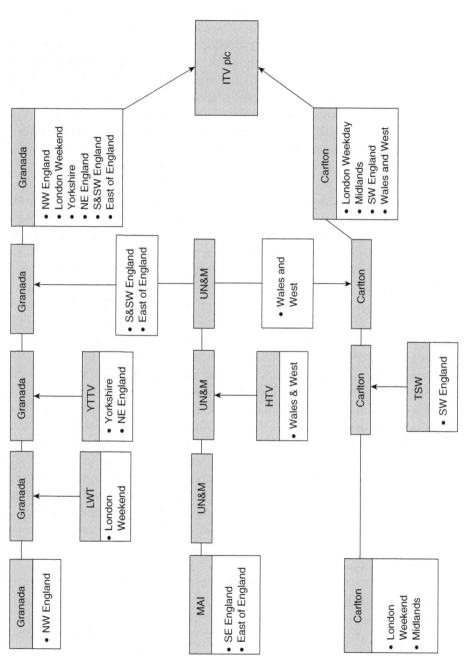

Figure 3.1 Corporate expansion from 1993 to 2004 leading to the formation of ITV plc

from 1993 onwards which culminated, in 2004, in the establishment of ITV plc – a consolidated entity which replaced numerous individual companies that previously had owned and operated separately most of the regional television services under the collective ITV brand.

The prevalence of economies of scope in the media explains the widespread tendency towards expansion and the very high incidence of multi-product firms. For example, the takeover by Global Radio (which owned 10 stations) of GCAP (which owned a further 72 stations across the UK) in 2008 created the largest commercial radio broadcaster in the country and a substantial multi-product entity (OFT, 2008). In the UK newspaper industry, all leading national and regional newspapers own not just one but several major titles. Likewise in the magazine publishing sector, all the leading players are multi-product firms.

For newspaper proprietors that publish more than one title, various economies of scope may arise. For example, large publishers may achieve better collective terms on input prices or support services (e.g. printing or distribution). Publishers of several titles may be able to combine and rationalize back-office functions or other shared activities such as advertising sales. However, for national newspaper publishers, the editorial process itself – sharing of journalistic resources – is generally not regarded as a principal area of opportunity when it comes to deriving economies of scope. Even though it is widely accepted that producing for multiple distribution formats is an integral aspect of journalism in the digital era, because the need for individual products to retain a distinctive tone is sacrosanct many publishers are sceptical about the feasibility of sharing journalists across multiple titles.

The presence of both economies of scale and scope in the media implies a natural gravitation towards oligopoly market structures and large-scale multi-product firms. Provided that product quality does not suffer through sharing or spreading costs among more consumers or over a greater number of media products, then strategies of horizontal expansion will yield efficiency gains which, in theory, ought to benefit societal welfare. However, if cost savings are achieved at the expense of viewers' or readers' utility then expansion will not serve to improve efficiency per se, albeit that it may increase the profit margins of the firm in question.

Aside from efficiency, another important advantage of having a large market presence in any sector of the media (or of cross-owning media products in several sectors) is that it gives the firm greater critical mass. Large firms have greater negotiating leverage in deals with suppliers and with buyers. For example, large newspaper and magazine publishers will tend to get a better deal on paper and newsprint prices.

A dominant firm has greater ability to exercise some control over the prices it charges its customers. Large media firms who control access to mass audiences are generally able to command premium prices for advertising (i.e. a higher cost-per-thousand rate than smaller firms). The tendency for large audiences to be worth more on a per-capita basis than small audiences appears to hold true for online media too, in that the most popular websites capture a disproportionately high share of online advertising relative to their share of audience attention (Napoli, 2011: 70).

The greater market power which large media firms command will enhance their profitability, but it may also potentially harm consumer interests (e.g. if prices charged are too high), and it may pose a threat to the operation of markets. To the extent that the exercise of market power by large media groups may serve to impede competition, the strategic advantage it confers upon the individual firm is simultaneously an obstacle to market efficiency and a disadvantage for consumers. In summary, then, strategies of horizontal expansion can potentially deliver a range of efficiency gains that contribute positively to societal welfare but, at the same time, they will pose a threat when individual firms are allowed to acquire excessive market power.

DIAGONAL AND CONGLOMERATE GROWTH

Another form of expansion common within the media industry is that of developing the business sideways or 'diagonally' into what may be perceived as complementary activities (e.g. newspapers plus magazines or television plus radio), or as new growth areas (e.g. traditional media companies acquiring digital players, such as New Corporation's acquisition of MySpace in 2005 or Disney's acquisition of Club Penguin in 2007). Many strategies of diagonal cross-media expansion result in positive synergies and efficiency gains. A very important potential advantage is the opportunity to share the use of specialized resources or expertise across more than one sort of media product. This will, of course, give rise to economies of scale and of scope.

The combinations of cross-media ownership that yield the most significant economic efficiencies tend to be those which enable the firm to share either common specialized forms of content or a common distribution infrastructure. When a media firm's output is characterized by a particular theme or subject matter, then expanding operations into several different sectors will usually create valuable synergies. For example, Pearson's specialization, through the *Financial Times*, in providing management and financial information enables it to exploit economies of scale and scope across several different products and modes of delivery (e.g. print, broadcast) for that content. A focus on one particular type of content may help the firm to build strong and recognizable brands that are more likely to be successful in crossing over from one platform to another.

The availability of economies of scale and scope depends largely on the extent to which specialist inputs – i.e. elements of media content – or other important resources can be reused or exploited more fully as the firm expands diagonally. It is worth noting that the repackaging of content into different forms has become somewhat easier in recent years thanks to digitization which facilitates the reduction of images, sounds and text to a common format and permits rapid electronic dissemination and exchange of raw and semi-processed materials for media content.

Different combinations of media activities within a conglomerate corporate configuration can yield numerous useful efficiency gains. However, expansion does not always lead to synergies and an improved performance (Peltier, 2004). As some media firms have discovered to their cost, the precise nature of efficiency gains that accompany different combinations of diagonal cross-ownership need to be appraised very carefully. For example, whereas expansion from one form of text-based activity to another (from print to electronic publishing; newspapers to magazines etc.) is likely to create opportunities for content sharing, it is not necessarily the case that combined ownership of text-based plus audio or text-based plus audiovisual (i.e. newspaper plus television) will give rise to any economies of scale or scope or to any other economic advantages. Notwithstanding the spread of digital technologies and the accompanying tendency for media companies to lean towards a multi-platform outlook, it remains true that some of the skills, techniques and equipment involved in producing and distributing, say, newspapers or television are still quite sector-specific. This is evidenced by the fact that many major diversified media conglomerates such as News Corporation continue to allow broadcasting and newspaper subsidiaries to operate virtually completely separately from each other. So, although a strategy of combining differing media activities under common ownership may well generate opportunities to rationalize resources, it is not the case that any and all combinations will automatically result in special efficiency gains (more so than would arise in any other merger situation involving loosely related sectors of activity).

Even if cross-ownership of, say, radio, television and newspapers fails to deliver any immediate opportunities to cut out waste or use collective resources more effectively, companies that engage in diagonal expansion may nonetheless derive some commercial or strategic benefits from cross-ownership. For example, diversified ownership brings with it an opportunity to cross-promote the firm's products. Whether cross-promotion is beneficial or damaging to the economy and society more widely depends on how it is used. When used to facilitate *de novo* expansion (i.e. the introduction of new products which increase choice) then welfare and competition should be enhanced, whereas the use of cross-promotion to build cross-sectoral dominance for existing media products will impact negatively on competition and on pluralism.

Risk-reduction is another driving force associated with diagonal expansion (Picard, 2002: 193). For example, a radio broadcaster whose income is derived wholly from advertising may expand operations into another media sector where revenues come directly from consumers in order to protect or cushion itself against cyclical downturns in advertising expenditure. A firm operating in a declining industry may wish to diversify into a perceived growth area. Aris and Bughin observe that the growth pattern of many dominant media players (e.g. the Lagardère Media Group which is one of the largest media companies in Europe) has been guided by the logic of 'portfolio optimization' with investment in emerging growth areas (e.g. television) providing a counterbalance for sectors which are mature or in slow decline (2009: 266).

In analysing gains that arise from any strategy of diagonal expansion, it is worth distinguishing between different sorts of advantages – i.e. efficiency gains versus risk-spreading etc. – and between different potential beneficiaries – i.e. the firm's shareholders or its managers versus society at large. The achievement of efficiency gains (e.g. economies or scale and scope) will not only serve the interests of the firm but should also contribute to the wider good of the economy by engendering an improved use of resources. Acquisition strategies that cut out unnecessary waste or that enable a restructuring of activities so as to underpin a firm's ongoing economic survival and success will naturally be regarded as congruent with more generalized goals of economic efficiency and growth. However, strategies of cross-media expansion that yield no efficiency gains and are predicated solely on the strategic interests of the firm's shareholders or managers may not give rise to any general economic gains.

On the contrary, the accumulation of greater size, more market power and dominant market positions can lead to behaviour and practices which run contrary to the public interest (Moschandreas, 2000: 362–3). Once a firm achieves a dominant position, the removal of competitive pressures may give rise to various inefficiencies, including excessive expenditure of resources aimed simply at maintaining dominance. Hence, competition policy – which applies to media as well other firms – strives to promote sufficient competition to induce firms to operate efficiently.

VERTICAL EXPANSION

The vertical supply chain outlined in Chapter 2 indicates how it is possible to break down into a few or indeed several stages the activities involved in making and then supplying a media product or service to the consumer. For instance, the newspaper industry can be disaggregated into news-gathering, editing, printing, distribution and retailing. The television industry can be broadly broken down into programme production, assembling the schedule, transmission and, in some cases, retail interface. Many media firms are vertically integrated in the sense that they are involved in activities at more than one stage in the supply process. Many broadcasters make their own programmes in-house, for example.

Why is vertical integration an attractive strategy? Broadly speaking, it makes sense to control both content production and distribution because the greater the distribution of your output, the lower your per-unit production costs will be. In television, per-viewer production costs can be reduced by 'selling' the same output to as many different audiences or segments of the audience as possible. As a distributor, vertical expansion upstream into production means that you have an assured supply of appropriate content to disseminate through your distribution infrastructure. As a content producer, vertical integration with a distributor means assured access to audiences.

Vertical expansion is not only about maximizing revenues and gaining more security or control over the market. Another advantage is that it can reduce transaction costs. These are all the costs involved in negotiating and conducting a transaction in the marketplace such as, for the purchaser, the time, effort and uncertainty involved in acquiring the right product (Lipsey and Chrystal, 2007: 116). Broadcasters who internalize the programme-production process rather than purchasing programme rights in the open market face fewer complications, delays and so on in securing exactly the sort of content they require.

So, as with other forms of expansion, the two main incentives associated with vertical growth are improved efficiency and the accumulation of market power. In any example of vertical expansion, it is possible that both motives may be present and that the two motives might be interrelated. Vertical integration may be motivated by the desire to minimize costs or by the desire for greater security (e.g. access to essential raw materials such as, for a broadcaster, attractive television programming), but then the latter – the desire to gain some control over the market environment – may itself result in market dominance.

Looking more closely at how vertical integration can help minimize costs, an important consideration is the difference between the expenses involved in buying from or selling to other firms – obtaining information, negotiating contracts, etc. – and, alternatively, the expenses involved in carrying out the functions performed by these other firms within one's own organization. Ronald Coase (1937) first introduced the idea that 'the market' and 'the firm' represent alternative modes for allocating resources. For Coase, firms exist because the co-ordination of economic activity through the firm (by hierarchies of managers) is less costly than through the market (by the pricing system). Integration of activities within the structure of a firm will occur because it creates transaction-cost savings and these act as an incentive to integrate vertically.

The potential for cost reductions within a firm may stem from improved information – e.g. about price or product specifications or, more generally, about the market. So in the television industry, for example, the costs (created by uncertainty, weaker informational flows, etc.) involved in inter-firm trade between programme produc-ers and broadcasters may well be higher than when both activities are carried out in-house. It may save time and hassle to be able to source the programmes that are needed directly from an in-house production division rather than having to shop around, negotiate and make deals with external programme-makers.

However, for media firms, the chief factor encouraging vertical expansion usually stems from the interdependent relation between different phases in the supply chain. Media content is no good without access to audiences, and vice versa. So the main driving force for firms to diversify into additional upstream or downstream phases is the desire to gain more security and control over the market environment. Integrated media firms can avoid the market power of dominant sup-pliers or buyers. Vertical expansion gives secure access to, for example, essential inputs or essential distribution outlets for output. This is a key advantage in the media, because firms depend on getting access both to content and to avenues for distribution of content.

A broadcaster that has to rely on external producers to supply all the hit programmes in its schedule will find itself vulnerable to the pos-sibility of post-contractual opportunistic behaviour on the part of these suppliers. If the supplier of a key programme series in a broadcaster's schedule threatens to withdraw that series or sell it at a higher price to a rival broadcaster, then high costs may have to be incurred to retain that particular programme. Vertical integration is a way of avoiding the higher costs associated with such behaviour (Martin, 2002: 405–6).

If monopoly power is present in the programme-production stage (say, because a supplier has control over a specific programme for which no perceived substitutes are available) then, even without vertical integration, the firm with upstream monopoly power may be able to appropriate some of any monopoly profits available at the broadcasting stage (Moschandreas, 2000: 260). It is rarely the situation that no substitutes are available for a particular product but, with powerful content brands, specificity of inputs (particular actors, writers or presenters) is a factor in their popularity and success. To avoid being held to ransom by important suppliers, broadcasters and other media distributors may have no choice other than to expand vertically into production.

From a content-producer's point of view, there are also numerous attractions in vertical integration. Ownership of, say, a popular online content service or of broadcasting activities ensures that the firm's output will find its way to audiences. Vertical integration may well lead to a more predictable and reliable stream of orders.

A steady and predictable production slate is an important advantage for content-makers. This, in turn, allows the vertically integrated production company to plan more effectively and to use its production resources, equipment, technicians and personnel more efficiently. The assured distribution enjoyed by a vertically integrated production firm also helps to build that producer's reputation, or brand name, as a supplier of content.

Digitization and growth of the Internet have encouraged new forms of vertical/diagonal expansion involving diversified media content-makers and digital platform operators. One example of traditional media content-making being combined with digital distribution was the merger of Time Warner with Internet service provider AOL in 2000, where subsequent well-publicized difficulties in integrating and making a success of this vast enterprise issued a costly lesson about the perils of over-expansion and over-valuation of 'new' media businesses (Gapper, 2005: 7). Nonetheless, the ambition to combine strengths in content creation with capability in fixed and mobile digital delivery has remained a major force driving corporate activity in the media sector. French media company Vivendi, for instance, started life as a water and waste-management firm but, through a series of business developments and acquisitions starting with Canal+, has gradually grown into a multinational media conglomerate with a range of content-making activities (including music and video games publishing, film and pay-TV) plus communication network businesses. Another example is US company Comcast which, through the acquisition of a major stake in NBC Universal in 2011, has developed from a heavily distribution-focused cable entity into a leading vertically integrated media player (Gelles, 2011b: 19).

When it comes to assessing the motives or merits of a media merger, it is sometimes difficult to disentangle the pursuit of greater efficiency and greater security from the pursuit of monopoly power (Griffiths and Wall, 2007: 75). A media firm might well expand vertically in order to gain greater security but then, the more control it acquires over all stages in the vertical supply chain, the more danger there is that it will start to dominate the market, with detrimental consequences for rivals and consumers. Vertical integration may protect the market power of incumbent firms by increasing barriers to entry. For example, if all the best programme-producers are cross-owned by broadcasters then, in order to secure its own supply of attractive programming, a new market entrant in the broadcasting arena would also be forced to adopt a vertically integrated structure, thus pushing up the costs of market entry. Put another way, '[v]ertical integration is a self-reinforcing process: once a few important players start to integrate, others feel forced to do the same in order to ensure future access to content (for platform operators) or to distribution (for media companies)' (Aris and Bughin, 2009: 271). So, vertical expansion can be seen, in one way, that of Coase, as a response to market failures and imperfections and, in another sense, as a source of such market imperfections.

TRANSNATIONAL GROWTH

Many large media conglomerates such as News Corporation, Bauer, Bertelsmann and Reed Elsevier are multinational companies. French company Vivendi, for example, acquired Universal Studios in the US for a time and has developed its Canal+ pay-television interests internationally across Europe, become a leading telecoms player in Morocco and, in 2009, acquired broadband distribution businesses in Brazil. Online Latin-American content provider Terra, a subsidiary of Spanish telecoms operator Telefonica, is expanding its business activities into European markets (Edgecliffe-Johnson, 2012: 21). Transnational growth, whether in the form of mergers and acquisitions of businesses in other territories or through international partnerships, is a well-rehearsed and commonplace phenomenon in the media industry (Terazono, 2007), and is driven largely by the same economic motives which underlie strategies of vertical, horizontal and conglomerate expansion in a domestic context but also by globalization.

Globalization, as discussed in the previous chapter, has resulted in much more intense international competition in many sectors of industry including, not least, media and communications (Lipsey and Chrystal, 2007: 183). Thanks to diminishing trade barriers, more mobility of capital and the spread of the Internet – an infrastructure for distribution that has little regard for national boundaries – local and national media businesses are no longer as insulated from competing international suppliers to the extent that they have been in the past. So, while many media organizations are still strongly oriented towards audiences and advertisers within their own home markets, most if not all have become more outward-looking in terms of ambitions to broaden the geographic reach of their products and businesses.

The popularity of strategies of international expansion has resulted in the emergence of some very large transnational media conglomerates across Europe and beyond (Sánchez-Tabernero, 2006: 489). In some cases, international growth may reflect saturation of home markets or curtailment over further domestic growth arising from local regulatory instruments related to competition or pluralism (Bruck et al., 2004: 9). In such circumstances, international expansion provides valuable opportunities to increase revenues, spread or reduce costs and derive economies (Picard, 2002: 213).

However, as with other forms of expansion, international growth is generally fuelled by conventional economic motives related to attainment of efficiency gains and greater critical mass. It reflects the prevalence of economies of scale and scope in the media industry which creates a natural incentive to expand consumption of your output to as wide an audience as possible. This includes expansion across international markets where this is feasible. Of course, internationalization can be achieved through partnerships with local firms (or, for example, franchise arrangements which, as discussed in more detail in Chapter 4, are common in magazine publishing), or through exports rather than by buying up businesses in overseas territories. However, in choosing to acquire or develop subsidiary operations in overseas markets, expanding organizations are attracted by opportunities to economize on transaction costs while reaping all available cost efficiencies and exploiting shared resources more effectively across the enlarged group. As processes of erosion of national boundaries take their course, such economic and strategic advantages ensure that multi-product and multinational firms will continue to predominate in the corporate media landscape.

4

Networks

Networks are a well-established but also an increasingly significant feature of media industries. Networks and other arrangements that allow shared use of content, brands, advertising relationships, etc. are found in television and radio broadcasting and sometimes in print publishing, for example, in magazines. These conventional media networks owe their existence at least partly to the long-standing availability of supply-side economies of scale, but digitization has introduced new players and magnified the importance of networks as systems of organization within media industries. This chapter examines the economics of media networks and explains how convergence raises new economic questions for media and communications organizations related to network externalities, opportunities to reap demand-side economies of scale, issues of market dominance and the growing significance of social networks.

After studying this chapter, you should be able to:

- identify and explain the incentives to form broadcast networks;
- analyse the features of transnational networks in publishing;
- understand the concept of network effects as they apply to digital media and communications;
- assess how digitization and interactivity have increased the significance of networks in media economics.

ECONOMICS OF NETWORKS

Networks exist in a range of contexts – social, organizational and industrial – and encompass numerous possible shapes and forms of relationships. Network industries are those characterized by structures that involve interconnections and links (Shy, 2003). Typical examples include electricity supply, transport and telecommunications. For instance, transport infrastructures such as railroads involve a network of nodes that enable users to move around. Similarly, telephone networks allow voice traffic to move freely from one point to another via central connections.

Because of the complex array of areas of economic activity it encompasses, the media sector cannot fairly be described as a 'typical' network industry, but it is one in which a number of differing sorts of networks can be found. The significance of networks as a feature of media businesses has grown and the characteristics of any given network will have a bearing on its economics. Directionality of traffic flow across the network is a key distinguishing characteristic (Economides, 2007). The sorts of networks traditionally found in, for example, broadcasting involve transmission of content *one-way* from suppliers in the direction of audiences that, in turn, may be used to attract advertisers. Where media networks involve a unidirectional flow of content towards audiences, the main economic incentive underpinning the arrangement is usually the availability of supply-side economies of scale. The formation of a geographically dispersed network of media outlets provides an effective means of spreading the high initial fixed costs involved in content-creation across additional audience groups and constituencies that share an interest in that content and are based in other localities.

A major change stemming from digitization and growth of the Internet has been the arrival of distribution infrastructures capable of conveying *two-way* and multidirectional traffic. Whereas multidirectional traffic has never been a feature of conventional systems of mass media provision, many other network industries are constructed to allow traffic to flow to and from all nodes reciprocally. When traffic is multidirectional rather than unidirectional, this gives rise to different sorts of benefits and the economic incentives that underpin network formation will be altered. The spread of digital technologies has introduced media suppliers to the question of how best to exploit the benefits arising from reciprocal as well as from one-to-many traffic flows.

The concept of 'network effects' is based on the idea that the value of a network will increase when others share it, and refers to the ways that higher or wider usage of certain products or services confers greater value for all users. For instance, when an extra member joins a business-related or professional online network such as LinkedIn, this confers a benefit on all other subscribers that have registered to use it. Early research into network effects focused on telecommunications, which is a good example of an industry where the more people that are signed up to participate in the service, the more valuable it becomes (Farrell and Saloner, 1985; Katz and Shapiro, 1985).

Online social and communication networks such as Facebook and Twitter enjoy network effects insofar as the more people that use these services, the greater the utility for each network participant. Metcalfe's law, named after computing engineer Robert Metcalfe, suggests a way of quantifying this by proposing that the total value of, say, a telecommunications network is proportional to the square of the number of users connected to the system (Shapiro and Varian, 1999). Whether the value that can be ascribed to each individual user is as high as Metcalfe proposed is disputed in more recent work on applied network effects theory (Odlyzko and Tilly, 2005), but the fundamental idea that extra participants add value to a communications network clearly holds true. However, the sources of network benefits are varied and are not confined solely to opportunities for reciprocal communication. Network effects often stem from technological compatibility and, for that reason, these effects are seen as particularly endemic to computing and electronic industries where capacity for synchronization between differing systems is a crucial concern.

In their seminal work on networks, Katz and Shapiro (1985) distinguish between 'direct' and 'indirect' effects which will arise depending on the nature of the network in question. When an additional person physically joins a communications network by, for example, purchasing and installing a fax machine or a telephone, other network users stand to benefit directly. But an indirect benefit will accrue, for example, to fellow users of a particular proprietary standard or system whenever an additional consumer purchases a product that is aligned to that particular system, because wider usage makes the system more popular and viable so that complementary goods will be available more widely and more cheaply (Katz and Shapiro, 1985: 424). Indirect network benefits are created when more usage of a product or service increases the value of goods that are complementary, e.g. software that is compatible.

A related concept, of particular relevance for media, is that of 'two-sided network effects'. Where two-sided markets exist, an increase in usage by one set of users generates benefits for another distinct user group. For example, payment card systems rely on wide usage on the part of both retailers and shoppers so as any payment card gains in popularity with merchants, the other user group – cardholders – stands to benefit from cross-side network effects (Rochet and Tirole, 2003). Many media operate in two-sided market industries in the sense that they serve both audiences and advertisers. Radio broadcast networks, for example, are reliant on the revenues they can earn from selling commercial airtime so, there are strong incentives to 'subsidize' adoption by one user group – i.e. listeners – in order to create cross-side network benefits so that charges can then be imposed on the other user group – i.e. advertisers (Evans and Schmalensee, 2008).

In some industries, technological compatibility is a source of network benefits, for instance, for some software and hardware products, high demand may result not only from the product's intrinsic features – the fact that it is superior to rival offerings, if indeed it is – but also simply because consumers want products that are in wide usage and least likely to pose problems in terms of compatibility and standards. In network markets where consumers derive more value from products or services that have wider acceptance, early market entrants will enjoy 'first-mover' advantages – i.e. 'the first technology that is introduced into the market may gain excess momentum when many early users join in anticipation of other users hopping on the bandwagon at a later stage' (Gottinger, 2003: 8–9).

The existence of network effects changes the nature of competition in an industry and may well encourage dominance by individual firms (Koski and Kretschmer, 2004; Tremblay, 2011). Normally, the main vectors through which market players compete with each other are price and product quality, but when network effects are present, the key imperative for competing suppliers is to win and maintain consumers' commitment to their own products or technological standards or brands. Because early leads are so decisive, it is argued that inferior products and services that capture such a lead can dominate over superior ones. This is because consumers are reluctant to bear the short-term costs of disconnecting from their established networks of users or switching to less popular brands or incompatible technologies (Farrell and Klemperer, 2007).

Switching costs and network effects serve to bind customers to particular brands or systems in what is sometimes called 'vendor lock-in'. The hassle and expense or the perceived loss of efficiency that would accompany a change serves to deter people from making a switch. Reluctance to switch greatly favours market incumbents, for example in the banking industry where customers are rarely keen to change their account to another bank. When technology is involved, as is frequently the case in media and communications industries, issues related to standardization and to the amount of time people spend training themselves to use existing standards will contribute to a reluctance to abandon that investment, 'even if new technology is better and a switch would be desirable for the sake of efficiency' (Gottinger, 2003:12).

Social networking sites (SNSs) provide an example of the potential for vendor lock-in in the context of developing communication markets. The two largest players in the industry, Facebook and MySpace, have invested heavily in recent years in competing for additional membership and for a strong market position (Johnson, 2008). The structure of the Web interface for services such as Facebook encourages network members to gradually build up an array of personal data, social interactions and links that comprise the individual's online profile and personality. But retrieving this data, whether with a view towards changing to another SNS or for other reasons, is not always easy. In the words of one industry analyst, '[t]he switching costs are very high, especially when you've built up a network of hundreds of friends and made an archive of your life and photos' (Smith, cited in Gelles and Waters, 2010).

Vendor lock-in is regarded as potentially detrimental to the development of markets because it gives some players excessive levels of market power. Whereas consumers may benefit in early stages when rival suppliers are competing intensively and working hard to build market share, the presence of network benefits implies that such competition is inherently unstable and there is a strong danger that it will eventually tip over into monopoly for the dominant system, thus closing off market entry and giving rise to all the inefficiencies commonly associated with monopolization (Farrell and Klemperer, 2007).

That dominance is a peril is not surprising, given that network effects naturally propel players in network industries towards achieving ever-larger numbers of users. Dominance is not the only worry that the expansion of networks can give rise to. The introduction of extra users to a network can also create capacity problems (Yoo, 2006), so the marginal value added by new participants may, at some point, start to diminish on account of congestion (e.g. where communication systems become overwhelmed by traffic).

In general, digitization and growth of the Internet have added to the opportunities and advantages available to media firms through the formation of networks and increased the economic significance of media networks. But network 'externalities' – the change imposed on third parties through the participation of an extra individual in a network – can be both negative and positive (Liebowitz and Margolis, 1994; Shy, 2011). As networks and network effects become more pervasive, new challenges arise not only for media market participants but also for policy-makers concerned with sustaining competition and efficiency within media provision.

BROADCASTING NETWORKS

In broadcasting, a network usually constitutes a group of players located in distinct geographic regions who have entered into a strategic alliance in order to create and then exploit some mutual advantages, usually built around shared use of content. The economic logic behind strategies of networking in broadcast industries is highly compelling, and broadcasting networks are often the market leaders within commercial television and radio markets. The most important benefit created is usually economies of scale in programming. The network enables a group of broadcasters to share more or less exactly the same schedule of programmes, thus reducing the per-viewer or per-listener costs of providing the service for each station in the network. Networks are a way of enlarging the audience for a single television or radio service.

In the UK, ITV is a good example of a television network. ITV or 'Channel 3' is a free-to-air, commercially funded national television broadcast channel made up of 15 regional licensed areas. ITV's audience share has been eroded steadily over recent years but nonetheless, it retains a viewing share of 18 per cent across all UK homes (Ofcom, 2010a: 163), ITV1 is still by far the most popular commercial channel in Britain. The network's 15 regional licences cover the whole of the UK. Ownership was originally spread across a number of regional television companies, but has been consolidating dramatically since the early 1990s: 11 are now controlled by ITV plc (see Figure 3.1, page 43), two by STV and one each by UTV and Channel Television. The ITV network shares programmes through a system where each of the 15 licensees contributes a payment into a collective budget for the ITV schedule of programmes and, in return, receives the right to broadcast that schedule (interspersed with some dedicated local output) in their own region. Each licensee makes money by selling advertising slots in and around transmissions of the ITV network schedule in their own regions.

Payments into the collective programme budget vary according to the respective revenue shares of participants in the network. So, albeit that controversy has occasionally flared up about the exact terms for participation (Fenton, 2011a), ITV's arrangements for sharing costs involve some cross-subsidization of smaller regional licensees by larger ones. Despite this, each participant – whether large or small – benefits greatly from being able to transmit a much more expensive schedule of programmes than it could afford if it were trying to operate independently.

In the US, the main television networks – ABC, NBC, CBS and Fox – carry out two key functions (Litman, 1998: 131; Lotz, 2007; Owen and Wildman, 1992: 153). Not only do they facilitate sharing the costs of programming in the same way as the ITV network, but the US networks also club together to sell advertising. Advertisers who want national coverage in the US can purchase it all in one go from the networks. This reduces transaction costs for national advertisers and increases demand for the airtime of local broadcasters participating in a network.

The US networks rely on a chain of local television stations or 'affiliates' – around 200 or more each – to provide national audiences for their programmes. Each of the networks owns a few of their own affiliates but many are independently owned. Local affiliates receive from the network a ready-made package for transmission comprised of a fairly comprehensive schedule of programmes together with advertisements. In return for carrying prime-time programmes supplied by the networks, affiliates are allowed opportunities to sell some commercial airtime of their own to both national and local advertisers.

Historically, affiliates have also received 'compensation' or a payment from the network, the amount of which has varied from station to station, in return for accepting the schedule. The bargaining position of network affiliates in relation to fees was helped in the 1990s by ever-growing competition in the upstream 'packaging' phase from newcomers such as Fox (Gapper, 1998: 22). Since then the declining fortunes of the networks has been accompanied by a whittling away of fees.

Network affiliates have managed to sustain their revenues by securing carriage payments from the pay-TV platforms that, in most cases, are now involved in retransmitting the network schedule onwards to US viewers (Li and Edgecliffe-Johnson, 2009). Competition between pay-TV operators has meant that 'none can afford to go without top networks' and this has helped local affiliates to negotiate increasing per-subscriber carriage fees (Brannon and Bargouth, 2010: 302). Broadcast networks have also turned their attention to retransmission fees as a valuable second stream of revenue at a time of ever-increasing competition for advertising. With the bargaining position of affiliates eroded by the emergence of alternative distribution platforms for network content, the previous situation whereby networks paid local stations to transmit their schedules has now been reversed, and affiliates frequently find themselves obliged to pay over a portion of their retransmission fee income to the broadcast network that is supplying their content (ibid.).

Although established television networks everywhere are faced with increasing competition from new terrestrial, cable, satellite, digital and online broadcasting rivals, the level of advertising revenue they are able to attract generally tends to decline at a slower pace than their audience share. This is true both of the US networks and of the ITV network in the UK (Gasson, 1996: 148–50). In an increasingly fragmented market, the ability to offer an immediate impact with mass audiences commands a special value. Advertisers are usually prepared to pay a premium on top of the usual cost per thousand (CPT) rate for airtime that gives them access to mass audiences.

Audiences during prime time and in the slots around particularly popular programmes typically sell at a higher CPT than in other periods. This was demonstrated, for example, by the $3m paid for each 30-second advertising slot transmitted to 111m US television viewers during the Super Bowl in March 2011 (Gelles and Edgecliffe-Johnson, 2011). Likewise, audiences for the most popular channels sell at a premium. The collective prime-time audience share for the major US networks – NBC, CBS and ABC – may well have declined steeply in recent decades, but these channels, now joined by Fox, still offer the easiest means of reaching a genuinely mass television audience in the US.

The advantages of scale that accrue to major networks can act as a barrier to entry in broadcasting. The economies of scale in programming available to established networks with large audiences make it very difficult for new entrants to break into the market. A new broadcaster usually has a long way to go before its audience reach will be sufficient to start earning the revenues needed to pay for a programme service that is directly competitive with existing networks. In the UK, for example, ITV's annual programme budget is running at around £800m, as compared with £135m for terrestrial rival Channel Five (Sweney, 2011) and less than £20m for some new pay-television channels.

When the strength of the networks is reinforced through strategies of vertical integration, the barriers to entry are even more difficult to overcome. The acquisition of NBC by Comcast Corporation, the largest Internet service provider in the US, provides an example of a forward vertical expansion strategy by combining the television and film content businesses of NBC Universal with Comcast's extensive cable and Internet distribution interests (Epstein, 2011). Backward vertical integration is another commonplace strategy and provides a means for broadcast networks to control inflation in content costs. According to the former chairman of USA Networks, Barry Diller: 'I don't think there is any way the [business] model can work unless you are making programming and owning it through every part of the value chain you can find' (cited in Gapper, 1998: 22).

This view is evidently widely shared by the major US networks as evidenced by, for example, the merger between ABC and Disney in 1995. Indeed, Fox took the concept of vertical expansion a stage further when its parent company, News Corporation, acquired the Los Angeles Dodgers baseball team in the late 1990s. A similar strategy was attempted when Murdoch-owned satellite broadcaster BSkyB tried to take over Manchester United Football Club but was prevented from doing so by UK competition authorities in 1999. These moves reflect the increasing importance of ownership of rights to sports programming in the ratings battle between broadcast networks, a point also underlined by the very high inflation in prices that US networks will pay for key sports events (Edgecliffe-Johnson, 2011a; Garrahan, 2011a).

In terms of viewer welfare, the prevalence of broadcasting networks can be criticized for contributing to uniformity of television output across different regions. On the other hand, because networks facilitate enormous economies of scale, it can be argued that the cost savings they create make it possible for local and regional audiences to have more expensive and better programme services than could be afforded if local or regional broadcasters were stand-alone operations. The cost savings enjoyed on prime-time programming by local stations who are part of a wider network should leave more resources available to invest in any parts of the schedule not supplied by the network – e.g. to dedicated regional programming.

GLOBAL NETWORKS IN TRANSNATIONAL PUBLISHING

Anyone who travels internationally will be familiar with the ubiquity of some broadcasting networks, such as CNN, but networks are not solely a feature of broadcasting. The magazine publishing industry provides numerous examples of international partnerships formed in order to facilitate cross-frontier expansion of media brands across additional geographic territories. As with many broadcasting networks, a typical modus operandi for cross-frontier networks of magazine publishing partners involves transmission of content outwards from the central co-ordinating headquarters or hub to partners based in different geographic regions who in turn convey that content onwards, usually in a slightly modified form, to local audiences.

Magazine publishing has long been an international business, and European companies have been among the most active in developing transfrontier titles and brands. In contrast with newspaper publishers who rarely manage to sell their wares across national frontiers, many consumer magazine companies in the US, Germany, France, the UK and Scandinavia have achieved much success in taking their products into new international territories (Doyle, 2011). In the face of growing competition, increased fragmentation of demand and saturation in their own local markets, overseas markets have provided fertile new territory for expansion. The needs of the advertising industry have played a role in encouraging this trend (Hafstrand, 1995). Globalization has engendered more ferocious competition at a transnational level among rival consumer goods and a desire, where possible, to build brands that have instant international recognition and appeal.

The fashion industry provides many examples of retail items (perfume, clothing, sunglasses, etc.) that are distributed and sold around the world. The formula for creation of a global brand involves extensive and sustained investment in worldwide advertising based on an expectation of substantial aggregate returns across numerous international territories over time (Arvidsson, 2006). For the creators and owners of global retail brands, access to global audiences is a highly valued and sought-after commodity. Not surprisingly then, transnational television networks such as MTV or magazines such as *Elle* that can offer access to a very specific demographic target group all around the world are well placed to cater to the emerging needs of the advertising industry.

A long history of success in internationalization by magazine publishers partly reflects the nature of the product which, relative to other media, has lent itself exceptionally well towards overseas expansion. Branding and segmentation techniques, which are discussed further in Chapter 5, are central to the business of magazine publishing. Often, the investment put into the creation of a magazine's distinctive brand image and the strength of its brand is sufficient to ensure that it will have some appeal for the same lifestyle group or niche across many different geographic and regional markets, albeit that some adaptation at the local level may be required. Because of their emphasis on visual material, many leisure and lifestyle titles are relatively easy to adapt into other languages and will not necessarily lose their core appeal in the process of translation.

These factors, which favour international expansion in magazine publishing, have triggered the creation of many sorts of formal and informal networks among international publishing partners. In order to widen the international readership for a magazine, its parent company will often adopt a strategy of publishing several different international versions in partnership with local publishing partners in different localities using a contract-based approach (Cabell and Greehan, 2004). As with broadcasting networks, the most compelling economic incentive underpinning the formation of a magazine publishing network is that it enables a group of companies in different localities to share significant elements of the same content, thus reducing the per-reader costs of supplying the product for each firm participating in the network. Again, networks provide a means of enlarging the audience for a single-content property.

Instances of magazine titles that sell in numerous modified versions across the globe abound. *FHM* – a magazine aimed at young men – provides a useful example. The title was purchased by UK media conglomerate EMAP (since acquired by Bauer Consumer Media) in 1994, and was transformed from a low-circulation product about mens' fashion distributed free in tailors' shops into a fashionable 'lad's mag' that soon came to dominate the emerging men's lifestyle category in the UK. Having developed *FHM* as a market-leading product in the home market, its parent company then embarked on a strategy of international expansion across a series of additional countries.

At the peak of its success in 2005–06, a series of 30 international editions comprised the *FHM* network (see Table 4.1), some published by wholly owned subsidiaries of the parent company (e.g. in the UK, the US and France) but most of which were published by overseas partners under a licence agreement. Since then, more intense competition and the contraction of the men's lifestyle magazine category as a whole has reduced the scale of the *FHM* network and, for instance, the US edition is no longer published in print form. Nonetheless *FHM* provides a vivid illustration of how the formation of a network of publishing partners can facilitate the rapid promulgation of a successful core brand and formula.

In setting up an international network, the key operational issues that need to be organized include choosing compatible partners, establishing systems for communication with and support of partners, the creation of a 'brand book' and negotiation of contract terms. The brand book for a magazine contains a detailed explanation of how an edition should look and feel, what its core values are and which standards and norms need to be adhered to in terms of design, layout, etc. Licensing terms vary from one deal to the next, but usually the licensee pays a percentage of revenues earned from copy sales and advertising to the licensor (Doyle, 2006).

In return for this payment, the magazine brand owner provides not only a tried-and-tested concept but also access for licensees to large amounts of editorial content. As is common in broadcasting networks, the magazine brand owner acts as a central hub, responsible

Table 4.1 The FHM international network in 2005

	Edition	Company	Ownership Status		Launch Date	Circulation ('000)
1	FHM UK	EMAP	100%	Market Leader	1985	560
2	FHM Singapore	EMAP	License	Market Leader	1997	40
3	FHM Australia	EMAP	100%	Market Leader	1998	140
4	FHM Turkey	Merkez Dergi	License	Market Leader	1998	30
5	FHM Malaysia	EMAP	License	Market Leader	1998	20
6	FHM France	EMAP	100%	Market Leader	1999	180
7	FHM South Africa	Media 24	JV	Market Leader	1999	115
8	FHM Philippines	Summit	License	Market Leader	2000	130
9	FHM US	EMAP	100%		2000	1,200
10	FHM Romania	Hearst Sanoma	License	Market Leader	2000	30
11	FHM Taiwan	King's International	License	Market Leader	2000	30
12	FHM Holland	TTG	License	Market Leader	2000	55
13	FHM Hungary	Hearst Sanoma	License	Market Leader	2000	50
14	FHM Germany	Attic Futura	License	Market Leader	2000	250
15	FHM Russia	Independent Media	License		2001	50
16	FHM Thailand	Siam Sport	License	Market Leader	2003	70
17	FHM Indonesia	MRA Group	License	Market Leader	2003	35
18	FHM Latvia	Lilita	License	Market Leader	2003	20
19	FHM Denmark	Benjamin/Bonnier	License		2003	40
20	FHM Mexico	Editorial Premiere	License		2003	70
21	FHM Spain	Focus Ediciones	License	Market Leader	2004	220
22	FHM Slovenia	Video Top	License		2004	5
23	FHM China	Trends	License		2004	80
24	FHM Norway	Bonnier Media	License	Market Leader	2004	60
25	FHM Estonia	I&L Publishing	License	Market Leader	2004	10
26	FHM Lithuania	I&L Publishing	License		2004	25
27	FHM Portugal	Edimpressa	License	Market Leader	2005	50
28	FHM Greece	Lambrakis	License	Market Leader	2005	50
29	FHM Sweden	Bonnier Media	License		2005	40
30	FHM Croatia	Video Top	License		2005	20
	TOTAL					3,565

Source: Based on company data supplied as at November 2005.

for assembling original content that is then transmitted onwards to local affiliates who, having made some adaptations and additions to suit local tastes, convey it outwards to local audiences. The resources on offer to the local publisher include, most obviously, the content and brand, but may also extend to guidance from the parent publisher on managing the business and on how best to develop and exploit the appeal of that particular magazine brand with advertisers.

Being a franchisee within an international magazine publishing network clearly offers benefits for local partners but it is also advantageous for the magazine brand owner because it minimizes many of the risks and costs associated with international expansion (Deresky, 2006). All participants in the network stand to benefit from economies of scale in content production and from shared expertise and joint branding and marketing.

However, sustaining a growing network of international local publishing partners can also involve complexity, particularly in the areas of communication and control over the brand (Doyle, 2006). The process of extending any cultural product or brand across numerous different international settings is inherently much more difficult than, say, internationalizing sales of shampoos or mobile phones. The main challenge stems from the need to adapt the product appropriately to fit indigenous circumstances, sensitivities, tastes, etc. When franchising is the chosen route, the brand book provides the local partner with a clear format and formula for editorial content, design, physical format and layout. However, in order to 'get it right' for the local audience, the partner publisher also has to be given sufficient freedom and scope to modify and adapt as required to fit local circumstances.

The emergence of global markets for consumer goods provides growing incentives for collaboration between media suppliers at transnational level. Some would argue that local cultural specificities are becoming ameliorated. Differences in tastes and preferences among international audiences are gradually being eroded by processes of globalization which magazines and other transnational media have facilitated and responded to, but which they have also accelerated (Cabell and Greehan, 2004: 8). However, the degree to which media globalization is really taking place is disputed by others (Hafez, 2007). In practice, awareness of the particularities of local tastes and values is essential in avoiding offensive or embarrassing editorial misjudgements, as some publishers have discovered only through making costly errors. Striking the right balance between protecting the core brand, which is clearly of paramount importance, and at the same time allowing sufficient editorial and operational latitude or trusting your local partner to understand what adaptations are needed is a major challenge for transnational brand owners (Doyle, 2006).

Although the literature of international management provides numerous warnings about the difficulties of sustaining transnational business alliances, the track record of companies such as Bauer, Hachette Filipacchi and Hearst in developing magazine brands that achieve positions of market leadership across the globe suggests that, at least in publishing, cross-border partnerships can work highly effectively. This is not perhaps surprising given the high financial rewards available to both brand owner and franchisee once a magazine title is successfully translated into new geographic territories.

Notwithstanding the challenges involved, the economic case in favour of extending consumption of a product through means of making minor adaptations to a basic or standard formula so that it appeals in international markets is very compelling. Expansion on this basis, whatever the product, generally involves low investment risks and enables the supplier to capitalize on economies of scale and scope. Expansion of media products on this basis is especially compelling because, in the case of media, once created, the raw material that is being shared between different international versions – the core content or intellectual property – costs little to reproduce. The same story, and/or variations of it, can be 'sold' to multiple different audiences around the globe without its value ever being impaired or diminished.

Technological advances, together with advertisers' needs for convenient access to global audiences, continue to favour the growth of international magazine publishing. Digitization and the use of electronic communications infrastructures have made it easier than ever for content (page proofs etc.) to be conveyed and exchanged back and forth across international publishing networks. The impetus for magazine publishers to form collaborative arrangements that enable the footprints of their most successful products to be extended across more territories is only likely to increase into the future.

ONLINE CONTENT DISTRIBUTION

Whereas conventional media networks are usually based on the notion of suppliers in different localities sharing a common body of content, in a digitized world where infrastructures for media and communications are converged and often indistinguishable, the idea of a network can involve quite different connotations. The Internet is, itself, a vast network of networks and, particularly for younger audiences, has radically transformed ways of relating to content (Borreau and

Lethiais, 2007). The ubiquity of the Internet and of Web-enabled functionality via PC screens, televisions, mobiles and tablets has enabled new forms of connectivity between suppliers and audiences or users and, alongside more widespread and enriched forms of connectivity, a range of new sorts of networks has started to appear and in many cases to prosper.

For some newly emerging media networks, the main *raison d'être*, as with conventional media networks, is simply to extend the audience for a core body of content, thus increasing the total audience value and the attention generated by that content. For example, Internet company Yahoo provides online communication and Web-user data monitoring services as well as news and content via its websites. The company now describes its content distribution business as a 'network', as a senior executive explains (Ross Levinsohn, Head of Americas, Yahoo cited in Edgecliffe-Johnson, 2011c):

> If you think about all the channels we are running, it looks very much like a network and it is something that advertisers and consumers understand ...

> We can all look back at articles written a decade ago that said 'network television is dead!' But ... in the fragmentation of the media landscape, when you are able to aggregate large amounts of people around good premium experiences, advertisers will be happy to pay for it. And I shift that to Yahoo where I think of us as a network where we are able to aggregate large numbers of people and match them with great content.

The claim that 'the network of Yahoo' should be accorded as much recognition by audiences and advertisers as a mainstream television network is supported by the growing popularity of its content. Yahoo currently accounts for nine out of the ten most-watched video series conveyed on the Internet in the US and, buoyed up by this, the company is making increased investments in original content creation (Menn, 2011). Yahoo's drive to exploit supply-side economies of scale in content production mirrors the strategy being pursued by any conventional media network.

Whereas conventional networks operate on the basis of building a sizeable aggregate audience from the smaller chunks that each of its local partners delivers, for an online content network such as Yahoo the construction of audiences takes place at a much more granular level. Yahoo's approach to aggregating audiences involves 'do[ing] it in a way that is *personalized*. That is the difference between digital businesses and traditional [media] businesses' (Levinsohn cited in Edgecliffe-Johnson, 2011c). For Yahoo, audience aggregation is based not on stitching together a patchwork of audiences based in different locations but rather on drawing together very sizeable numbers of viewers or readers through the use of the sophisticated individualized targeting made possible by digital technology. Levinsohn explains: 'our secret sauce is the technology we have that is powering everything underneath ... So we can deliver a piece of content and advertising in context for *you*, personalized' (ibid.).

The tailoring of content offerings to suit individual preferences may take place at the level of a home page where what is displayed can vary slightly from one receiving device or individual to the next, dependent on the associated history of 'data collection events' (Story, 2008). By, for example, tracking which pages are selected for display, which links are clicked through to, what search enquiries are made, which media content is accessed or downloaded, which advertisements are connected with, etc., large Internet companies have become increasingly adept at collecting data about the tastes and preferences exhibited by individuals visiting their sites. Such data is of immense value to marketers and advertisers. It also enables Internet-based media suppliers who have this feedback to modify the interface to their content offerings at an individual level – say, the home page to a media website – giving greater prominence to whichever sort of material is likely to appeal to that particular consumer.

Yahoo recently introduced this technique and currently serves 13m variations of its home page in order 'to optimize the experience for each individual consumer' (Levinsohn cited in Edgecliffe-Johnson, 2011c). Personalization of content offering has proved an 'incredibly powerful' strategy and, in the space of three months, has resulted in an increase of 200 per cent in the rate of click conversion (ibid.). Yahoo is by no means alone in recognizing the value of data gathered through the return path on digital platforms. Many media companies are keen to take advantage of the range of relatively cheap and unobtrusive means that the Internet provides of surveying audience preferences (Napoli, 2011). Such intelligence can feed into more effective upstream content decisions on the part of traditional media suppliers. For example, a broadcaster may decide, in the light of positive online 'chatter', to elevate a show to a more prominent time slot. Web-connected content delivery services enjoy a significant advantage over conventional unidirectional media products and services in that audience data collected can be deployed to adjust, modify and improve content offerings at the level of every individual.

The traditional concept of a media network based on distribution of a largely identical package of content via a number of geographically dispersed nodes involves collaboration among partners in modifying that content in order to extend its attractions for additional geographic segments. Local affiliates or partners or subsidiaries usually play a part – sometimes a crucial and active role – in shaping content to the needs and preferences of a specific regional or national audience. By contrast, the model provided by the Yahoo online service does not involve local intermediaries. Instead, the tailoring function is performed by embedded technologies which track, analyse and respond to revealed audience preferences.

Reciprocity of traffic flows is generally considered a defining feature of networks in the communications industry, but whether interactivity alone provides a sufficient qualification for status as a media network seems doubtful. Companies involved both in communications and media tend to conform more readily with the structural norms of one sector rather than another but, increasingly, lines are blurring. From the point of view of the consumer, the distinction between new 'networks' such as Yahoo which, through adept personalizing of content, are able to deliver very sizeable aggregate audiences, and other 'non-network' Internet portals, online film subscription services, content aggregation sites and catch-up services such as Hulu or Netflix is not always obvious. Indeed, the popularity of such services as an alternative to conventional network television has led to the growing phenomenon of 'cord-cutting' where viewers discontinue their regular subscription for pay-television and instead rely on cheaper online video services (Garrahan, 2010). While a growing variety of linear and non-linear, one-to-many and two-way services compete for audience attention, it is clear that, in the emerging order, considerable advantages attach to the capacity to gather data about people's preferences and, on the strength of that, to target content with increasing efficiency.

SOCIAL NETWORKS AND MICROBLOGGING

The phenomenon of online social networking has boomed in recent years. Social networks – conduits of information between 'contacts' – have a long history and the role they play, for example, in exchanges of information about business opportunities, labour markets and jobs, long predates the arrival of the Internet. Early economic studies of social networks have focused on how they form and on their characteristics, utility and costs (Jackson, 2006). The rapid growth of online social networking in recent years demonstrates the highly effective role the Internet can play in enabling the formation and growth of networks or communities of users that want to relate and engage in multiple conversations with each other. As a result, a new generation of companies such as Facebook, LinkedIn and Twitter which have been at the forefront of 'the social wave' have projected the online communicative space to far greater prominence in how social and business exchanges are now conducted.

Online social networks such as Facebook or MySpace or, in China, Renren are centred around sites where members are encouraged to generate individual personal profiles through posting up content such as videos and photos. Social network sites (SNSs) allow users to send messages and interact with other members and their capabilities have gradually developed over time. The growing popularity of SNSs is demonstrated by amount of time people are spending using them. In the UK, for example, whereas nine per cent of time spent online was accounted for by SNSs in 2007, by 2010 this rose to 23 per cent of users' Internet time (Ofcom, 2010a: 238).

A major difference between traditional media networks and online social networks is that, in the case of the former, a clear distinction exists between suppliers and consumers of content. In order to attract audiences, media networks need to invest in creating or acquiring compelling original content. With social networking sites, members serve the role of both producers *and* consumers of content. Although audience attention can be monetized by the online social network owner, no cost burden stemming from the need to originate content will arise.

The economics of operating an online social network are different from running a conventional media network. In both cases, growth of the network is advantageous but the nature of the incentives to expand are different. SNSs benefit from network effects in that the more people who join a social network the greater its usefulness to each member because each user will be able to communicate and interact with more people. For conventional media networks, the value of the service does not change simply because new audience members sign up, rather the chief advantage of wider participation is that it enables the high fixed costs involved in content production to be spread across more individuals.

It follows that in general, the operating costs of a SNS are apt to be lower than that of a traditional media content provider, but this depends on the range of value-added features and functions that the SNS is seeking to provide. And the business models deployed by SNSs to cover their costs vary. The approach taken by, for instance, LinkedIn, a business-focused online network, involves a 'freemium' model. The freemium approach – where a basic service is made available for free but then for upgraded and enhanced services a subscription charge is levied – has proven popular with some Internet content services such as online gaming (Moules, 2009). As a niche service focused on professionals, LinkedIn is relatively well-placed to attract subscriptions but, even so, the company needs to draw on revenue streams from additional sources, in particular from recruitment deals and from marketing.

Many SNSs rely on multiple revenue streams and typically advertising and marketing will play an important role. Facebook has emerged as by far the most popular networking site, with some 700m active users who spend on average more than six hours each per month using the site (Dembosky, 2011). Not surprisingly, this level of user attention has enabled the network's owners to earn considerable revenues from advertising, and Facebook is now estimated to account for almost one-third of all online display (i.e. excluding Google search) advertising (ibid.). But sales of straightforward display advertisements and banners are by no means the only revenue stream open to SNSs.

At Facebook, investment in developing additional ways of monetizing user engagement increased ahead of a public flotation of the company's shares in May 2012. One initiative has been that companies can create 'like' pages in Facebook where enthusiasts for a product or service, brand or concept may join as a fan and, as these pages are integrated with Facebook's advertising system, a means becomes established for subsequent targeting of commercial messages. A recent survey suggests that '[e]ach new fan acquired on a Facebook page drives 20 additional visits to a typical retailer's website over the course of a year' (Experian Hitwise, 2011). SNSs can play a powerful role in raising the profile of a brand, and major advertisers' need to utilize these tools has spawned the development of a growing industry in how best to use online social space effectively for marketing purposes. As acknowledged by Paul Polman the chief executive of leading advertiser Unilever, the ability of SNSs to provide detailed data about the tastes and preferences of individuals is of particular value:

> The influence of Facebook and a handful of other companies cannot be underestimated ... These companies have the capability to know their – and ours – customers intimately. The implications for the marketing industry are enormous. (Paul Polman cited in Bradshaw, 2011b)

Owners of any popular website can derive significant revenues by collecting detailed data about the tastes, preferences and habits of visitors and selling that data onwards to companies that wish to target site visitors as customers (Angwin, 2010). Owners of SNSs have access to particular rich user data and, as social networks emerge as the most visited part of the Internet, the incentives to monetize that data are clear. For the most part, collection of information is unobtrusive and has little immediate effect on the user experience. Despite this, data-harvesting by SNSs has raised concerns about protection of privacy for members who may not want their behaviours to be tracked nor their data to be sold onwards, nor to become targets for messages from advertisers (ibid.).

SNSs have been working closely with major brands and advertisers to find new ways to monetize their knowledge and also their power to connect with specific sorts of individuals and demographic groupings (Dembosky, 2011). Such efforts have, at times, risked alienating users. One advertising format Facebook has adopted is the 'sponsored story' where comments left by fans on the 'like' pages of companies or brands are then repackaged into advertising messages, including the individual's profile photo, which are then sent to the home or profile pages of that person's friends. While personalized advertisements may achieve greater reach and impact, they are also regarded as intrusive and exploitative by some who resent the difficulty of opting out of such methods for commercialization of social networks.

Because the value of social networks is predicated on scale of user participation, risks of user alienation should act as a deterrent against revenue strategies that members may dislike. However, because of network effects and switching costs, the momentum created by an early market lead in the SNS industry may prove self-perpetuating despite any deficiencies emerging that cause dissatisfaction with the predominant service on offer. Perceived flaws can, however, act as a spur for competition. At the launch of Google+, Google sought to distinguish its own new SNS offering from market-leader Facebook by emphasizing the enhanced features it will provide for protecting privacy and security of personal data (Waters, Nuttall and Bradshaw, 2011).

New entrants to the social networking industry face an uphill struggle in competing against the brand recognition and network effects enjoyed by early market leaders. However, the technology dependent and youth-oriented nature of the online social sphere means it is always open to innovation and to the vagaries of fashion. The arrival of microblogging site Twitter provides an example of how, in a very short space of time, new services can emerge unforeseen and achieve widespread popularity around the globe. Its potential was powerfully demonstrated during the 'Arab Spring' when Twitter became one of the main conduits for information about unfolding developments in an eventful but highly restricted setting for delivery of news.

Twitter is a social media tool that allows users to interact with each other using less than 140 characters. Five years after being founded in 2006, the service had an estimated 300m registered users worldwide (Arthur, 2011). Twitter enables users to connect instantly via the Internet or smartphones with large groups of others and to share snippets of information or news or to ask questions. As with Facebook, MySpace and other successful players in the SNS domain, the spread of the Twitter network has contributed to the development of a global online social media space that is rich with many reciprocal links and ongoing cross-currents of discussion.

The user experience on Twitter's microblogging service is different – simpler and more immediate – from interactions that typify online networks such as Facebook. Even so, the nature of the service has enabled and encouraged the formation of many communities and constituencies of shared interest. The ability of Twitter, in common with other social network owners, to identify and connect with groups that share common profiles and interests holds out numerous opportunities in terms of marketing. Although Twitter has been slower than rivals in exploiting commercial revenue streams, ideas for income generation are being developed and include 'promoted tweets' which started in 2010 and the introduction of bolder marketing products such as straightforward advertisements (Bradshaw, 2011a). While the company has been willing to, for example, disseminate sponsored messages about time-sensitive retailing offers, it has not engaged in more controversial data-mining strategies that might threaten user privacy. The key challenge for Twitter, as for other social network owners, is how to integrate commercial into social intercourse without intruding to the point where user dissatisfaction harms popularity and threatens to slow down or halt network expansion.

THE CHANGING ROLE OF NETWORKS IN MEDIA ECONOMICS

Within traditional media supply businesses such as broadcasting and publishing a number of sorts of networking arrangements have occurred historically and networks remain important today. But networks are a much more prevalent and essential feature in many other industries, especially communications and information technology. As the spread of digital technology has brought the media, communications and IT industries closer together, the role of networks has assumed far greater prominence in the converged order. The Internet – a global network made up of interconnected networks linking together PCs and other Web-enabled devices such as mobile phones and tablets – is by far the most important new network of recent years (Economides, 2007), and its growth as a force in distribution and exchange of content has naturally increased the significance of networks as systems of organization within media industries in recent years.

The many examples of networks to be found in the broadcasting industry are usually founded on the notion of a shared schedule of television or radio content which is assembled at the hub and moves outwards from suppliers to viewers via local affiliates (or nodes) in different localities. Likewise the less formalized networks that occur in international magazine publishing are predicated on shared use of a common brand and body of content by partners based in separate localities. So networking arrangements can enable media content suppliers to work together to exploit supply-side economies of scale. Economies of scale arise not in the sense that costs fall with increasing output – initial production costs will, of course, remain the same – but rather in the sense that, by increasing consumption of a body of media content, media networks enable the costs of creating that content to be spread more widely, thus reducing per-consumer production costs for all participants in the network.

Growth of the Internet and of Web-enabled functionality has introduced two-way and multidirectional flows between suppliers and consumers of media content, and this development has resulted in the emergence of new sorts of networks. As these networks grow in sophistication and capacity, they often exhibit qualities of 'intelligence' (Gershon, 2011) or an ability to adapt and improve or 'evolve' through self-learning (Monge, Heiss and Magolin, 2008). Online content networks such as Yahoo, using the digital return path to gather signals about individual tastes and interests, can target and shape delivery of content not on the basis of geography but rather on the preferences individuals have demonstrated over time. The matching of content offerings to individual preferences enables content to be exploited more fully and, as Internet-based consumption of media grows, new online media networks have been able to construct sizeable audiences for specific properties using this approach. As traditional media networks migrate towards multi-platform delivery, they too have benefited from opportunities to use two-way connectivity to extend consumption of their output (e.g. through catch-up services). The introduction of the digital return path has enabled more effective approaches towards aggregating audience demand and, in turn, facilitated cost spreading and economies of scale on the part of online content networks.

Capacity for reciprocal traffic flows across the Internet has led to a flowering of new communication and interactive content-related networks including SNSs and online social gaming. When positive network effects are present, higher or wider usage confers greater value for all users, as is the case for telecommunications networks or social network sites such as Facebook. The new sorts of networks which have risen to prominence under the category of 'social media', many of which are virtual rather than real, are generally predicated on positive network effects. The content that circulates on social media is largely self-generated by members, and this constitutes a very significant difference between social networks and conventional media networks.

The nature of the network and the economic incentives for network formation will differ in the case of, on the one hand, communication and social networking sites and, on the other, conventional media suppliers. Positive network effects are crucial for interactive networks such as Facebook and Twitter, whereas economies of scale in content production are an important (though by no means the only) advantage driving more traditional forms of media networks. In both cases, it is notable that the same incentives which encourage network formation are also liable to encourage expansion and domination, thus making it difficult for other firms to gain a foothold and raising potential concerns about monopolization.

The growth of SNSs is a source of both threat and opportunity for conventional media suppliers. Not only do social media account for an ever-growing portion of online advertising, they also contribute to an ethos of non-payment for content which some would argue is an endemic and irreversible aspect of the rise of digital technology (Anderson, 2009). The existence of network effects militates against SNS owners making any charges to users because this might deter participation. The adoption of a freemium model by services such as LinkedIn or Skype also reflects network effects and the need to encourage wide usage. Even though social media and traditional content services are not substitutes for each other, traditional media can suffer from the chasing downwards of consumers' willingness to pay for online content. At the same time, many conventional media organizations have sought to buttress themselves against these developments by diversifying into communications and SNS provision. The progressive integration within conventional media of differing sorts of network businesses not only provides a means of diversifying revenues but also, by promoting a rethink of the architecture of relationships with audiences, it may well prove a source of inspiration and innovation in the shaping of future media provision.

5

Demand: Push to Pull

Fragmentation of mass audiences and the progressive empowerment of individuals to express preferences via the digital return path have, in a fundamental way, altered modes of interaction between the forces of demand and supply. This chapter focuses on the economic implications of a changing relationship between suppliers of media content and audiences or demand. It examines how changes in technology have introduced improved signalling of audience preferences to media suppliers and engendered a shift from mass to niche markets. These developments have encouraged strategies of segmentation of market demand and have increased the importance of effective branding techniques. At the same time, changes in distribution and viewer empowerment have posed new challenges in relation to the management of television audience flows. While the introduction of the digital return path has provided unprecedented opportunities for the demands of individual audience members to find expression, this development does not entirely eradicate market failures in broadcasting which have long supported the case in favour of publicly funded content provision.

After studying this chapter, you should be able to:

- assess how changes in demand and greater user empowerment are affecting the economics of media;
- analyse the implications of transition from mass to niche markets;
- understand the growing importance of branding and segmentation of market demand;
- appreciate, from an economic perspective, why techniques for the management of television audience flows are changing;
- explain the concept of market failure and assess key positions in the debate over publicly funded content provision.

MASS TO NICHE

The traditional conception of media involves organizations delivering products or services, e.g. a newspaper or a television schedule, to mass audiences. Because support is drawn both from charging consumers directly for content and from the sale of audience attention, the demand-side factors which play a role in shaping market provision reflect not only the preferences of readers, viewers and listeners but also the interests of major advertisers. With success generally dependent on amassing audiences of significant size, the focus within many media organizations has been on creating, assembling or distributing product that is designed to appeal widely. The supply of identical products and services to mass audiences has facilitated vast economies of scale but variant strategies – such as networks – have evolved which also enable scale economies to be captured through modifying content to suit the tastes of particular audience subgroups.

However, advancing technology and especially digitization and growth of the Internet have transformed the relationship between media suppliers and audiences and have accorded unprecedented prominence to individual consumer demand. The main changes brought on by recent technological advances have been a steady rise in avenues available for distribution of media and the rapid spread of delivery platforms and devices that enable more connectivity and different forms of user engagement with content. The result has been a gradual shift from the 'one-to-many' model that has typified mass media provision throughout its history towards a more mixed economy in which 'one-to-one' also features quite strongly. The growing ability of individual media users to assert preferences and to access content on their own terms has altered the traditional mode of interaction between media suppliers and audiences from a situation in which 'push' was predominant to one in which 'pull' is now also part of the equation (Reding, 2006: 33).

One aspect of advancing technology has been a vast expansion in distribution avenues with the arrival of innumerable websites, the rapid uptake of devices for receiving and engaging with content and explosive growth in the number of channels for broadcasting. In the television and radio industries, following on from the proliferation of new channels made possible by cable and satellite technologies in the 1980s and 1990s, digital compression techniques and webstreaming have driven a further and ongoing phase of expansion in distribution since the start of the twenty-first century.

In the UK for example, data from regulator Ofcom suggests that there were more than 500 licensed television channels in operation in 2011 compared to just four in the early 1980s. Figure 5.1 which shows how multichannel television has increased in popularity in the UK is indicative of wider international patterns of growth. At the level of

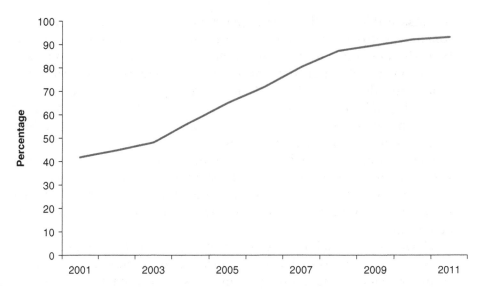

Figure 5.1   Household uptake of multichannel TV in the UK, 2001–2011 (%)

Source: Annual Q1 data from Ofcom CMR (Ofcom, 2011a: 132).

the EU, it is estimated that some 9,800 licensed channels had been established by 2010 compared with just 47 television channels back in 1989.[3] As the number of broadcast distribution outlets has increased so too has competition among television companies, who are obliged to work much harder now than in the past to capture the attention of audiences (Brannon and Bargouth, 2010). Additional competition has, in turn, resulted in different forms of content, with many more thematic or niche products and services emerging.

A number of economic theorists have considered how, in any industry characterized by growing competition, suppliers will adjust their product offerings in response to the arrival of competition. The Hotelling model, for example, uses the analogy of two ice-cream sellers arriving at a beach on which swimmers and sunbathers are spread evenly from one end to the other and its asks the question: where, along the beach, should each seller locate their ice-cream stall? The answer is that rather than spreading out and locating one at either end, in equilibrium both vendors will locate together in the middle. Assuming that they don't compete with each other on price, then the most competitive solution for each ice-cream seller will be to locate side-by-side in the middle of the beach. If either seller were to move to

---

[3]Cited on the website of the Association of Commercial Television in Europe (ACTE).

the right or the left, then they would lose market share to the other. This model can be translated to the context of the television industry in order to understand the competitive scheduling strategies deployed by broadcasters in an environment with few channels where more-or-less identical offerings aimed at mainstream tastes may predominate (Hughes and Vines, 1989: 44).

If you look at the distribution of consumer preferences across many classes of products, you'll generally find that some are more popular than others. The same is true for television. As was shown by the experience of the US television industry in the 1970s and 1980s, in a situation where a small number of channels – in this case, the main over-the-air networks – competed with each other for market share, as with the ice-cream sellers, you are likely to see a tendency towards all suppliers locating side-by-side in the middle instead of a spreading out to better serve audiences right across the spectrum.

Why so? US economists developed what are called programme choice models to understand the phenomenon known as competitive duplication in broadcasting schedules. The Beebe model, which typifies these models, highlights various factors that determine the range of programmes offered including the structure of viewer preferences among different programme types, the number of television channels in existence, the competitive structure of the markets they operate in and the means of support for their services (Owen and Wildman, 1992: 99). Programme choice models suggest that if most viewers want the same types of programmes and television is supported by advertising payments, competing broadcasters are likely to offer highly similar programmes targeted to this mass audience. The number of programmes designed to satisfy majority tastes will be excessive because competing channels will find it more profitable to carve up the majority-taste audience (by offering close substitutes) than to cater for minority tastes by alienating the majority.

Clearly the number of competing suppliers and how content is paid for are crucial determinants of what sort of media output is supplied. In an unregulated television market, it is only when the number of channels is large enough to exhaust the profits in competitive duplication, making minority-taste programming as profitable as majority-taste programming at the margin, that serving the interests of minorities and specialist interest groups will become attractive. With advances in technology, the number of channels has soared in most developed countries and growth in Internet distribution capacity has made possible further exponential increases. The arrival and rapid growth of direct viewer payments or subscription funding has introduced an increasingly important revenue stream for broadcasting which has supported the development of many new channels. These developments have radically altered the structure of television broadcasting markets, and the implications for the competitive behaviour of market participants are far-reaching.

As history has shown, the number of programmes and channels designed to satisfy majority tastes will be excessive when you have only a few competing broadcasters in an unregulated advertising-supported economy. The increasingly complex and pluralistic environment in which the television industry now operates supports a wide array of competing players – advertiser-supported and pay; linear and non-linear – all vying for a share of viewers' attention. As a consequence, for a new TV channel setting up now, the choices about how to locate and what sort of programmes to offer are much more complicated. Notably, however, in many if not most television markets, the point at which the profit available from catering to a niche or minority-taste audience – particularly an affluent audience segment – is very likely to exceed that from competing for a small share of the majority-taste audience.

Ever-widening opportunities for distribution and growth in subscription funding have propelled a shift from mass to niche television content. It makes sense that if direct payments can be charged then the juncture at which it is financially feasible to cater to specialist interests will arrive more quickly than under a purely advertising-supported model. This holds true not only for television. Increased income to publishers from higher cover prices for specialist monthlies was one of the factors which helped fuel an increase in niche consumer magazine titles in the 1980s and 1990s.

USER EMPOWERMENT

Another crucially important change stemming from digitization has been the introduction of a digital return path. The use of digital delivery platforms and in particular the Internet has not only vastly increased distribution capacity but also allows for the use of search tools that, in turn, facilitate much more personalized media consumption (Küng, Picard and Towse, 2008: 22). The two-way communication made possible by the Internet makes it easier for content suppliers to learn about their customers (Shapiro and Varian, 1999: 34). No longer confined by scheduling constraints, and thanks to improved means for identifying and monitoring the interests of audiences, television suppliers are now far better placed than before to ensure that the universe of content properties they own is matched to the specific wants and needs of individuals and of audience segments.

On new digital platforms, the mode of interaction between media suppliers and consumers is very different from how it has been with analogue channels (Bennett and Strange, 2011). With conventional broadcast channels, channel owners provide viewers with a linear schedule and viewers are passive receivers of that given schedule of content assembled for them and supplied by the broadcaster. Digital platforms enable television suppliers to offer access to their content properties on a non-linear as well as a linear basis – they allow video on demand (VOD) and near video on demand (NVOD) services as well as broadcast services. Instead of the broadcaster acting as 'overseer in the great treasure house of content' (Duncan, 2006: 21), on digital platforms the viewer can become their own scheduler enjoying much wider choice and greater control.

That distinction is sometimes referred to as 'lean-forward' versus 'lean-back' services – instead of being couch potatoes in a lean-back world, digitization gives us the option to lean forward and decide what we as individuals or households want to watch and when. Lean-forward services are possible because, when content properties are created in a digital format, they are then easy to store and to redistribute. Low storage costs mean that many digital files can be housed simultaneously on servers and over long periods, so consumers can be given access to a very wide range of content options.

Greater choice of content would be of limited use without a means for consumers to find what they want, but digital platforms provide unparalleled searchability. The tagging of digital content and use of search algorithms enables files containing content to be found and called up speedily (Highfield, 2006: 50). It is therefore both easy and convenient for the consumer to exercise and make use of the greater choice made possible by low-cost storage of vast amounts of digital content.

One of the most prominent theorists on the effect of the Internet is Chris Anderson, who coined the phrase 'the long tail' to describe how the arrival of the online marketplace has affected retail sales (Anderson: 2006). Anderson notes that some products are more popular than others and it is commonly accepted that most sales will be accounted for by just a handful of best-sellers. As much as 80 per cent of sales are accounted for by the 20 per cent or so of products or brands that happen to be popular with consumers.

However, the arrival of the Internet challenges this traditional understanding of how the marketplace functions. With lower storage costs for online retailers such as Amazon, consumers can be offered extended access to a wider range of less popular products. This overcomes the issue normally evident in retailing: that shelf space is limited and so is naturally going to be dominated by best-sellers. The Internet marketplace is extended and this favours the position of niche items that may sell well over time.

The essence of Anderson's argument is that if relatively unpopular products are made available to consumers over longer periods, they too will manage to generate high levels of sales. The capacity for sales generated by numerous less popular products to match those accounted for by the handful of best-sellers is illustrated in the classic graph in Figure 5.2. The 'long tail' (depicting the aggregate value of sales from numerous less popular products) equals the 'head' (denoting sales achieved by best-sellers) in size.

Strategies of deriving returns from content properties, both mainstream and niche, over extended periods of time are completely integral to the business of supplying media, so, in some sense, the concept of the long tail is not new in the context of the economics of media. However, if Anderson's theory is correct, then specialist content ought to fare particularly well thanks to the Internet and the arrival of relatively

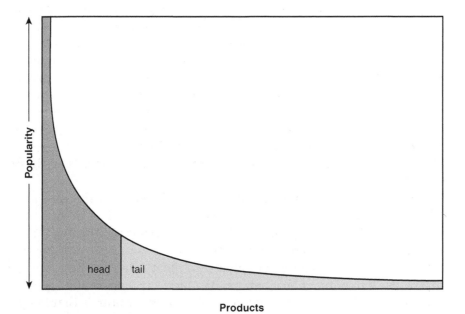

Figure 5.2 The 'long tail'

Source: Based on Anderson, 2006.

low storage costs and easy searchability. However, even on the Internet, storage and transmission of data does involve at least some costs, and therefore it remains the case that some content is simply too narrow in its appeal to generate a return large enough to make publication economically viable, even when that content is made widely available over an extended period of time. In analysing how 'zero-cost content' (ZCC) services such as YouTube have struggled to achieve profitability, Wildman, Lee and Song (2012) point out that because advertisers are willing to pay much more for opportunities to advertise around some forms of content than others (professionally produced videos generally command a much high 'per-thousand views' advertising rate than user-generated content), and because service costs are lower if usage is concentrated on a small fraction of hosted content, there is an incentive for the service to try to induce more uploads of viable content and to direct a greater proportion of traffic towards a minority of popular content.

It is certainly true that the Internet has extended the range and diversity of content offerings that audiences can tap into should they choose. However, so far at least, whether extended choice has engendered any rebalancing of media consumption away from hits and bestsellers in favour of niche content appears questionable (Napoli, 2011: 63). Looking at the BBC iPlayer for instance, which offers online access to an extremely wide assortment of programme content offerings following scheduled transmissions on television and radio, the dispersion of demand revealed through requested downloads on this catch-up service is strongly skewed in favour of popular high-profile shows such as *Dr Who* and *Top Gear* (BBC, 2010).

Although an ever-widening profusion of niche content offerings via the Internet may do little to counteract the long-standing propensity towards a predominance, within overall patterns of media consumption, of 'hits' with popular taste, there is no doubt that additional channels and choice have brought about an ongoing fragmentation in the media environment. Audiences are embracing the additional choice, control and opportunities for participation offered by the Internet and mobile connectivity and new sorts of services that capitalize on the interactive dimensions of digital distribution, e.g. ZCCs and social networking sites, have grown rapidly as many people have shown enthusiasm for creating and connecting with user-generated content. More delivery platforms, greater connectivity, wider access to content and a rise in user-generated material have all contributed to a relentless fragmentation and spreading of audience attention across the variety of options on offer.

SEGMENTATION AND BRANDING

Given an ever-wider array of content offerings competing for attention, strategies of segmentation of market demand, targeting and brand-building have become crucial aspects of maximizing the value of digital content assets (Duffy, 2006; Ots, 2008). In a world of potentially over-whelming choice, the ability to segment market demand effectively, to target content towards specific audience groups and forge relation-ships with that constituency have become important sources of advan-tage for media suppliers.

Market segmentation is based on the notion that '[h]eterogeneity in demand functions exists such that market demand can be disag-gregated into segments with distinct demand functions' (Dickson and Ginter, 1987: 4). It describes the approach of offering differentiated products that are designed to cater to and capitalize on variations in consumer preferences. Differentiations may be to do with the actual properties of the product or just its packaging or image. Product dif-ferentiation can be seen as a response to naturally occurring variations in taste. However, some have argued that segmentation is based more on contrived rather than on real differences and is really about suppli-ers seeking to distort and manipulate consumer demand (Samuelson, 1976). It is about ensuring demand for the products that firms want to supply and is often supported by heavy advertising that, likewise, may serve to distort consumer demand (Galbraith, 1967).

Be that as it may, in an increasingly fragmented media environ-ment, the targeting of particular market segments provides an impor-tant means through which content suppliers can and do seek to sustain demand for their output. In the context of media, market segmentation refers to how suppliers use audience analysis to identify heterogeneity in demand and to develop differentiated products aimed at differing audience groups. Growth in Web-enabled connectivity, provided by online media suppliers with rich data for use in segmentation analysis, points towards a future in which strategies of segmentation of mar-ket demand will become easier to execute and more commonplace. In an increasingly crowded and competitive media environment, a more targeted customer-oriented approach seems a natural corollary of the broader shift from push to pull.

Although relatively new to some mass media suppliers, strategies of segmentation of market demand are right at the core of magazine publishing (Doyle, 2011). A notable feature of the way in which the magazine publishing industry has developed in recent decades has been the trend towards increased segmentation of readership or

increased subdivision of demand into more and more narrow specialisms. A number of issues explain why strategies of segmentation and
targeting have become more prevalent in the magazine sector.

Long-term trends in demand for magazines are dictated by factors
including levels of literacy and, in particular, available leisure time
and disposable incomes. Long periods of sustained growth in expenditure on consumer magazines across Europe in the 1980s and 1990s
were fuelled by increases in leisure time and in incomes during these
periods. Publishers in wealthier European countries (especially Germany, France and the UK) and in the US were well placed to capitalize
on growth in demand for high-quality entertainment products in the
1980s and 1990s but, looking to the future, it is in China, India and
other developing economies where literacy rates, levels of leisure time
and disposable incomes are growing fastest. In the longer term, these
emerging territories are likely to provide a stimulus for future expansion in demand for magazines (Doyle, 2011).

A shift towards ever-narrower segmentation took place partly
because of increased demand, especially in middle- and upper-market
sectors in wealthier countries, for more specialist and higher-quality
entertainment, features and hobby magazines with a focus on, for
example, photography, sport, cooking and home improvement. To take
advantage of these trends, many magazine publishers embarked on a
strategy of launching new titles aimed at more specialized segments
of the market. At the same time, changes that took place in the cost
structure and economic organization of the printing industry during
the 1980s reduced the costs of publishing high-quality magazines.
This made it possible to cater for increasingly fragmented consumer
demand by launching new low-circulation titles. A move from hot to
cold metal technology and the introduction of desktop publishing radically reduced the costs involved in printing and made it possible for
publishers to introduce new titles with lower print runs. Many new
titles aimed at ever-narrower audience groups – e.g. large boat enthusiasts; small boat enthusiasts, etc. – began to appear.

Until the 1980s, major magazine publishers such as EMAP and IPC
in the UK, Time Warner in the US and Condé Nast or Hachette in
France tended to produce and print a relatively higher proportion of
large-circulation (often general interest weekly) titles. This strategy
meant that magazine publishers relied quite heavily on economies of
scale rather than economies of scope. Advancing technology made it
much cheaper to produce new titles with lower print runs and this
encouraged publishers to change their approach (Cox and Mowatt,
2008). By 2009, the number of consumer titles being published in the

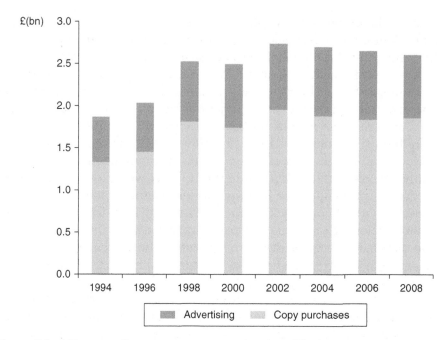

Figure 5.3   UK expenditure on consumer magazines (£bn)

Source: Data from Warc/Advertising Association (2005: 117; 2009: 122).

UK was 3,243 as compared with 1,383 in 1980 (BRAD/PPA 2009).
Strategies of targeting particular audience groups with similar tastes
or preferences and of segmentation of market demand, whereby audiences are subdivided into ever-narrower specialisms, took over from
publication of mass-market titles, and this has left readers better supplied in terms of range and diversity of leisure titles than ever before.

Many of the new and more narrowly focused titles that have been
launched are attractive vehicles for advertisers. Even so, as Figure 5.3
shows, the proliferation of new titles in recent times has also been strongly
supported by growth in cover sales income, reflecting rising prosperity and
changing patterns of demand. The size of the UK market has contracted
slightly in real terms over recent years. As well as the impact of economic
recession, this partly reflects a slowdown for the sector following two decades
of very strong growth but also, according to Küng, sales have fallen 'because
consumers are increasingly "time poor" and much of the expert information
that [specialist titles] contain is now easily available online' (2008: 44).

Like other sectors of the print media, magazine publishing has suffered from the ongoing migration of consumers away from reading as
a form of leisure and towards screen-based entertainment activities.
Recent trends in advertising confirm that the share of total expenditure

accounted for by the Internet has grown sharply since the start of the twenty-first century and these gains have taken place largely at the expense of print media, especially newspapers but including consumer magazines. Magazines have also suffered a diversion of revenues caused by the arrival of a growing range of free colour supplements attached to newspapers which can be attractive for advertisers.

Notwithstanding these challenges, a key advantage that magazine publishers can claim is the strength of their expertise in targeting and addressing niche audience segments through the development of strong media brands – for example *Vogue, Cosmopolitan, GQ* and *Reader's Digest* – that appeal to particular audience segments and constituencies of shared interest. This strength should be a source of opportunity for magazine brand owners as digital platforms develop. Virtually all magazine titles now have a well-developed Web presence (a small handful are available only in electronic format) and some also offer mobile content services. Digital media platforms, with their capacity for interactivity, are not just venues for electronic versions of the print media version of a magazine, rather they offer an opportunity to deepen and strengthen the relationship between a magazine brand and its target readership and to recruit additional subscribers by providing a more comprehensive and richly layered range of content-based services (Küng, 2008: 49).

As discussed in Chapter 2, the fact that digitization allows suppliers to forge new sorts of relationships with audiences has been identified by a number of leading media players as key to the development of successful strategies for the future. Magazine publishers are well ahead of rivals in other sectors in recognizing the value of understanding and engaging closely with audiences. Expertise in communicating with specific audience segments – for instance those interested in high-performance cars or weddings or interior decoration – has frequently been used by publishers to develop complementary products and services such as live events or exhibitions and trade fairs aimed at the interest groups who subscribe to specific titles. Even though competition from online rivals and the ease with which content can be intermediated illegally are potential threats, magazine publishers also stand to gain from the possibilities offered by the Internet to exercise competencies in building, sustaining and then finding ways to capitalize on relationships with niche audiences that, for players in this sector, are well-established.

A magazine's main asset is its title or brand, but magazine brands are subject to the vagaries of time and fashion and not all will last indefinitely. Although a few well-known titles, such as *Elle*, have survived over numerous decades, most magazines have a much shorter life expectancy. Those that succeed over longer periods require ongoing adaptation to ensure they maintain a viable constituency (Gasson, 1996: 86). To sustain and replenish the portfolios that help reduce the risks inherent in magazine publishing, new products need to be innovated and launched on a regular basis. The dynamic nature of markets for magazines is such that publishers must pay close attention to the many cultural and social trends and the transient fads and fashions that help shape demand within and across product genres. Through building expert knowledge of particular lifestyle groups and areas of special interest, publishers become adept in recognizing shifts and trends and in identifying opportunities for new product launches (Cox and Mowatt, 2008).

An important challenge for any newly launched magazine title is to survive long enough to justify the considerable investment and promotional costs involved in its launch (Gasson, 1996: 87). The vast majority of magazines have a limited life expectancy, and success depends on whether the publisher has identified and valued the target market segment for that title correctly. Magazine publishing revolves around identifying viable constituencies of interest and establishing powerful titles that command sufficient brand appeal and will stay in business long enough to cover their launch costs and provide a profitable return to their owner. The cost of new launches can be extremely high, so fewer will take place in times of recession than normally (Jarvis, 2009: 6). Nonetheless, new launches are essential in sustaining the industry. A systematic strategy for maximizing the available returns from any successful magazine brand will take into account a number of streams of revenue that the title may generate across its expected lifetime. These include not only domestic and international sales of the magazine but also the potential to extend and exploit the brand across additional delivery platforms and in complementary product markets.

AUDIENCE FLOW MANAGEMENT

The fragmentation of mass audiences that has accompanied explosive growth in distribution and an ever-widening array of content offerings has posed particular challenges for television content suppliers. In the post-linear era of television, the process of 'windowing' or planning the release sequence for content and ancillary material so as to maximize the value of television properties has grown much more complex (as discussed in Chapter 6). At the same time, greater competition for audiences and more choice and control on the part of viewers over which content to access and when has sapped power away from broadcasters and called for a rethink of techniques traditionally used to manage audience exposure to content.

The general concept of managing audience flows is not new. In broadcasting, 'flow' relates to how channels attract and retain audiences through careful sequencing of the transmissions of programmes that make up their linear schedule. The term 'audience flow' was coined by one of the pioneers of television studies, Raymond Williams, to describe the techniques and tactics used by broadcasting schedulers to build up and hold on to their audiences (Williams, 1974). For many years these techniques have been central to maximizing and sustaining audience attention and, in turn, broadcasting revenues. A number of economists working in the area of television have modelled and analysed competitive scheduling techniques under differing market circumstances (Bourreau, 2003), but as multichannel television has multiplied the choice of linear content offerings available to audiences at any given time of the day or week, the task of devising suitable scheduling strategies to counter rivals has become much more complex (Doyle, 2012b; Ihlebæk, Syvertsen and Ytreberg, 2012).

The factors a scheduler has traditionally taken account of in seeking to build audience flows include budgets, programmes available, the availability of audiences in any given time slot, the interests of target audiences, advertiser preferences and last, but certainly not least, the likely scheduling behaviour of competitors (Pringle and Starr, 2006: 123–5). As the market context has evolved from one involving just a handful of rivals to a multifaceted and multilayered landscape of competing alternatives, it has become much more difficult to weigh up the range of uncertainties involved in attracting and sustaining audience attention. Indeed, some would argue that the very status of television has changed from once having being an event laid on by a scheduler to 'merely a[nother] form of audiovisual content – to be watched whenever and wherever users demand, on whatever device they choose' (Bennett, 2011: 1).

However, the impact of non-linear offerings on consumption habits should not be exaggerated. Research from UK communications regulator Ofcom shows that, despite a tidal wave of competing alternatives, watching television remains buoyant and non-linear viewing, although growing, still accounts for only a relatively small proportion of all television viewing – 17 per cent on average (Ofcom, 2010a: 106). Despite the transition to digital, most television consumption is still accounted for by linear broadcasts and with viewers in 'couch potato' mode rather than lean-forward mode. As a result, the old scheduling techniques that rely on habit formation and passivity among audiences (e.g. use of lead-in effects, or building off common junction points with rivals' schedules, etc.) are still potent for a sizeable proportion of viewers. Broadcasters still need to programme strategically and opportunistically around what is known about rivals' schedules.

However, adjustments in viewing habits are evident and particularly so among younger audiences, who are much more adept at media multitasking than their elders and who tend to spend more time watching DVDs and on-demand or downloaded content on PCs and mobile devices (Ofcom, 2010a: 107). As audiences have become active, new opportunities have arrived in relation to capturing and sustaining audience attention. Digitization provides extra platforms and interfaces through which broadcasters can guide viewers towards engaging with television content and content brands via whichever form of expression of that content delivers the best return. Typically, it is the conventional television transmission which delivers the highest advertising return per viewer. At MTV UK, for instance, schedulers have found that through 'seeding' fragments of content online a couple of months ahead of the conventional linear transmission of a television show, it is possible to generate considerable advance interest on the part of audiences. And provision of tie-ins to that television show via the Internet and mobile and through social networking sites helps to keep up audience attention in between linear transmissions as one executive explains:

> If we want to continue to grow our business there's no point saying 'let's make a great TV show and then put a bit of content online' ... [W]e *create* an audience and build it prior to a linear broadcast. Any of our shows start online, on mobile, on social networking sites and we build an audience. They migrate to television and when they're not watching on television they can continue to have a relationship with that media property on any platform ...[4]

Multi-platform engagement can be an important contributor to success, as evidenced by, for example, the Fox production *Glee* which benefited from building strong relationships with a devoted fanbase, especially in the US, of so-called Gleeks. The extent to which a television programme becomes a topic of conversation on Twitter or Facebook and the tenor of the online chatter surrounding it are perceived as indicators of success

---

[4] 'O' Ferrall: interviewed in London in 2009.

and these factors bear an influence over programme commissioning decisions (Bulkley, 2011). The use of 'talent' is an increasingly common aspect of strategies to engage viewers. To the extent that, for example, cast members, scriptwriters or directors are willing to participate actively in social media which greatly enriches the scope to build forums through which audiences can engage and connect with the wider community experience a television property is able to offer.

Another change relates to the role of audience data in content selection and scheduling decisions. Use of audience information has always featured in audience flow management, but online delivery of content yields unprecedented depth and detail about the preferences and behaviours of audience members at aggregate and individual level. The Internet provides broadcasters with numerous means of monitoring tastes and fads and the market intelligence gathered via online interfaces can feed directly into content selection decisions which, accordingly, become more closely attuned to audience tastes. As one senior BBC executive put it, broadcasters in the Web 2.0 world have much to gain from '[h]arnessing "the wisdom of crowds" or social software, from buddy recommendations to most downloaded' (Highfield, 2006: 50).

Although greater competition and fragmentation of the media environment has made it more difficult for broadcasters to devise strategies which ensure that content costs will be spread across significant-sized audiences, digital delivery has also provided some new tools and techniques to help address an increasingly fragmented media environment. In the increasingly complex competitive environment of the twenty-first century, selecting particular time slots for linear transmission has receded somewhat in importance as, at the same time, the ability to forge a sense of connection between specific television content properties and a target audience and also to use the multiplicity of digital platforms available both to gather and use audience feedback effectively have become more crucial. According to one executive at Viacom International with scheduling experience at the BBC, Channel 4 and MTV, the key challenges for the scheduler or programmer are to identify what sort of content ideas will work for a brand across *multiple* distribution platforms and how that content can be used to secure engagement over an *extended* time period:

> For young audiences, portability is everything ... If they love something ... and have that emotional connection, they will find it when they want it and they will come to it wherever they want it. We don't see ourselves now as a traditional broadcaster – we see ourselves as a brand and our content is part of a brand

experience and our brand is on different platforms ... Portability of programming is key.[5]

MARKET FAILURE IN BROADCASTING

In properly functioning competitive markets, interaction between the forces of demand and supply should bring about a socially optimal provision of the good or service in question. Consumers signal their wants and preferences through the prices they are prepared to pay and producers respond accordingly by supplying goods and services in the right quantities and to the desired level of quality. Historically, broadcasting has not taken place in normally functioning competitive markets. Instead, the industry has been prone to market failure. Market entry to broadcasting has been restricted by scarcity of spectrum and interaction between demand and supply has been impaired by the one-way nature of transmissions from suppliers to consumers and by an absence of means to charge viewers and listeners directly.

However, advancing technology has added many more distribution channels and has introduced viewer payments to support increased diversity of output. Digitization has changed the nature of the marketplace for supply of broadcast content from one in which push was highly predominant to the current situation where pull also now features to some extent. No longer confined to the constraints of a linear schedule, and thanks to improved means for identifying and monitoring the interests of audiences, broadcasters – including those devoted to public service content provision – are now far better placed than before to ensure that the universe of content properties that they assemble and distribute can be matched to the specific wants and needs of individuals and of audience segments. Does this mean that market failure in broadcasting is now a thing of the past?

In the context of broadcasting, the term 'market failure' tends to be used in two different ways. In one sense it refers to any failure by the market system – the unbridled forces of demand and supply – to allocate resources efficiently. In another sense, it may refer to the failure of the market to advance socially desirable goals other than efficiency, e.g. preserving democracy and social cohesion.

Looking first at efficiency problems, the most striking case of market failure in broadcasting is that radio and television would not, in the first place, have been produced at all by private profit-seeking firms were they reliant on the conventional mechanism of market

---

[5]Booth: interviewed in Glasgow in 2011.

funding – i.e. direct payments from consumers. The market system could not have compelled payment for broadcasting because, first, there was no way to identify those who were receiving it and, second, there was no way to prevent anyone who refused to pay for broadcasting from being able to receive it anyway.

Public goods often have the characteristic of being 'non-excludable'. Non-excludable refers to the difficulty of excluding those who don't want to pay for something. For example, a national defence establishment protects everybody in a country, whether they want it or not and whether they are prepared to pay for it or not. Terrestrial broadcasting services are usually available to everyone, whether individual viewers are willing to pay for them or not. With any good or service that is non-excludable and where customers do not have exclusive rights to consume the good in question, it is difficult to make 'free riders' pay for it (Griffiths and Wall, 2007: 148). The free market is unlikely to provide these sorts of goods efficiently.

Public goods also have the characteristic of being 'non-exhaustible' (ibid.). Non-exhaustible refers to the fact that there are zero marginal costs involved in supplying the service to one additional viewer. Because there are no extra costs, and because extra 'consumption' of television output does not reduce the supply available to other viewers, this implies that no one should be prevented from receiving any broadcast service. 'Restricting the viewing of programmes that, once produced, could be made available to everyone at no extra cost, leads to inefficiency and welfare losses' (Davies, 1999: 203). On the other hand, if no one can be excluded from receiving broadcast services, then payment for broadcasting cannot be compelled and the economic incentive to supply some forms of output will be removed.

Another cause of failure in broadcasting markets relates to the problem of asymmetric information. What consumers are offered by broadcasters is the opportunity for new knowledge or a new entertainment experience, but viewers cannot know in advance whether they will value this experience or not and how much it is worth to them. It is only by 'consuming' what is on offer that viewers will get a sense of its worth but, once they have watched a television show, there is no longer any incentive to pay for it. In short, '[p]eople do not know what they are "buying" until they have experienced it, yet once they have experienced it they no longer need to buy it!' (Graham and Davies, 1997: 19).

An important source of market failure stems from what are referred to as 'externalities' or external effects. Externalities are costs or, in some cases, benefits imposed on third parties. They arise when the private costs to a firm of engaging in a certain activity are out of line with its social costs. Pollution provides a good example of a negative externality. An individual firm may neglect the external effects of its actions when it discharges hazardous waste into rivers because its own profits are not affected by this activity. Broadcasting can have adverse external effects. The provision of some sorts of content may engender a wider cost to society, for example, by increasing levels of violence or the fear of violence in society. The fact that these costs are not borne by the broadcaster results in market failure because more resources may be devoted to providing television output with negative external affects than is socially optimal.

There are several ways in which a completely unregulated broadcasting market might fail to allocate resources efficiently but because of technological change, the nature and extent of market failures is changing. The arrival of many additional channels, of more on-demand viewing and of encryption and pay-TV models have resulted in a marketplace that is now much more varied and, broadly speaking, more capable of meeting the array of differing demands and preferences exhibited by individuals and groups across the audience population (Ofcom, 2008). The ability of digital broadcasting to give audiences wider access to a richer and more diverse range of content options 'greatly mitigates traditional market failures' (Armstrong and Weeds, 2007: 82). As well as facilitating more channels and more responsive modes of interfacing with audience demand, digital delivery enables encryption technologies that sidestep earlier problems of non-excludability. These developments have brought about more effectively functioning markets and welfare improvements for many listeners and viewers. As a result, some have argued that '[i]t is hard to see what is left, in the digital age, of the market failure justification for public service broadcasting' (Elstein, 2004: 10).

However, whether the rise of multichannel television and of viewer sovereignty has eradicated sources of market failure in broadcasting is questionable. Despite digitization, the nature of broadcast content is such that it continues to be non-exhaustible or non-rivalrous so that 'exclusion is not only inefficient with respect to the value of private value of viewing but is also socially undesirable' (Ofcom, 2008: para 1.15). Old problems with regard to informational asymmetries persist in that '[v]iewers cannot perform an accurate valuation of a programme's worth until after it has finished' (Rossiter, 2005: 13) and, as online content widens choice, new problems of information deficiency in relation to navigating the extended possibilities may arise (Ofcom, 2008).

Despite the many opportunities and advantages created by the spread of digital technology, it is possible to identify ways in which a completely unregulated market might fail to allocate resources efficiently. However, it is worth remembering that any notion that the market *should* act as the main determinant of how resources are allocated depends, in the first instance, on the belief that individuals and households are the best judges of their own interests. Opinions tend to differ on whether television viewers are, in fact, the best judges of their own interests. Some favour a more paternalistic approach towards broadcasting.

A 'merit good' (or service) is one where the government takes the view that more of it should be produced than people would choose to consume if left to their own devices. Public health care or educational provision are examples, but merit good arguments also play a part in justifying public support for arts and culture (Towse, 2011: 6). If something is classified as a merit good, this implies that it has an inherent value for society that extends beyond what can be measured or expressed in market terms.

Broadcasting is often perceived in this way. It can confer positive externalities. There are some forms of content that are collectively desirable and that everyone benefits from (e.g. documentaries, educational and cultural programmes) but which viewers, on an individual basis, might not tune in to or be prepared to pay for. Just as with education or training, consumers tend to buy less 'good' programming than is in their own long-term interests. Notwithstanding the effects of digitization, it remains highly likely that under free market circumstances programming that is intrinsically 'good' will be under-supplied (Armstrong and Weeds, 2007: 116). Davies' argument that '[i]f all television is provided via the free market, there is a danger that consumers will under-invest in their own tastes, experience and capacity to comprehend because it is only in retrospect that the benefits of such investment become apparent' (1999: 203) remains as true now as ever in the past.

PUBLIC SERVICE CONTENT PROVISION

Although the shift to digital technology has had a transformative effect, it has not entirely removed some of the root causes of market failure in broadcasting. These stem from the public good qualities of broadcast output, from externalities, informational deficiencies and (on account of the availability of economies of scale) from a tendency towards monopolization within the industry (Davies, 2004: 12–13).

The most commonly used policy tools to address market failures in broadcasting are regulation and public ownership. Licensing and regulation of commercial television broadcasting are carried out in the UK by Ofcom, the regulatory and competition authority for communications industries. The relevant authority for broadcasting in the US is the Federal Communications Commission (FCC). Regulation (both structural and content-related) is a common feature of television markets and, typically, it involves rules that encourage privately owned broadcasters to deviate from profit-maximizing strategies where necessary to meet public requirements concerning quality of output. Broadcasting has always been one of the most heavily regulated sectors of the economy and regulation is one of the key factors influencing the financial performance and prospects for commercial television companies (Gasson, 1996: 8–9).

A second and, arguably, more effective way of counteracting market failures is through public ownership of broadcasting. The public good characteristic of broadcasting which gives rise to the fact that it is non-exhaustible implies that it would best be supplied by the public sector at zero price, using public funds to finance provision. Another advantage of public as opposed to private ownership is that, rather than worrying about shareholders, managers can devote themselves exclusively to 'public service' broadcasting. Indeed, most countries have established some sort of publicly funded and state-owned broadcasting entity to provide public service broadcasting (PSB).

However, as spectrum constraints give way to an ever-increasing choice of channels and other TV-like services and as audiences continue to fragment, the use of public funds to finance broadcasting has grown increasingly controversial. One of the main points of concern is that support through public funding denies consumer sovereignty. Some people believe that, in principle, the provision of any service – including broadcasting – is best left up to market forces. This begs the question of whether, as was suggested above, the peculiarities of broadcasting remain such that the market system would fail to provide people with the broadcasting services they want.

For many years, the main source of market funding for broadcasting was advertising. Advertising is a faulty funding mechanism in that it creates an incentive for the broadcaster to maximize not overall viewer welfare but, instead, the supply of whatever mix of programming yields the audiences that advertisers particularly want to reach. Reliance on advertising creates a particular focus on attaining large audience volumes, while patterns of intensity of viewer demand between different sorts of output may be ignored.

However, advertising is no longer the only funding option: thanks to advances in encryption technology, direct payments from viewers now represent an important revenue stream for commercial broadcasters. Indeed, subscription funding now accounts for over 40 per cent of global television revenues, and the proportion is growing (Ofcom, 2009: 14). With direct viewer payments, a properly functioning market in television broadcasting seems more feasible. The spread of digital broadcast delivery platforms promises to make possible more individualized provision and charging on a per-channel and even a per-programme basis. The option of direct viewer payments for public service broadcasting in many ways undermines the case for continued use of 'distorted' funding mechanisms or public funds.

In the UK, the BBC's public service output is funded through a compulsory licence fee imposed on all homes where a television set is owned (irrespective of whether or not BBC services are watched). Peacock (1996), Graham (1999) and current communications regulator Ofcom (2008) have focused attention on the question of whether or not, in an increasingly competitive broadcasting market, this form of public funding has now become outdated. Positions are divided. Arguments against the licence fee highlight the fact that we no longer suffer from spectrum scarcity, that audiences are fragmenting and that the necessary technology to allow viewers to make payments directly for whatever broadcasting services they want has existed for some time. Since it is unfair to make everyone pay for services they may not want to watch, a voluntary payment would be preferable to a compulsory universal tax as a means of supporting public service broadcasting. An old-fashioned paternalistic PSB system is undesirable when a free market in television broadcasting is now entirely feasible and would give viewers exactly what they want.

Others, however, take the view that, although 'for most goods and services, governments should get out of the way and watch the price system do its magical work', the broadcasting industry remains an exception on account of market failures that 'have not disappeared simply because technology has gone digital' (Davies, 2004: 12, 13). It is still the case that '[a]lthough private markets in broadcasting may be good in some areas, on their own they will generally fail to produce the overall quality of broadcasting that consumers individually or collectively would desire' (Porter, 1999: 36). As discussed earlier, some forms of PSB content which are desirable and which everybody benefits from, but which viewers do not always want to tune in to or pay for on an individual basis, will be under-supplied in a free market. Conversely, television output which creates negative externalities may be over-supplied. So, even with direct viewer payments, market failures still persist. The problem remains that in charging for broadcast services, some viewers will be excluded whose enjoyment would exceed the marginal cost of providing the service.

An unregulated free market for broadcasting will result in some deficiencies, but the use of public funds to finance broadcasting also raises problems. Among those who agree that the provision of PSB is desirable and that a free market will not adequately supply this, opinions are divided about which methods of public finance ought to be used. Some regard the compulsory licence fee favoured in the UK as inherently unfair. Peacock (1996) accepts that there are arguments for continuing with the licence fee but has questioned whether the proceeds should be put out to competitive tender (thus allowing other broadcasters to bid for the opportunity to supply UK viewers and listeners with PSB) rather than it simply be awarded to the BBC. The idea of introducing a contestable element to the BBC licence fee has been called for by rivals (Fenton, 2010) but although considered by policy-makers, it has so far not achieved any broad consensus of support.

In Australia, public service broadcasting output is paid for through a public grant. State funding, however, raises questions about how the independence of public broadcasters can be preserved. In Greece, PSB is partly paid for through a levy imposed on consumers' electricity bills. As with a compulsory licence fee, however, the incidence and level of charges imposed for PSB bear no relation to patterns of usage or demand so this may be considered an unfair system. Across Europe, many public service broadcasters are funded partly by advertising and partly from public finances. Reliance on advertising creates an incentive for PSBs to compete with private broadcasters for audience ratings and this practice has resulted in complaints to the European Commission's competition directorate from commercial television rivals about unfair competition.

The arrival of digital distribution has opened up numerous possibilities for PSBs to offer new sorts of services and output to audiences (Born, 2003; Enli, 2008; Graham, 1999; Trappel, 2008). But it has also instigated new concerns about the role played by PSBs and the potential for crowding out of commercial competition (Donders and Pauwels, 2008). For PSBs, digital distribution plus longer time frames during which content may be accessed have greatly extended the potential value available to the public from provision of public service output. A good example of this is the BBC iPlayer catch-up service for television and radio, which has grown rapidly in popularity and usage and throughout 2010 – only three years after its launch – catered for more than 1.3 billion requests for programmes (BBC, 2010).

PSBs can deliver greater value to audiences, not only because of extended opportunities to consume content, but also because modes of engagement in a digital multi-platform context allow for provision of improved and enriched audience experiences. Not surprisingly, the spread of digital technology has been accompanied by a widespread re-envisaging of missions on the part of PSBs with increased emphasis on platform-neutral content provision rather than broadcasting per se. But a widening in the scope of public service entities to embrace digital platforms has precipitated a new round of concerns, particularly at the level of the EU, about the extent to which the activities of PSBs may impede competition and potentially crowd out commercial rivals (Humphreys, 2010; Wheeler, 2010).

A continued consensus favouring licence-fee-funded broadcasting is also threatened by advancing technology because, with increased broadband and greater mobile Web-enabled connectivity, the ways and means of consuming television content have multiplied and so, from the viewer's perspective, the rationale for a funding system based solely on ownership of broadcast receiving equipment is no longer clear. A blurring of the distinction between the television set and other devices renders 'a licence fee that applies to one but not the rest increasingly arbitrary' (Armstrong and Weeds, 2007: 118). Discussions which have taken place in a number of European countries about switching to a more broadly based 'media tax' reflect concerns about how to ensure funding mechanisms remain in step with the way public service content is being consumed and used by audiences (Bron, 2010). But, however much consumption has changed, any remapping of the way charges for public service content are imposed that extends the incidence to a wider array of digital devices promises to be both highly controversial and difficult to enforce. Despite propelling the development of pay-TV, digitization seems to add to as much as it diminishes quandaries about the efficacy and appropriateness of alternative funding mechanisms for PSB.

6

Economics of Content Supply

Converging technologies have created challenges for some existing types of media content while opening up opportunities for new ones. Generally, however, processes of content-creation involve elements of novelty and uncertainty. This chapter explains the strategies used by media suppliers to spread and minimize risk and, more broadly, to maximize the value of their content properties. The ongoing relevance and value of the concept of windowing for content creators is examined in the context of a digital environment where patterns of usage are increasingly complex and protracted, resulting in the phenomenon of the long tail (see page 82). In addition, this chapter introduces and analyses successful models of risk spreading, notably portfolios, the Hollywood model, the use of stars, branding and reliance on repetition and imitation.

After studying this chapter, you should be able to:

- understand the need for and strategies involved in risk spreading in content creation;
- explain the economic success of the Hollywood majors;
- analyse the significance of alternative financing models for rights creators;
- appreciate the relevance, for programme-makers and other suppliers of digital content, of strategies of windowing.

NOVELTY AND RISK SPREADING

Production of media content is an expensive business. Each television programme, film, newspaper and magazine edition must offer messages, images or stories that are novel and unique. The persistent need for creative input – for novelty and innovation – makes content production a labour-intensive process. The production of commodities in the cultural industries as a whole (i.e. in the arts as well as film, television, etc.) is said to suffer from 'Baumol's disease' – named after US economist William

Baumol – in that, because creativity is inherently labour-intensive and because labour costs tend to rise more quickly than others, costs across these sectors will tend to rise at a faster rate than inflation. Audiovisual content-creation is particularly expensive because of the need for specialist capital (as well as human) resources such as cameras, studios, recording and editing equipment.

The media industry has long been characterized by high initial or 'first-run' production costs and, on account of the public good characteristics of content, relatively low marginal distribution costs, which is why economies of scale are such a prevalent feature of the sector. Sometimes, a higher level of initial investment in the processes and elements involved in creating, say, a film or magazine or radio programme will positively enhance the attractiveness of the finished product and increase the likely overall size of the audience that will want to consume it. But this is by no means guaranteed.

Uncertainty about likely demand for an as yet unproduced item of content is a fact of life in all industries devoted to making creative products. Because a creative product is an 'experience good', the extent to which it will please and satisfy is a subjective matter and, as Richard Caves has put it, 'nobody knows' how consumers will respond or what will work (Caves, 2000: 3). At the same time, creation of media products and services typically requires very sizeable investments in production. Publishers, television production companies and film-makers are obliged to take on major risks. With uncertainty about demand, media suppliers need to deploy a number of strategies aimed at reducing risks.

Of course, the spread of digital technology has made it possible to produce and distribute media content at a much lower cost than in the past. Much user-generated digital content is created at extremely low cost and such material is available in ever-increasing quantities on the Internet. Because digitization has reduced content production costs, it can be argued that publishing does not entail the same risks and uncertainties as it did in the past (Shirky, 2010). Low production costs and free copying of digital files means that virtually anyone can publish anything so decisions about quality – about what will or will not be produced – are not necessary.

Ultra low-cost user-generated content combined with ease of copying and distribution of digital files across the Internet has made it more feasible now than in the past to publish for micro-audiences (Aris and Bughin, 2009: 101). The role of the Internet in making access to a much wider diversity of content offerings possible has enabled far more widespread publication and enjoyment of low-cost and less-popular content items. In some content areas, e.g. news provision, conventional suppliers have clearly suffered from the rise of online alternatives. Nonetheless, overall patterns of media consumption continue to strongly favour expensive professionally crafted content (e.g. popular television shows such as *Mad Men*) over low-cost user-produced alternatives. Digitization and the arrival of micropublishing have not seriously dented the general popularity of professionally constructed media properties. The conventional model of publishing based on high initial investment and hopes of wide distribution to yield economies of scale still predominates in the digital era, therefore necessitating the use of a range of strategies aimed at risk reduction.

PORTFOLIOS

In industries where uncertainty is endemic and needs to be managed (e.g. investment), one approach commonly used is to spread risk across a portfolio. This mode of operation has long been evident in television and radio, for example, where broadcasters deploy content portfolio strategies designed to counteract some of the risks inherent in the business. It is commonplace for the broadcaster to offer a whole range of products (elements of programming), with some parts of the schedule designed to appeal to some parts of the audience and others to a different set of individuals (Blumler and Nossiter, 1991: 12–13; Collins, Graham and Locksley, 1988: 11). Consumers will tune in so long as a high enough proportion is to their taste. This control over a range of products greatly increases the broadcaster's chances of making a 'hit' with consumer taste. The revenue (or audience value) from a hit compensates the broadcaster for the cost of producing the whole schedule or portfolio of programmes. In other words, the strength of individual programmes in a schedule is used to spread risk and equalize costs across a range of total output designed to generate the greatest possible audience value or appeal.

The more efficient use of bandwidth made possible by digital compression techniques has multiplied the number of distribution channels available to broadcasters and facilitated new portfolio strategies based on more extensive diversification and targeted development of content. In the UK, for example, additional digital frequencies have enabled most of the main television broadcasters to establish additional channels, many of which are themed or aimed at specific segments of the audience (e.g. children) and some of which simply shift, delay or repeat transmissions of material already shown on flagship channels. The range of 'sister' channels offered by MTV (MTV Music, MTV Base, MTV Hits, MTV Dance, MTV Classic, etc.) provides an example of a portfolio strategy whereby each narrowly differentiated service is designed to extend the exposure of MTV content to a different set of individuals. Because uncertainty exists about which channels or strands or items of content will perform better than others, a portfolio approach enables the broadcaster to disseminate an array of elements based on the expectation that the success of some will subsidize the provision of all others.

The more hit or miss the business, the more compelling the case will be for reliance on portfolios. Such strategies are common, for example, in book and in music publishing where prospects are determined at least partly by fads and fashions that are highly unpredictable. Management of the portfolio is not simply about countering risk by developing as wide an array of products as possible; rather the aim is to discriminate and filter so that those innovations and product ideas that are most likely to succeed receive an appropriate level of attention and investment (Aris and Bughin, 2009: 97).

The use of content portfolio strategies is widespread across the media and, for example, most major magazine publishers such as IPC, Bauer, Time Inc. and Hachette Filipacchi offer not just one or two titles but an extensive range. Because magazine publishing is a sector characterized by products with life cycles, a portfolio strategy can help to stabilize revenues by combining a number of products at different stages in their life and portfolios of titles help ensure the replenishment and renewal of publishers' revenue streams (Picard, 2005). By producing many rather than few products, the risk of failure that is endemic in magazine publishing can be managed and ameliorated.

REPETITION AND FORMATS

The risks and uncertainties associated with producing high-cost audiovisual output are sometimes offset by the use of strategies which, through processes of repetition and imitation, seek to capitalize on characters, storylines and formats that have already worked successfully with audiences (Bielby and Bielby, 1994). For example, programmes that perform successfully on US networks are routinely screened for potential spin-offs, such as the construction of a new show centred around one of the secondary characters (Caves, 2005: 31).

Typical of the reliance on repetition of a formula that works is the production of television programmes in a series of several episodes which allows repeated use of a familiar format and characters in order to build and exploit audience loyalty (Hoskins, McFadyen and Finn, 1997: 120). After the initial outlay associated with devising the format, developing the characters and creating the set, the production of a series with many episodes ought to give rise to some reduction in per-unit production costs. However, such cost advantages may prove transitory because the success of any long-running television series is prone to improve the negotiating position of its core 'talent' and with a resulting transfer in rents (ibid.). Even so, the popularity of producing programmes in series rather than as single stand-alone events (and of spin-offs that deploy elements which have worked well in a previous series) underlines the importance of repetition and reuse of successful formulae as a means of countering some of the costs and risks involved in an industry that calls for constant innovation and novelty.

Another means through which the risks involved in developing new products can be avoided is through acquiring just the format for a programme that is already successfully established elsewhere. A television format describes the core elements or features or the basic formula of a television programme (Moran with Malbon, 2006) and, although formal protection through copyright is limited, international trade in television formats is a growing business (Altmeppen, Lantzsch and Will, 2007; Singh and Kretschmer, 2012). International trade in formats enables broadcasters to buy the rights to make a local version of a show that has already done well in an overseas territory. Although the US remains by far the largest exporter of finished television programmes in the world, the UK production sector is currently the largest supplier to the international market in television formats with successful exports, such as the BBC's *Strictly come Dancing* (which has been made into *Dancing with the Stars* in the US) or *The Office* and Fremantle's *Britain's got Talent* (Colwell and Price, 2005; Oliver & Ohlbaum, 2006; PACT, 2010). The genres which feature in international trade in formats are broad-ranging, but quiz or game shows (e.g. *Who wants to be a Millionaire*) and talent competitions (e.g. *Pop Idol*) are especially popular, as these can easily be remade in local versions without losing any of their essential flavour and appeal. The advantages of relying on formats are manifold, and broadcasters worldwide are increasingly reliant on them as a major element within their daily schedules (Esser, 2010). With a tried-and-tested product, the high costs and risks associated with innovating and launching an entirely new product are eliminated. A content property such as *Top Gear* or *MasterChef* brings not only a market-tested format that can be nuanced and adapted to suit local sensibilities, but also a high-profile format such as *Who Wants to be a Millionaire* or *Ramsay's Kitchen Nightmares* offers the local broad-caster the opportunity to gain leverage with local audiences and adver-tisers from the recognition and credibility an established brand will confer. In addition, the sorts of programmes that work well as interna-tional formats often offer high potential for generation of incremental revenues via sales of merchandise, telephone voting systems or other forms of multi-platform exploitation.

HOLLYWOOD AND RISK

The high costs involved in feature production and uncertainty surround-ing which finished products may appeal to audiences make film an industry in which the use of strategies aimed at risk reduction is criti-cal. It has been argued that film companies impose risks on themselves through their heavy expenditures on 'star-studded features promoted by massive marketing campaigns' (Wasko, 2005: 15). Nevertheless, the film industry is characterized by extreme uncertainty about the revenue prospects for any new production (Walls, 2005) and therefore achieving success on a sustained basis is dependent on managing and countering that uncertainty effectively.

Risk-reduction strategies often focus on enhancing the chances of creating hit content. One means of courting success is through use of texts that have already worked well with audiences, for example through adaptation of plays or novels or remakes of stories that have worked in other languages and cultures. Recent empirical research indicates that a large proportion of Hollywood output is drawn from literary sources, and that 'artistic imitation essentially stems from a commercial strategy aimed at minimising risk and introducing some (financial) security in a very unsure business' (Joye, 2009). Similarly, the use of sequels that build on a successful format or popular char-acter (for example the *Star Wars* series or the James Bond films) can provide another widely used means of reducing the uncertainty inher-ent in developing new film projects.

Marketing plays an important role is seeking to shape and stabi-lize demand for films: marketing activities do not simply occur after the movie has been made but 'can shape the aesthetic identity of film from its conception' (Grainge, 2008: 10). The use of established actors and directors, to whom some brand loyalty may attach, forms part of the marketing strategy for a film (Hoskins, McFayden and Finn, 1997: 121). Film-makers have long relied on the use of stars to try to give new productions a higher chance of success with audiences (Rosen, 1981). The use of a well-known actor helps to make a film project a more reliable 'banker', so the participation of a prominent name will usually assist in ensuring that a film project secures financial backing. However, the presence of box-office stars is not a guarantee of success and nor will it necessarily mitigate the effects of negative critical reviews (Suárez-Vásquez, 2011). In addition, stars are often successful in capturing all if not more than the likely contribution that their participation might make to a film's revenue through fees charged by their agents – a phenomenon de Vany has referred to as 'the curse of the superstar' (de Vany, 2004: 225).

Setting aside content and marketing strategies, the size (or scale of operations) and vertical structure adopted by a film company can also play an important role in risk reduction, as demonstrated by the success of the Hollywood 'majors'. A very notable characteristic of global markets for film is the predominance of output from the US (WTO, 2010). Consumer expenditure on films has generally been buoyant in recent years but a problem for the UK, as well as for many other countries worldwide, is that the bulk of domestic expenditure on films is generated by and ploughed back into the dominant Hollywood-based US film production industry. In the UK and Ireland, for example, some 90 per cent of box-office receipts were accounted for films partly or wholly made by US film companies in 2010 (BFI, 2011: 14). A similar situation exists across Europe where, in 2009, US studios accounted for 64 percent of the box-office revenues generated by the top 100 distributors (Hancock and Zhang, 2010).

A small handful of multinational companies called the majors account for the overwhelming success of US films in world markets. The major studios – Disney, 20th Century Fox, Paramount Pictures, Sony/Columbia Pictures, Universal Pictures and Warner Brothers – are large, well-resourced and vertically integrated film companies that are generally part of larger media conglomerates (e.g. Fox is owned by News Corporation and Paramount by Viacom). The films produced by these six companies tend to dominate international film markets across the globe year after year. The US industry is also comprised of numerous 'independent' studios which, in general, tend to be only minor players in the international market compared with the Hollywood majors.

One of the main factors favouring the majors is size. This is important, not only in terms of demand (i.e. the size of domestic US market available to support their output), but also in terms of supply (i.e. the scale of productive activity in which each of the majors is engaged). The value of global cinema box-office receipts reached US$31.8bn in 2010, and of that, the North American box office accounted for

US$10.6bn (MPAA, 2011). But the box office represents only one slice of total expenditure on filmed entertainment, with the majority coming from video rental and retail (both online and in DVD or Blu-ray disc format) plus television payments. Industry estimates suggest that in North America the film industry will generate total revenues of over US$40bn in 2011 (PwC, 2011). A vast amount is spent in the US each year on consuming domestically made feature films, and this expenditure provides very considerable resources to support new production of high-budget movies. The ability of the major studios to make sizeable 'slates' of high-budget well-promoted movies every year, as opposed to only being involved in one-off film projects, means that these companies are particularly well-positioned to spread their risks and to sustain a high share of the market. Effectively, the scale of the US majors enables them to adopt a portfolio approach to investment in film production.

Structure is the other area where the US industry has a big advantage over the UK and other would-be rivals. The distinction between majors and independents is important here. The US majors consist of integrated film companies whose activities span across both production and distribution. The major studios produce and release only around 160 films in-house between them each year (MPAA, 2011), but it is these 160 films that dominate international markets for feature films. Films distributed by the majors usually account for well over 90 per cent of takings at the US box office and everywhere else their market share is usually above 50 per cent of total revenues.

The independent sector is made up of all film producers worldwide except the majors. It comprises 'those companies – both within the US and around the world – that develop, finance and distribute feature films independently of the US major studios' (Lewis and Marris, 1991: 4). In a few cases, independence from the majors is not absolute. A handful of the more successful independents are now backed by much larger parent corporations with cross-ownership interests in the Hollywood majors, e.g. New Line Cinema is owned by Time Warner and Pixar by Disney. Aside from these, there is a large international population of genuinely independent film-production companies. In the US, for example, independents produce around three times as many films as the Hollywood studios each year. However, only a small proportion of films made by independents in the US manage to gain a theatrical release and, elsewhere in the world, independent film producers experience similar difficulties in gaining access to exhibition.

The main difference between the Hollywood major studios and independents is that the majors are all vertically integrated companies that incorporate both production and distribution. The distribution divisions of the majors cover virtually all territories in the world and, crucially, this gives companies such as Fox and Warner Brothers control over domestic and international distribution of their product. 'With control of distribution, the risks of film-making can be spread across a large number of films, and between production and distribution' (Lewis and Marris, 1991: 4). With assured distribution, the majors are able to commit significant resources to production and to marketing or 'P&A' (prints and advertising) so as to build audience awareness for their own product. Independent producers who lack such control over distribution are clearly at a considerable disadvantage. They can only reduce the risks involved in production by separately pre-selling the distribution rights to several territories before a film is made.

So, the vertical structure of the Hollywood majors plays an important role in reducing risk. In the so-called 'classic' film economy, vertically integrated companies – i.e. the Hollywood majors – provide the finance for film production and use their own distribution networks to disseminate their films onwards to exhibition outlets. They exhibit where possible in their own cinemas. Then, a proportion of their profits is reinvested in new production so as to keep the virtuous circle going. Typically, the distribution division will have a say in which projects are pursued and which are not, so that production is strongly influenced by marketing considerations. The success of this model stems from two factors: control over distribution plus the ability to produce a steady outflow of films. This ensures that income from the few hits or blockbusters produced by each of the majors each year is available to cover whatever losses are incurred by the flops and the average performers.

Like fashion and popular music, film production is a hit-or-miss business. Film production is not only risky but also highly expensive. In 2007, average production budgets for a major Hollywood movie were running at some US$71m plus an additional US$36m or so for marketing (McClintock, 2008). Production budgets are subject to fairly constant upward pressure, mainly because of inflation in the fees that brand-name stars are able to command. The heavy investment and high risks involved in the film industry have led to it being likened to the oil-exploration sector. As Headland and Relph put it, '[a] great deal of money can be spent drilling wells that trickle rather than gush' (1991: 6).

Investment in production of feature films, wherever it is carried out, is regarded as highly speculative. Typically, only two out of every ten films made even by the most successful Hollywood studios make profits (Gasson, 1996: 184). In other words, the majority of films lose money. The scale of revenues created by hits at the box office is enormous, even relative to the sizeable budgets which are necessary to create them in the first place. For the Hollywood majors, revenues from just two successes out of every ten films provide the cash-flow needed to, first, continue replenishing the stream of well-promoted big-budget Hollywood movies in between the hits and, second, provide a return to shareholders. For independent producers, it is almost impossible to break into the virtuous cash-flow circle enjoyed by the majors.

All the finance needed to fund development, production and marketing of a film has to be raised in advance, but returns do not start to flow until after the completed film reaches the cinemas, which is often some three years later or more. If the producer is attached to one of the major studios, then the studio will organize production finance internally. Independent producers must seek finance through an advance from a distributor against future box-office revenues and through borrowing and investment by third parties. The latter is difficult to come by and expensive because all the working capital involved in the film represents 'risk capital' insofar as, apart from the film itself (which is not yet made), there are no assets against which borrowing can be secured.

When the film's release date arrives and theatrical revenues begin to flow, the cinema covers its own costs first, often taking 50 per cent of box-office income (although terms vary according to the film, the duration of the theatrical run and other circumstances). The balance or 'distributor's gross' goes back to the distributor who deducts commission and costs, including all advertising and promotional costs. Anything left after this is then passed on to the equity investors or financiers who have covered production costs, and who deduct a premium for covering risks etc. Finally, any profit remaining goes back to the producer and (if appropriate) the production studio.

Generally speaking, the investor or financier (unless it happens to be a distributor) is second from last in the repayment chain from the film's proceeds, followed only by the producer. Their place in the queue may be pushed back even further if some of the key people involved in producing the film decide to take a proportion of their fee in the form of a participation in gross revenues. Top film stars can jump to the front of the queue by negotiating a cut of the film's so-called 'first dollar' receipts – i.e. box-office receipts before deduction of any distribution costs. For example, a so-called '20 and 20' package' – i.e. a US$20m up-front fee for participation plus 20 per cent of the film's first dollar receipts is not uncommon for prominent actors (Garrahan, 2009).

Going back to the example of the oil industry, companies such as Shell, Esso and BP are normally involved in the whole cycle from exploration to refining to sales of petrol at the filling-station forecourt. Consequently, they can absorb the costs of the riskiest element (drilling) across the return from the whole process. The Hollywood majors work on the same principle. They control production and distribution and, in many cases, are also involved in exhibition. In the UK, for example, several multiplex cinema sites are run by subsidiaries of the US majors. As with the large oil companies, the expensive risk phase (i.e. production) is covered by total returns to the film company on each phase of the entire and ongoing process of supply to the consumer.

The accumulation of market power stretching across all phases in the vertical supply chain creates a number of important advantages for the US major studios. It ensures wide exhibition and therefore a dominant market position for the supply of their own products. Every film produced, even the failures, can be fed into the distribution business to achieve some earnings. Because of their control over the supply chain, major distributors can engage in trade practices such as block booking – i.e. when exhibitors are required to take a bundle of films, including some they might not otherwise have wanted to exhibit – which help to reduce their risks (Hoskins, McFayden and Finn, 1997: 55–6). Vertical integration also means that there are no (or fewer) third-party distributors or other middle-men taking a cut from the return to the original investor – i.e. the studios themselves.

FUNDING MODELS: COST PLUS VERSUS DEFICIT FINANCING

Whereas a variety of approaches can be used to try to mitigate the risks inherent in making media content, the fact remains that production is an expensive process. Once the 'first copy' of, say, a television programme has been created, it then costs little or nothing to reproduce and supply it to extra customers. This is because the main value of broadcast content is generally to do with attributes that are immaterial (i.e. its messages or meanings) and these do not get used up in the act of consumption. Increasing marginal returns will be enjoyed as more and more customers for a television programme are added. The wider the audience for a programme, the more profitable it will become.

An important question for any media content production firm is who will reap the benefit (of reducing per-capita production costs) as consumption of its output expands? In the television industry, the powerful position occupied by dominant broadcasters may result in a situation where producers are unable to share in any of the benefits associated with the public good attributes of their output. If, for example, broadcasters manage to purchase all the retransmission rights to the programmes they acquire from producers, then it is broadcasters and not producers who will benefit from all the economies of scale that arise should that programming be sold to additional audiences.

The issue of rights ownership is crucial in the creative industries. The experience of many creators of intellectual property who have achieved financial success underlines the importance of retaining copyright and of exploiting rights as fully as possible. The ability of producers to exploit copyright effectively may depend on how market power is distributed along the vertical supply chain that stretches between the producer and the consumer. Theoretically, each of the different stages along the way is interdependent – e.g. distribution facilities are no good without supplies of content and vice versa. In reality, strategic bottlenecks and concentrations of market power can develop. The problem both for producers and for distributors is that a monopolist or dominant player at any other stage along the supply chain may be able to appropriate some or all of their profits.

In the television production sector, a distinction can be drawn between two alternative models of financing which, in turn, have important implications for rights ownership. The term 'deficit financing' describes a system, prevalent in the US, where programme-makers share a portion of the financial risks involved in production in return for ownership of secondary and tertiary rights to their programmes (Litman, 1998: 140). Thus, producers (rather than broadcasters) are able to exploit their own hit programmes. By contrast, the system that has prevailed historically in the UK and elsewhere across Europe is one in which broadcasters tend to pay all production costs, so that producers are not exposed to any financial risk, but in return broadcasters also retain the majority of secondary rights.

Deficit-financing works in the following way. In return for the right to transmit a programme made by independent producers, the US networks systematically offer a fee which is less than the production budget for that programme, often by as much as one-third (ibid.: 149). The programme-maker has to make up the difference or deficit themselves, and the programme producers are obliged to take a share in the financial risk associated with a new programme. If the programme flops then the producer loses out on the share of the production budget they have invested in it, because the programme has little or no residual value in secondary markets. On the other hand, if the programme is a hit, then the programme-maker stands to gain significantly from selling their programmes again either to other broadcasters in the US (a process known as secondary syndication), or to video distributors, or to overseas broadcasters.

This contrasts with the 'cost plus' system under which broadcasters who commission programmes from independent producers are prepared to cover the production budget in full and also to pay the programme-maker a small up-front production fee or 'profit', usually of around 10 per cent of the total production budget. However, in return, the broadcaster acquires not only the primary rights (or first right to transmit the programme itself) but also, generally, the majority of secondary rights (e.g. for DVD retail, online distribution and overseas sales).

The pattern of apportionment of risks and profits between broadcasters and programme-makers has important implications for the financial performance of both sectors. In the late 1990s, UK independent producers increasingly recognized that financial success requires participation in the risks and rewards from their output and they lobbied for change in the then prevalent cost-plus arrangements (Woodward, 1998: 18). They complained that for years broadcasters had 'tried wherever possible to control all rights in a programme "brand" (including copyright, distribution rights, trademarks, secondary rights and other rights not directly connected to broadcasting) when in fact all they have really needed is a right to broadcast' (Gutteridge et al., 2000: 3).

In response, the then regulator of UK television broadcasting, the ITC, conducted a major review and concluded that lack of negotiating power on the part of independent producers was indeed a significant problem (ITC, 2002). On account of their weak bargaining position, television content producers were left with little or no ownership of secondary rights, and had little economic incentive to build up and exploit their programme brands, for example, by developing formats suitable for digital media. Television broadcasters tended to retain all rights in perpetuity but often would do little to exploit the works in their possession. Thus retention of blanket rights by broadcasters was seen as inefficient as well as unfair to producers.

This problem was addressed in legislation[6] which required a new regulator, Ofcom, to oversee the implementation of suitable Codes of Practice governing transactions between broadcasters and independent producers. From 2004, new Codes were implemented that improved transparency in dealings between broadcasters and independent producers and offered better opportunities for unbundling of primary from secondary rights. This initiative paved the way for

---

[6]Through the Communications Act 2003.

a fundamental improvement in the economic position of independent producers and coincided with a restructuring within the sector characterized by a trend towards the development of larger-sized or so-called 'super indies' such as IMG, Endemol and All3Media who, on account of their scale and track records, have managed to achieve considerable status and financial success (Doyle and Paterson, 2008).

Among the larger independents that have emerged, a more risk-positive and entrepreneurial culture is evident with 'business models geared to production for the world market and to the maximization of the global value of ... rights' (Colwell and Price, 2005: 6). Bigger firms are better placed to become important suppliers and to acquire negotiating leverage in their transactions with broadcasters and they also enjoy advantages in relation to being able to spread their risks over a number of programme titles and differing genres. The change in policy which has enabled producers to retain more of their rights and 'become asset-owning businesses' has encouraged the development of production entities that are better adapted to competing in international television markets (Chalaby, 2010: 675).

However, it is worth noting that the majority of the 400 or so independent production companies that are currently active in the UK are still relatively small enterprises who typically earn very slender, if any, profits (Oliver & Ohlbaum Associates Ltd, 2006; Parker, 2011). To participate successfully in strategies of cross-subsidization and risk-spreading, production companies need to be of a certain size and to have 'a portfolio of programs of different vintages in their inventory' (Litman, 1998: 135). So while the industry remains, in general, fragmented and highly populated by small under-funded firms with small back catalogues and low volumes of work, opportunities associated with a deficit financing approach will not be fully open to exploitation for a majority of UK programme-makers for some time to come.

This contrasts with the situation in the US where, with historically much fuller participation in both the risks and rewards of programme-making, many successful production companies have built up significant financial resources and developed a strong market presence both domestically and internationally. The development of a mature and an exceptionally well-funded production sector in the US is, of course, a reflection of other aspects of its unique history and circumstances, including the large size and wealth of domestic US television audiences plus the existence, within the US, of very well-developed secondary and tertiary markets to which programme-makers can sell their wares. UK secondary broadcasting markets are small by comparison and have developed only slowly (Levy, 2008: 210). However, as multichannel viewing continues to grow, the transition from a cost-plus to a deficit financing model clearly augers well for the commercial prospects of the UK television production sector over the longer term.

WINDOWING

Rights ownership is of central importance when it comes to exploiting the value that resides in media content. Part of the business of supplying television content on a profit-maximizing basis involves giving attention to how best to organize the sale or release of that content to differing segments of the television audience or 'windows'. Owen and Wildman (1992: 26) have explained how programme suppliers try to maximize the exploitation of programme assets by regarding primary, secondary and tertiary television audiences as different windows. Suppliers of television content set about maximizing the value of their assets by not only selling programmes through as many avenues or windows as possible but also in a pattern or order that yields the greatest return.

   The concept of windowing or maximizing the returns from ownership of rights long predates the transition to convergent digital technology but, in principle, this technique is as relevant as ever for media suppliers, albeit that, in the context of a multi-platform approach to content distribution, modelling the range of distributive outlets and the factors likely to dictate their sequencing is more complex. Figure 6.1 gives an example of the sorts of windows a television programme supplier will consider, although the order in which windows will be ranked and their relative value depends on the nature of the content property, the territory in question, the size of the audience that each window makes available and the profit margin per viewer in each case. In the UK, for instance, the most important domestic television windows are the primary free-to-air terrestrial channels, followed by cable or satellite and DTT distributed channels (which may be categorized as 'premium' or 'basic', depending on whether subscription charges apply). The proportion of revenues being derived from primary broadcast channels as opposed to 'other' sources has gradually reduced over time reflecting

Figure 6.1   Possible distribution outlets or windows for television content

changed consumption patterns and ongoing fragmentation of audiences (Foster and Broughton, 2011: 26).

Windowing can be regarded as a form of price discrimination, in that it involves the same product being sold at different prices to different groups of consumers for reasons not associated with differences in costs (Moschandreas, 2000: 145). The total value that is placed on being able to watch a particular television programme will vary from individual to individual and may also vary across time. Because the size of consumers' surplus for access to programmes varies among individual viewers and over time, a uniform viewing charge will not allow suppliers to maximize their income. A uniform charge that is too low would imply that only a small part of the consumers' surplus is transferred to the supplier. A uniform fee that is too high drives out of the market those viewers whose surplus is lower than the charge. Selling the programme at a different price to each viewer – a practice known as 'first-degree price discrimination' – would be efficient but (albeit that digital distribution infrastructures make it likely that more individualized charging will evolve) is difficult to implement. For the time being, price discrimination between different groups of viewers or different distribution channels or windows – a form of 'third-degree' price discrimination – offers programme suppliers an approach that is both practical and advantageous.

A number of issues will affect the placing of each window within the overall release sequence. Given that the perceived appeal of any programme tends to diminish over time, it generally makes sense to try to schedule outlets with high per-viewer profit margins early in the release sequence and ahead of channels with lower per-viewer margins (Owen and Wildman, 1992: 33). The size of the audience reached is another consideration, and if per-viewer profit margins are exactly the same in all windows, then scheduling large audiences that yield bigger receipts before small ones will help maximize revenue. However, in the era of digitization and the Internet, piracy has become an even more influential factor in determining release sequences.

Advances in technology impact on windowing strategies in a number of ways. On account of channel proliferation, content suppliers have benefited from increased competition among distributors in need of attractive television material. At the same time, ongoing fragmentation of the media environment has meant that organizing a release strategy which achieves exposure to sizeable segments of the population is much more difficult to accomplish now than in the past.

Suppliers of television content are faced with the problem that, at all times, multitudes of competing linear and non-linear offerings are simultaneously vying for viewers' attention and for viewer payments.

Massive growth in Internet-based distribution of audiovisual material has made it more difficult to execute strategies that rely on dividing audiences into distinct groups and on controlling retransmission of content between separate audience segments. Third-degree price discrimination is feasible 'only if markets can be effectively segregated so that resale from the lower to the higher priced market is not possible' (Moschandreas, 2000: 147). With the introduction of digital platforms, prevention of seepage between audience groups can be problematic because of the relative ease with which digital files can be downloaded, stored, reproduced and recirculated. Because piracy can result in the loss of significant potential revenues from secondary and tertiary markets, an obvious concern for any profit-maximizing content producer in organizing its windowing strategy is how prone each distributive outlet or window is to illegal copying.

The Internet is highly vulnerable in this respect but, with Web connectivity among consumers increasing all the time, online distribution can only gain in prominence as an aspect of windowing strategies. This dilemma has spurred vigorous efforts on the part of content producers to develop technological solutions such as encryption systems that enable content to be watched but not illegally copied (Burt, 2004) and legal solutions such as requiring Internet service providers (ISPs) to block access to websites offering illegal downloads of music and audiovisual material (Bradshaw and Croft, 2011). Interventions of the latter kind help address the problem of asymmetry in the economic impact of illegal downloading between content-makers and communication infrastructure providers.

Windowing strategies in the film industry have adjusted over time in line with advancing technology. The once-dominant cinema or theatrical window now represents only around a quarter of film revenues (UKFC, 2010), but the box office remains an important barometer of what sort of appeal any film might generate and how it is likely to perform in other release windows. Sales and rentals of DVDs, Blu-ray discs and videos – including online rental and retail – now account for some 40 per cent of film revenues (PwC, 2011). It is likely that as viewers migrate to Web-connected television sets that offer ready access to Internet-based film and VOD services online windows will become more important (Loeffler, 2010). The television industry accounts for a further significant slice of income for film through content payments from movie subscription channels and free-to-air television services. And some feature films, e.g. the *Harry Potter* series, can also earn sizeable revenues in associated markets, for example, though sale of merchandise and, of growing importance, through games (either packaged or online) that draw on key characters and features within a film property.

Although overall expenditure on consuming feature films has been buoyant in recent years, the timing, duration and relative value of the differing windows in the release sequence have changed. Piracy is a general concern and has tended to create pressure towards shorter release periods, but windowing strategies in the film industry are influenced by a variety of other technological and market developments. For example, the Hollywood majors recently reduced the duration of the cinema window for their output from around four months to just two months by bringing forward the time at which their films are available via on-demand services in the home (Davoudi, 2011). Earlier studies have indicated that around 60–70 per cent of the revenues a film will earn at the box office are collected during the first three weeks after its release (Jedidi, Krider and Weinberg, 1998), but nonetheless cinema owners have voiced understandable concern about how this move is likely to impact on future cinema admission trends. However, the majors hope that developing a 'premium VOD' window (where viewers are charged around US$30 to view films that are still relatively new in the comfort of their homes) will help counteract declining revenues from DVD sales. From the point of view of the major studios, another incentive for this change is that, compared with the box-office window where cinema owners usually retain 50 per cent of ticket sales income, the profit margins available through an on-demand screening window are much higher (Halliday, 2011).

Windowing affects content production budgets, with extra potential cumulative revenue in a number of windows justifying a larger budget than would be feasible if the content were destined for release in just one distribution channel. A television series can be highly profitable even though none of the individual windows it sells through would, on its own, provide sufficient revenues to cover the costs of production. Production decisions often reflect the various distributive outlets a production firm is targeting. Sometimes a particular actor or storyline is fed into a television production precisely because that element is expected to increase the attractiveness of the programme for audiences in a specific window. For example, the inclusion of a popular actor from the US within a European television production might be designed to ensure that the programme will be purchased by US television channels.

So, windowing involves not only domestic outlets but also overseas ones. To maximize the value of their assets, programme suppliers need to devise a strategy for exploiting all available transmission and other rights in as many territories as possible across the globe. Overseas markets represent increasingly important windows for television content, as is evidenced by the popularity in the UK and elsewhere of imported television programmes such as *Mad Men* and *The Sopranos*. The prices that broadcasters are willing (and able to afford) to pay in different geographic markets for, say, the same half-hour comedy show will vary widely. A wide discrepancy exists between, for example, what European broadcasters and African broadcasters are willing to pay for an hour of US programming (Hoskins, McFayden and Finn, 1997: 69). Consequently, in order to maximize international revenues, programme suppliers need to discriminate on price between different overseas territories as well as between primary and secondary markets.

The sale of programmes in international markets by dominant US producers is sometimes regarded as being akin to 'dumping'. Dumping occurs where a good is sold in an overseas market at a price below the real cost of production. It is generally frowned upon as a practice because of its damaging effects on local producers. In the case of television exports, the good is almost certainly sold into foreign markets at a price well below initial production costs. On the other hand, the price at which the programme is sold is bound to be well above the marginal cost of supplying it (i.e. the cost of making and supplying one extra copy of the original to the importing broadcaster). Whether or not programme exports correspond with the technical description of dumping depends on which definition of cost is used. Since what is being sold is not the programme per se but merely the right to transmit it in one territory, marginal costs seem in some ways to provide the more relevant benchmark.

The perception of US producers dumping product on to foreign markets also overlooks the fact that programme-makers often set out with the intention of recouping their costs not just through domestic primary and secondary sales but also through a series of releases into additional geographic markets. The US domestic market is large, but it may not necessarily provide all the revenues needed to ensure that a television programme will be produced. The targeting of international markets may sometimes play an important part in a producer's windowing strategy, to the extent that international preferences will exert some influence over production decisions (Noam, 1993: 47). Spreading production costs across as many different release windows and territories as possible is, after all, the fundamental recipe for success for any media-content producer.

As well as gaining income through the sale of television transmission rights in various release windows, creators of successful programme brands may also be able to derive revenues from exploitation of copyright in related and complementary goods. This is especially true for children's television programming where many internationally renowned character brands have been created, such as *The Simpsons*. For example, the BBC's *Teletubbies* series has given rise to vast revenues for the BBC from licensing the sale of a wide array of books, magazines, DVDs and toys and other merchandise bearing the *Teletubbies* brand. Other high-profile successes for UK television content-makers include the *Bob the Builder* children's programme, which was developed by the BBC and HIT Entertainment in the late 1990s. According to Andrew Carley of Entertainment One, the maker of *Peppa Pig,* which has sold in some 180 territories internationally, revenues from licensing have grown as a proportion of income for children's television content to the point where '[w]hen we're looking at new shows, it can be difficult to work out how to finance them if there's not the licensing component' (cited in Conlon, 2010).

The concept of windowing, as elucidated by Owen and Wildman (1992), involves careful planning of the release sequence for a television programme – a single identical item of content – in order to maximize returns. As digitization encourages greater convergence across the media industry, strong incentives exist to exploit any successful television content property or brand not only via television windows but via a wider multiplicity of distribution modes and platforms (Doyle, 2010a). A multi-platform approach to distribution may well call for strategies of adaptation of content and for production of multiple versions of narratives and ancillary material. The notion of multi-platform distribution is *different* from windowing – it involves migrating content across differing media formats as well as organizing the sequencing of delivery – but similarly it is driven by the logic of seeking to exploit the value in content as fully as possible. The reuse of and reformatting of content to facilitate wider consumption across a multiplicity of platforms and modes of delivery means that, as audiences expand, average per-viewer costs reduce sharply and significant economies of scale and scope can be earned.

In the context of a digital media environment, ease of reformatting plus the availability of multiple distribution outlets and extended time frames are key to maximizing the value of content assets. As a result, more time and care is needed now than in the past in planning the sequence of releases for a content property into differing distribution channels. According to a commissioning scheduler at MTV UK, it is no longer the case that first transmission on linear television is the sole concern. His reflections indicate both the necessity for and the complexity of strategies of windowing in a digital multi-platform context:

> It is about *aggregate* viewing … When we commission something we're thinking: what is the longevity of this show? You could have six 30-minute episodes – that doesn't mean the show is over in six weeks' time. You've probably got two years sweating that content on different platforms … I spend a lot of my time with strategy and finance working out the return on investment across different platforms of doing an idea.[7]

---

[7]Booth: interviewed in London in 2009.

7

Copyright

Copyright is central to the business of earning returns from media content, but a rise in unauthorized content-sharing, facilitated by digitization and growth of the Internet, has raised doubts about the ability to police and control intellectual property rights. This chapter examines the key economic issues and arguments behind copyright and assesses in what ways these are affected by changes in technology and in market structures. Is copyright essential in incentivizing creativity, or are there workable alternatives for financing content production? What is the relationship between copyright and innovation? This chapter aims to unravel the core underlying welfare issues associated with copyright enforcement in the media. The role played by copyright in sustaining investment in media content creation is considered here alongside the challenges posed by digital piracy and by the need to adapt to the 'open' Internet.

After studying this chapter, you should be able to:

- identify and understand the main economic principles underlying the development of systems of legal protection for copyright;
- analyse how the spread of digital technology has affected the economic case in favour of and against copyright;
- appreciate the challenges to existing copyright regimes posed by the increased internationalization of media;
- assess the merits of copyright versus alternative mechanisms for incentivizing and supporting content creation.

THE ECONOMIC ORIGINS OF COPYRIGHT

Copyright plays a crucial role in enabling the creators of media content to exploit the value that resides in their output. It relates to whatever entitlements the law will protect in respect of an author's ownership of their original creations. The fundamental idea is to protect authors and artists against unauthorized use of their work and also to ensure that they can share in any earnings from its use by the public. So copyright is centrally concerned with the right conferred on authors to monopolize rents from their own creative work and to control its usage. However, copyright recognizes two different sorts of entitlements on the part of creators. First, a property right or an exclusive right to earn revenues from the work for a given period and, second, what is sometimes called a 'moral' right – i.e. the right to have the work attributed to you as its author and to prevent any distortion or misuse of it.

One of the central ideas behind copyright is that the assured reward for the author is what stimulates the creativity from which society ultimately benefits. Reward is assured through the granting of a monopoly to the author for a limited time to allow them to earn a living from uses of their work. Monopolies are usually frowned upon by economists because it is recognized that competition plays a key role in promoting and sustaining efficiency among rival suppliers. However, cultural industries, including media, are prone to market failure. Even the founder of economics, Adam Smith, recognized that the special quasi-public attributes of cultural output may sometimes result in a failure of the market to provide outcomes which are in line with the best interests of society (Towse, 2004: 56). Albeit that the 'abhorrence of monopoly has permeated economic thinking' down through the ages and has engendered a certain ambivalence about copyright in some quarters, it nonetheless remains the case that copyright is supported by an economic justification (Handke, 2010: 22).

This justification stems from the public good nature of informational goods and, in particular, the fact that consumption of these is non-rivalrous. Unlike normal private goods, the locus of value in informational goods is often intangible in nature and therefore not prone to getting used up in the act of consumption. For example, one person watching a film will not diminish its availability to supply to others. Making copies is generally quick and easy – all the more so in the digital era – but the problem is that unrestricted copying would prevent the author of a creative work from being able to earn rewards from it. And while marginal replication costs are small or sometimes zero, the initial production costs involved in creating media content are typically very high. So, in the absence of any system that restricts copying and resupplying of informational goods, it is not obvious how the producer of original media output could recoup the initial production costs involved or what financial incentive there would be to create that content in the first place (Landes and Posner, 1989: 26).

Therefore, national and international regimes of protection for intellectual property rights (IPRs), of which copyright is a part, are based on the assumption that it is desirable to incentivize the production of informational goods (Withers, 2006). The existence of copyright is partly underpinned by the view that authors of creative work are naturally entitled to benefit from their own output. The economic case in favour of copyright goes beyond questions of natural entitlement to the notion that incentives to creativity are a good thing not just for the individual author but for society more widely. Copyright addresses the problem that, in a free market, fewer creative works would be produced than is socially desirable (Lilley, 2006: 3). Without the system of rewards that copyright law manages to enshrine, fewer creative outputs – including films and other media outputs – would be produced and all would lose out.

The development of copyright has traditionally been underpinned by the view that public interventions to foster and encourage creativity are economically desirable. In recent years, the viewpoint that creativity ought to be supported has gained momentum on account of the rise of 'creative industries' thinking (Hesmondhalgh and Pratt, 2005; Schlesinger, 2007). Spurred on by Richard Florida's influential work on the role of creativity in regional and urban economic development (Florida, 2002), the idea that creative sectors of the economy are growing rapidly and that creativity acts as a driver to growth in the wider economy have achieved widespread recognition and been embraced by public policy-makers in the UK and around the globe (Andari et al., 2007). The role of measures to support the creative industries – copyright being a case in point – has therefore become a subject of growing interest.

Still, the extent to which a rights regime is essential in incentivizing creativity is a matter of divided opinions. Some have noted that although returns to artists (despite being highly skewed) are typically low, this does not necessarily appear to diminish the general willingness of artists to work (Towse, 2001). Indeed, some artists' labour markets are characterized by a persistent over-supply of creative workers (WIPO, 2003: 24). Since the motives that encourage authors and artists to engage in production of creative outputs are varied and to some extent intrinsic, it cannot be assumed that strengthening copyright or extending its term will automatically translate into higher levels of creative output (Kay, 2011; Withers, 2006: 15).

Even if some or many creators are not driven primarily by pursuit of financial rewards, it remains that the production of good-quality media content – television programmes, films, newspapers, etc. – is generally a resource-intensive activity that requires investment. Some media organizations are non-market players (e.g. public service broadcasters) but the majority of content production is carried out by commercial entities – commercial publishing houses and audiovisual production firms – for whom success and indeed survival hinges on being able to derive revenues from exploitation of their intellectual property assets. As noted earlier, media content-creation is characterized by risk, uncertainty and incessant pursuit of novelty. This implies a need for well-resourced production and publishing firms who, unlike individuals, are generally better placed to attract capital, spread risks and conduct portfolio strategies (WIPO, 2003: 25). The support that a rights regime provides to commercial publishing and content production firms can be seen as crucial in fuelling the ongoing process of replenishment of the creative work that constitutes their output.

While copyright mitigates a potential problem in relation to incentives to produce information goods, it also involves costs. As suggested by Landes and Posner (1989), copyright involves a trade-off. The existence of copyright protection ensures incentives for creators but, at the same time, it means that artists who want to build on or integrate earlier work within a newly created and original piece of output are obliged, first of all, to trace and secure permissions from relevant owners of copyright. This process can be very time-consuming and complex, so copyright imposes transaction costs on later creators (Towse, 2010).

Can excessive copyright protection, itself, impose a restriction on creativity? Because copyright stops authors from producing works that follow up on or derive too closely from earlier works, it has been argued that copyright, in a sense, stifles innovation and creativity as well as encouraging it. Copyright is supposed to strike a fair balance 'between the rights of the creators to be rewarded for their artistic endeavour and the needs of a flourishing cultural and democratic society to have access to and be able to build upon existing creative works' (Withers, 2006: 16). It is intended to balance the advantages to society of encouraging extra works to be created against the significant disadvantages and costs of reducing public access to creative works. However, striking that balance is not easy, as evidenced by the strength of opposing viewpoints among differing interest groups in relation to whether protections for copyright need to be strengthened or liberalized or whether protection periods ought to be lengthened or reduced.

The potentially stifling effect that copyright can have on follow-up creations has long been recognized as a drawback of the system and a cost for society at large (Landes and Posner, 1989). Boldrin and Levine suggest that copyright and patents are 'intellectual monopolies' that hinder the operations of the free market needed to deliver innovations and, as such, are detrimental rather than helpful to economic development (Boldrin and Levine, 2008). Given that the digital era has brought greater emphasis on the mixing together and integration of existing copyright material within new creative works, the prevailing approach towards copyright can be said to tilt the balance of interests too far in favour of first-generation creators at the expense of new artists and forms of creative expression (Lilley, 2006: 6). Most notably, Lawrence Lessig has argued that in the wake of digitization copyright laws are out of date and need to be liberalized to accommodate rather than criminalize the 'remix' creativity (Lessig, 2009).

It is not just new creators for whom the brunt of compliance can be a burden. Copyright in a work is usually not just a single right but a complex bundle relating to the entitlements of the various creative individuals and parties whose input has given rise to its production. Before a copyright-protected work can be disseminated publicly, there is an obligation to trace and gain permissions from all relevant copyright holders. For media organizations that are bulk users of third-party copyright-protected material, the amount of time spent on administering and securing clearance of rights can be enormous. For example the BBC 'spends some £230m per year on acquiring third party intellectual property right' and the level of man-hours involved in ensuring compliance with relevant copyright and licensing requirements is 'really quite significant', especially so in the context of a digital multi-platform environment (Freeman, 2008: 119). Even for historic archive programming material created by the BBC itself, the level of work and uncertainty involved in tracing key contributors and in gaining clearance can make exploitation of the work unfeasible (ibid.: 120).

In short, the transaction costs involved in trading, negotiating and clearing rights represent a significant burden on would-be users of copyright-protected works. The existence of such costs naturally serves to depress consumption of creative outputs below what might be considered an ideal level. Copyright restricts access to goods that could be enjoyed at no marginal cost. In a sense, copyright entails a trade-off between production efficiency – i.e. making sure that there are sufficient incentives to produce goods – and, on the other hand, consumption efficiency – i.e. maximizing the value that consumers can extract from protected works (Liebowitz, 2003: 2–3). Copyright involves a trade-off between under-production and under-consumption of creative outputs (Handke, 2010: 7).

COPYRIGHT AND WELFARE LOSSES

It is worth noting that many of the arguments of principle in debates about copyright are largely unaffected by changes in technology. One potent argument concerns how copyright enforcement causes reductions in consumer welfare that are wasteful.

Economics is built around the notion of scarcity: scarcity of resources generally implies a need to make choices and to ration, typically through prices charged for output. However, because of the peculiar public good attributes of informational goods which allow for additional consumption to take place often at little or no extra cost, the conventional scarcity-based rationale for imposing charges becomes ameliorated. A new feature film or music album may costs millions of pounds to create, but making extra copies of it costs next to nothing, especially if these are distributed as digital files over the Internet. Once media content has been created, providing access to it involves little or no marginal cost because scarcity is not a problem, and it therefore becomes questionable whether a sound case can be made in favour of denying and restricting consumer access.

The laws of economics would have it that an 'optimal' or ideal situation has been achieved only when it is not possible, through any further reorganization of available resources, to make anyone better off without making someone else worse off (Doyle, 2002: 154–5). This implies that inefficiencies are created every time someone is denied access to copyright-protected intellectual property. Providing free access to a copyright-protected product for those who would otherwise be unwilling or unable to pay for it would add positively to the sum of human welfare and would do so, it may be argued, without making anyone worse off. To avoid a suboptimal allocation of resources, copyright protection ought *not* to be enforced.

The view that copyright enforcement is inherently wasteful suggests that a new order in which creative works are made available to consumers for free would be preferable. Yet without copyright it is far from obvious how authors, musicians, media producers, etc. could earn a commercial living from their work on a scale sufficiently generous to support production of output at anything like current rates. The standard arguments that favour proper enforcement of copyright stem from the view that, without it, quality and quantity of creative output would naturally deteriorate and societal welfare would suffer accordingly. The effects of copyright differ in the short and long run (Handke, 2010: 7). In the short run, the clear beneficiaries are rights holders whose advantage comes at the expense of consumers denied access to the work. However, when looked at over a longer time frame, copyright may serve the interests of consumers (in diverse output) as much as rights owners. Notwithstanding 'unnecessary' welfare losses, there are very powerful counterarguments to support maintenance of copyright protection.

Changes in technology are in many senses irrelevant to these fundamental arguments of principle about whether or not writers, musicians or film-makers ought to be allowed to monopolize the returns from their work. However, with the spread of digital technology and the arrival of the Internet, the task of policing and enforcing copyright protection has become more difficult. The challenges associated with preserving copyright in the context of digitization and the Internet are increasing all the time. Enforcement problems have serious implications for the economics of media-content production and publishing and this has caused many to question whether it makes sense to continue the current reliance on copyright as a means of supporting content-creation industries.

DIGITIZATION AND ENFORCEMENT

Unauthorized copying has always existed, but digital technology has brought the costs of copying and redistributing copies to virtually zero in many cases. In the Internet era, the opportunities and temptations to make and pass on copies of protected works through digital file-sharing have increased vastly. As copying and transnational exchange of content has become almost effortless, it has become increasingly difficult for content suppliers to retain control over unauthorized usages of their work. Tracing and tracking down online infringers of copyright can be quite difficult because of the amount of detailed information that needs to be secured from Internet service providers (Freeman, 2008: 122) and because of the porous and borderless nature of the Internet.

From the point of view of many owners and producers of rights to media content, the relative ease of digital copying and redistribution has simply served to amplify the need for an effective copyright regime (Levine, 2011). The power to monopolize returns is as important as ever and therefore the need for an effective regime, and for a regime that is co-ordinated and enforced internationally, is stronger than ever. However, from a societal point of view, the balance between the costs and benefits of strictly policing copyright has shifted.

While digitization and growth of the Internet have increased enforcement costs, the extent to which infringement of copyright is really harming incentives to produce creative output has been questioned by some. Results from earlier research about the effects of unauthorized copying and file-sharing on commercial sales of music (and, in turn, on incentives to produce new work) have varied. One explanation for this could be the difficulty of obtaining reliable data on file-sharing and other infringing behaviours (Handke, 2010: 63). Nonetheless, many earlier surveys point to a correlation between upward trends in file-sharing and the remorselessly downward trajectory in legal sales of physical CDs, etc. Liebowitz (2006), for example, takes the view that file-sharing harms revenues and cuts across the interests of copyright owners. Oberholzer-Gee and Strumpf (2007), on the other hand, have argued that illegal downloads only have a negligible affect on sales. Some authors have suggested that free downloads for sampling purposes can have a positive rather than a negative effect on subsequent sales (Peitz and Waelbroek, 2006). Whether piracy of music always harms sales and whether it negates incentives to produce new creative output is a subject for divided opinions.

The general effect, in the context of the music industry, of unauthorized copying on willingness to purchase legitimate copies is in some ways different from other areas of media content-creation. In the case of music, a single exposure to the product – e.g. a song – will not necessarily diminish the value of that item for a consumer. On the contrary, because music lovers want repeat access to tracks which they like, it follows that illegal downloading and sampling will sometimes stimulate legitimate sales. For other forms of media content (e.g. an edition of a magazine or a television programme), a single exposure is often all that is required, and once the item has been enjoyed on a single occasion then typically its value will be substantially depleted. Whereas in the case of music former pirates may become purchasers, there is perhaps less reason to hope or suppose that this will be the case for other forms of media content.

GLOBALIZATION

The development of online piracy has been a major concern for media rights owners. As the infrastructure of the Internet continues to improve around the globe, making way for more transfrontier distribution of media content, existing frameworks for transnational co-ordination of copyright face a number of challenges. International harmonization of copyright has historically been based on agreements that provide minimum levels of protection across borders, such as the Berne Convention for the Protection of Literary and Artistic Works (1886) and the UNESCO Universal Copyright Convention (1952). However, because of tensions between differing ideological positions and interest groups, and uncertainties caused by changing technologies and other inherent complexities, achieving consensus is difficult, particularly at international level (Doyle, 2012a).

Despite international agreements, the will to actually implement and uphold copyright at ground level is not shared with equal enthusiasm in all territories around the globe and some countries, such as China and the Philippines, have been characterized by weak enforcement (Cocq and Levy, 2006: 79; Edgecliffe-Johnson, 2011b). Digital piracy has been prevalent in South Korea, for instance, where levels of connection to an exceptionally well-advanced Internet infrastructure are high and, according to the Motion Picture Association of America (MPAA), digital piracy is growing in other territories too including Europe, North America, South Africa and China (MPAA, 2010).

Work on updating trade agreements via the World Trade Organisation (WTO) and the World Intellectual Property Organization (WIPO) has been important in addressing inconsistencies in approach but even so, the future fate of transnational co-ordination of copyright is uncertain because, against a background of ongoing technological change, copyright is increasingly a subject that gives rise to opposing opinions. Tensions exist between differing camps and interest groups whose interpretations of the implications of changing technology are markedly different. A key battleground here is between those who believe that whatever the nature of new delivery platforms, what is required is strict enforcement of copyright measures in order to protect the interests of content-owners and production industries versus, on the other hand, those who think that because of the radically different nature of digital platforms, copyright is perhaps no longer a feasible way to incentivize and reward content-creation (Brown, 2009).

It is well recognized that copyright involves a trade-off between under-production and under-consumption of creative outputs (Handke, 2010). For some, including the MPAA, continued and strengthened protections for copyright are seen as vital to the successful development of audiovisual content supply industries, notwithstanding digital platforms (USITC, 2011: 3–11). Others, however, take the view that adjustment and liberalization of current approaches are necessary because the assumptions underlying traditional copyright law are now out-of-date and apt to stifle innovation (Hargreaves, 2011: 1). The prevailing approach tilts the balance of interests too far in favour of first-generation creators at the expense of new forms of innovation (Lessig, 2009; Lilley, 2006).

Digitization has caused a reassessment of the costs and benefits involved in allowing owners to monopolize their works, and has made it more challenging for national and international regulators to build consensus around what constitutes the correct balance between incentivizing and rewarding creative production and ensuring that consumers can extract maximum value from protected works.

Contention about where exactly the line should be drawn between rewards for creators and freedom for those who want to use existing ideas is exemplified in debates about copyright term – the period for which creators should be allowed to monopolize returns from their work. Whereas earlier research suggests that longer periods of protection will result in only modest improvements to incentives (Akerlof et al., 2002), and whereas longer copyright terms clearly add to the costs suffered by consumers, many media companies have persistently lobbied for extensions in copyright in order to strengthen their ability to profit from back catalogues of IP assets. Such lobbying has frequently, though not always, met with success. A review of copyright law in the UK in 2007 concluded that extending the term of copyright protection would impose costs on consumers while benefiting only a few performers (Gowers, 2006) and so should not be permitted. By contrast, a recommendation to extend the term of protection for sound recordings across Europe from 50 to 70 years was approved by the EU Council of Ministers in 2011 (Edgecliffe-Johnson and Pignal, 2011).

TERRITORIALITY AND FREE TRADE AREAS

One of the challenges for international co-ordination of copyright is that regulators in differing localities and operating at different levels will, on occasion, adopt conflicting positions. In the EU, conflicting positions have been evident in relation to the potentially highly economically significant question of what stance ought to be taken in relation to transfrontier overspill of television content. Does unauthorized cross-frontier spillage need to be stamped out because it constitutes a threat to the livelihoods of owners of intellectual property rights? Or should retransmission across national frontiers be embraced as part and parcel of the growth of free trade areas from which the industry at large and consumers stand to gain? These are troublesome questions in the context of collective free trade areas such as the European Union, as was demonstrated by the recent so-called 'pub landlady' case.

This case centres around UK-based publican Karen Murphy who, rather than paying high tariffs to local broadcaster BSkyB, instead chose to show English Premier League football games using an imported satellite card from a Greek broadcaster. However, because BSkyB had bought the rights to screen league matches in the UK, a UK court in 2006 fined Ms Murphy £8,000 for breach of copyright. When the case was appealed at European level, the European Court of Justice (ECJ), rather than upholding the national position, instead ruled in favour of the landlady (Blitz and Fenton, 2011). The European Court held that 'national legislation which prohibits the import, sale or use of foreign decoder cards is contrary to the freedom to provide services and cannot be justified' (ECJ, 2011). The ECJ's position is that European broadcasters should be allowed to offer their content across Europe regardless of existing exclusivity deals, and viewers should be free to choose to watch whichever European broadcast service is offering access to football games at the cheapest price.

The Court of Justice ruling makes it clear that protection of copyright does not provide a sufficient justification to impede the free movement of goods and services across Europe. From the point of view of promoting the free market, the ECJ's reluctance to penalize retransmission of services across European frontiers is understandable. On the other hand, the prospect that audiovisual content owners may find it difficult in future to market their rights on a territory-by-territory basis has far-reaching commercial implications.

Market demarcations across Europe historically may have been shaped at least partly by culture and language, but the logic driving contemporary strategies of territorial segmentation on the part of television rights owners is economic, the aim being to extract as much consumers' surplus as possible in each national market. The accepted convention over many years has been that, in order to maximize revenue from exploitation of content assets, rights owners can and will market their wares on an exclusive territory-by-territory basis with differential pricing based on local demand and other market conditions. The UK, Norway, France or Greece are all separate territories for purposes of licensing television rights and the acquisition of rights by a broadcaster in one country is always accompanied by an obligation to ensure compliance with territorial limitations. The notion that such obligations are incompatible with EU law raises a potentially serious threat to the revenue strategies of content-creation industries (Fenton, 2011b).

Territoriality is 'the linchpin for making money from intellectual property rights – the strategy of selling rights on an exclusive territory-by-territory basis is essential to maximizing revenues and therefore encouraging reinvestment in content production (Garrett, 2011). Outlawing territoriality will make it more difficult for rights owners to unlock the full value of their IP assets. One possible response on the part of the owners of rights would be, in order to protect against diminution of revenues from the larger and more lucrative pay-television markets in the EU, to simply stop selling into smaller EU markets which yield a relatively low commercial return but a high risk of transfrontier leakage. Such a curtailment would be paradoxical, given that the intention behind the EJC ruling is to support greater cross-border trade. This situation exemplifies the growing complexity involved in coordinating and updating approaches to copyright at international level.

COMMERCIAL MODELS OTHER THAN COPYRIGHT

The growing challenges surrounding enforcement and co-ordination of copyright in the digital era have provoked questions about whether alternative mechanisms should be utilized to reward creative work. What other forms of policy intervention that avoid the disadvantages and costs associated with enforcement of IP rights could be called upon to support production of creative output? Or is it possible, as some economists have argued (Plant, cited in Towse, 2010: 355; Romer, 2002), that allowing free and unregulated markets to operate would provide some other solution – a sufficient commercial incentive to produce creative output – without need for deployment of special interventions by the state? The essence of many economic objections to copyright is that markets can and should be allowed to function freely (Handke, 2010: 42–3). If copyright were abandoned in favour of a market approach then commercial businesses would have to adapt and produce creative outputs in forms that consumers are prepared to pay for.

One alternative to using the law to enforce protection of owners' rights to restrict copying would be to ensure that the inherent costs and effort involved in copying are very high, for example through investment in anti-copying technologies (Bates, 2008: Varian, 2005). This approach has been adopted by, for example, the Hollywood major studios who have worked with the computer industry to develop technologically advanced methods of restraining and controlling copying of digital film content (Young, Gong and Van der Stede, 2010: 40). Use of digital rights management (DRM) – technologies that limit access to the use of digital content, including copying – has produced mixed results but investment continues. It is recognized that such systems can be costly, restrictive and off-putting for consumers (Bates, 2008). Even so, an uncertain outlook for copyright enforcement suggests that media companies will have to look to innovations in digital rights management to help sustain their ability to control and monopolize commercial exploitation of content properties into the future.

Copyright establishes a period of time during which the law will enforce the copyright owners' right to monopolize returns. However, it has been argued that even without the formal protection of intellectual property law, innovators would nonetheless enjoy a brief period after the production of a new idea or work in which, on account of first-mover advantages, they would be able to capture all of the returns on their own original work, thus enabling initial production costs to be recouped (Boldrin and Levine, 2008). Of course, the length of the period of 'natural' monopoly is partly determined by how difficult or easy it is for aspiring free-riders to make and circulate copies.

It is interesting to note that whereas television formats (e.g. *Who wants to be a Millionaire* or *Big Brother*) lack the formal protection enjoyed by finished television programmes, this nonetheless does not seem to prevent popular formats from selling well in international markets (Humphreys, 2008). Format suppliers recognize the need to move quickly to capitalize on first-mover advantages or, in the words of Martyn Freeman, Director of Business at BBC Worldwide, the need to 'get out there and sell it to as many places as you can before the copycat formats – which inevitably will crop up – get in the market and steal your thunder' (Freeman, 2008: 115). At the same time, because what is supplied to purchasers of formats is not just the idea but more typically comprises detailed and valuable expert advice about the specificities of production management and marketing for that particular show which are integral to successful re-staging, the originators and owners of programme formats do benefit from some level of protection from copycats. The informational advantages enjoyed by format sellers are not shared by all content suppliers, however. Although speed to market matters (Lilley, 2006: 4), it is doubtful whether, across the media content-creation industries at large, the brief period of 'natural' monopoly prior to encroachment by free riders capitalizing on the ease and low costs involved in copying and retransmission of finished media output would, in a world where copyright were abandoned altogether, be sufficient to sustain origination and production of high-cost content at anything like current levels.

Varian has proposed several alternative business models that creators might use to support themselves in an environment in which copyright is no longer a feasible option. One example is to rely on the support that embedded advertising and/or product placement can provide (Varian, 2005: 135). Another approach is for the owners of rights to engage in joint sale of complementary products where the package on offer to consumers, in addition to the content property (e.g. the physical CD or DVD) whose value is primarily intangible, also consists of complementary physical goods (e.g. a poster or T-shirt) which are difficult to reproduce and would not be available to those helping themselves to illicit downloads (ibid.). Another suggested model is to sell versions of content which are highly personalized or tailored to the needs of individual consumers (ibid.).

Growth of digital delivery platforms has encouraged the development of many different sorts of personalized content services, often opening up valuable new revenue streams for content suppliers. Niche services focused on affluent market segments (such as financial news services) have fared especially well in attracting paying subscribers. Some have experimented with 'freemium' models. The *Financial Times (FT)*, for example, offers a basic service – access to a limited number of articles – on a free basis to users willing to register and thereby provide the *FT* with access to data about preferences which can be sold on to advertisers. The *FT* also attracts many subscribers willing to pay for upgraded and enhanced access to content, not least because they value the convenience of being able to tailor consumption and make searches of back archives of news on an individualized basis (Kirwan, 2010).

However, in the era of the Internet, all suppliers of content services, including specialist content services such as the *FT*, appear vulnerable to the predations of free riders if the protections offered by copyright were removed. Because the costs involved in providing personalized content services on interactive digital platforms are relatively low, this feature provides little protection against copying activity. The marginal costs of copying and remediating content, whether specialist or otherwise, are typically very far below the high initial fixed costs involved in creating that content. Therefore copiers stand to benefit because remediated content can be supplied at a much lower cost than newly originated work and because recycling of successful content avoids the risks and uncertainties inherent to investment in original creative output (Towse, 2004). Even where content services are personalized, commercial survival may well still hinge on the existence of a copyright regime that is effective in deterring free riders

'Indirect appropriability' offers another possible response to the shortcomings of copyright. This concept was pioneered by Stan Liebowitz based on research into the impact of photocopying of academic journals which found that publishers do not lose out from unauthorized copying because they can discriminate on pricing (charging much higher subscription fees to libraries than to individuals) and, in this way, publishers manage to appropriate revenues that more than compensate them for such photocopying (Liebowitz, 1985). The general idea here is that creators of original works can collect revenue from unauthorized copiers by charging higher prices for the originals from which unauthorized copies are subsequently going to be made. However, one difficulty with this approach is that in the context of contemporary markets for the supply of media content, it is generally not possible to identify which legitimate purchases may subsequently be used to make or facilitate copies and which not. Critics have argued that given the extent to which digitization and the Internet have transformed and facilitated copying, indirect appropiability is now only of limited value and applicability in real-life situations (Johnson and Waldman, 2005).

One of the initiatives which US-based producers of television and film hope will help to sustain future sales revenues is to foster demand for audiovisual content in a digital format which can be streamed remotely from cloud-based servers. Several of the Hollywood majors – Warner Brothers, Universal, Paramount and Sony – announced the launch of a cloud-based 'rights locker' system called Ultraviolet which will enable consumers to purchase movies or television programmes that are then stored remotely in personalized libraries that are available to access via any device (Garrahan, 2011b: 5). It is hoped that cloud-based streaming, because it cuts out the need to store DVDs, Blu-ray discs or digital files, may reinvigorate consumers' appetites to spend on owning film and television content (ibid.). Streaming from remote servers avoids both the inconveniences involved in downloading and/or storing extremely large digital files and the problems caused by lack of interoperability between the various devices (PC, tablet, mobile phone, etc.) consumers may want to use to watch their content.

Although the detachment of ownership from custodianship offers what seems, in many respects, an innovative response to the problems of digital abundance, it is questionable how great levels of demand for 'electronic sell-through' of films and television will be, given the existing popularity and wide availability of services (e.g. Netflix) that offer streaming on a far cheaper rental basis and also given the number of sites offering illegal access to content. Downward trends in sales of DVDs over recent years tend to reinforce the view that, in the digital era, actual ownership has become less attractive to consumers (Greenfield, cited in Garrahan, 2011b). But whether content-creation industries pin their hopes on electronic sell-through or rental, the chief problem with streaming as an initiative designed to sustain future revenues is that, far from reducing the long-standing reliance on being able to monopolize and tightly control access to use of their works, this approach extends and perpetuates copyright as the core model for recouping production costs. Despite all the concerns occasioned by digital piracy and the threat that copyright may become increasingly difficult to enforce, most commercial media content producers and publishers continue to rely heavily on business models centred around exploitation of copyright.

NON-MARKET ALTERNATIVE MEANS OF INCENTIVIZING CREATIVITY

Copyright law has been around since the eighteenth and nineteenth centuries and has been adapted many times to keep pace with technological changes. While concerns about its restrictiveness have gathered pace in recent years, the survival of copyright over time is at least partly accounted for by the lack of viable alternatives. Another contributing factor has been indifference among the public at large towards debates about the legitimacy of copyright which, historically, has enabled lobbyists acting on behalf of the publishing industries to ensure that corporate interests in relation to the rationale underpinning copyright law have received plentiful airplay (Frith and Marshall, 2004: 4). However, interest in the subject has grown in recent years, driven by a sense that a system intended to benefit under-resourced artists has become excessively restrictive at the expense of consumers and creativity and, in the twenty-first century is out of step with the ethos of the Internet where content 'wants to be free' (Anderson, 2009).

The prevailing orthodoxy of non-payment for content which has accompanied growth of the Internet has placed immense pressure on commercial media content suppliers to innovate and evolve their business models. Anderson has argued that expectations that content be supplied for free are an endemic and irreversible aspect of the transition to a digital world (ibid.). According to Anderson, firms that want to survive need to accept this situation and adjust to lower revenues and/or find other ways to cross-subsidize production.

Anderson's viewpoint seems to ignore the core problem that production of professionally crafted media content on a commercial basis is reliant on firms having a realistic prospect of recouping the typically not insubstantial costs involved in initial production. For newspapers, publishers and television companies, etc., although advertising plays a very helpful role in supporting content production costs, it remains the case that advertising alone is not sufficient to support and safeguard

future creation and provision of the full range of high-quality professionally crafted content for which consumers currently exhibit high
levels of demand. Certainly, production and circulation of user-generated content has vastly expanded the availability of low-cost content
on digital platforms in recent years, but professionally crafted media
content still predominates in audience preferences and this typically
involves significant production costs. The view that supplying content
free is not a sustainable business model for the digital era was underlined forcefully by Rupert Murdoch who, in announcing plans to start
charging for online access to the content of News Corporation newspaper
titles, declared 'We are in the midst of an epochal debate over the value
of content, and it is clear to many newspapers the current model is
malfunctioning' (Murdoch, cited in Edgecliffe-Johnson, 2009).

Notwithstanding the prevailing ethos of non-payment for online
content, most media businesses have found great difficulty in evolving
their strategies beyond the model which has served them so well in the
past: reliance on payments from advertisers and also from audiences
and readers. Investment in high-quality media content production is
expensive and charging for content remains the linchpin to the prosperity of most if not all content-creation businesses. This, in turn, implies
a need on the part of producers to be able to exercise some control over
copying and distribution. So, although copyright may be a 'second-best
solution to intellectual property provision' (Varian, 2005: 136), because
other market solutions or business models are scant and beset by their
own deficiencies, content-creation industries are naturally very keen to
retain the protections offered by copyright law.

Even so, with disputes about the restrictiveness of copyright and
the treatment of infringers growing ever noisier, one of the questions policy-makers are confronted with is whether there are any
other forms of policy intervention which avoid the disadvantages
associated with enforcement of copyright? Aside from copyright,
are there alternative sorts of interventions or non-market solutions
that could be called upon to encourage and ensure production of
creative output?

One way of stimulating additional production of creative output
is to provide grants, prizes and subsidies to support individuals and
firms involved in businesses in this area (Towse, 2010: 365). Historically many countries, regions and indeed cities have provided grants
and public funding incentives to boost indigenous cultural and creative
production activity based on the expectation that this investment may
result in a variety of social, cultural and economic benefits to society
at large. The general efficacy of policies of providing grants and

subsidies to media content providers is assessed in Chapter 9. For present purposes, it is noteworthy that any general move to deploy public subsidies and grants *in place of* copyright as the primary means of encouraging and rewarding creative activity raises at least two serious problems. First, replacing the rights-based revenue streams which are currently the lifeblood of content-creation industries would place impossibly burdensome demands on the public purse. Second, such a move would trigger inefficiencies by replacing market demand with some form of centralized control.

Whatever the disadvantages of copyright, it does manage to preserve a link between sales and rewards which ensures that production decisions are informed and shaped by market considerations. By contrast, a system of public subsidies to support the production of creative work would require administration by some form of public funding body, with attendant inefficiencies. Likewise any solution based on private patronage (support from wealthy private individuals and corporations) – albeit that such support from kings, merchants, etc. represents a model of support for creativity that long predates copyright – raises the problem that production decisions and allocation will be skewed by the tastes, preferences or value judgements of a handful of private sponsors.

Another form of invention is for the state to impose taxes on a good that is related to or complementary to the information good, such as the imposition of a tax on top of the price of blank tapes, and to use this income to compensate the originators of creative work (Varian, 2005: 136). Across Europe, the imposition of copyright levies – taxes on any hardware and equipment (such as PCs) that may be used for copying – is increasingly commonplace and this provides a mechanism for transferring rewards from potential copiers onwards to rights holders via national copyright collecting societies. This mechanism has been criticized as too crude because levies are targeted at devices rather than at copying activity (Oxera, 2011). Also, the system for subsequent distribution of funds involves allocation 'in a fairly arbitrary way between the different groups of rights holders whose work may or may not have been copied' (Towse, 2010: 367) – in short, a blunderbuss approach.

ADJUSTING COPYRIGHT TO THE 'OPEN' INTERNET

Although copyright may be regarded as a second-best solution, there appear to be few viable alternative reward systems through which the desired outcome of safeguarding plentiful provision of creative output could otherwise be achieved. Therefore, rather than abandoning or replacing copyright, another solution which has attracted much attention is that of adjusting the copyright regime to fit better with the prevailing ethos and needs of the 'open' Internet. Many see this as the best solution to ongoing conflict between those who argue that, despite digitization, copyright is essential and should be strengthened versus those who see it as out of date and believe it enriches a few at the expense of creativity.

The general drift of policy-making over many years, particularly in the US but also in Europe, has been in sympathy with the need to strengthen copyright, through, for example, term extension – extending the period after the death of an author or artist in which copyright can be enforced (Kay, 2011). Opponents argue that such restrictions are excessive and, since the arrival of Internet, unenforceable and that criminalization of online information-sharing impinges on free speech.

Prominent among the campaigners for a rebalancing away from excessively strict protection for industry incumbents and in favour of more freedom for consumers and other creators is Lawrence Lessig who, along with others, founded the Creative Commons movement in 2001. The intention with this scheme is to introduce flexibility by providing a set of template licences which authors can use in order to communicate to the public which rights they want to reserve and which they are willing to waive so that others – consumers and second-generation creators – can use their works freely (Lessig, 2002). A number of content owners have experimented with Creative Commons and as the community of users 'has grown from only a few thousand to millions of users, its members have retained a strong focus on fostering creativity through reuse' (Coates, 2007: 76).

As policy-makers struggle to reshape copyright for the Internet, some echoes may be found, for example in the Hargreaves review of UK copyright policy (Hargreaves, 2011), of the view that existing copyright frameworks need to be at least partially loosened up so as to avoid damaging innovation. This augurs well as, despite the objections of those who say that copyright no longer works, the arrival of the Internet has not, in fact, obviated the basic rationale which supported the development of copyright in the first place (Gapper, 2011; Levine, 2011). Certainly the spread of digital technology has increased enforcement costs and, in many ways, has made it even more difficult for policy-makers to strike an appropriate balance between assured support for content-creators and securing the widest possible access to creative output for consumers (Kay, 2011).

'Governments need to tread lightly to avoid damaging innovation' (Gapper 2011: 13) but at the same time, it makes little sense to remove altogether what clearly remains a crucial mechanism for sustaining media content and creative production industries. The continued use of rights as a rewards system is dependent on the ability of policy-makers to find an effective way of recalibrating 'the balance of the deal between creators, users and investors' for the needs of a digital future (Haynes, 2005: 142).

8

Media and Advertising

One of the key sources of revenue for media is advertising. Consequently, patterns of advertising activity exert a very significant influence over the fortunes of the media industry as a whole. This chapter is concerned with the key arguments surrounding the economic role played by advertising, and with its impact on market structures and on consumer decision-making. It introduces you to the economic forces and factors which determine the extent of advertising activity in an economy, examining why levels of advertising vary from one country to another, and over time. It also considers the significant impact of digitization and growth of the Internet on patterns of advertising. With the advent of online intermediaries such as search engines, aggregators and social networking sites, the sale of audience attention has in some cases become dislocated from investment in professionally crafted original content production. Focusing on Internet advertising and the growth of search, this chapter considers the crucial role played by advertising in supporting and shaping the ongoing development of media.

After studying this chapter, you should be able to:

- understand why advertising takes place;
- identify and explain the main factors that influence the amount of advertising activity taking place in an economy, including the significance of the Internet in bolstering advertising, and understand why advertising tends to be cyclical;
- explain the determinants of the firm's advertising decision;
- analyse the implications of disintermediation;
- assess whether advertising is a beneficial or a harmful economic force.

THE ADVERTISING INDUSTRY

Advertising is ubiquitous. Its roots can be traced back to the cave but, in the twenty-first century, its reach and influence have become virtually inescapable. Over the last 60 years, an increased willingness on the part of firms to invest in building awareness of themselves and of their wares has been matched by the rapid development of the advertising, marketing and public relations sectors. Advertising agencies have generated catchphrases, jingles and images to accompany brands that are familiar to audiences across the globe and across generations.

Advertising is big business, and the industry it has spawned has grown quickly and diversified to keep pace with ongoing market changes and with the development of digital media. Alongside the basic function of creating advertising messages, many agencies can offer an array of specialist communication services including, for example, provision of sophisticated market research information or consultancy related to sponsorship deals. The major advertising agencies in the world, such as WPP, Omnicom, Interpublic and Publicis, are all diversified multinational corporations with networks of operating subsidiaries and strategic alliances that provide clients with global audience reach as well as creative advertising ideas.

As advertising expenditure has grown in response to rising economic prosperity in the developed world, the advertising industry has flourished. According to estimates from Zenith (cited in Edgecliffe-Johnson, 2011d), global expenditure on advertising reached some US$460bn in 2011 – a sizeable slice of our collective resources. Even this may understate the extent of advertising, because industry estimates often exclude some of the investment made in emerging platforms and vehicles.

The advertising market is perpetually evolving and, in recent years, a striking trend has been growth in expenditure on online advertising. The migration of advertising investment away from traditional media to online reflects the migration of consumer attention towards the Internet – a trend which has accelerated over the past 10 years and to which traditional sectors, such as television and especially newspapers, are still struggling to adjust.

Statistics compiled by advertising and market research agencies such as Warc provide a helpful account of the state of advertising both across the media as a whole and within individual sectors, e.g. television or radio. Figure 8.1 demonstrates vividly how established patterns of growth in overall global expenditure on advertising were disrupted by economic recession in 2009. It also shows how, propelled by growth in investment in online advertising, the distribution of total global advertising expenditure among differing sectors of the media has altered considerably in recent years. In the sections

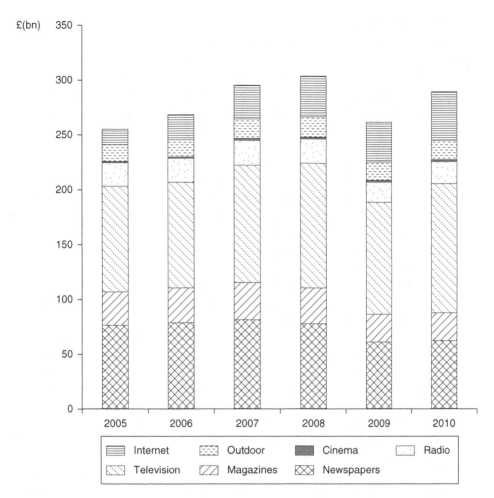

Figure 8.1   Global advertising spend by medium (£bn)

Source: Warc data in Ofcom, 2011b: 20.

which follow, the relationship between the economy and advertising and the effect of digitization on advertising markets will be explored further.

WHY DOES ADVERTISING TAKE PLACE?

Why does all this advertising take place? Clearly, firms spend money on advertising in the hope of persuading consumers to buy their products. The general aim behind advertising expenditure is to try to increase sales and to reinforce consumers' loyalty to particular brands.[8] Advertising is a form of competitive behaviour. It is one of the main tools that firms can use to compete with each other in order to entice consumers to switch to their own product rather than that of a rival. Other tactics that a firm might use to try to gain advantage over its competitors include making changes to the quality of the product so as to increase its attractiveness, or simply making adjustments to its price so as to undercut rivals.

According to the economic theory of firms, whether or not an organization is likely to engage in competitive behaviour depends on which kind of market structure it is operating within. As discussed earlier, the term 'competitive market structure' describes the kind of market situation a firm can find itself in, and is primarily to do with how many rivals it has, whether the market is open to new entrants, how similar the goods on offer are and how much power each firm has over market demand and over prices. Advertising will generally take place in market situations where firms have an incentive to engage in some form of competitive behaviour (Chiplin and Sturgess, 1981).

Broadly speaking, the more competition present in a market, the greater the need to advertise. Thanks to globalization, most sectors of industry are now operating in a much more competitive environment than at any time in the past. In addition, deregulation and the wider availability of inexpensive technological know-how today have served to intensify competitive pressures across many areas of industry. Consequently, there is an ever-increasing trend for firms to regard advertising as the best means of differentiating and drawing attention to their own brands, and this, in turn, is reflected by a general long-term pattern of growth in overall levels of advertising.

Nonetheless, the decision taken by specific firms about whether or not to engage in advertising or other sorts of competitive behaviour is determined, to a large extent, by which kind of market structure the company is operating within. Perhaps surprisingly, firms that operate in 'perfectly' competitive markets do not need to compete actively with each other to stoke up demand for their own product because, in theory, none has any influence over the market. It is assumed that in the rather utopian circumstances of perfect competition, there is no point in any individual firm spending money to advertise its wares

---

[8]When advertising is successful, it may cause the demand curve to shift outwards (reflecting an increased market share) and also to become steeper (as price elasticity is reduced).

because each firm's goods are exactly the same as everyone else's and consumers are perfectly well aware of this.

At the other end of the scale, in very uncompetitive market circumstances such as a monopoly or a monopolistic market structure – i.e. where there are no close substitutes for an organization's products – the firm has no rivals to worry about, so monopolists also have relatively little to gain from expending resources on advertising.

On the other hand, firms operating in an oligopoly market structure are strongly motivated to advertise. Oligopolists do, indeed, have a degree of market power but they are aware that their rivals also have some power to influence the market. Competitive behaviour – e.g. advertising or price competition – is a particular feature of oligopolistic market structures. And in the real world, a very great and increasing number of industries operate in imperfectly competitive or oligopoly situations. At the most basic level, it is the competitive behaviour of firms operating in oligopoly market structures which fuels advertising activity. As global competition continues to intensify, so too will patterns of advertising expenditure reflect this trend.

ARE FIRMS IN CONTROL OF THEIR OWN MARKETS?

One of the most prominent thinkers in economics in the twentieth century was Professor J.K. Galbraith, who put forward an interesting theory about the role of advertising. He suggested that firms use advertising to control their own markets (Lipsey and Chrystal, 1995: 321). Galbraith pointed out that firms have to make sizeable investments in developing and launching new products but, notwithstanding market research, they cannot be entirely certain how well these new products will be appreciated by consumers and how profitable they will turn out to be. Firms are exposed to and threatened by the unpredictability of future events, especially changes in patterns of demand or fashions or technology. To make the future less unpredictable, firms invest vast sums of money in advertising.

According to Galbraith, expenditure on advertising is intended to manipulate market demand and to guard against sudden unexpected shifts in public tastes. Advertising expenditure enables companies to sell what they themselves want to produce rather than what consumers would want to buy. At the same time, firms decide not to produce some new products that consumers might actually like to buy. This allows them to cut the risks and expenses involved in launching untried products which, even if they are successful, might well simply undermine the market for existing products.

From Galbraith's point of view, consumers appear to be the hapless victims of corporations. We are forced, through the manipulative power of advertising, to buy things we do not necessarily want and we are deprived of those products we might like to have. Can this really be true?

Even though the purpose underlying firms' expenditure on advertising is to try to increase demand for particular products, it is also the case that sometimes, wholly unexpected shifts in consumer demand occur. Sometimes, the demand for new categories of products or services cannot just be explained by manipulative advertising; it has to do with more basic changes, or with some new technological innovation. For example, the general success of the motor car or of the washing machine can hardly be put down to brainwashing by advertisers, albeit that advertising may persuade us to opt for one brand of these products rather than another. Likewise, the explanation for escalating interest in online services and mobile devices over recent years seems to owe more to technology, consumer convenience and fashion than to the efforts of advertisers. Although advertising plays an important part in shaping demand, the view that firms can effectively control their own markets is not entirely a convincing one.

Where advertising seems to be most effective is in shifting and determining the pattern of demand among existing products which are similar to each other. In other words, advertising is likely to have more of a bearing on which *brands* rather than which *products* consumers will want to buy. It undoubtedly helps to create and sustain loyalty to particular brands, but it is unable to dictate overall trends in consumer demand and nor can it hope to overcome the influence of, for example, technology, fashion or the media on the sorts of products people express a wish for.

INFORMATIVE VERSUS PERSUASIVE ADVERTISING

Advertising has two related aspects. First, it sets out to inform consumers of the characteristics of the various products available and, second, it also tries to influence consumers by altering their tastes or preferences and hence their purchasing decisions. Informative advertising – giving consumers more information about what is available to them – can be seen as playing a useful role in making the market system work more effectively. It performs a valuable function in facilitating the interaction between consumers and producers. However, the second function – persuasion – is more questionable in terms of its impact on consumer welfare.

The distinction between information and persuasion has been a major preoccupation in historic texts devoted to the economics of advertising. To summarize briefly, those who see advertising as being informative in nature tend to see it as a necessary expenditure that keeps markets competitive in a world where imperfect knowledge is a fact of life. They argue that if we didn't have advertising, the transaction costs (i.e. all of the costs involved in negotiating and completing a deal) of any sale or purchase – and particularly those to do with the search for goods and for knowledge about their attributes – would be higher and, as a result, buyers would be worse off. Not only would they have to pay more for their goods and services, but also the probability of their making a wrong choice would be increased. The greater the variety of goods and services offered for sale, the more difficult it is for the consumer to judge the capacity of the good to satisfy a particular want before they buy it and the more they will value objective information to help them make the right choice.

Not surprisingly, many who work in the advertising industry take the view that advertising helps people to make choices in an over-supplied world. But if the information provided by advertising is not objective, the choices it engenders may not be good ones and the effect of advertising will be to diminish rather than to enhance the overall welfare or utility of consumers. Those who view advertising as being primarily persuasive regard it as leading to excessive differentiation of products, resulting in prices and profits higher than those arising in an ideal competitive world (Chiplin and Sturgess, 1981: 74–7). Think, for example, of the amount Coca-Cola and Pepsi spend on advertising when, arguably, there is relatively little difference between their products. Those who criticize advertising and argue that too many resources are being allocated to it are, to some extent, saying that consumers are being bombarded with rather too much information and that it pays an enterprise to advertise beyond the point at which the advertising provides any benefit to consumers. They are also suggesting that the persuasive spin put upon product information by advertisers results in incomplete, misleading or distorted messages rather than a useful resource for consumers.

Is advertising generally harmful or beneficial to the operation of markets? On the one hand, consumers have to pay a higher price for products to cover the cost of advertising but, on the other, they benefit from widespread information about the range and availability of competing goods and services which facilitates their decision-making. In its role as a source of information for consumers, advertising can be a pro-competitive force leading to an improved allocation of resources. Counteracting such a force, however, is a possible anti-competitive effect through the use of advertising as a means of preventing potential rivals from gaining entry to markets.

ADVERTISING AS A BARRIER TO MARKET ENTRY

An important criticism of advertising relates to its effect on competitive market structures. It is suggested that firms use advertising to put up barriers to market entry which prevent other firms from competing with them (Chiplin and Sturgess, 1981: 112). The basic argument here is that the millions of pounds invested every year in building up recognition for their brands, by, for example, Procter & Gamble or Kellogg's, make it difficult or impossible for potential new entrants to encroach on their product markets unless they also have the scale of resources and the will to match this expenditure. In other words, heavy advertising is a means of imposing high set-up costs on new entrants and this, in turn, serves to deter would-be rivals.

Advertising is a feature of oligopoly market structures. Oligopolists not only have to worry about competing with their existing rivals to build and defend market share, they also have to worry about potential competitors from firms that might be tempted to enter their industry. If there are no natural barriers to entry, oligopolist firms will earn pure profits just in the short run and until such time as other firms enter their industry. Oligopolists can protect their profitability in the long run only if they can find ways of creating barriers that prevent entry.

One method of keeping out potential new entrants is called 'brand proliferation' (Lipsey and Chrystal, 2007: 269). Differentiated products – i.e. products, such as breakfast cereals, that are similar but with some discernible differences in their attributes – usually have several characteristics that can be varied over a wide range. Thus there is room in the market for a large number of similar products each with a somewhat different range of features or characteristics. Consider, for example, the current range of breakfast cereals or cars. Although the numerous brands that manufacturers make available is, undoubtedly, at least partly a reflection of efforts to cater to variations in consumers' tastes, it may also be partly the result of a deliberate attempt by existing players to discourage the entry of new firms. When existing suppliers sell a wide array of differentiated products, this makes it difficult for a new firm to gain entry on a small scale. Brand proliferation means that, in effect, all the potential niches are already occupied. The larger the number of differentiated products already being sold by existing oligopolists, the smaller the market available to a new firm entering with a single new product.

Alternatively, existing firms can create barriers to entry by impos-ing significant fixed costs associated with setting up operations in that market on new entrants. This is an important tactic if there are no economies of large-scale production to provide 'natural' barriers to entry. Advertising is one means by which existing firms can impose heavy set-up costs on new entrants (Griffiths and Wall, 2007: 109). Advertising, of course, has effects other than creating barriers to entry. As discussed above, it may perform the useful function of informing buyers of their alternatives. Indeed, a new firm may find it necessary to advertise even if existing firms don't bother, simply to call attention to their entry into an industry.

Nonetheless, advertising can operate as a potent entry barrier. Effective brand-image advertising means that a new firm will have to advertise in order to catch the public's attention. If the firm's sales are small then advertising costs per unit sold will be large (Lipsey and Chrystal, 2007: 196). Unit costs will only be reduced sufficiently to make a new entrant profitable when sales volumes are large, so that the fixed advertising costs needed to break into the market are spread over a large number of units.

The combined use of brand proliferation and of heavy advertis-ing sometimes acts as a formidable entry barrier. This explains why some of the biggest advertisers often sell multiple brands of the same product. For example, among the top 30 advertisers in the UK in 2008 were washing powder manufacturers Procter & Gamble and Unilever; shampoo manufacturers L'Oréal Paris and Garnier; car manufactur-ers Ford, Renault and Vauxhall; and breakfast cereal manufacturers Kellogg's and Nestlé (Advertising Association, 2009: 254).

To some extent, the debate about advertising and market structures is not really about the effects of advertising per se, because both sides agree that it can work as a powerful barrier to entry. Instead, it is about whether or not barriers to market entry are a good thing and whether one market structure is better than another. Competition is normally considered a prerequisite for efficiency, therefore open and more compet-itive markets seem preferable to monopolized ones. If, however, by keep-ing rivals out of the market, advertising enables firms to increase their output and to achieve economies of large-scale production, then arguably this might serve to benefit consumers. The economies of scale created by concentration of ownership in the washing powder industry, for example, means that (provided there is sufficient competition to prevent monopoly pricing) consumers should enjoy lower product prices than would be pos-sible under a more fragmented and competitive market structure. Pro-vided that firms do not become so large that they can extract monopoly profits, consumers might occasionally benefit from the anti-competitive effects of advertising (Parkin, Powell and Matthews, 2008: 278).

ADVERTISING AND THE PERFORMANCE OF THE ECONOMY

A great deal of detailed analysis of advertising and economic data is undertaken by commercial agencies for the purposes of forecasting future advertising trends. When this data is analysed it provides compelling evidence of a historic link between levels of economic wealth and of advertising activity. Although growth in UK investment in advertising has cooled off over the past decade, when trends in expenditure are examined over long periods of time it is apparent that advertising has tended to grow as a proportion of the national economy.

Advertising expenditure can be defined in various ways, for example including or excluding production costs, new media and alternative promotional expenditures. Likewise, the performance of the economy can be defined and calculated in a number of different ways, including by gross domestic product (GDP). GDP measures the total value of all productive output in the whole economy over a given period – usually a year – and is probably the most widely used benchmark of general economic performance. When expenditure on advertising is calculated as a percentage of GDP, the pattern that emerges indicates that as the national economy has grown over time in real terms, advertising has not just grown in parallel, it has grown faster.

However, the tendency for increases in advertising expenditure to exceed growth in the economy has been ameliorated in recent years – see Figure 8.2. A weakening in overall levels of advertising in developed economies in the first decade of the twenty-first century – coinciding with structural shifts related to the transition to digital technology and, latterly, with economic recession – has called into question the constancy of the historic relationship between advertising expenditure and GDP. The downward realignment in advertising expenditure relative to GDP is partly a reflection of a wholesale shift in investment over recent years away from relatively costly conventional media advertising towards online vehicles which are typically less expensive (Shaw in Bradshaw and Edgecliffe-Johnson, 2009). And while this shift is underway, slow adjustment in the conventional metrics used to record advertising expenditure may account for further digital leakage.

It remains to be seen whether recent divergences between growth rates for GDP and for advertising expenditure reflect transient side effects of the transition to digital or whether they signal a permanent weakening in the relationship between advertising and the state of the economy. However, the weight of historic evidence clearly suggests that the amount of advertising activity in an economy is related to the size and growth rates of the economy itself, and advertising has generally tended to account for a progressively more significant proportion of GDP as time goes on. In the UK for example, whereas advertising represented 1.14 per cent of GDP in 1960, the equivalent figure in 2008 was 1.20 per cent (Advertising Association, 2009: 5).

The general relationship between wealth and levels of advertising does not apply solely to the UK. It is also observable in other developed economies and can be demonstrated by a bivariate analysis of GDP per capita (i.e. the productive output of the country divided by the number of inhabitants) and advertising expenditure per capita (Nayarodou, 2006). Albeit that patterns of interaction between GDP and advertising can be complex (van der Wurff, Bakker and Picard, 2008), the general pattern which emerges from international comparisons shows a positive association between economic wealth in any country and the level of advertising expenditure it enjoys. This correlation may be disturbed occasionally when, for example, government restrictions on advertising hold back levels of expenditure on commercial airtime. Generally speaking, richer countries such as Switzerland enjoy a much higher level of advertising expenditure than poorer countries such as Greece and Portugal (Advertising Association, 2000: 22). Although other factors may play a part, GDP appears to be the main explanatory variable underlying a country's advertising expenditure (Chang and Chan-Olmsted, 2005).

Why is this? There have been two arguments about the relationship between advertising and living standards. One is that advertising stimulates the levels of consumption that are found in countries with high per capita incomes – that 'strong and lasting economic growth is necessarily associated with a high rate of media advertising investment' (Nayarodou, 2006: 34). This perspective implies a causal connection between high levels of advertising, high consumption and, in turn, higher levels of economic activity and growth. The other viewpoint is that advertising is a 'waste of resources' that can only be afforded by rich countries (Chiplin and Sturgess, 1981: 7).

Historic UK data shows that the growth in advertising as a proportion of GDP is not exactly steady and continuous. Advertising growth is cyclical and it reflects, in an exaggerated way, the ups and downs of the economy at large. In periods of economic expansion, the proportion of GDP spent on advertising increases, but the converse is true in recession. Figure 8.2 shows advertising as a proportion of GDP over the past

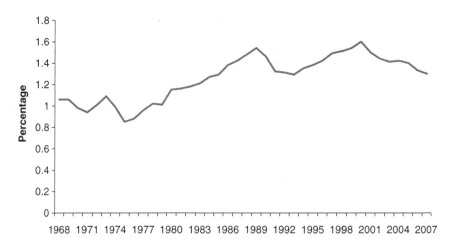

Figure 8.2   UK advertising expenditure as a percentage of GDP, 1968–2007

Source: Warc data in Advertising Association, 2008: 7.

50 years. It demonstrates how advertising expenditure, when expressed as a percentage of GDP, peaks at the top of economic boom periods such as in 1973, in 1989 and again in the late 1990s. By the same token, expenditure on advertising bottoms out at the lowest point in the economic cycle, such as in 1975 at the height of the oil crisis, in the recession of 1993 or more recently in the financial crisis and recession of 2007–08. Advertising tends to gallop ahead more quickly than the economy in boom periods, but then it slumps more quickly in recession.

To understand why advertising is cyclical, it is helpful to carry out more detailed analysis of advertising expenditure data. Advertising is sometimes broken down between 'display' and 'classified'. Display advertising (which forms the bulk of advertising expenditure) is total advertising minus financial notices, classified and advertising in trade or technical journals etc. Classified is employment, housing, personal advertisements, etc. Different sets of factors will affect the performance of each of these two categories of advertising expenditure.

The two primary forces which appear to determine the growth or decline of display advertising expenditure are consumers' expenditure and company profits (Advertising Association, 2009: 5). The close correlation between company profits and display advertising expenditure suggests that, perhaps not surprisingly, companies can afford to and *do* spend more on advertising when times are good. Plentiful evidence exists to confirm that lower earnings and lower prospective earnings during recessions serve to depress firms' spending on advertising

(Graham and Frankenberger, 2011). Likewise, the correlation between consumers' expenditure and display advertising expenditure suggests that companies are willing to spend more when consumer spending and confidence is buoyant, i.e. when advertising expenditure is more likely to translate itself into increased sales. In short, advertising expenditure expands along with consumer expenditure, but is reined back when company profits are under pressure.

Classified advertising expenditure is dependent on a variety of factors, e.g. the state of the housing market, the second-hand car market and levels of unfilled job vacancies. Statistics gathered by bodies such as the Advertising Association (2009: 6) suggest a close and consistent (counter-)relationship between levels of unemployment and recruitment classified expenditure. It is mainly recruitment advertising which pushes up classified and thus total advertising expenditure during economic booms.

It has been argued that the state of the economy should not play such an important determining role in levels of advertising investment. Barwise (1999) suggests that advertising by firms with established brands is essentially a defensive activity, carried out in order to protect their market share rather than in the hope of boosting sales. Others argue that because advertising is about sustaining market positioning relative to rivals, recessions offer firms a useful chance to gain competitive advantage by investing more in advertising (O'Malley, Story and O'Sullivan, 2011). Be that as it may, historic trends in advertising clearly demonstrate the prevalent tendency for firms to cut back on their advertising expenditure as soon as an economic downturn looms into view. As John Hegarty, creative director of advertising agency Bartle Bogle Hegarty has explained: '[r]ecession is always a problem for the advertising industry, in the sense that clients feel that advertising is the first thing they can switch off' (cited in Smith, 1998: 1).

The apportionment of advertising between different sectors of the economy is not static but varies in response to alterations in the market structure for particular industry sectors. Such alterations might occur, for instance, because of policy changes that are designed to promote or limit competition in a particular market. For example, advertising expenditure data by product sector in the UK in the 1980s shows how the deregulation of the UK financial services industry in the mid-1980s and the accompanying increase in competitive behaviour on the part of banks and building societies was reflected in an immediate and sharp increase in advertising expenditure by banks and building societies. Similarly in the late 1990s, there was something of a mini boom in dot.com advertising because of the growth in competition between major rivals in the online business sector, in this case spurred on by advancing technology. Therefore it is worth remembering that although the significance of economic wealth as a broad determinant of advertising activity is inescapable, there is plentiful scope for developments within individual sectors of the economy also to contribute strongly to how patterns of advertising expenditure unfold over time.

THE RISE OF INTERNET ADVERTISING

The steady rise of the Internet has had a sizeable impact on advertising markets in the twenty-first century. To some extent advertisers have benefited from digitization and the development of vast additional supplies of 'online' access to audiences which have provided more low-cost and more specialist and targeted advertising opportunities. On the other hand, the popularity of the Internet has accelerated processes of erosion and fragmentation of mass audiences which, from the point of view of many advertisers, makes consumers more difficult to reach.

In response to ongoing changes in patterns of consumption and engagement with media, much advertising investment has migrated away from traditional media to online. As a consequence, the apportionment of total advertising expenditure across differing sectors of the media has changed markedly over the last decade. Table 8.1 shows how the breakdown of total advertising expenditure across different media has changed in recent years in the UK. In 2000, newspapers and magazines accounted for more than half of all advertising expenditures, whereas a decade later the share of spending accounted for by print

Table 8.1   UK advertising expenditure by medium (%)

	2001	2002	2003	2004	2005	2006	2007	2008	2009[9]	2010
Press (newspapers & mags)	51.8	49.9	48.4	47.5	45.3	43.3	40.9	37.6	30.2	27.4
Television	23.5	24.2	23.6	23.5	23.8	22.5	22.2	22.1	24.3	26.0
Direct mail	14.8	15.6	15.6	14.7	13.8	13.4	12.0	11.8	11.6	10.9
Outdoor & transport	4.5	4.6	5.0	5.0	5.2	5.4	5.4	5.4	5.4	5.6
Radio	3.2	3.2	3.3	3.2	3.0	2.8	2.7	2.6	2.8	2.7
Cinema	1.1	1.2	1.1	1.1	1.1	1.1	1.1	1.2	1.2	1.2
Internet	1.1	1.3	2.9	4.9	7.9	11.6	15.6	19.3	24.4	26.1
TOTAL	100.0	100.0	100.0	100.0	100.0	100.0	100.0	100.0	100.0	100.0

Source: Advertising Association, 2009; Warc Expenditure Report.

[9]The basis of calculation for post-2009 data from the Warc *Expenditure Report* differs from earlier data from the Advertising Association/Warc (2009: 13–14).

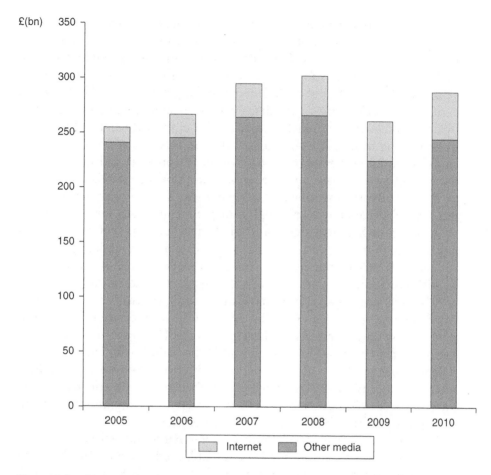

£(bn)

Figure 8.3   Global advertising expenditure: Internet vs other media (£bn)
Source: Warc data in Ofcom, 2011b: 20.

media fell to around a quarter. This has exerted a significant squeeze on the finances of many publishers. At the same time as newspapers have lost ground, investment in online advertising has increased dramatically from just one per cent of total UK advertising expenditures in the year 2000 to more than 26 per cent by 2010.

Structural changes in the apportionment of advertising caused by digitization and growth of the Internet are a global phenomenon. The propensity exhibited by UK advertisers to invest more in online media is widely shared internationally, albeit that analysis of recent advertising trends across different territories suggests that redistribution in favour of the Internet has occurred more speedily in the UK than in other countries (Ofcom, 2011b: 24).

By 2008, investment in Internet advertising added £37bn to global expenditures on other media advertising that year of £266bn (see Figure 8.3). It is evident that the enthusiasm of advertisers to embrace this new platform and all it may offer has, to some extent, stimulated and inflated global demand for advertising. At the same time, substitution effects are discernable through patterns of redistribution of advertising investment in favour of the Internet. Advertisers are choosing to invest their budgets in the Internet – for example, in search-related advertising – *rather than* in conventional media, such as through purchasing commercial airtime slots on television or radio or buying advertising space in newspapers. Visible within the broad pattern of expansion in the value of global markets for advertising that occurred between 2005 and 2010 are both market growth and substitution effects caused by the rise of Internet advertising.

A switch in advertising investment in favour of the Internet is the inevitable corollary of extensive changes in technology and lifestyle which have positioned the Internet much more centrally in how people communicate and imbibe media. In the UK, for example, broadband penetration had reached 74 subscriptions per 100 homes in 2010, compared with 77 per 100 in France and 70 per 100 in the United States (Ofcom, 2011b: 24). In addition, many now access the Internet via their mobile phones (ibid.: 194). As levels of Web connectivity and Web usage have surged, the migration of advertising, content and audience attention to the Internet has become self-reinforcing.

The propensity to increase online advertising and switch from conventional media to online vehicles is explained not only by the need to keep pace with evolving patterns of audience behaviour, but also reflects ways in which the Internet is seen as more effective than, say, newspapers or radio. The capacity for interactivity which, in turn, provides numerous opportunities for targeting is a crucial advantage enjoyed by the Internet. Much Internet advertising is accounted for by paid-for search (Ofcom, 2010a: 241). The use by consumers of online search engines to, for example, identify and compare products and services can create opportunities for tailored advertising messages relevant to an intended purchase that are highly valuable to advertisers. This ability to provide a close and immediate match between buyers and sellers is clearly a major advantage.

More broadly, the use of a two-way communication infrastructure means that online media providers can collect plentiful information which is of value to advertisers about the tastes, preferences and habits of particular sections of the audience. The facility for online media to get to know their target customer base – to learn about and speak to individual tastes among niche audiences – is a valuable strategic advantage. In addition, the ability to collect and pass on data that better facilitates advertisers who want to target consumers based on exhibited behaviours and preferences is a major selling point for online media, albeit that this has raised concerns about intrusions against the privacy of Internet users (Evans, 2009).

The threat to traditional media posed by the Internet stems not only from additional competition for audience attention and more fragmentation of audiences but also from the superiority of this digital platform in delivering certain sorts of advertising opportunities, e.g. search advertising, targeted advertising via social media such as Twitter and Facebook. The advantages that the Internet enjoys in terms of proficiency in aiming commercial messages at specific audience subgroups and the fact that it is clearly better suited to some forms of advertising than others – i.e. to providing classified rather than display advertisements – is reflected in how advertising expenditure has gradually redistributed itself across different sectors of the media in recent years (see Table 8.1).

The ongoing resilience of television reflects the strength of this industry in delivering the sort of mass high-profile audience access which meets the needs of many big-brand advertisers. Even as audiences fragment across media catering to ever-narrower sets of tastes, many advertisers continue to rely primarily on mainstream conventional media to create the mass consumer brands of the future. The greater ability of such channels to reach mass audiences and to establish famous brands still remains a strong selling point. By contrast, newspapers (especially at regional and local level) that have traditionally relied heavily on targeted classified advertising have suffered extensive losses as investment has switched to online and, similarly, there has been significant encroachment upon the advertising revenues of many specialist and niche magazines.

Current patterns of displacement in favour of the Internet appear to conform with an evolutionary process to which the media industry, because of its reliance on ever-improving delivery technologies, has long been prone. Just as radio took away audiences from newspapers and, in turn, television wooed audiences away from radio and newspapers, the Internet is now taking audiences away from other established media. However, as new platforms and delivery formats arrive and take over from old ones, the investment advertisers are willing to make in supporting media content does not cease – instead it redistributes itself. Given the two-sidedness of media markets, any 'new' platform that succeeds in diverting attention from the existing alternatives or otherwise in generating large audiences on its own account will be well-positioned to displace and capture accompanying revenues from advertising. Theoretically, the process of redistribution of advertising should help complete the evolutionary process by ensuring the availability of resources for innovation and development of content for the new delivery platform or format which, in turn, facilitates a reshaping and improvement in the technological quality and composition of the universe of media content offerings.

However, one concern related to the rise of the Internet and the accompanying redistribution of advertising is that at least some of the investment by advertisers in the attention of online audiences is being siphoned off by intermediaries who are not, themselves, investing anything in the content that is attracting audiences to the Internet. When advertising is diverted thus, it impedes the process of renewal, improvement and replenishment of professionally crafted media content upon which the future revenue-generating ability of the media industry is reliant. This process may be viewed as a form of 'disintermediation' or the cutting out of the middle man – i.e. the media distributor. Disintermediation effectively reduces the subsidy available from advertisers to support production and to constrain the direct charge to consumers.

In the conventional media model, newspaper publishers, broadcasters, etc. supply content to an audience. The attention of that audience is sold by the publisher or broadcaster to advertisers and advertising income then pays for more content-creation. Digitization and growth of the Internet has made possible a new model in which players such as search engines, social networking sites and aggregators, as part of performing their own functions, occupy an intermediary position between the media publisher and their audience. Instead of the publisher being able to convert audience attention into revenue, it becomes the aggregator or search engine who is able to 'monetize' the audience attention in part or in full (Wimmer, 2010). As a result, at least a portion of advertising that otherwise may have come to the media publisher is being siphoned off.

Conventional media are finding themselves disintermediated because, as the scope for consumption of media to be driven by personalized choice has increased, the content-packaging functions they have traditionally carried out have become less essential. To the extent that the consumer is taking more control, the need for the previously crucial role that media suppliers have played in assembling and packaging content on behalf of consumers into what are judged to be attractive parcels has diminished in importance. Online purveyors of media content (aggregation sites, search engines, etc.) who are facilitating and accelerating the trend towards greater personalized choice – and some of whom, in particular Google, have achieved considerable dominance in online advertising markets – are well placed to benefit from a gradual attenuation of one of the key value-added roles played by traditional media suppliers.

A diminution in potential flows of advertising back into content-creation is clearly unwelcome from the point of view of news and other media content production industries. Any contraction in resources available for media content production also has wider societal implications. Evans has argued that because the Internet is so efficient at matching buyers and sellers, an economically beneficial aspect of online advertising is that '[s]ociety may not need to invest as much in magazines, newspapers, and other media whose main purpose is aggregating the right eyeballs for advertisers' (Evans, 2009: 43). In other words, it is to be welcomed if fewer resources are tied up unnecessarily in content production. However, notwithstanding the two-sidedness of media markets, it is highly questionable whether 'delivery of eyeballs' is the function of media which society values most. To the extent that audiences and the public at large value the presence of a rich array of professionally crafted media-content offerings, erosion of investment in content production will have harmful implications.

It is not only media companies but also advertising agencies who have been threatened by processes of disintermediation. Sinclair and Wilken (2009) explain how agencies have suffered from the rise of the Internet and the predominance of Google and other search services. For decades, the advertising industry has earned its living from brokering and orchestrating campaigns via an assortment of advertising media channels and outlets. Although the major advertising agencies such as WPP and Publicis are still getting most business from advertisers, the fastest-growing area of advertising at present is online search. In the UK, 61 per cent of *online* advertising in 2009 was accounted for by search (Ofcom, 2010a: 241), but search advertising diminishes the need for input from agencies (Sinclair and Wilken, 2009). Advertisers can go straight to a search engine such as Google, which has an auction system for placing advertisements next to key words or terms used in online searches, with the advertiser usually paying on a 'pay-per-click' basis. For advertising agencies as for television companies and publishers, the intrinsic nature of the Internet as an interactive medium has removed the need for some of the value-added functions they traditionally carried out.

THE FIRM'S ADVERTISING DECISION

Albeit that the arrival and growth of the Internet has affected advertisers' perception of which media are more attractive than others, the broad decision each firm takes about how much of its resources to devote to advertising depends on what it believes this investment can achieve. What companies expect in return for their expenditure on advertising can vary and whereas some simply want an effective marketing campaign, others believe that advertising agencies play a broader role in creating and managing their long-term brand strategies.

Systems of remuneration for advertising agencies have changed over time (Grande, 2007). For a long time it was customary for agencies to rely on a fee of 15 per cent of 'gross billings' (i.e. the cost of all advertising space purchased on behalf of the client). Hence, US radio comedian Fred Allen coined the following definition of an advertising agency: 85 per cent confusion and 15 per cent commission. A greater separation between media-buying activities (which attract commissions or discounts of up to 15 per cent of media placement budgets) and, on the other hand, the creative work that advertising agencies carry out for clients has led to increased emphasis on payment of negotiated time-based fees for the latter in recent years.

The traditional commission-based mode of payment was frequently criticized, not only because it encouraged agencies to concentrate their efforts on expensive media outlets but also because it ignored whether the advertising campaign supplied to the client was in any way effective or not. However, systems of payment based on the actual costs incurred by agencies in carrying out creative work are also open to criticism. When fees are time-based, creative agencies may invest too much energy in pacing their work rather than coming up with the most effective ideas quickly.

A 'payment by results' approach is attractive from the point of advertising clients, but it raises a perplexing and long-standing question surrounding firms' expenditure on advertising – namely, how can the effectiveness of advertising be measured? Some advertising clients favour a sales-based model of compensation whereby agency fees are calculated by reference to the impact of the advertising campaign on client sales. This seems fair, to the extent that the primary motivation behind advertising is to sustain or improve demand for the firms' products or services. However, others regard this as too simplistic and prefer to adopt a more a holistic approach towards measuring their agencies' success including, for example, tracking how sentiment and perceptions towards the firm and its brands have changed over time.

The question of how to measure the effectiveness of advertising expenditure is important because unless some idea can be gained about what return advertising will bring, firms will naturally find it very difficult to decide what level of resources to devote to this activity.

The two most common types of approach taken to research the effectiveness of advertising involve either measuring the success of advertising in communicating its message or direct tests of the effects of advertising on sales or profits. Both of these methods, however, have serious weaknesses.

In the case of testing people's ability to recall advertising messages, the obvious weakness is that this approach doesn't yield any reliable information about the impact on sales. How often does a clever visual or punchline in an advertisement create a lasting impression but without successfully projecting the brand or having a discernible effect on demand (van Kuilenburg, de Jong and van Rompay (2011)? Studies which focus more broadly on how advertising has affected perceptions of the firm and on its brands suffer from the same problem – the impact of this expenditure on the firm's financial performance is not addressed.

Growing use of interactive digital platforms has brought new ways of gauging how many responses an advertisement elicits. For Internet advertising, metrics commonly used include counting the number of clicks or page view requests which follow from viewing an online advertisement, but discerning the exact impact of digital advertising is not always straightforward. Advertisers' use of social media such as Twitter and Facebook to convey promotional messages has grown in popularity. However, the general shift away from a one-to-many mode of address to, instead, a more interactive conversational mode of engagement clearly involves difficulty in terms of isolating and measuring impact (Handley, 2012). Whereas with online search and display advertising, click-through rates are available to be counted and analysed, with expenditure on social media advertising, assessing the impact on sentiment and purchasing intentions is much more challenging and techniques commonly used such as counting fans and followers are only of limited use (Gelles, 2012: 2).

All in all, proof that advertising has engaged viewers' attention, has communicated a message successfully or has improved a brand or a corporate image is not the same as demonstrating an impact on profits. So for many advertisers, the second method – looking directly at sales – seems more useful, because the whole point of advertising is usually to boost sales. Advertising on the Internet often provides an immediate and reliable means of assessing the impact on sales – advertisers can count 'conversion' rates by tracking how many people click through from the advertisement to a purchase. Some would argue that higher levels of accountability in terms of the effect of online advertising expenditures on sales is precisely what has helped drive the switch away from conventional media to the Internet in recent years (Philipson, cited in

Bradshaw, 2009). But not all forms of online advertising are open to analysis of how effectively expenditure converts into sales, and across the media more generally, measuring the effects of advertising is beset by a number of problems to do with establishing any direct causal link between what you spend on advertising and what happens to sales.

One problem to be taken into account with direct testing is that advertising is not, itself, a homogeneous product. The effect on sales that a given expenditure on advertising will achieve depends, to a great extent, on the quality of the particular advertising campaign that has been purchased. Not all advertising agencies have equal talent and, in the UK for example, those advertising campaigns which seem to most clearly demonstrate a profitable or an effective return for clients are acknowledged each year by the Institute of Practitioners in Advertising (IPA) effectiveness awards competition. The way in which a firm's sales move or fail to move as a result of a campaign devised by one particular agency may not prove to be a reliable indicator of how sales will typically or more generally respond to investment on advertising.

The spread of click-through technology on the Internet has improved the immediacy of some forms of advertising by reducing the time and distance between advertising and the point of sale. With advertising more generally, time lags are common in the sense of delays between when an advertisement appears and when it starts to have the desired impact on sales. Advertising might inspire an initial trial which might then result in positive recommendations to friends and, in turn, be followed by further purchases. Advertising may communicate its message successfully but at a time when the consumer is not yet in a position to make a purchase. So it may take some time before advertising has a visible impact on sales. It is often argued that consumers need to be exposed to a certain amount of advertising before they will respond but once they do respond, not much advertising is required to retain their loyalty. Advertising gradually builds up and then reinforces the positive perceptions of a product or brand or, in a sense, the 'goodwill' that is needed to ensure habitual purchasing of it. Indeed, the future earnings potential that investment on advertising is thought to have generated for a firm is sometimes recognized when famous brands are valued and accounted for as assets on a company's balance sheet.

When it comes to measuring the effect of advertising, a regressive model is sometimes used to deal with this problem of time lags. In other words, advertising which has taken place in a previous period (say, the first quarter of 2011) is compared against current sales (in the first quarter of the following year). But a further and more insurmountable difficulty with measuring the effectiveness of a firm's expenditure on advertising is that of the behaviour of rivals. How do you disentangle the effect of advertising on demand for your product from the effect caused by whatever your rivals have been up to simultaneously in terms of advertising or not advertising their own wares, or implementing competitive price reductions, or instigating product changes or other special promotional efforts? It is virtually impossible for any firm in an oligopoly or a competitive market situation to isolate the impact of its own advertising investment from the impact on demand caused by the behaviour of its rivals.

The problems of measuring the effects of advertising are not simple and, in particular, it is very difficult to establish proof of some degree of causality, i.e. that x expenditure on advertising will have y given effect on sales (Carter, 1998: 6). How, then, do firms decide on their advertising budgets?

Many economists and other theorists who have considered this question (such as Chiplin and Sturgess, 1981; Duncan, 1981; Shimp, 2010) acknowledge that firms often simply use some kind of 'rule of thumb'. The decision taken about what level of resources to devote to advertising is often based on customary practice or what amounts to intuition rather than on any attempt to calculate expected returns. Sometimes, advertising is regarded as discretionary rather than necessary expenditure and firms simply spend whatever they think they can afford at a given time. This approach is reflected in historic data, discussed above, which demonstrates the sensitivity of overall levels of advertising to company profits and to fluctuations in the economy at large, but the discretionary approach is often criticized on the basis of being too unscientific and unlikely to achieve great results.

Many firms take the approach of setting their advertising budget as a given proportion of sales or of assets. The predetermined percentage of either previous or predicted sales is a particularly popular method – e.g. this year's advertising budget may be set at the rate of 10 per cent of last year's sales – and it offers various advantages. It is easy to calculate and it is quite manageable in financial terms, in the sense that the advertising budget will go up or down directly in accordance with the firm's fortunes.

But how does the firm decide what proportion of sales the advertising budget should represent? Analysis of historic sales and advertising figures reveals some very wide disparities between the proportions opted for by different firms. Should the advertising budget be set at 5 or 40 per cent of sales? Many firms examine what their competitors are spending and set their own advertising budget as a similar proportion of sales or assets. In many consumer markets, competition between leading firms (such as Colgate-Palmolive, Proctor & Gamble and Unilever) acts as a spur to not only match but outspend the percentage rivals are investing in advertising where possible (Jopson, 2012: 15), but there is no guarantee that the sort of level set by competitors is optimal.

Some economic theorists have tried to provide a more scientific answer to this question. Dorfman and Steiner have suggested that when it comes to deciding what proportion of sales income to devote to advertising, there are two things that firms should take into account: first, how responsive sales are to advertising expenditure and second, 'price elasticity' or how responsive sales are to any reduction in price (Chiplin and Sturgess, 1981: 45). The reason why consumers' reactions to any price change should be taken into account in setting the advertising budget is because it would be inefficient to spend money on advertising if the same money invested in a price reduction would boost sales by a greater amount. If sales are more responsive to fluctuations in price than to changes in levels of advertising, this implies that a lower proportion of sales income should be devoted to advertising.

The Dorfman–Steiner approach may have merit in theory but it is by no means easy to put into operation. Price elasticity refers to the responsiveness or sensitivity of demand to upward or downward movements in the price of a product. Likewise, the concept of 'advertising elasticity' refers to the responsiveness of demand to changes in levels of advertising expenditure on that product. The problem is that it is virtually impossible to calculate advertising elasticity in real-world circumstances because of constant changes and the unpredictable behaviour of competitors. When it comes to setting a firm's overall budget for advertising, it seems unlikely that advertisers will abandon the tradition of adopting a rule of thumb approach in the near future.

9

Media Economics and Public Policy

Since the earliest days of printing, the ability to communicate with mass audiences has been subject to many forms of intervention by state authorities. Media industries are affected not only by 'normal' economic and industrial policy concerns (e.g. growth and efficiency), but also by a range of special considerations that reflect the sociopolitical and cultural importance of mass communications. In recent years, a sense that 'creative' industries (which include, for example, publishers and television producers) are instrumental in propelling growth in the wider economy has added to the range of concerns that, from the point of view of public policy, distinguish media from other areas of activity. In addition, the growth of the Internet and the development of new sorts of dominant players has raised questions about what role competition policy can play, in the digital era, in fostering the development of a healthy media industry.

For a variety of reasons, media industries are frequently subject to special concerns and policy interventions and such measures can have a strong determining influence over the economic performance of media markets and media firms. This chapter considers what role economic theory and analysis can play in helping to address media-related policy questions.

After studying this chapter, you should be able to:

- identify areas where government intervention might help to improve the economic performance of media firms or markets;
- evaluate what outcomes can be expected of special support initiatives for media-content creators, including subsidies and protectionist measures;
- analyse the significance of gatekeeper functions and associated competition concerns;
- assess what the economic advantages and disadvantages of policy measures which restrict levels of media ownership are.

FREE MARKET VERSUS INTERVENTION

The broad ideological case in favour of relying on free markets to allocate resources is based on the notion that decentralized decision-taking is usually better than decision-making carried out by the government. Consumers and firms are thought to be the best judges of their own interests. The price system may not always be perfect but, compared with a centrally planned economy, it is relatively effective in co-ordinating resource allocation decisions.

Recent changes in the approach towards allocation of spectrum provide an example of how media regulators are moving towards greater reliance on market mechanisms to allocate resources where this is feasible. The right to transmit signals over specific bands of electromagnetic spectrum – a valuable public resource – is generally managed by national authorities (such as Ofcom in the UK or the FCC in the US) who license and co-ordinate usage of the airwaves and ensure problems of interference are minimized. In the past, all key decisions about who can use spectrum and for what purpose have been centrally managed, but economists have long argued that the use of a market force to determine spectrum allocation would provide a more optimal outcome (Cave, 2002 and 2005; Coase, 1959). The use of an auction system would ensure that spectrum is allocated to whichever user/s can derive the highest value from it as well as providing funds to the state (Cramton, 2002). Removal of restrictions over how allocated spectrum is used would encourage trade – i.e. enable spectrum owners to sell their rights onwards to alternative users – thus helping to avoid potential waste of this resource.

Since the beginning of the twenty-first century, national communication regulators in European countries including the UK, Germany and France have moved from a centralized control model of spectrum allocation towards the more market-driven approach adopted in the US where, since 1994, the FCC has conducted auctions to price and sell access to the airwaves. Although in the UK as elsewhere some organizations (including broadcasters) still enjoy usage of the airwaves that is relatively free of market pressures, the gradual introduction of spectrum pricing, auctions and trading has brought a shift towards a system where market signals now play a much greater role in determining how spectrum is deployed (Richards, 2011: 2–3). A number of factors have contributed to European and national regulators embracing a more liberalized approach. The transition from analogue to digital broadcasting has brought reorganization and, typically, a release of available spectrum, thus prompting national regulators to consider how best to maximize its value. At the same time, increased demand from the mobile communications sector has driven up the prices bidders are prepared to pay for national spectrum, in some cases resulting in great windfalls to national governments from spectrum auctions (Leahy, 2010; Thomas, 2011).

Proponents of auctions take the view that this is a much more efficient means of allocating an important and valuable resource than the old 'beauty contest' approach to spectrum allocation (Davies and Lam, 2001: 4). Auctions provide a way of pricing and selling an asset where asymmetric information exists in relation to valuations of the resource (Fisher, Prentice and Waschik, 2010: 343). Critics argue that if firms are required to make large bids to secure spectrum this is liable to result in higher prices being charged to consumers and under-investment in new services. Those who favour auctions say this is impossible because rational profit-maximizing firms make bids based on estimates of future profits – i.e. prices and investment plans are determined *prior to* and not after decisions about what amount to bid (ibid.). However, in reality, over-payment for spectrum licences has occurred and, in some cases, impeded subsequent investment in services by mobile service operators (Leahy, 2010; Thomas, 2011). This highlights an inherent problem with auctions, which is that misallocations will occur when bidders fail to or are unable to value the resource correctly. Where significant uncertainty exists about the value of the asset, participants in an auction are exposed to the so-called 'winner's curse' of paying too much.

Whatever presumption may exist in favour of market-driven rather than centrally organized allocation, it remains the case that intervention by the government is sometimes called for to counteract deficiencies arising from the free operation of markets. The standard economic case in favour of government intervention in any industry is that a market failure has occurred and needs to be corrected. As far as the media are concerned, the most important economic reasons why government intervention may be required are to address market failures, to deal with the problem of externalities and to restrict the exercise of monopoly power by media firms. Of course, governments may also have cause to intervene in media markets for non-economic reasons, but these are not considered here.

Many of the market failures associated with media have been discussed in earlier chapters. The most serious cases stem from the public good characteristics of broadcast output discussed in Chapter 1. For example, based on conventional methods of market support (i.e. direct consumer payments), broadcasting might not have been supplied at all because, until relatively recently, it was not feasible to collect payments directly from consumers. Many broadcasting services are non-excludable (which leads to free-rider problems) and all exhibit the characteristic of being non-rivalrous. Non-rivalrous refers to the fact that there are zero marginal costs involved in supplying the service to one additional viewer. As Davies has pointed out, '[r]estricting the viewing of programmes that, once produced, could be made available to everyone at no extra cost, leads to inefficiency and welfare losses' (1999: 203).

Externalities constitute another important and enduring source of market failure in the media. These are external effects, usually costs, imposed on third parties and they arise when the private costs to a firm of engaging in a certain activity are out of line with its social costs. For example, the provision of some forms of media content may impose a wider cost on society by encouraging violence or increasing fear of violence within society. But these costs do not have to be borne by the media supplier. The misalignment between private and social costs constitutes a market failure because more resources may be devoted to providing media content with negative external affects than is socially optimal.

In addition, other forms of media content which confer positive external affects may be under-supplied under free market circumstances. There are some types of content that are collectively desirable and that everyone benefits from (e.g. documentaries, educational and cultural output) but which audiences, on an individual basis, might not tune in to or be prepared to pay for. A 'merit good' is one where the government takes the view that more of it should be produced than people would choose to consume on their own account (e.g. health support, education). Various categories of broadcast output which are considered to be inherently good are often treated as merit goods.

So there are several ways in which a completely unregulated market for the supply of media might fail to allocate resources efficiently or in accordance with the best interests of society. It is up to the government to step in with policy measures that correct these failures. As discussed earlier, two of the main policy tools used to address market failures in broadcasting are regulation and public ownership. Regulation is used to encourage privately owned broadcasters to deviate from profit-maximizing strategies where necessary in order to meet public requirements concerning the quality of their output. Broadcasters may be prohibited from supplying some types of programming that are considered damaging to society's interests and they may be required to include other sorts of 'meritorious' content within their schedules. In the UK, for example, Ofcom has power to impose financial penalties on any commercial broadcaster that fails to comply with the Ofcom

Broadcasting Code which governs basic standards in relation to content on all licensed television channels.

Another measure commonly used is to organize provision of public service broadcasting (PSB) provision through the public sector using some form of public funding. Most countries have their own publicly funded and state-owned broadcasting entity to provide PSB. However, as discussed in Chapter 5, the use of public funds to finance broadcasting has become increasingly controversial in the era of direct payments and abundant multichannel competition. A further source of controversy, analysed in more depth below, stems from the potential for crowding out to occur which, as PSB organizations have extended their content delivery activities across additional digital platforms including especially the Internet, has become a more manifest threat for commercial rivals, including newspapers.

Other ways in which governments can encourage the dissemination of particular sorts of media content include provision of public subsidies directed not at organizations per se but at encouraging production or distribution of whatever sort of content is favoured. The use of subsidies and other support measures to encourage supply and consumption of meritorious content is considered in more detail below.

Finally, one of the most important concerns that arises from the free operation of markets is the accumulation of excessive market power by individual firms. As firms grow in size and gain monopoly power there is a risk that this power will be abused, with negative implications both for consumers and for rival firms. As discussed in Chapter 3, media industries will naturally gravitate towards monopoly and oligopoly market structures because of the prevalence of economies of scale. The economic characteristics of the media sector strongly encourage strategies of vertical, horizontal and diagonal growth but expansion inevitably leads to the accumulation of dominant positions by individual media firms. In addition, the diffusion of digital technologies has created new concerns in relation to monopolized control over gateways between media content and audiences or end-users. Public policy interventions are required to ensure that competition is maintained and to prevent abuses of market power. Policies to counteract monopoly problems are considered in further detail below.

SUPPORT MEASURES FOR MEDIA CONTENT

The extent to which special support measures are used to encourage greater supply and consumption of media content that confers positive externalities varies from one country to the next. Across Europe, such interventions are relatively widespread and are usually aimed at creators of audiovisual content – i.e. film-makers and independent television production companies. Support measures for content-creators can be divided into two broad categories. First, some policy interventions are designed to help domestic producers by restricting the volume of imports of competing non-domestic feature films and programme material. Second, an alternative policy approach is to provide subsidies to domestic producers so as to improve their competitiveness at home and in international markets.

A typical example of the first approach – that of using protectionist measures – would be quotas or limits in relation to how much locally made versus how much foreign-made content suppliers may provide to audiences. Quotas are common in audiovisual industries and reflect concerns about the vulnerability of domestic television and film markets to a predominance of imported material. Recent data in Table 9.1 about trends in imports and exports of film and television confirms how international trade tends to be dominated by English-language content and by the output of one country in particular – the US. Although the growth in global demand for television content which has accompanied digitization and channel proliferation has encouraged the development of strong regional markets in Latin America, the Arab countries and the countries of east Asia including China, South Korea and Japan (CMM-I, 2007), data from a variety of sources confirms that the US is and remains far and away the largest exporter of television and also film content (WTO, 2010: USITC, 2011).

A variety of factors explain the success of US exporters including, not least, advantages of scale, wealth and language. The US is home to an audience of 116m television households and, in addition, per capita expenditure on television in the US is considerably higher than in any other country (Ofcom, 2010b: 132). However, the predominance of US audiovisual exports has given rise to concerns about balance of trade problems and also in relation to the impact on diversity, local cultures and languages (Guerrieri, Iapadre and Koopman, 2004). A common response has been to impose compulsory quotas on broadcasters. Typically, quotas restrict the level of time that can be given over to transmission of imported works, especially during peak time or prime time or else they require broadcasters to ensure that a certain minimum proportion of content which is transmitted is made locally. Quotas set out to redistribute demand in favour of local television content producers but, to the extent that domestic prices may be higher than import prices (for the same performance characteristics), they are also criticized in terms of their impact on broadcasters' operating costs.

Table 9.1 Major exporters and importers of AV and related services, 2007

Rank	Major Exporters	Value (US$m)	Share of top 15 (%)	Annual change (%)	Rank	Major Importers	Value (US$m)	Share of top 15 (%)	Annual change (%)
1	United States	15,043	51.5	23	1	European Union (27)	13,893	63.7	1
2	European Union (27)	9,962	34.1	14		Extra-EU (27) imports	6,315	29.0	−16
	Extra-EU (27) exports	4,063	13.9	6	2	Canada	2,001	9.2	6
3	Canada	2,021	6.9	−3	3	United States	1,440	6.6	32
4	China	316	1.1	130	4	Japan	1,044	4.8	6
5	Mexico	308	1.1	−19	5	Australia	798	3.7	13
6	Argentina	294	1.0	21	6	Russian Federation	624	2.9	36
7	Norway	272	0.9	18	7	Brazil	456	2.1	18
8	Hong Kong, China	249	0.9	−3	8	Korea, Republic of	381	1.7	66
9	Russian Federation	196	0.7	28	9	Norway	300	1.4	−21
10	Korea, Republic of	183	0.6	8	10	Mexico	259	1.2	−21
11	Australia	139	0.5	−8	11	Argentina	212	1.0	24
12	Japan	126	0.4	22	12	China	154	0.7	27
13	Albania	61	0.2	59	13	Ecuador	126	0.6	9
14	Ecuador	44	0.1	7	14	Albania	59	0.3	83
15	Colombia	21	0.1	−24	15	Croatia	55	0.3	64
	Above 15	**29,235**	**100.0**	–		**Above 15**	**21,800**	**100.0**	–

Source: WTO Secretariat estimates from 2009 based on available trade statistics (WTO, 2010: 4).

Whether or not quotas affect trade depends on how strictly they are enforced. The general failure of a loosely phrased 'compulsory' quota for European-made content contained in the Audiovisual Media Services Directive 2007 (previously the Television Without Frontiers Directive) to reshape patterns of trade in television content across Europe provides a good case in point (Cocq and Messerlin, 2004: 22–3). Lax enforcement often results in content quotas having only a limited impact. However, in the few instances where very tight compulsory content quotas exist and cut across local demand preferences and where they *are* properly implemented this will certainly influence international trade. For example, China operates a quota system that curbs the number of foreign feature films which are permitted access to the domestic market to 20 per year, and this is highly effective in restricting the inflow of films into China (*Screen Digest*, 2010). The fact that the 20 foreign titles which are allowed into the market, despite competing with some 500 locally made Chinese films, have accounted for around 45 per cent of Chinese box-office revenues (Jaffe, 2011) suggests that without a strictly enforced quota trade flows in film might look very different.

Measures such as quotas and tariffs will help domestic content producers by transferring demand away from imports and in favour of local output. The main problem with protectionism is that by encouraging local production of goods that can be made more cost-efficiently elsewhere, it promotes what is perceived to be a misallocation of resources. Protectionism can also give rise to retaliatory measures and the risk of a tit-for-tat trade war breaking out, which would leave everyone worse off.

The need to avoid waste and to avoid trade disputes are important policy considerations in every country. However, at the same time, many countries regard cultural industries as a 'special case' and are highly concerned to preserve the positive externalities associated with the availability of domestically made audiovisual content. As well as subscribing to interventions that restrict audiovisual imports, many European countries also provide direct subsidies to local film-makers and television producers. Unlike quotas or tariffs, direct subsidies to support local producers extend the range and variety of indigenous provision without erecting trade barriers, so subsidies are sometimes seen as more appropriate and less trade-distorting instruments (Burri, 2011; Voon, 2007: 20). The opportunity cost to society of sustaining these support measures is considerable, albeit that subsidies for media production appear modest when compared with those allocated to sectors such as agriculture and manufacturing in recent years.

Special subsidies and taxes are effective tools for correcting any divergences that occur between private and social costs or benefits. For example, a tax per unit of pollution is an effective way of encouraging firms to internalize what would otherwise be purely an externality – i.e. the cost of its pollution. Likewise, the provision of grants for production of locally made films in indigenous languages enables production firms to enter into their own internal calculations of costs and benefits the third-party gains associated with their output. Production grants allow the positive gains to society arising from the availability of indigenously made content to be internalized by the production firm, thus correcting the failure of the market system to adequately supply such content.

European countries such as France and Germany have a long tradition of providing public subsidies and grants to indigenous producers of audiovisual content. In addition, a variety of public funding awards are available to European film-makers through schemes administered by the EU such as Eurimages and the MEDIA programme. Even in the UK, where attitudes towards support schemes for industry generally tend to be more laissez-faire than in most other EU member states, some £27m of National Lottery funding is available to support film-making every year and this is expected to increase to £40m by 2014 (Smith, 2012: 87).

In providing these subsidies, the aim is to try to encourage private decisions about what audiovisual content is produced to be taken in accordance with the wider public interest. Grants and subsidies are not only intended to encourage wider dissemination to audiences of indigenous audiovisual product but are also supposed to improve the competitiveness of domestic content-creators in home and world markets. However, some would argue that subsidies can have precisely the opposite effect. The provision of public grants for film-makers is more likely to delay and prevent the development of the necessary skills to compete in domestic and international markets than it is to foster improved competitiveness.

One of the main criticisms of public grants for content-creators, then, is that they encourage the production of films and television programming which lack commercial appeal. Subsidies for programme-makers may well help to promote wider distribution and consumption of certain kinds of meritorious indigenous television content, but in so doing, they encourage local producers to depart from profit-maximizing strategies of creating content that is as popular and as commercially competitive as possible.

Hoskins, McFayden and Finn point out that '[t]he subsidy partially insulates the producer financially from the commercial performance of the film/programme and hence lessens the motivation to be efficient'

(1997: 96). If a significant proportion of production costs is going to be covered by a public grant then the producer has relatively little incentive to constrain the budget. In fact, if a cost-plus system of financing is favoured then producers may find it advantageous to inflate production budgets (ibid.). While special support measures can encourage higher levels of local production of audiovisual content, there is also a risk that protective interventions may prove counterproductive by, for example, contributing to a culture of dependence among indigenous content creators.

PROTECTIONISM

International trade in cultural output gets caught at the crossroads between conflicting sociopolitical, cultural and economic interests. The public good characteristics of media content – the fact that however many times it is consumed it does not get used up – means that, unlike most products, it can be sold over and over and over again to new audiences. Reproduction costs are negligible and scarcity is not a problem, so media content seems well suited to wide international distribution. From a producer's point of view, spreading production costs across as many additional geographic markets as possible is the ideal strategy.

At the same time, however, any threat to indigenous producers of cultural output tends to bring out protective impulses. Notwithstanding language barriers, domestic television producers in Europe and elsewhere often find it difficult to compete in their own home markets with attractive, high-budget second-hand programme exports from the US that are readily available at a low cost. Profit-seeking broadcasters will naturally want to avail themselves of this supply of inexpensive programming. This places domestic producers at a perceived disadvantage. Concerns about the need for indigenous programming and the potential harm to indigenous cultures, languages and values that may be caused by high levels of import penetration television have occupied considerable importance in European debates about audiovisual policy.

However, the invocation of cultural concerns is sometimes regarded as a disguise for straightforward, old-fashioned protectionism. Television production is a major international business, employing tens of thousands of individuals across the globe and generating billions of pounds in commercial revenue every year, not only for US suppliers but for producers in many other countries too. Some would argue that television is not really that different from any other business sector and that the use of subsidies, quotas or other special measures to prop up local producers is not only unnecessary but is also wasteful.

To analyse the arguments for and against protection of indigenous producers, it is worth understanding some of the fundamentals of international trade theory. The basic theory of 'gains from trade' was developed by David Ricardo in 1817. Ricardo was extending Adam Smith's earlier notion about the benefits of division of labour to a global level. Smith observed that specialization of labour – i.e. the allocation of different jobs to different people on the basis of what each person does best – and voluntary exchange of goods and services is a much more efficient way or organizing things than expecting everyone to be self-sufficient. Modern economies are based on this notion of specialization and division of labour. Ricardo took the idea further by suggesting that each country should specialize in those goods that it can produce most efficiently, e.g. Brazil should produce coffee, Scotland should produce sheep, etc.

With free international trade, each country or region can concentrate on producing whatever it happens to be good at making or whatever it produces most cost-efficiently. If each area specializes in producing commodities for which it has some natural or acquired advantage and buys in whatever it does not produce efficiently from other countries, then the world's limited resources will be used as efficiently as possible and, in theory, everyone can enjoy a higher standard of living. But what happens if one country is more efficient than another in the production of all goods? Ricardo pointed out that there are still gains to be made (i.e. world output will be maximized) so long as each country specializes in whatever it is relatively good at producing or whatever it happens to have a 'comparative advantage' in and then we trade with each other freely.

Does the US have a comparative advantage in television production? The traditional notion of comparative advantage relies on the assumption that certain countries or regions are inherently better suited to producing some commodities rather than others, probably because of endowments of natural resources or local climatic conditions. A competing view is that comparative advantages are not necessarily nature-given and fixed but are, in fact, acquired and may change over time. The US is clearly the world's most successful exporter of audiovisual goods and services, yet most of the major factors involved in production of television programming (particularly, the human capital) seem to be internationally mobile rather than fixed. Its comparative advantage may, to a large extent, be acquired rather than naturally occurring.

The fact that television production in the US results in an English-language product is certainly one important factor which inherently favours US suppliers, as it does producers in other English-speaking countries including the UK, Canada and Ireland. The size and wealth of the domestic market is also clearly a major advantage for US television producers. The ability to spread production costs over such an enormous home market means that US producers are able to offer television programmes to overseas audiences at extremely competitive prices.

But if the economies of scale available in the US market were enough to guarantee international success for its television producers, then why don't US producers predominate in all areas of cultural production? Why is it that in the area of pop music, for example, UK producers have managed to become a more important international force? Evidently, US audiovisual producers have some special flair for creating output with a wide appeal that is not fully shared by US producers of other forms of cultural output.

Television producers in the US also benefit from a concentration of talent, technical equipment and specialist support services related to audiovisual production. However, these are acquired rather than natural resources. Judging by its current trade surplus, it appears that the US does, indeed, enjoy a comparative advantage in production of television content, but natural endowments of raw materials or climate cannot adequately account for this.

If relatively few of the factors that contribute to the US's comparative advantage in television production are innate and immutable, this implies that other countries could similarly acquire a comparative advantage over time. Theoretically, many of the US's advantages in television production are contestable. In reality, it would be foolish to assume that the conditions which currently favour US television suppliers in international markets could easily be replicated elsewhere.

The desire to build up competitive indigenous audiovisual production sectors has resulted in the use of a variety of methods of protection in different countries over the years including, as noted above, quotas and subsidies. Tariffs provide another example. These are taxes levied on imported television programmes or films. Tariffs protect indigenous producers by increasing the costs of imports and, at the same time, they provide a source of revenue for the government.

According to international trade theory, the introduction of any artificial support measures to encourage local production of a commodity – cultural or otherwise – which can be created more cheaply or cost-efficiently elsewhere will lead to a suboptimal use of resources. The use of special policies to develop indigenous industries that do not have, and will never achieve, comparative advantages is generally a waste of time. Protectionism may serve the interests of domestic producers but, on the other hand, encouraging high-cost local production inevitably results in a misallocation of resources with concomitant welfare losses. Another major drawback of introducing protectionist measures is that they invite the prospect of retaliation.

There may, however, be some situations when a degree of selective protectionism is justified. For example, when 'dumping' takes place then a typical response is to impose a tariff. Dumping occurs when goods are sold in a foreign market 'at a price below the real cost of production' (Griffiths and Wall, 2007: 581) or, in other words, at below the real cost of supplying them. For example, if agricultural goods whose production has been subsidized in their country of origin are then sold or dumped into overseas markets, local producers will find it very difficult to compete with these imports on price. As discussed in Chapter 6, it is sometimes argued that US audiovisual producers dump low-cost material on to foreign markets. But the sale of programmes into overseas territories does not really fit with the technical description of dumping because, although programmes are sold at well below their production costs, it is not the show as a whole which is being sold but rather just the right to provide one or two transmissions of it in a particular territory.

Another circumstance where protectionism is considered justifiable is in order to nurture an 'infant industry'. The infant industry argument suggests that new domestic industries, because of a lack of experience, may not be able to compete with more established firms in other countries and therefore interventions such as trade barriers or subsidies can and should be tolerated temporarily (Lipsey and Chrystal, 2007: 618–19). The use of protective measures to help establish new industries is reasonably widely accepted and, indeed, is explicitly provided for under Article 18 of the original General Agreement on Tariffs and Trade (GATT) – the principal rule book guiding the work of the WTO, an international institution devoted to fostering trade and reducing trade barriers (Griffith and Wall, 2007: 572). If there is a belief that a period of time is required for the local industry to 'go down a learning curve' until it becomes fully competitive then there would be a valid argument for protecting the industry for a limited period until it matures and becomes competitive in the international market and no longer needs protection.

Whether or not this sort of argument is applicable to, for instance, television production industries across Europe is debatable. The most obvious disadvantage for European programme-makers is that they operate in much smaller domestic markets than US programme-makers, which makes it is difficult for them to build up the same critical mass.

Some scholars dismiss the use of infant industry arguments to support European quotas as illegitimate (Hoskins, McFayden and Finn, 1997: 85–6). Production of television programmes is by no means a new activity in most developed countries so the retention of subsidies and other protective intervention over extended periods cannot really be justified on the grounds of temporarily supporting an infant industry.

Other arguments in favour of protection of domestic television producers focus on the fact that patterns of trade in media products have important cultural implications. The availability of domestically made audiovisual content creates positive externalities (beneficial side effects for society, including a strengthened sense of community, etc.) So, for example, even if Hollywood has a comparative advantage in making English-language programmes because of economies of scale in a market as large as the US, that does not necessarily imply that the UK should just give up domestic television production and import all their programmes. Protective measures for television producers can undoubtedly be justified on non-economic or cultural grounds.

CONCENTRATED MEDIA OWNERSHIP

Concern about the potential for exercise of monopoly power has become an increasingly important issue for media policy-makers in recent years. Across the media industry and in related communications sectors, mergers and alliances have taken place on a massive level and have created enormous transnational conglomerates with significant amounts of market power. Policy-makers are confronted by at least two major challenges. First, there is the question of how best to address high levels of concentrated media ownership. Are media empires a problem and, if so, how should they be tackled? As a related issue, policy-makers have increasingly been faced with the question of how to deal with monopolized control over specific access points and bottlenecks along the vertical supply chain for media (Vick, 2006: 37).

The various advantages associated with strategies of vertical, horizontal and diagonal growth that encourage media firms to expand are discussed in Chapter 3. In theory, the main benefits that accrue to firms as they expand are to do either with increased efficiency or increased market power (Davies and Lam, 2001: 65). Economics generally attributes expansion – whether through internal growth or through mergers and takeovers – to these two key incentives associated with profit-maximizing behaviour. As far as the collective economic welfare of society is concerned, the net impact of industrial concentration depends on the trade-off between these two possible outcomes. Efficiency gains that allow for an improved used of society's resources are beneficial to the economy as a whole. On the other hand, increased market power in the hands of individual firms poses a threat to rivals and consumers and thus is damaging to the public interest.

Policy-makers are sometimes confronted by the problem that proposed mergers and expansion strategies may potentially result in *both* outcomes. For example, as a media firm enlarges, it may well be able to exploit greater economies of scale and economies of scope, thus allowing for a more productive use of resources. So consolidation appears to be warranted and desirable on the grounds of increased efficiency. At the same time, however, the greater market power associated with increased size might create new opportunities for the enlarged media firm to raise prices or otherwise abuse its dominant market position. Although enlargement may, in the first place, have been predicated on improvements in efficiency (e.g. the realization of economies of scale), it might well then be accompanied by the accumulation of a dominant market position which, in turn, can lead to behaviour and practices that run contrary to the public interest (Moschandreas, 2000: 363). Once a firm achieves a dominant position, the removal of competitive pressures may give rise to various inefficiencies, including excessive expenditure of resources aimed simply at maintaining dominance.

A major economic concern associated with concentrated media ownership is its impact on competition. Competition is generally regarded as an essential means of fostering economic efficiency and of averting abusive behaviour by dominant firms. In essence, competition – the presence of several competing suppliers – helps to ensure that firms keep their costs and prices down, which encourages a more efficient use of resources (Scherer and Ross, 1990: 20). If there are few or no rivals in a market, then suppliers can more easily get away with offering goods and services that are costly or inferior. Competitive pressures incentivize managers to improve the performance of their firm relative to rivals and this, in turn, benefits consumers and society at large. Monopolists – whether in the media or in other sectors – are usually seen as less efficient than competitive firms. Monopolists may suppress new innovatory products and may, sometimes, engage in unfair competition.

On the other hand, a media industry in which ownership is too fragmented is also susceptible to inefficiency. It is often argued that because of the availability of economies of scale in the media, large firms are needed in order to ensure the most cost-effective possible use of resources. If promoting cost-efficiency in the media industry is regarded as the dominant policy objective, encouraging greater concentration of media ownership may be consistent with the public interest.

In short, the need to sustain competition and the desire to maximize efficiency are the two main economic policy goals affected by concentrations of media ownership. These goals are related, in that fair and plentiful competition is seen as an essential means of sustaining efficiency. On the other hand, the two objectives may pull in opposite directions. If because of the availability of economies of scale the optimal size of a firm in some media markets is so large as to preclude rivals, then a trade-off will occur between encouraging more competition and achieving maximum efficiency gains.

PROMOTING COMPETITION

One of the traditional concerns associated with allowing individual firms to establish dominance in particular markets is that they may charge prices that are too high and become careless about their costs (Scherer and Ross, 1990: 19–23). Monopolists may become complacent about product quality and about the need to innovate new products, to the detriment of consumers. Another important worry is that dominant firms will waste too much of their resources in activities designed to maintain their market dominance. They may engage in business practices that are intended to squeeze rivals out the market or to deter new rivals, who are offering products which consumers may want, from entering.

Conventional economic theory suggests that perfect competition (i.e. the existence of many suppliers, in open markets, offering homogeneous products to buyers who have perfect knowledge of all available substitutes) is one route towards bringing about an efficient allocation of resources. However, in the real world, there are few if any examples of perfect competition. Instead, very many markets in modern industrialized economies are dominated by a small number of large firms who have some degree of market power. The potential for this market power to be abused, and to result in a misallocation of resources, is the main economic rationale underlying competition policy (George, Joll and Lynk, 1992: 314).

The media industry is prone to oligopoly and, in turn, to the many forms of resource misallocation which accompany concentrated market power. In the UK, for example, very high inflation in prices charged for television advertising during the 1980s can be associated with monopolized control of commercial airtime during this period. The price war which affected UK national daily newspaper markets in the 1990s provided an example of how dominant media suppliers can use their strength and resources to reinforce and extend positions of market dominance. Monopolized control within the UK pay-TV market has resulted in various instances of abuse of market power, such as consumers being charged too much for premium film content in the view of the UK competition authorities (Competition Commission, 2011: 18). Bottlenecks can occur not only in upstream content stages of the supply chain but also throughout distribution and on any of the platforms and interfaces made possible by digital technology. In recent years, the potential to monopolize key access points and gateways between media content and audiences or end-users' ability has extended to new sorts of players including, for example, search engines and SNSs, thus creating new challenges for competition regulators.

The standard provisions of national and European competition law apply to all sectors of industry including media although, as discussed below, PSBs are exempt. Competition policy has become an increasingly active area of media policy intervention at European level in recent years (Ungerer, 2005). Competition policy has traditionally worked on the assumption that the efficiency of markets depends directly on their competitive structure and, especially, on the extent of seller concentration. So competition policy may sometimes involve structural interventions – i.e. attempts to bring about market structures which are less concentrated – on the assumption that this, in turn, will ensure good behaviour by competing firms and promote an improved industrial performance (Moschandreas, 2000: 363).

Upper restrictions on levels of media and cross-media ownership represent a means of structural intervention through which competition among media can be promoted and seller concentration can be avoided. Special restrictions on media ownership are still a common feature in most European countries and elsewhere, but they usually owe their existence to concerns about pluralism and not competition. Media ownership restrictions are generally intended to protect political and cultural pluralism which, as a policy objective, is quite different from promoting competition. Nonetheless, ownership limits intended to preserve pluralism may, at the same time, also serve to prevent the development and subsequent possible abuse of excessive market power by dominant media firms.

However, the use of ownership rules to alter the structure of a market represents what some economists would consider to be a fairly extreme form of intervention. In recent years, the emphasis of competition policy has shifted away from such structural interventions towards alternative behavioural measures which regulate the conduct of dominant firms in such a way as to ensure that market power is not abused. In the UK, for example, the 1998 Competition Act brought the UK approach more into line with that of the European Union, whereby the focus is on remedies to anti-competitive behaviour rather than on corporate structures (Feintuck, 1999: 91).

The change in emphasis from structural to behavioural regulation reflects important theoretical developments in the area of industrial organization over recent decades. It is now widely recognized that what matters for efficiency is not necessarily the number of rival suppliers that exist in a market per se but whether competitive pressure from incumbent or even potential market entrants is sufficient to induce firms to operate efficiently and to deter anti-competitive behaviour (Moschandreas, 2000: 364).

When interventions are called for to promote competition, ownership restrictions offer one possibility and regulation aimed at encouraging monopolistic firms into behaviour consistent with the public interest offers another. Behavioural interventions are less disruptive and controversial than requiring divestitures, but they do not curb market power directly in the way that structural remedies do and they are more easily evaded than other measures (OECD, 2008: 3–4). The behavioural approach holds out advantages in circumstances where monopolistic ownership is considered inevitable, for example, in the case of 'natural' monopoly. 'A natural monopoly arises when technology is such that economies of scale exist which are exhausted at a scale of operation which is so large in relation to the market that only one firm can operate efficiently' (Moschandreas, 2000: 364). Where there is only room in the market for one supplier, or just a few suppliers (i.e. a natural oligopoly), this implies that increased competition would only result in higher costs and less efficiency.

Many subsectors of the media have some natural monopoly or natural oligopoly characteristics. The prevalence of both economies of scale and scope means that joint production – i.e. production within one firm – of a set of media outputs may well be demonstrably cheaper than their production by a multitude of separate firms. In addition to supply-side economies of scale, for digitally delivered services the presence of network effects may act as a further stimulus towards expansion and monopolization. This situation presents a dilemma for policy-making. Whereas competition is generally seen as an essential stimulus to efficiency, the counter-argument may be mounted that ownership ceilings which promote competition result in an economic welfare loss by stopping media firms from realizing all available efficiencies and economies of scale and scope.

However, even when securing diversity of ownership involves sacrificing some potential efficiency gains, the advantages of having more than one supplier are often considered to take precedence. In the

UK, the general approach towards regulation of so-called natural monopolies such as gas, electricity and telephony has changed markedly since the 1980s (George, Joll and Lynk, 1992: 340). The post-war policy of exclusive public ownership of such activities has been reversed via a programme of privatization, regulation and efforts to promote competition. This new approach to 'the natural monopoly problem' highlights the perceived importance of introducing competitive pressures into industries that are prone to monopoly wherever this is feasible and whether or not it involves the loss of some potential efficiency gains (ibid.: 361).

MONOPOLIES AND TECHNOLOGICAL CHANGE

Digitization and growth of the Internet and of mobile devices have been major forces for change, vastly increasing competition in some media markets while also encouraging innovation and the development of new platforms, players and services. Alongside these developments, one of the most difficult challenges posed for media policy-makers has been that of how to deal with monopolies during periods of rapid technological change.

Digital convergence has prompted numerous mergers across communications and media and encouraged the development of major, enlarged vertically integrated businesses with interests in all stages of the vertical supply chain and that span digital as well as conventional delivery platforms. Much investment in digital infrastructures and content has come from existing large players in the media and communications industries such as BT, Telefonica, AOL Time Warner and Bertelsmann AG. Investment in new services in some cases has resulted in the emergence of de facto vertical and horizontal monopoly situations. For example, in the UK, the competition authorities have on numerous occasions considered complaints about BSkyB's position of dominance in relation to premium content inputs for pay-TV (i.e. sports and film) and its control over the prevalent conditional access technology for pay-TV (Grant and Wood, 2004: 184).

The spread of digital technology has also introduced many new and additional players into the business of selling advertising and supplying content. Growth of the Internet has spawned the development of innumerable online start-ups and new forms of communication and media-related services, such as content aggregators and online social media, many of which have grown in popularity with remarkable rapidity. Thanks to digitization, the landscape of media provision has expanded dramatically in the twenty-first century and the arrival of new functions and forms of service provision has, in turn, resulted in the development of several new dominant players in digital markets. For example, search engines have become indispensible in how people interface with media content on digital platforms (van Eijk, 2009). The transformation of digital start-ups such as Facebook and Google into enormous global players has precipitated concerns about new bottle-necks, gateway monopolies and control over access points to media.

The problem with monopolized control of specific phases or dimensions of the supply chain for digital media – e.g. navigation systems such as electronic programme guides (EPGs) or search engines – is that these functions are often located centrally between new service providers and viewers and so they occupy what is potentially a very powerful position. When individual firms have exclusive control over a vital activity or piece of infrastructure that all media suppliers need in order to reach viewers or to collect charges then, because of their control over the bottleneck, these firms are in a position to act as gate-keepers and to decide who may or may not be allowed market access. This has important implications for the public interest.

Gatekeepers are often vertically integrated firms with control not only of the gateway in question but also with an involvement in upstream and downstream activities. The problem is that vertically integrated gatekeepers have both the means and the incentive to favour their own services and to exclude rivals. Gateway monopolists can abuse their position either by denying access to rival service providers or by offering access on terms that are very disadvantageous to potential competitors. Like monopolists in any other situation, gatekeepers have the power to raise prices, restrict output and engage in other forms of behaviour that run contrary to the interests of consumers.

Search engines, whose function is to trawl the Internet for content and to structure and index it so that it becomes traceable, provide an example of a new bottleneck (Schulz, Held and Laudien, 2005; van Eijk, 2009). The costs involved in establishing and sustaining a database of up-to-date traceable content are considerable but income is derived through sale of advertisements, usually next to particular search terms on a 'pay per click' basis. Search engines are now a crucial gateway between digital content and audiences and, in how they rank and position responses to specific enquiries, they wield enormous power to shape and influence content-accessing decisions and therefore media consumption behaviours. At the same time, because economies of scale and network effects are prevalent, the industry is highly prone to monopolization. Despite the presence of a handful of rival players such as Yahoo, Ask and Baidu (in China), Google is by far the most dominant player in search across the globe with a market share of some 66 per cent in the US and in excess of 80 per cent in many European countries (Bradshaw, 2011c; comScore, 2012; Fairsearch, 2011).

Such dominance creates many possibilities for abuse of market power. The ranking which results from use of a search engine is determined by the underlying algorithm but search results can be and sometimes are manipulated by the service provider – search engines can simply sell higher positioning – or by investment in 'search engine optimization' techniques on the part of content providers (van Eijk, 2009). Manipulation of results is often not transparently visible to users. Search engines are increasingly investing in the development of upstream content services, thus establishing vertical market power and a clear incentive to give preferential treatment to in-house information services (Fairsearch, 2011: 14–28; van Eijk, 2009: 152). Abuses may occur if, in seeking to privilege certain content properties rather than others, some rival offerings are deliberately excluded against the wishes of content providers (Fairsearch, 2011). A position of predominance in the supply of search advertising also lays open the possibility of overcharging for advertising.

The function of online social networks such as Facebook and Twitter is quite different from that of search engines but they too, to a lesser extent, enjoy power to shape media selection choices and preferences, for example through systems of onward recommendation. As with Google, the rapid growth of Facebook has raised concerns about market dominance and about escalating charges for online advertising. Industry data suggests that the cost per click of advertising on Facebook in four of the world's largest markets increased by some 74 per cent in the 12 months to June 2011 (TBG Digital, cited in Bradshaw, 2011c: 17). As with Google, Facebook's strategy for commercial exploitation of users' personal data has been subject to much criticism, but the powerful position occupied by these companies (underlined, in the case of Facebook, by high switching costs for those choosing to withdraw from the world's most popular social network) means there has been little incentive to provide the privacy protections that consumers may want or need.

The relationship between monopoly and technological innovation is not altogether straightforward. Whereas some economists believe that monopolists tend to suppress the rate of new product innovation, others (following on from Schumpeter) take the view that 'firms need protection from competition before they will bear the risks and costs of invention' and so monopoly offers the ideal situation for innovation (Scherer and Ross, 1990: 31). Schumpeter put forward the argument that the incentive of being able to reap monopoly profits, at least in the short term, is absolutely vital in encouraging firms to innovate new products and, thus, in stimulating overall economic growth and technological progress.

Debates about the extent to which investors in the infrastructure of the Internet should be allowed to manage traffic in order to maximize their financial returns underline a conflict between, on the one hand, the Schumpeterian view that innovation ought to bring as its reward the right to exploit monopoly power at least temporarily versus, on the other, the conviction that the Internet is and should remain a completely open and free platform. Part of the concern to preserve 'net neutrality' stems from a wish to protect plurality of information sources and democracy (Lessig and McChesney, 2006). Arguments against allowing major telecommunications players and infrastructure owners to discriminate in how they treat Internet traffic, e.g. by prioritizing some types of traffic and slowing down or blocking others, also reflect worries about the potential for anti-competitive behaviour (Richards, 2010; Xavier and Paltridge, 2011: 25). Control over the Internet distribution pipeline may be abused by, for example, discriminating against or attempting to squeeze access to content services that compete with those provided by the infrastructure owner. As acknowledged by Ofcom's Chief Executive Ed Richards, the difficult challenge for media regulators in dealing with new bottlenecks is to 'avoid suppressing reward for innovation and risk' while, at the same time, 'avoid allowing the creation of an enduring monopoly with associated consequences' (Richards, 2010: 5).

In discussing the problems posed by regulation of gateway monopolies, Collins and Murroni point out that 'the characteristic regulatory response of imposing structural constraints on dominant firms is often at odds with the need to allow firms find their own shape during phases of transformation' (1996: 37). The high cost of activities such as laying broadband cable infrastructures or developing conditional access systems or developing databases of traceable data for a search engine service often militates against duplication by rivals, at least in the short term. Thus, structural interventions to prevent monopolized ownership of new technologies may have the unwelcome outcome of simply choking off rates of investment and innovation.

This implies that in order to encourage the development of new media monopolies may have to tolerated, at least in the short term, and their conduct regulated in such a way as to prevent anti-competitive behaviour. For some, the best response in a situation of dynamic technological change is to regulate behaviour to ensure that monopoly power is not abused (ibid.). For example, if implemented effectively, the requirement that gateway monopolists provide third-party access (for rivals to their vital facilities) on fair and non-discriminatory terms will help to promote wider market access. Under European competition law, natural monopoly bottlenecks are usually dealt with in this way under what is known as the 'essential facilities doctrine', which places a duty on monopolists to facilitate market access for rivals on fair and equal terms (Cowie, 1997; Nikolinakos, 2006).

The close interdependence between access to media content and access to distribution infrastructures has led to numerous calls for strengthened policies to tackle vertical cross-ownership. Some favour restrictions on cross-ownership between distribution activities and those that confer gatekeeping powers. Others are concerned about the need to avoid stifling innovation by introducing too much regulation. Most, however, emphasize the need for regulators to enforce open standards and procedures that allow interconnection and interoperability between rival technologies and that safeguard access points to the media for suppliers that are independent and unaffiliated.

The development of the computer tablet market, since the launch of the iPad in 2010, demonstrates how the potential for monopolization of key gateways can extend beyond content services, distribution pipelines and crucial interfaces to actual devices. Consumer take-up of tablets has been rapid – three million units of the third-generation iPad were sold in the first three days after its launch in March 2012 (Nutall, 2012) – and Apple has remained at the forefront with a share of the global tablet market in the order of 60 per cent (Alexander, 2012). Apple was also the initiator of mobile apps – a short form and simple version of software applications usually designed to run on smartphones and tablets – which have ballooned in popularity alongside growth in ownership of mobile devices. Many print publishers, having struggled to derive revenues from the Internet, have embraced iPad and other tablet apps as the ideal mode for development of digital versions of newspaper and magazine titles (Gelles, 2011a: 24). Investment is being propelled by evidence of strong consumer appetites for 'print' content on tablet apps which facilitate a more immersive and consumer-friendly experience. But Apple charges third-party content providers 'a 30 percent cut of all subscriber content sold directly through its iPads and iPhones' (Edgecliffe-Johnson and Gelles, 2011: 17). The company's predominance in the tablet market – its control over a key gateway to digital subscribers – is reflected in the terms publishers who want to use this platform to charge for content must accept.

Usage of tablets is growing rapidly, and some believe this will become the main platform over which most Web-connected media consumption will eventually take place. So the degree of gatekeeper power wielded by Apple in tablet and apps markets creates potential for distortions which could be far-reaching. One area of concern relates to Apple's decision not to support cross-platform software players such as Flash (made by Adobe) and Silverlight (made by Microsoft) on the iPad. The exclusion is defended on the basis that Flash is cumbersome and impairs the browsing experience of iPad and iPhone users so Apple wants to encourage software developers to use a new computer language, HTML5, instead. Critics note that because cross-platform players offer a means of delivering app-style functionality that is independent of specific devices and is universally accessible, their development poses a threat to the continuation of Apple's gatekeeping powers in the app market and its future revenues (Arah, 2011). So a wish to sustain and exploit vertical monopoly power provides an incentive to choke off the development of rival software initiatives whose development could benefit consumers and publishers by facilitating more open and competitive access to rich app-style functionality in the future.

Regulation of technical standards to promote open access and close supervision of the behaviour of dominant players are important means of avoiding problems that arise from bottlenecks and gateway monopolies. They cannot, however, guarantee to eliminate all inefficiencies associated with market dominance. The exercise of dominance across the supply chain for media does not simply imply the possibility of unfair pricing, vertical restraints and other restrictive practices which run contrary to public welfare. It may also involve an excessive expenditure of resources in order to gain strategic advantages over existing or potential competitors. A range of other inefficiencies, sometimes referred to as 'X-inefficiencies', may set in because of the adverse affect on managerial incentives and controls caused by lack of competitive pressure.

MAXIMIZING EFFICIENCY

Effective competition, involving many rather than just one or two rival suppliers, is clearly an ideal way to avoid the substantial range of economic deficiencies associated with excessive market dominance. To that end, the imposition of upper limits on media or cross-media ownership seems to offer useful safeguards for the process of competition and for the interests of media consumers. However, restrictions on media ownership also play a role in determining whether or not firms are allowed to reach their 'optimal' size and corporate configuration. Because of the economic characteristics of media discussed in earlier chapters, strategies of expansion within and across media industries *do*, in fact, quite often allow firms to make better use of the resources available for media provision. The fact that expansion gives rise to efficiency gains provides a compelling public interest case in favour of media ownership policies which encourage rather than curb such growth strategies.

Economies of scale are clearly a central feature of the economics of media. However, the potential efficiency gains arising from concentrated media ownership do not necessarily end there. The realization of scale economies by enlarged media firms may arguably, in turn, facilitate higher levels of gross investment and speedier adoption of new technologies. Faster-growing media firms may attract better-quality personnel. Expansion strategies may create the opportunity for cost reductions through elimination of overlapping or excess capacity (e.g. surplus printing or production capacity). In theory, all such efficiency gains represent a benefit not only for media firms but also for society at large.

The availability of a range of potential cost savings and improvements in efficiency as media firms expand and diversify suggests that the design of media and cross-media ownership policies will have important economic implications. Ownership policies determine whether firms operating in the media industry are permitted to arrive at the size and corporate structure most conducive to exploiting economies of scale and scope. Large and diversified media firms who can spread production costs across wider product and geographic markets will clearly benefit from a range of economies. A strong economic case can be made in favour of encouraging firms to exploit all such economies to the full so that unnecessary waste can be eliminated and the resources available for media provision can be used to best effect. Indeed, the desire to cultivate strong and efficient indigenous media firms capable of competing in global markets encouraged media policy-makers in many European countries to progressively deregulate media ownership restrictions from the 1990s onwards.

However, the concept of industrial efficiency is not just about minimizing costs. Efficiency implies producing output of the right quality and quantity to satisfy the needs and wants of society. Product diversity represents one aspect of quality. To the extent that diversity of media output is of greater value to society than uniformity of output, some duplication of media production resources need not be seen as wasteful but rather as contributing to efficiency.

As mentioned above, special policies to deal with ownership of the media generally owe their existence to concerns about pluralism, not economics. Even so, economic arguments have gained steadily and substantially greater importance in debates about media ownership policy over time. But a sharp reminder that special policies to deal with ownership of the media generally owe their existence to concerns about pluralism, not economics, was delivered when, in the course of investigations into illegal phone-hacking among journalists in the UK in 2011–12, the damaging ways in which high levels of corporate media ownership translate into political influence received widespread public attention. Pluralism and diversity remain the key concerns underlying public policy in this area. Nonetheless, economic analysis can play a useful role by helping policy-makers weigh up potential efficiency losses caused by fragmented ownership against the benefits of sustaining effective levels of competition.

PSBs AND STATE AID RULES

In regulating to promote competition in the media industry, one of the difficult questions regulators face is how to deal with PSBs (Jakubowicz, 2007). PSB entities are an integral aspect of the broadcasting ecology in many countries but their activities are open to criticism as harmful for competition (Cave, Collins and Crowther, 2004). As digitization has transformed patterns of media consumption, PSBs have sought to adjust accordingly and some have played important roles in pioneering multi-platform approaches to content distribution (Doyle, 2010a; Enli, 2008). The BBC's online news service, its additional niche channels on digital platforms and the iPlayer are all examples of initiatives that have met with popular audience approval. But expansion across digitally converged platforms has exacerbated concern among commercial rivals about potential anti-competitive impacts.

Whether or not PSBs fall under the scope of European competition rules has long been a controversial issue. Concerns that the sizeable funding received annually by Europe's public broadcasters creates an unlevel playing field led many rivals to complain to the Competition Directorate of the European Union in the 1990s. They argued that PSB funding amounted to state aid (where public authorities confer advantages on a selective basis to local companies) and, since state aid is prohibited under EU competition rules, should not be allowed. These concerns were debated and, in the end, the Commission's response was to clearly formalize the notion that the exceptional nature of broadcasting justifies an exclusion for PSBs from normal EU competition rules (CEC, 2001).

Despite this, the success of Europe's PSBs in extending the scope of their activities across new digital fixed and mobile platforms triggered a further resurgence of concerns about market dominance and unfair competition in the early twenty-first century. Rivals argued that PSBs use their public funding to invest not just in broadcasting (which, under the terms of the so-called Amsterdam Protocol, is exempt from state aid rules) but *also* in new digital services (which are not exempt). The involvement of well-funded PSB players in new digital media services has held back investment on the part of commercial rivals thus, they argue, holding back the competitiveness of the European commercial audiovisual sector in a wider global context.

Such complaints led to a revised communication on PSBs and state aid which introduces a requirement for a test of the impact on the market to be carried out each time a PSB entity decides it wishes to set up a 'significant' new media service (CEC, 2009). A transparent evaluation is required, prior to any launch, to assess whether the new service is really justified in terms of delivering some positive value to the public and also to consider what impact it may have on existing markets. However, some have questioned whether the public value test will be applied fairly and consistently in all EU member states and whether it will be rigorous enough (Donders and Pauwels, 2008). From the point of view of newspaper publishers, the fact that PSBs are prolific suppliers of high-quality news content that is available free of charge online has made it much more difficult to erect paywalls around their own offerings. The controversy surrounding PSBs and state aid exemplifies the increasingly complex challenges faced by regulators in weighing up how to integrate non-market with market provision of media content and services in the context of fundamental market transformations brought about by the digital revolution.

References

Advertising Association (2000) *The Advertising Statistics Yearbook 2000*. Henley-on-Thames: NTC Publications/Advertising Association.

Advertising Association (2005) *The Advertising Statistics Yearbook 2005*. London: Warc/Advertising Association.

Advertising Association (2008) *The Advertising Statistics Yearbook 2008*. London: Warc/Advertising Association.

Advertising Association (2009) *The Advertising Statistics Yearbook 2009*. London: Warc/Advertising Association.

Advertising Association/Warc, *Warc Expenditure Report*, at http://expenditure report.warc.com.

Aghion, P. and Howitt, P. (1992) 'A model of growth through creative destruction', *Econometrica*, 60 (2): 323–51.

Akerlof, G., Arrow, K., Bresnahan, T., Buchanan, J., Coase, R., Cohen, L., Friedman, M., Green, J., Hazlett, T., Hemphill, C., Noll, R., Schmalensee, R., Shavall, S., Varian, H. and Zeckhauser, R. (2002) *The Copyright Term Extension Act of 1998: An Economic Analysis*. AEI-Brookings Joint Center for Regulatory Studies, Brief 02-1 in support of petitioners in the Writ of Certiorari (Supreme Court of the U.S., E. Eldred et al. vs Ashcroft). Washington DC: AEI-Brookings Joint Center for Regulatory Studies.

Albarran, A. (2002) *Media Economics: Understanding Markets, Industries, and Concepts*, 2nd edn. Ames, IA: Iowa State Press.

Albarran, A. (2004) 'Media economics', in J. Downing, D. McQuail, P. Schlesinger and E. Wartella (eds), *The Sage Handbook of Media Studies*. Thousand Oaks, CA: Sage, pp. 291–308.

Alexander, R. (2012) 'Apple set to regain media tablet market share with release of new iPad model', IHS iSuppli press release. California: IHS iSuppli.

Allen, W., Doherty, N., Weigelt, K. and Mansfield, E. (2005) *Managerial Economics: Theory, Applications and Cases*, 6th edn. New York: W.W. Norton & Co.

Altmeppen, K., Lantzsch, K. and Will, A. (2007) 'Flowing networks in entertainment business: organizing international TV format trade', *The International Journal on Media Management*, 9 (3): 94–104.

Andari, R., Bakhshi, H., Hutton, W., O'Keeffe, A. and Schneider, P. (2007) *Staying Ahead: The Economic Performance of the UK's Creative Industries*. London: The Work Foundation.

Anderson, C. (2006) *The Long Tail: Why the Future of Business Is Selling Less of More*. New York: Hyperion.

Anderson, C. (2009) *Free: The Future of a Radical Price*. New York: Hyperion.

Angwin, J. (2010) 'The web's new gold mine: your secrets', *The Wall Street Journal*, 30 July, online.wsj.com/article/SB10001424052748703940904575395073512989404.html

Arah, T. (2011) 'The iPad 2: looks nice, plays ugly', *Pro PC* – blog posted 9 March, http://www.pcpro.co.uk/blogs/2011/03/09/the-ipad-2-looks-nice-plays-ugly.

Aris, A. and Bughin, J. (2009) *Managing Media Companies: Harnessing Creative Value*, 2nd edn. Chichester: John Wiley & Sons.

Armstrong, M. and Weeds, H. (2007) 'Public service broadcasting in the digital world', in P. Seabright and J. von Hagen (eds), *The Economic Regulation of Broadcasting Markets*. Cambridge: Cambridge University Press, pp. 81–149.

Arthur, C. (2011) 'It's fight or flight for Twitter', *Guardian*, Media Supplement, 5 May: 1.

Arvidsson, A. (2006) *Brands: Meaning and Value*. London: Routledge.

Bain, J. (1951) 'Relation of profit rate to industry concentration: American manufacturing (1936–1944)', *The Quarterly Journal of Economics*, 65 (3): 293–324.

Barwise, P. (1999) *Advertising in a Recession: The Benefits of Investing for the Long Term*. London: NTC Publications.

Bates, B. (2008) 'Commentary: value and digital rights management – a social economics approach', *Journal of Media Economics*, 21 (1): 53–77.

Baumol, W. (2002) *The Free-market Innovation Machine: Analyzing the Growth Miracle of Capitalism*. Princeton, NJ: Princeton University Press.

Baumol, W. and Blinder, A. (2011) *Macroeconomics: Principles and Policy*, 12th edn. Mason, OH: South-Western Cengage.

BBC (2010) 'BBC iPlayer celebrates a record-breaking 2010', BBC press release, 23 December.

Bennett, J. (2011) 'Introduction', in J. Bennett and N. Strange (eds), *Television as Digital Media*. Durham, NC: Duke University Press, pp. 1–30.

Bennett, J. and Strange, N. (eds) (2011) *Television as Digital Media*. Durham, NC: Duke University Press.

BFI (2011) *BFI Statistical Yearbook*. London: British Film Institute.

Bielby, W. and Bielby, D. (1994) 'All hits are flukes: institutionalized decision-making and the rhetoric of prime-time program development', *American Journal of Sociology*, 99 (5): 1287–313.

Blitz, R. and Fenton, B. (2011) 'Premier League faces TV rights shake-up', *Financial Times*, 4 November.

Blumler, J. and Nossiter, T. (eds) (1991) *Broadcasting Finance in Transition: A Comparative Handbook*. Oxford: Oxford University Press.

Boldrin, M. and Levine, D. (2008) *Against Intellectual Monopoly*. Cambridge: Cambridge University Press.

Born, G. (2003) 'Strategy, positioning and projection in digital television: Channel Four and the commercialization of PSB in the UK', *Media, Culture & Society*, 25: 773–99.

Bourreau, M. (2003) 'Mimicking vs. counter-programming strategies for television programs', *Information Economics and Policy*, 15: 35–54.

Bourreau, M. and Lethiais, V. (2007) 'Pricing information goods: free vs. pay content', in E. Brousseau and N. Curien (eds), *Internet and Digital Economics: Principle, Methods and Applications*. Cambridge: Cambridge University Press, pp. 345–67.

BRAD/PPA (2009) *Consumer Magazine Facts & Figures 2009*. www.ppamarketing.net/cgi-bin/go.pl/data-trends/article.html?uid=348.

Bradshaw, B. and Croft, J. (2011) 'Hollywood studios launch landmark online piracy case', *Financial Times*, 28 July: 1.

Bradshaw, T. (2009) 'Web beats TV to biggest advertising share', *Financial Times*, 30 September.

Bradshaw, T. (2011a) 'Twitter risks backlash with bolder adverts', *Financial Times*, 24 June: 15.

Bradshaw, T. (2011b) 'Havas chief backs Twitter over Facebook ads', *Financial Times*, 24 June: 15.

Bradshaw, T. (2011c) 'Facebook ad prices soar as brands shift spending online', *Financial Times*, 19 July: 17.

Bradshaw, T. and Edgecliffe-Johnson, A. (2009) 'Out of the box', *Financial Times*, 28 August, http://www.ft.com/cms/s/0/04b5a80c-9369-11de-b146-00144feabdc0.html#axzz2DbG90GJ6.

Brannon, E. and Bargouth, A. (2010) 'US cable networks pass broadband', *Screen Digest*, October: 301–08.

Bron, C. (2010) 'Financing and supervision of public service', in S. Nikoltchev (ed.), *Broadcasting Public Service Media: Money for Content, IRIS plus 2010-4*. Strasbourg: European Audiovisual Observatory, pp. 7–25.

Brown, D. (1999) *European Cable and Satellite Economics*. London: Screen Digest.

Brown, I. (2009) 'Can creative industries survive the digital onslaught?', *Financial Times*, 2 November, http://www.ft.com/cms/s/0/4f35215e-c745-11de-bb6f-00144feab49a.html#axzz1kwIlHU8B.

Bruck, P., Dorr, D., Cole, M., Favre, J., Gramstad, S., Monaco, M. and Culek, Z. (2004) *Transnational Media Concentrations in Europe*. Report prepared by the Advisory Panel on Media Concentrations, Pluralism and Diversity (AP-MD), Media Directorate, November. Strasbourg: Council of Europe.

Bulkley, K. (2011) 'The impact of Twitter on TV shows', *Guardian*, 6 June, http://www.guardian.co.uk/film/2011/jun/06/twitter-facebook-television-shows.

Burri, M. (2011) 'Reconciling trade and culture: a global law perspective', *The Journal of Arts Management, Law and Society*, 41: 1–21.

Burt, T. (2004) 'Breakthrough in TV's battle against piracy', *Financial Times*, 28 July: 7.

Caballero, R. (2006) *The Macroeconomics of Specificity and Restructuring*. Cambridge, MA: MIT Press.

Cabell, J. and Greehan, M. (2004) *International Magazine Publishing Handbook* (prepared by Cue Ball LLC for the International Federation of the Periodical Press). London: FIPP.

Caldwell, J. (2003) 'Second shift media aesthetics: programming, interactivity and user flows', in J. Caldwell and A. Everett (eds), *New Media: Theories and Practices of Digitextuality*. London: Routledge, pp. 127–44.

Caldwell, J. (2006) 'Critical industrial practice: branding, repurposing, and the migratory patterns of industrial texts', *Television & New Media*, 7 (2): 99–134.

Carlaw, K., Oxley, L., Walker, P., Thorns, D. and Nuth, M. (2006) 'Beyond the hype: intellectual property and the knowledge society/knowledge economy', *Journal of Economic Surveys*, 20 (4): 633–90.

Carter, M. (1998) 'Methodologies can bewilder', in The Advertising Industry, eight-page special report, *Financial Times*, 11 November: 6.

Cave, M. (1989) 'An introduction to television economics', in G. Hughes and D. Vines (eds), *Deregulation and the Future of Commercial Television, Hume Paper No 12*. Aberdeen: Aberdeen University Press, pp. 9–37.

Cave, M. (2002) *Review of Radio Spectrum Management: An Independent Review for Department of Trade and Industry and HM Treasury*. London: DTI/HM Treasury.

Cave, M. (2005) *Independent Audit of Spectrum Holdings: A Report for HM Treasury*. London: TSO.

Cave, M., Collins, R. and Crowther, P. (2004) 'Regulating the BBC', *Telecommunications Policy*, 28 (3–4): 249–72.

Caves, R. (2000) *Creative Industries: Contracts between Art and Commerce*. Cambridge, MA: Harvard University Press.

Caves, R. (2005) *Switching Channels: Organization and Change in TV Broadcasting*. Cambridge, MA: Harvard University Press.

CEC (2001) *Communication from the Commission on the Application of State Aid Rules to Public Service Broadcasting*, http://ec.europa.eu/competition/state_aid/legislation/broadcasting_communication_en.pdf.

CEC (2009) *Communication from the Commission on the Application of State Aid Rules to Public Service Broadcasting,* http://eur-lex.europa.eu/LexUriServ/LexUriServ.do?uri=CELEX:52009XC1027(01):EN:NOT.

Chalaby, J. (2010) 'The rise of Britain's super-indies: policy-making in the age of the global media market', *International Communication Gazette,* 72 (8): 675–93.

Chan-Olmsted, S. and Chang, B.-H. (2003) 'Diversification strategy of global media conglomerates: examining its patterns and determinants', *Journal of Media Economics,* 16 (4): 213–33.

Chang, B.-H. and Chan-Olmsted, S. (2005) 'Relative constancy of advertising spending: a cross-national examination of advertising expenditures and their determinants', *Gazette,* 67 (4): 339–57.

Chiplin, B. and Sturgess, B. (1981) *Economics of Advertising.* London: Advertising Association.

CMM-I (2007) *Trends in Audiovisual Markets: China, Mongolia and South Korea.* Beijing: UNESCO.

Coase, R. (1937) 'The nature of the firm', reprinted in O. Williamson and S. Winter, *The Nature of the Firm: Origins, Evolution and Development.* Oxford University Press, pp. 18–74.

Coase, R. (1959) 'The Federal Communications Commission', *Journal of Law and Economics,* 2: 1–40.

Coates, J. (2007) 'Creative commons – the next generation: creative commons licence use five years on', *SCRIPTed,* 4 (1): 72–94.

Cocq, E. and Levy, F. (2006) 'Audiovisual markets in the developing world: statistical assessment of 11 countries', in V. Gai (ed.), *Trends in Audiovisual Markets: Regional Perspectives from the South.* Paris: UNESCO, pp. 21–85.

Cocq, E. and Messerlin, P. (2004) 'French audio-visual policy: impact and compatibility with trade negotiations', in P. Guerrieri, L. Iapadre and G. Koopman (eds), *Cultural Diversity and International Economic Integration: The Global Governance of the Audiovisual Sector.* Cheltenham: Edward Elgar, pp. 21–51.

Cole, J. (2008) *Creative Destruction in the Digital Media Age.* Insead Knowledge, http://knowledge.insead.edu/CreativeDestructionDigitalMedia081112.cfm.

Collins, R., Garnham, N. and Locksley, G. (1988) *The Economics of Television: The UK Case.* London: Sage.

Collins, R. and Murroni, C. (1996) *New Media, New Policies: Media and Communications Strategies for the Future.* London: Polity Press.

Colwell, T. and Price, D. (2005) *Rights of Passage: British Television in the Global Market.* London: BTDA.

Competition Commission (2011) *Movies on Pay-TV Market Investigation: Provisional Findings Report,* 19 August. London: Competition Commission.

comScore (2012) *comScore Releases February 2012 US Search Engine Rankings*. Press release. New York: comScore.

Conlon, T. (2010) 'The next generation', *Guardian*, Media Supplement, 27 September: 1.

Cowie, C. (1997) 'Competition problems in the transition to digital television', *Media Culture & Society*, 19: 679–85.

Cox, H. and Mowatt, S. (2008) 'Technological change and forms of innovation in consumer magazine publishing: a UK-based study', *Technology Analysis & Strategic Management*, 20 (4): 503–20.

Cramton, P. (2002) 'Spectrum auctions', in M. Cave, S. Majumdar and I. Vogelsang (eds), *Handbook of Telecommunications Economics*. Amsterdam: Elsevier Science B.V., pp. 605–39.

Davies, G. (1999) *The Future Funding of the BBC, Report of the Independent Review Panel*. London: Department for Culture, Media and Sport.

Davies, G. (2004) *The BBC and Public Value*. London: The Social Market Foundation.

Davies, H. and Lam, P.-L. (2001) *Managerial Economics: An Analysis of Business Issues*, 3rd edn. London: FT Prentice Hall.

Davoudi, S. (2011) 'Cinemas set for Hollywood battle', *Financial Times*, 2 May: 3.

de Vany, A. (2004) *Hollywood Economics: How Extreme Uncertainty Shapes the Film Industry*. London: Routledge.

Dembosky, A. (2011) 'Facebook pokes big brands into action', *Financial Times*, 25 June: 10.

Demers, D. (1999) *Global Media: Menace or Messiah?* Creskill, NJ: Hampton Press.

Deresky, H. (2006) *International Management: Managing Across Borders and Cultures*, 5th edn. Upper Saddle River, NJ: Pearson Prentice Hall.

Dickson, P. and Ginter, J. (1987) 'Market segmentation, product differentiation, and marketing strategy', *The Journal of Marketing*, 51 (2): 1–10.

Donders, K. and Pauwels, C. (2008) 'Does EU policy challenge the digital future of public service broadcasting? An Analysis of the Commission's state aid approach to digitization and the public service remit of public broadcasting organizations, *Convergence*, 14 (3): 295–311.

Doyle, G. (2000) 'The economics of monomedia and cross-media expansion', *Journal of Cultural Economics*, 24: 1–26.

Doyle, G. (2002) *Media Ownership: The Economics and Politics of Convergence and Concentration in the UK and European Media*. London: Sage.

Doyle, G. (2006) 'Managing global expansion of media products and brands: a case study of FHM', *International Journal on Media Management*, 8 (3): 105–15.

Doyle, G. (2010a) 'From television to multi-platform: more for less or less from more?', *Convergence*, 16 (4): 1–19.

Doyle, G. (2010b) 'Why culture attracts and resists economic analysis', *Journal of Cultural Economics*, 34 (4): 245–59.

Doyle, G. (2011) 'Magazines', in S. Cameron (ed.), *The Economics of Leisure*, Cheltenham: Edward Elgar Publishing, pp. 720–51.

Doyle, G. (2012a) 'Audiovisual services: international trade and cultural policy', *ADBI Working Paper 355,* Tokyo, Japan: Asian Development Bank Institute.

Doyle, G. (2012b) 'Innovation in use of digital infrastructures: TV scheduling strategies and reflections on public policy'. Paper presented at the International Symposium on Media Innovations, University of Oslo, Oslo, 20 April.

Doyle, G. and Paterson, R. (2008) 'Public policy and independent television production in the UK', *Journal of Media Business Studies*, 5 (3): 17–33.

Duffy, S. (2006) 'Internet protocol versus intellectual property', in C. Sinclair (ed.), *Transforming Television: Strategies for Convergence*. Glasgow: The Research Centre, pp. 36–41.

Duncan, A. (2006) 'Maximising public value in the "now" media world', in C. Sinclair (ed.), *Transforming Television: Strategies for Convergence*. Glasgow: The Research Centre, pp. 18–29.

Duncan, W.D. (1981) *The Economics of Advertising*. London: Macmillan.

ECJ (2011) 'Judgement in Cases C-403/08 and C-429/08', press release No 102/11, 4 October. Luxembourg: Court of Justice of the European Union.

Economides, N. (2007) 'The internet and network economics', in E. Brousseau and N. Curien (eds), *Internet and Digital Economics: Principle, Methods and Applications*. Cambridge: Cambridge University Press, pp. 239–67.

Edgecliffe-Johnson, A. (2009) 'A want to break free', *Financial Times*, 18 May: 11.

Edgecliffe-Johnson, A. (2011a) 'TV economics rests on Super Bowl's shoulders', *Financial Times*, 26 January: 22.

Edgecliffe-Johnson, A. (2011b) 'Murdoch makes film plea to China', *Financial Times*, 13 June: 24.

Edgecliffe-Johnson, A. (2011c) 'Internet chief plays to the audience', *Financial Times*, 20 June: 23.

Edgecliffe-Johnson, A. (2011d) 'Zenith to cut media spending forecasts', *Financial Times*, 5 December: 5.

Edgecliffe-Johnson, A. (2012) 'ABC and Univision eye English-speaking Hispanics', *Financial Times*, 8 May: 21.

Edgecliffe-Johnson, A. and Gelles, D. (2011) 'Apple demands 30% slice of subscriptions sold via apps', *Financial Times*, 16 February: 17.

Edgecliffe-Johnson, A. and Pignal, S. (2011) 'EMI scores a hit as Brussels agrees to extend copyright on recordings', *Financial Times*, 9 September: 17.

Elstein, D. (2004) 'Building public value: a new definition of public service broadcasting.' 19th IEA Current Controversies Paper. London: Institute of Economic Affairs.

Enli, G. (2008) 'Redefining public service broadcasting: multi-platform participation', *Convergence: The International Journal of Research into New Media Technologies*, 14 (1): 105–20.

Epstein, R. (2011) Regulators take the wrong path on Comcast-NBC, *Financial Times*, FT.com New Technology Policy Forum, 9 February, http://www.ft.com/cms/s/0/c5245b60-34a3-11e0-9ebc-00144feabdc0.html#axzz2CreJ4jPp.

Esser, A. (2010) 'Television formats: primetime staple, global market', *Popular Communication*, 8 (4): 273–92.

Evans, D. (2009) 'The online advertising industry: economics, evolution, and privacy', *Journal of Economic Perspectives*, 23 (3): 37–60.

Evans, D. and Schmalensee, R. (2008) 'Industrial organization of markets with two-sided platforms' in W. Collins (ed.) *Issues in Competition Law and Policy*. Chicago: American Bar Association, pp. 667–93.

Experian Hitwise (2011) 'Experian launches new tool to help retailers drive Facebook fans to their websites', *Hitwise* press release, 23 June, http://www.hitwise.com/uk/press-centre/press-releases/experian-launches-facebook-tool-to-help-retailer/.

Fairsearch (2011) *Google's Transformation From Gateway To Gatekeeper: How Google's Exclusionary And Anticompetitive Conduct Restricts Innovation And Deceives Consumers*. US Fairsearch Coalition, October, http://www.fairsearch.org/wp-content/uploads/2011/10/Googles-Transformation-from-Gateway-to-Gatekeeper.pdf.

Farrell, J. and Klemperer, P. (2007) 'Coordination and lock-in: competition with switching costs and network effects', in M. Armstrong and R. Porter (eds), *Handbook of Industrial Organisation*, vol. 3. New York: Elsevier, pp. 1967–2072.

Farrell, J. and Saloner, G. (1985) 'Standardization, compatibility, and innovation', *Rand Journal*, 16: 70–83.

Feintuck, M. (1999) *Media Regulation, Public Interest and the Law*. Edinburgh: Edinburgh University Press.

Fenton, B. (2010) 'Grade urges BBC and C4 to share licence fee', *Financial Times*, 25 November: 4.

Fenton, B. (2011a) 'STV rebounds as legal fight with ITV ends', *Financial Times*, 28 April: 21.

Fenton, B. (2011b) 'Ruling draws in music and films', *Financial Times*, 5 October: 3.

Fisher, T., Prentice, D. and Waschik, R. (2010) *Managerial Economics: A Strategic Approach*, 2nd edn. London: Routledge.

Flew, T. (2009) 'Online media and user-created content: case studies in news media repositioning in the Australian media environment'. Paper presented to the Australian and New Zealand Communications Association (ANZCA) Conference, ANZCA09: Communication, Creativity and Global Citizenship, Queensland University of Technology, Brisbane, Australia, 8–10 July 2009.

Florida, R. (2002) *The Rise of the Creative Class*. New York: Basic Books.

Foster, R. and Broughton, T. (2011) *Creative UK: The Audiovisual Sector and Economic Success*. London: Communications Chambers.

Freeman, M. (2008) 'The changing media landscape: an industry perspective', in E. Humphreys (ed.), *International Copyright and Intellectual Property Law*, JIBS Research Report Series No 2008–2. Jonkoping: Jonkoping International Business School, pp. 111–26.

Friedrichsen, M. and Mühl-Benninhaus, W. (2012) 'Convergence and business models: innovation in daily newspaper economy – case of Germany'. Paper presented at the 10th World Media Economics & Management Conference, Aristotle University of Thessaloniki, Thessaloniki, 26 May.

Frith, S. and Marshall, L. (2004) 'Making sense of copyright', in S. Frith and L. Marshall (eds), *Music and Copyright*, 2nd edn. Edinburgh: Edinburgh University Press, pp. 1–18.

Galbraith, J.K. (1967) *The New Industrial State*. Boston, MA: Houghton-Mifflin Company.

Gapper, J. (1998) 'America's networks take a stern look at prospects', *Financial Times*, 6 April: 22.

Gapper, J. (2005) 'A variety act from the comedians at Time Warner's gate', *Financial Times*, 11/12 February: 7.

Gapper, J. (2011) 'Why it is right to fight web pirates', *Financial Times*, 26 May: 13.

García Avilés, J., and Carvajal, M. (2008) 'Integrated and cross-media newsroom convergence', *Convergence: The International Journal of Research into New Media Technologies*, 14 (2): 221–39.

Garrahan, M. (2009) 'Hollywood braced for budget cuts', *Financial Times*, 7 October: 15.

Garrahan, M. (2010) 'Cable groups suffer as viewers switch to video streaming', *Financial Times*, 29 November: 22.

Garrahan, M. (2011a) 'Show me the money: US sport cashes in on broadcasting', *Financial Times*, 23 June, http://www.ft.com/cms/s/0/5eec9f78-9ccd-11e0-bf57-00144feabdc0.html#axzz2DbG90GJ6.

Garrahan, M. (2011b) 'A cloud up in the air', *Financial Times*, 1 August: 5.

Garrett, S. (2011) 'One football result could be the end for Spooks', *Times*, 4 November: 11.

Gasson, C. (1996) *Media Equities: Evaluation and Trading*. Cambridge: Woodhead Publishing Ltd.

Gelles, D. (2011a) 'Comcast buoyed by integration', *Financial Times*, 4 August: 19.

Gelles, D. (2011b) 'Magazines pin hope on new app', *Financial Times*, 30 September: 24.

Gelles, D. (2012) 'Advertisers rush to master fresh set of skills', Digital & Social Media Marketing, four-page special report, *Financial Times*, 7 March: 1–2.

Gelles, D. and Edgecliffe-Johnson, A. (2011) 'Television: inflated assets', *Financial Times*, 24 March, http://www.ft.com/cms/s/0/d2a693b2-5653-11e0-82aa-00144feab49a.html#axzz2DbG90GJ6.

Gelles, D. and Waters, R. (2010) 'Google prepares for head-to-head battle with Facebook', *Financial Times*, 16 August: 22.

George, K., Joll, C. and Lynk, E. (1992) *Industrial Organization: Competition, Growth and Structural Change*, 4th edn. London: Routledge.

Gershon, R. (2011) 'Intelligent networks and international business communication: a systems theory interpretation', *Media Markets Monographs*, Issue 12. Pamplona: Servicio de Publicaciones de la Universidad de Navarra.

Gershon, R. (2012) 'Media innovation: three strategic approaches to business transformation'. Paper presented at the 10th World Media Economics & Management Conference, Aristotle University of Thessaloniki, Thessaloniki, 24 May.

Gottinger, H. (2003) *Economics of Network Industries*. London: Routledge.

Gowers, A. (2006) *The Gowers Review of Intellectual Property*. London: TSO.

Graham, A. (ed.) (1999) *Public Purposes in Broadcasting: Funding the BBC*. Luton: University of Luton Press.

Graham, A. and Davies G. (1997) *Broadcasting, Society and Policy in the Multimedia Age*. Luton: John Libbey.

Graham, R., and Frankenburger, K. (2011) 'The earnings effects of marketing communication expenditures during recessions', *Journal of Advertising*, 40(2): 5–24.

Grainge, P. (2008) *Brand Hollywood: Selling Entertainment in a Global Media Age*. London: Routledge.

Grande, C. (2007) 'New advertising genre with few rules', *Financial Times*, 10 April, http://www.ft.com/cms/s/0/8805c9f4-e636-11db-9fcf-000b5df10621.html#axzz2DbG90GJ6.

Grant, P. and Wood, C. (2004) *Blockbusters and Trade Wars: Popular Culture in a Globalized World*. Toronto: Douglas and Mclnytre.

Griffiths, A. and Wall, S. (2007) *Applied Economics*, 11th edn. Harlow: Pearson Education.

Guerrieri, P., Iapadre, L. and Koopman, G. (2004) *Cultural Diversity and International Economic Integration: The Global Governance of the Audiovisual Sector*. Cheltenham: Edward Elgar.

Gutteridge, T., O'Donoghue, D., Mulville, J., Brand, C. and Smith, P. (2000), 'We will fight for our rights', *Guardian,* Media Supplement, 4 December: 2–3.

Hafez, K. (2007) *The Myth of Media Globalisation*. Cambridge: Polity.

Hafstrand, H. (1995) 'Consumer magazines in transition: a study of approaches to internationalisation', *Journal of Media Economics*, 8 (1): 1–12.

Halliday, J. (2011) 'Hollywood offers films at home within weeks of cinema release', *Guardian*, 2 April: 43.

Hancock, D. and Zhang, X. (2010) 'Europe's top 100 film distributors: Hollywood accounts for nearly two-thirds of revenues', *Screen Digest*, November: 330–31.

Handke, C. (2010) *The Economics of Copyright and Digitisation: A Report on the Literature and the Need for Further Research*. London: SABIP.

Handley, L. (2012) 'Getting the measure of social media success', *Marketing Week*, 16 February: 12–16.

Hargreaves, I. (2011) *Digital Opportunity: A Review of Intellectual Property and Growth*. London: TSO.

Haynes, R. (2005) *Media Rights and Intellectual Property*. Edinburgh: Edinburgh University Press.

Headland, J. and Relph, S. (1991) *The View From Downing Street. UK Film Initiatives 1*. London: BFI.

Hesmondhalgh, D. (2002) *The Cultural Industries*. London: Sage.

Hesmondhalgh, D. and Pratt, A. (2005) 'Cultural industries and cultural policy', *International Journal of Cultural Policy*, 11 (1): 1–14.

Highfield, A. (2006) 'The future role of the BBC as a broadcaster on the web', in C. Sinclair (ed.), *Transforming Television: Strategies for Convergence*. Glasgow: TRC, pp. 48–52.

Hoskins, C., McFadyen, S. and Finn, A. (1997) *Global Television and Film: An Introduction to the Economics of the Business*. Oxford: Oxford University Press.

Hoskins, C., McFadyen, S. and Finn, A. (2004) *Media Economics: Applying Economics to New and Traditional Media*. Thousand Oaks, CA: Sage.

Hughes, G. and Vines, D. (1989) *Deregulation and the Future of Commercial Television*. Aberdeen: The David Hume Institute, Aberdeen University Press.

Humphreys, E. (2008) 'International copyright and the TV format industry', in E. Humphreys (ed.), *International Copyright and Intellectual Property Law*. JIBS Research Report Series No 2008–2, Jonkoping: Jonkoping International Business School, pp. 71–9.

Humphreys, P. (2010) 'Public policies for public service media: the UK and German cases'. Paper presented at RIPE Conference on Public Service after the Recession, University of Westminster, 8–11 September, http://ripeat.org/?s=humphreys&cat=411.

Ihlebæk, K., Syvertsen, T. and Ytreberg, E. (2012) 'Transformations of TV scheduling in a time of channel fragmentation and multi-platform development'. Paper presented at the International Symposium on Media Innovations, University of Oslo, Oslo, 20 April.

ITC (2002) *Programme Supply Review*. London: Independent Television.

Jackson, M. (2006) 'The economics of social networks', in R. Blundell, W. Newey and T. Persson (eds), *Advances in Economics and Econometrics, Theory and Applications: Ninth World Congress of the Econometric Society*. Cambridge: Cambridge University Press, pp. 1–56.

Jaffe, G. (2011) 'Will the great film quota wall of China come down?', *Guardian*, Film & Music Supplement, 25 March: 4.

Jakubowicz, K. (2007) *Public Service Broadcasting: A New Beginning, or the Beginning of the End?*www.knowledgepolitics.org.uk.

Jarvis, J. (2009) 'Digital media: another one bites the dust', *Guardian*, Media Supplement, 4 May: 6.

Jedidi, K., Krider, R. and Weinberg, C. (1998) 'Clustering at the movies', *Marketing Letters*, 9 (4): 393–405.

Jenkins, H. (2006) *Convergence Culture*. New York: New York University Press.

Johnson, C. (2007) 'Tele-branding in TVIII: the network as brand and the programme as brand', *New Review of Film and Television Studies*, 5 (1): 5–24.

Johnson, J. and Waldman, M. (2005) 'The limits of indirect appropriability in markets for copiable goods', *Review of Economic Research on Copyright Issues*, 2 (1): 19–37.

Johnson, R. (2008) 'Facebook and MySpace lock horns for social networking future', *Guardian*, 7 November. http://www.guardian.co.uk/technology/2008/nov/07/facebook-myspace.

Jopson, B. (2012) 'Colgate vows to brush up on its advertising spend', *Financial Times*, 27 January: 15.

Joye, S. (2009) 'Novelty through repetition: exploring the success of artistic imitation in the contemporary film industry', *Scope: an online journal of film & tv studies*, 15.

Katz, M. and Shapiro, C. (1985) 'Network externalities, competition, and compatibility', *American Economic Review*, 75: 424–40.

Kay, J. (2011) 'It's mad to give my heirs rights to a student lit crit essay', *Financial Times*, 23 March: 15.

Kirwan, P. (2010) 'Is the *Financial Times* the perfect digital model?', *Guardian*, Media Supplement, 5 April: 9.

Kolo, C. and Vogt, P. (2003) 'Strategies for growth in the media and communication industry: does size really matter?' *International Journal on Media Management*, 5 (4): 251–61.

Koski, H. and Kretschmer, T. (2004) 'Survey on competing in network industries: firm strategies, market outcomes, and policy implications', *Journal of Industry, Competition and Trade*, 4 (1): 5–31.

Krone, J. and Grueblbauer, J. (2012) 'Convergence and business models: innovation in daily newspaper economy – case of Austria'. Paper presented at the 10th World Media Economics & Management Conference, Aristotle University of Thessaloniki, Thessaloniki, 26 May.

Krumsvik, A., Skogerbø, E. and Storsul, T. (2012) 'Size, ownership, and innovations in newspapers'. Paper presented at the International Symposium on Media Innovations, University of Oslo, Oslo, 20 April.

Küng, L (2008) *Strategic Management in the Media: Theory to Practice*. London: Sage.

Küng, L., Picard, R. and Towse, R. (2008) *The Internet and the Mass Media*. London: Sage.

Landes, W. and Posner, R. (1989) 'An economic analysis of copyright law', *Journal of Legal Studies*, 8: 325–63.

Leahy, J. (2010) 'Battle for 3G licences in India hots up', *Financial Times* (Asia), 28 April: 16.

Lessig, L. (2002) *The Future of Ideas: The Fate of the Commons in a Connected World*. London: Vintage.

Lessig, L. (2009) *Remix: Making Art and Commerce Thrive in the Hybrid Economy*. London: Bloomsbury.

Lessig, L and McChesney, R. (2006) 'No tolls on the internet', *Washington Post*, 8 June: A23.

Levine, R. (2011) *Free Ride: How the Internet is Destroying the Culture Business and how the Culture Business can Fight Back*. London: Bodley Head.

Levy, D. (2008) 'The way ahead: towards a new Communications Act', in T. Gardam and D. Levy, *The Price of Plurality: Choice, Diversity and Broadcasting Institutions in the Digital Age*. Oxford: OFCOM, Reuters Institute for the Study of Journalism, pp. 209–16.

Lewis, R. and Marris, P. (1991) *Promoting the Industry, UK Film Initiatives 3*. London: British Film Institute.

Li, K. and Edgecliffe-Johnson, A. (2009) 'Three-way battle to reshape TV economics', *Financial Times*, 31 October: 20.

Liebowitz, S. (1985) 'Copying and indirect appropriability: photocopying of journals', *Journal of Political Economy*, 93 (5): 945–57.

Liebowitz, S. (2003) 'Back to the future: can copyright owners appropriate revenues in the face of new copying technologies?', in W.J. Gordon and R. Watt (eds), *The Economics of Copyright: Developments in Research and Analysis*. Cheltenham, UK and Northampton, MA, Edward Elgar, pp. 1–25.

Liebowitz, S. (2006) 'File sharing: creative destruction or just plain destruction?', *Journal of Law and Economics*, 49 (1): 1–28.

Liebowitz, S. and Margolis, S. (1994) 'Network externality – an uncommon tragedy', *Journal of Economic Perspectives*, 8 (2): 133–50.

Lilley, A. (2006) *Inside the Creative Industries: Copyright on the Ground*. London: Institute for Public Policy Research.

Lipsey, R. and Chrystal, A. (1995) *Positive Economics*, 8th edn. Oxford: Oxford University Press.

Lipsey, R. and Chrystal, A (2007) *Positive Economics*, 11th edn Oxford: Oxford University Press.

Litman, B. (1998) 'The economics of television networks: new dimensions and new alliances', in A. Alexander, J. Owers and R. Carveth, *Media Economics: Theory and Practice*, 2nd edn. NJ: Lawrence Erlbaum Associates, pp. 131–50.

Loeffler, T. (2010) 'Online film spending near doubled', *Screen Digest*, April: 105.

Lotz, A. (2007) *The Television will be Revolutionized*. New York: New York University Press.

Luft, O. (2009) 'Stuck in the middle', *Guardian*, Media Supplement, 5 January: 5.

Martin, S. (2002) *Advanced Industrial Economics*, 2nd edn. Oxford: Blackwell.

McClintock, P. (2008) 'MPAA: specialty films see rising costs; 2007 the best year on record for box office', *Variety*, 5 March, accessed 25 July 2011, http://variety.com/article/VR1117981882?refcatid=18.

McCraw, T. (2007) *Prophet of Destruction: Joesph Schumpter and Creative Destruction*. Cambridge, MA: Harvard University Press.

Medina, M. and Prario, B. (2012) 'The impact of digital convergence and mobile devices on traditional media companies: Mediaset and Antena 3'. Paper presented at the 10th World Media Economics & Management Conference, Aristotle University of Thessaloniki, Thessaloniki, 26 May.

Menn, J. (2011) 'Yahoo talks up video, content strategy', *Financial Times*, 26 May. Accessed at FT.com tech blog at http://blogs.ft.com/tech-blog/2011/05/yahoo-talks-up-video-content-strategy/#axzz2DdTpGzxS.

Metcalfe, J. (1998) *Evolutionary Economics and Creative Destruction*. London: Routledge.

Monge, P., Heiss, B. and Magolin, D. (2008) 'Communication network evolution in organizational communities', *Communication Theory*, 18 (4): 449–77.

Moran, A. with Malbon, J. (2006) *Understanding the Global TV Format*. Bristol: Intellect.

Moschandreas, M. (2000) *Business Economics*, 2nd edn. London: Thomson Learning.

Moules, J. (2009) 'The schoolboy dream grows up', *Financial Times*, 8 July: 20.

MPAA (Motion Pictures Association of America) (2010) *Trade Barriers to US Filmed Entertainment*. Washington, DC: Motion Pictures Association of America.

MPAA (2011) *Theatrical Market Statistics 2010*. Los Angeles, CA: Motion Pictures Association of America.

Murray, S. (2005) 'Brand loyalties: rethinking content within global corporate media', *Media Culture & Society*, 27 (3): 415–35.

Napoli, P. (2011) *Audience Evolution: New Technologies and the Transformation of Media Audiences*. New York: Columbia University Press.

Nayarodou, M. (2006) Advertising and economic growth, summary of doctoral thesis in economics. Paris: Unions des Annonceurs (UDA).

Nieminen, H., Koikkalainen, K. and Karppinen, K. (2012) 'Convergence and business models: innovation in daily newspaper economy – case of Finland'. Paper presented at the 10th World Media Economics & Management Conference, Aristotle University of Thessaloniki, Thessaloniki, 26 May.

Nikolinakos, N. (2006) *EU Competition Law and Regulation in the Converging Telecommunications Media and IT Sectors*. Gravenhage: Kluwer Law International.

Noam, E. (1993) 'Media Americanization, national culture, and forces of integration', in E. Noam and J. Millonzi (eds), *The International Market in Film and Television Programs*. Norwood, NJ: Ablex, pp. 41–58.

Noll, M. (2003) 'The myth of convergence', *The International Journal on Media Management*, 5 (1): 12–13.

Nutall, C. (2012) 'Apple sells 3m iPads in 4 days', *Financial Times*, 18 March, www.ft.com/cms/s/0/012da836-7216-11e1-90b5-00144feab49a.html #axzz2DbG90GJ6.

O'Malley, L., Story, V. and O'Sullivan, V. (2011) 'Marketing in a recession: retrench or invest?', *Journal of Strategic Marketing*, 19 (3): 285–310.

Oberholzer-Gee, F. and Strumpf, K. (2007) 'The effect of file sharing on record sales: an empirical analysis', *Journal of Political Economy*, 115 (1): 1–42.

Odlyzko, A. and Tilly, B. (2005) *A Refutation of Metcalfe's Law and a Better Estimate for the Value of Networks and Network Interconnections*, http://www.dtc.umn.edu/~odlyzko/doc/metcalfe.pdf.

OECD (2008) *Remedies and Sanctions for Abuse of Market Dominance, Policy Brief*. Paris: Organisation for Economic Co-operation and Development (OECD).

Ofcom (2008) *Ofcom's Second PSB Review – Phase One: The Digital Opportunity, Annex 11: Market Failure in Broadcasting, April*. London: Ofcom.

Ofcom (2009) *International Communications Market Report,* December. London: Ofcom.

Ofcom (2010a) *Communications Market Report,* 19 August. London: Ofcom.

Ofcom (2010b) *International Communications Market Report,* 2 December. London: Ofcom.

Ofcom (2011a) *Communications Market Report,* August. London: Ofcom.

Ofcom (2011b) *International Communications Market Report,* 14 December. London: Ofcom.

OFT (Office of Fair Trading) (2008) *Completed Acquisition by Global Radio UK Limited of GCap Media plc.* Decision: ME/3638 /08, 27 August. London: OFT.

Oliver & Ohlbaum Associates Ltd (2006) *UK Television Content in the Digital Age: Opportunities and Challenges, Report for PACT.* London: PACT.

Ots, M. (ed.) (2008) *Media Brands and Branding.* JIBS Research Report Series No. 2008-1, MMTC. Jonkoping: Jonkoping International Business School.

Owen, B. and Wildman, S. (1992) *Video Economics.* Cambridge, MA: Harvard University Press.

Owers, J. Carveth R. and Alexander, A. (2002) 'An introduction to media economics theory and practice', in A. Alexander, J. Owers, R. Carveth, A. Hollifield and A. Greco (eds), *Media Economics: Theory and Practice,* 3rd edn. Mahwah, NJ: Erlbaum, pp. 3–48.

Oxera (2011) *Is There a Case for Copyright Levies: An Economic Impact Analysis?* London: Oxera Consulting Ltd.

PACT (2010) Written Evidence to Business, Innovation and Skills Committee, 24 September.

Pardo, A., Guerrero, E. and Diego, P. (2012) 'Multiplatform strategies of the Spanish TV industry'. Paper presented at the 10th World Media Economics & Management Conference, Aristotle University of Thessaloniki, Thessaloniki, 24 May.

Parker, R. (2007) 'Focus: 360-degree commissioning', *Broadcast,* 13 September: 11.

Parker, R. (ed.) (2011) 'Indies: the annual survey of the UK's independent TV producers 2011', *Broadcast Supplement,* 18 March.

Parkin, M., Powell, M. and Matthews, K. (2008) *Economics,* 7th edn. Harlow: Pearson Education.

Patterson, T. (2007) *Creative Destruction: An Exploratory Look at News on the Internet,* Report from the Joan Shorenstein Center on the Press, Politics and Public Policy. New York: Harvard University.

Peacock, A. (1996) *The Political Economy of Broadcasting, Essays in Regulation No. 7.* Oxford: Regulatory Policy Institute.

Peitz, M. and Waelbroeck, P. (2006) 'Why the music industry may gain from free downloading: the role of sampling', *International Journal of Industrial Organization*, 24 (5): 907–13.

Peltier, S. (2004) 'Mergers and acquisitions in the media industries: were failures really unforeseeable?', *Journal of Media Economics*, 17 (4): 261–78.

Picard, R. (1989) *Media Economics: Concepts and Issues*. London: Sage.

Picard, R. (2002) *The Economics and Financing of Media Companies*. New York: Fordham University Press.

Picard, R. (ed.) (2005) *Media Product Portfolios: Issues in Management of Multiple Products and Services*. Mahwah, NJ: Lawrence Erlbaum Associates.

Picard, R. (2006) 'Comparative aspects of media economics and its development in Europe and the USA', in J. Heinrich and G. Kopper (eds), *Media Economics on Europe*. Berlin: Vistas Verlag, pp. 15–23.

Porter, M. (1985) *Competitive Advantage*. New York: Free Press.

Porter, V. (1999) 'Public service broadcasting and the new global information order', *InterMedia*, 27 (4): 34–7.

Pringle, P and Starr, M. (2006) *Electronic Media Management*. Burlington, MA: Elsevier.

PwC (2011) *Global entertainment and media outlook: 2011–2015*. London: PricewaterhouseCoopers LLP.

PwC (2012) 'PwC analysis – M&A trends in the European entertainment & media industry', *PwC Press Release*, 31 January. London: Pricewaterhouse Coopers.

Reding, V. (2006) 'Digital convergence: a whole new way of life', in C. Sinclair (ed.), *Transforming Television: Strategies for Convergence*. Glasgow: TRC, pp. 30–34.

Richards, E. (2010) 'Competition law and the communications sector'. Speech by Ofcom Chief Executive for UCL Jevons Institute for Competition Law and Economics Annual Colloquium, 13 July. London: Ofcom.

Richards, E. (2011) 'Spectrum in an age of innovation'. Speech by Ofcom Chief Executive for The European Competitive Telecommunications Association (ECTA) Regulatory Conference 2011, 29 November. London: Ofcom.

Rochet, J. and Tirole, J. (2003) 'Platform competition in two-sided markets', *Journal of the European Economic Association*, 1 (4): 990–1029.

Romer, P. (2002) 'When should we use intellectual property rights?', *American Economic Review: Papers & Proceedings*, 92 (2): 213–16.

Roscoe, J. (2004) 'Multi-platform event television: reconceptualizing our relationship with television', *The Communications Review*, 7: 363–69.

Rosen, S. (1981) 'The economics of superstars', *American Economic Review*, 71 (5): 845–58.

Rossiter, A. (2005) *News Broadcasting in the Digital Age The Need for PSB Genre Licences*. London: The Social Market Foundation.

Samuelson, P. (1976) *Economics*. New York: McGraw Hill.

Sánchez-Tabernero, A. (2006) 'Issues in media globalisation', in A. Albarran, S. Chan-Olmsted and M. Wirth (eds), *Handbook of Media Management and Economics*. Mahwah, NJ: Lawrence Erlbaum Associates, pp. 463–91.

Sánchez-Tabernero, A. and Carvajal, M. (2002) *Media Concentrations in the European Market, New Trends and Challenges, Media Markets Monograph*. Pamplona, Spain: Servicio de Publiciones de la Universidad de Navarra.

Scherer, F. and Ross, D. (1990) *Industrial Market Structure and Economic Performance*, 3rd edn. Boston, MA: Houghton Mifflin.

Schlesinger, P (2007) 'Creativity: from discourse to doctrine?', *Screen*, 48 (3): 377–87.

Schulz, W., Held, T. and Laudien, A. (2005) 'Search engines as gatekeepers of public communication: analysis of the German framework applicable to internet search engines including media law and anti trust law', *German Law Journal*, 6 (10): 1419–33.

Schumpeter, J. (1942) *Capitalism, Socialism and Democracy*. Harper: New York.

Screen Digest (2010) 'International film trade with China', *Screen Digest*, 463: 107.

Shapiro, C. and Varian, H. (1999) *Information Rules: A Strategic Guide to the Network Economy*. Boston, MA: Harvard Business School Press.

Shimp, T. (2010) *Integrated Marketing Communications in Advertising and Promotions*, 8th edn. Mason, OH: South-Western Cengage Learning.

Shirky, C. (2010) *Cognitive Surplus: Creativity and Generosity in a Connected Age*. New York: Penguin Press.

Shy, O. (2003) *The Economics of Network Industries*. Cambridge: Cambridge University Press.

Shy, O. (2011) 'A short survey of network economics', *Review of Industrial Organisation*, 38: 119–49.

Sinclair, J. and Wilken, R. (2009) 'Sleeping with the enemy: disintermediation in internet advertising', *Media International Australia*, 132: 93–104.

Singh, S. and Kretschmer, M. (2012) 'Strategic behaviour in the international exploitation of tv formats – a case study of the *Idols* format', in A. Zwaan and J. de Bruin (eds), *Adapting Idols: Authenticity, Identity and Performance in a Global Television Format*. Farnham: Ashgate Publishing Ltd, pp. 11–26.

Slattery, J. (2009) 'Where the hell do we go now?', *Guardian*, Media Supplement, 5 January: 1.

Smith, A. (1998) 'Displaying a stronger hand', in The Advertising Industry, eight-page special report, *Financial Times*, 11 November: 1.

Smith, C. (2012) *A Future for British Film: It Begins with the Audience, Report by the Film Review Panel*. London: DCMS.

Story, L. (2008) 'How do they track you? Let us count the ways', *New York Times*, 9 March, http://bits.blogs.nytimes.com/2008/03/09/how-do-they-track-you-let-us-count-the-ways/.

Strange, N. (2011) 'Multiplatforming public service: the BBC's "Bundled Project"', in J. Bennett and N. Strange (eds), *Television as Digital Media*. London: Duke University Press, pp. 132–57.

Suárez-Vázquez, A. (2011) 'Critic power or star power? The influence of hallmarks of quality of motion pictures: an experimental approach,' *Journal of Cultural Economics,* 35 (2): 119–135.

Sweney, M. (2011) 'National TV bidder Channel 6 pledges bigger budget than Channel 5', *Guardian*, 15 February, http://www.guardian.co.uk/media/2011/feb/15/channel-6-channel-5.

Terazono, E. (2007) 'European media deals rise by 75%', *Financial Times*, 30 January: 21.

Thomas, D. (2011) 'Warning over 4G spectrum auction', *Financial Times*, 11 December: 20.

Thompson, M (2006) 'BBC creative future' in C. Sinclair (ed.) (2006), *Transforming Television: Strategies for Convergence*. Glasgow: The Research Centre, pp 10–17.

Towse, R. (2001) *Creativity, Incentive and Reward: An Economic Analysis of Copyright and Culture in the Information Age*. Cheltenham: Edward Elgar Publishing.

Towse, R. (2004) 'Copyright and economics', in S. Frith and L. Marshall (eds), *Music and Copyright*, 2nd edn. Edinburgh: Edinburgh University Press, pp. 70–85.

Towse, R. (2010) *A Textbook of Cultural Economics*. Cambridge: Cambridge University Press.

Towse, R. (2011) 'Introduction', in R. Towse (ed.), *A Handbook of Cultural Economics*, 2nd edn. Cheltenham: Edward Elgar, pp. 1–8.

Trappel, J. (2008) 'Online media within the public service realm?', *Convergence: The International Journal of Research into New Media Technologies*, 14 (3): 313–22.

Tremblay, V. (2011) 'Introduction: issues in network economics', *Review of Industrial Organisation*, Special edition, 38: 117–18.

Tremblay, V. (2012) 'Introduction: market structure and efficiency', *Review of Industrial Organisation*, 40 (2): 85–86.

UKFC (2010) *2010 Statistical Yearbook*. London: UK Film Council.

Ungerer, H. (2005) 'Competition in the media sector – how long can the future be delayed?' Speech to PCLMP 2005, COMP/C2/HU, 19 January, Brussels: CEC.

USITC (2011) *Recent Trends in US Services Trade: 2011 Annual Report*. Investigation No 332–345; Publication No 4243, July. Washington, DC: United States International Trade Commission.

van der Wurff, R., Bakker, P. and Picard, R. (2008) 'Economic growth and advertising expenditures in different media in different countries', *Journal of Media Economics*, 21: 28–52.

van Eijk, N. (2009) 'Search engines, the new bottleneck for content access', in B. Preissel, J. Haucap and P. Curwen (eds), *Telecommunications Markets: Drivers and Impediments*. Heidelberg: Springer Phsica-Verlag HD, pp. 141–56.

Van Kranenburg, H. and Hogenbirk, A. (2006) 'Issues in market structure', in A. Albarrran, S. Chan-Olmsted and M. Wirth (eds), *Handbook of Media Management and Economics*. Mahwah, NJ: Lawrence Erlbaum Associates, pp. 325–44.

van Kuilenburg, P., de Jong, M. and van Rompay, T (2011) '"That was funny but what was the brand again?": Humorous television commercials and brand linkage', *International Journal of Advertising*, 30 (5): 795–814.

Varian, H. (2005) 'Copying and copyright', *Journal of Economic Perspectives*, 19 (2): 121–38.

Vatanova, E., Makeenko, M. and Vyrkovsky, A. (2012) 'Convergence and business models: innovation in daily newspaper economy – case of Russia'. Paper presented at the 10th World Media Economics & Management Conference, Aristotle University of Thessaloniki, Thessaloniki, 26 May.

Vick, D. (2006) 'Regulatory convergence?', *Legal Studies*, 26 (1): 26–64.

Voon, T. (2007) 'A new approach to audiovisual products in the WTO: rebalancing GATT and GATS', *UCLA Entertainment Law Review*, 14: 1–32.

Vukanovic, Z. (2009) 'Global paradigm shift: strategic management of new and digital media in new and digital economics', *The International Journal on Media Management*, 11 (2): 81–90.

Walls, W. (2005) 'Modeling movie success when 'nobody knows anything': conditional stable-distribution analysis of film returns', *Journal of Cultural Economics*, 9 (3): 177–190.

Wasko, J. (2005) 'Critiquing Hollywood: the political economy of motion pictures', in C. Moul (ed.), *The Concise Handbook of Movie Industry Economics*. New York: Cambridge University Press, pp. 32–58.

Waters, R. (2010) 'Unrest over Google's secret formula', *Financial Times*, 12 July: 22.

Waters, R., Nuttall, C. and Bradshaw, T. (2011) 'Google social networking takes on Facebook', *Financial Times*, 29 June. Accessed at FT.com tech blog at http://www.ft.com/cms/s/2/fdcb2aae-a1bb-11e0-b9f9-00144feabdc0.html#axzz2DbG90GJ6.

Wheeler, M. (2010) 'The EU Competition Directorate's 2009 Communication on the application of state aid rules to PSB'. Paper presented at RIPE Conference on Public Service after the Recession, University of Westminster, 8–11 September, http://ripeat.org/?s=wheeler&cat=411.

Wildman, S. (2006) 'Paradigms and analytical frameworks in modern economics and media economics', in A. Albarran, S. Chan-Olmsted and M. Wirth (eds), *Handbook of Media Management and Economics*. Mahwah, NJ: Lawrence Earlbaum Associates, pp. 67–90.

Wildman, S., Lee, S-Y. and Song, S-Y. (2012) 'How to make money by giving away content you get for free'. Paper presented at the 10th World Media Economics & Management Conference, Aristotle University of Thessaloniki, Thessaloniki, 24 May.

Williams, R. (1974) *Television: Technology and Cultural Form*. London: Collins.

Wimmer, K. (2010) 'Digital journalism: the audience in here but who is monetizing the content?', *Issue Papers (Policy Views)* No. 5, The Media Institute, www.mediainstitute.org/IssuePapers.php.

Wimmer, K. (2010) 'Digital journalism: the audience in here but who is monetizing the content?' *Policy Views*, Arlington, VA: The Media Institute.

WIPO (2003) *Guide on Surveying the Economic Contribution of the Copyright-Based Industries*. Geneva: WIPO.

Wirth, M. and Bloch, H. (1995) 'Industrial organization theory and media industry analysis', *Journal of Media Economics*, 8 (2): 15–26.

Withers, K. (2006) *Intellectual Property and the Knowledge Economy*. London: Institute for Public Policy Research.

Woodward, J. (1998) 'Our time has come', *Broadcast*, 30 January: 18–19.

WTO (2010) *Audiovisual Services; Background Note by the Secretariat*. 12 January, S/C/W/310. Geneva: WTO.

Xavier, P. and Paltridge, S. (2011) *Next Generation Market Access Networks and Market Structure, Report of Working Party on Communication Infrastructures and Services Policy*, DSTI/ICCP/CISP(2010)5/FINAL, 20 June. Paris: OECD Directorate for Science, Technology and Industry.

Yoo, C. (2006) 'Network neutrality and the economics of congestion', *Georgetown Law Journal*, 94 (6): 1847–908.

Young, S., Gong, J. and Van der Stede, W. (2010) 'The business of making money with movies', *Strategic Finance*, February: 35–40.

Index

And I have a terrible past.
For three years now,
I've been living with a
saxophone player.

I forgive you.

And I can never have children.

We'll adopt some.

But you don't understand.
I'm a MAN!

Well -- nobody's perfect.

Glenn Hopp

BILLY WILDER

The Cinema of Wit 1906 –2002

TASCHEN

KÖLN LONDON LOS ANGELES MADRID PARIS TOKYO

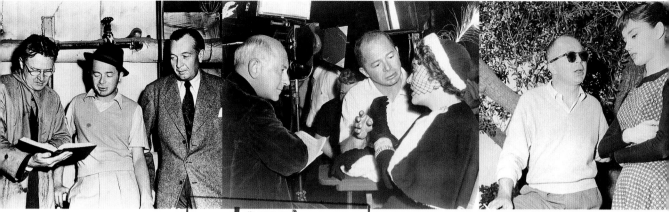

FRONT COVER
On the set of 'Some Like It Hot' (1959)
Tony Curtis and Marilyn Monroe prepare to embark on a night of lovemaking.

FIRST PAGE
Stills from 'Some Like It Hot' (1959)
Jerry/Daphne (Jack Lemmon, right) reveals to his fiancé Osgood Fielding
(Joe E. Brown, left) that he is a man.

FRONTISPIECE
On the set of 'A Foreign Affair' (1948)
Billy Wilder looks on in disbelief as Hedy Lamarr and Marlene Dietrich are about to kiss.

THIS PAGE
1 **On the set of 'Five Graves to Cairo' (1943)** Although Charles Brackett (left) and Billy Wilder were
a successful writing team up until 1950, it not often acknowledged that Doane Harrison (right) was
Billy's editorial advisor from 1942 until his death in 1967. 2 **On the set of 'Sunset Boulevard' (1950)**
During the film Norma Desmond visits the set of 'Samson and Delilah' to speak with her friend Cecil
B. DeMille (left). 3 **On the set of 'Sabrina' (1954)** The top female stars were attracted to Wilder's films
because he wrote strong female characters. Audrey Hepburn appeared in two of his films.

OPPOSITE PAGE
1 **On the set of 'Avanti!' (1972)** Jack Lemmon (in the background) developed his Everyman persona in
seven films with Wilder. 2 **Publicity still for 'The Front Page' (1974)** I. A. L. Diamond was Wilder's
writing partner from 1957 onwards. 3 **On the set of 'The Front Page' (1974)** Wilder originally wanted
Walter Matthau for the lead in 'The Seven Year Itch' and eventually cast him eleven years later in
'The Fortune Cookie', the film that began the Lemmon/Matthau screen partnership.

PAGES 6/7
On the set of 'Avanti!' (1972)
Billy Wilder is behind the camera on a makeshift platform off the Italian coast.

BACK COVER
Billy Wilder, Los Angeles (1998)
Copyright by William Claxton, 2000

© 2003 TASCHEN GmbH
Hohenzollernring 53, D–50672 Köln
www.taschen.com
Editor/Layout: Paul Duncan/Wordsmith Solutions
Typeface Design: Sense/Net, Andy Disl, Cologne

Printed in Italy
ISBN 3–8228–1595–0

Dedication
To my mother and father, Marvine Hopp and Bill Hopp.

Notes
A superscript number indicates a reference to a note on page 191.

Images
British Film Institute Stills, Posters and Designs, London: 4 (3), 5 (3),
6/7, 8, 10, 11, 13, 14, 20, 21, 23, 24, 25, 28 (2), 29left, 34l, 35
(2), 36, 37 (2), 38/39, 40 (2), 41, 44, 45, 47, 49 (2), 50/51, 52,
54 (2), 55 (2), 56, 59, 60, 61 (2), 62, 63, 64bottom, 66top, 67,
68, 70/71, 74, 76, 77, 79 (2), 80 (2), 81, 83, 84 (2), 85 (2), 86,
87, 101, 102/103, 104 (2), 105, 108 (2), 109, 112, 113, 114,
115, 116, 117, 118, 121, 122, 123, 128, 129, 130/131, 132,
133, 136, 138, 139, 144, 145, 150 (3), 151, 154/155, 156top
right+b, 157, 159, 160 (2), 164, 165, 166/167, 168 (2), 170b,
173t, 174b, 175, 178, 179, 188 (2), 189 (2), 190 (2)
PWE Verlag / defd-movies, Hamburg: 12, 15, 18 (2), 22, 26, 27,
29r, 32, 34r, 58, 64t, 66b, 72/73, 78, 82, 110, 111, 137,
140/141, 142, 143, 148, 156tl, 158, 169, 170t, 171, 172 (2),
173b, 174t, 183t+br, 185 (2)
The Kobal Collection, London/New York: 2, 46, 53, 69, 88/89, 124,
127, 134/135, 152, 153, 161, 162/163
Sam Shaw. Licensed by Shaw Family Archives/USA: 92, 93, 94, 95,
96, 97, 98/99
Corbis, London: 65, 119 (Sunset Boulevard/Corbis Sygma), 120
(Sunset Boulevard/Corbis Sygma), 125 (Bettmann/Corbis)
Timepix, New York: 16 (Peter Stackpole), 31 (Ralph Crane), 42/43
(Peter Stackpole), 106 (Gjon Mili)
MPTV, Los Angeles: Front Cover, 91 (Mark Shaw), 126, 180 (Richard
Miller)
Dennis Stock/Magnum Photos, London: 90, 176
Herbert Klemens / Filmbild Fundus Robert Fischer, Munich: 100
Hulton Getty Archive, London: 181 (© Archive Photos)
Helmut Newton: 192 (© 2003)

Copyright
The film images in this book are copyright to the respective distri-
butors: Paramount Pictures (*Bluebeard's Eighth Wife, Midnight,
Arise, My Love, Hold Back the Dawn, The Major and the Minor,
Five Graves to Cairo, Double Indemnity, The Lost Weekend, The
Emperor Waltz, A Foreign Affair, Sunset Boulevard, Ace in the Hole,
Stalag 17, Sabrina*), MGM (*Ninotchka, Buddy Buddy*), Samuel
Goldwyn (*Ball of Fire*), Twentieth Century-Fox (*The Seven Year Itch*),
Warner Brothers (*The Spirit of St. Louis*), Allied Artists (*Love in the
Afternoon*), United Artists (*Witness for the Prosecution, Irma la
Douce*), United Artists/Mirisch Company/Ashton Productions (*Some
Like It Hot*), United Artists/Mirisch Company (*The Apartment, The
Private Life of Sherlock Holmes*), United Artists/Mirisch Company/
Pyramid Productions (*One, Two, Three*), Mirisch Company/Lopert
Pictures (*Kiss Me, Stupid*), United Artists/Mirisch Company/Phalanx/
Jalem (*The Fortune Cookie*), Mirisch Corporation/Phalanx/Jalem
(*Avanti!*), Universal International (*The Front Page*), Geria-Bavaria
(*Fedora*). We deeply regret it if, despite our concerted efforts, any
copyright owners have been unintentionally overlooked and omitted.
Obviously we will amend any such errors in the next edition if they
are brought to the attention of the publisher.

From Europe to America 1906–1935

In Richard Attenborough's movie biography *Chaplin* (1992), a curious scene appears that would resonate for many film-makers coming to America from abroad. Douglas Fairbanks has been visited by government agents investigating Chaplin's supposed subversive behavior. Fairbanks gently advises his friend to be careful, saying, "You've never understood this country." Chaplin shrugs off the warning: "It's a good country underneath." Fairbanks scoffs a bit and corrects him: "It's a good country *on top*." What Fairbanks understands and what Chaplin seems to puzzle over – the gap between how Americans see themselves and how they really are – became for writer-director Billy Wilder a healthy tension that resulted in some of the most admired films of all time. Wilder's European sensibility blended his adopted homeland with the unorthodox morality of the Yankee maverick and allowed him to explore in comic and dramatic ways the deceptions that humans practice on others and on themselves.

This healthy tension usually saves a Wilder film from the extremes of cynicism and of sentiment. In a famous essay on Wilder, Stephen Farber writes that 'Wilder's chief gift to the American film is intelligence.' This smartness balances a Wilder film between the corrosive and the mawkish and often emerges in surprising ironies, reversals in plotting, and a love of paradox. Sometimes respected individuals may be revealed as heels – like the American G.I.s in post-war Berlin in *A Foreign Affair* (1948), the security chief in *Stalag 17* (1953) or the dignified boss of an insurance company in *The Apartment* (1960). Sometimes a seeming scoundrel may turn out to be a *mensch* – a person of integrity, a full human being. Wilder knows that people are usually not as good as they think they are 'on top' nor as craven as they fear they are 'underneath.' Such a view of reality won him honors (twenty-one Academy Award nominations and six wins) but also caused controversy. When some critics noticed integrity turning up in unlikely places in the Wilder film world, they faulted the director for compromising his cynicism. When, watching the same films, some audiences (and even one collaborator) noticed corruption among those who should know better, they became offended at the very idea. Stripping off a false sense of who we think we are and finding out who we really are started with a mixture of the old world and the new.

On the set of 'The Spirit of St. Louis' (1957)
Billy Wilder gives the evil eye during a night-time shoot in Paris.

In a segment from a documentary prepared for American television, Billy Wilder describes the Austro-Hungarian Empire into which he was born. He sounds as if he knows he is talking about a different world. And so he is. That world may be glimpsed, or at least a Hollywood version of it, in Wilder's film *The Emperor Waltz* (1948). Richard Haydn plays the tired Emperor Franz-Josef, who talks to an American phonograph salesman played by Bing Crosby. The film is probably set around 1906, the year Billy Wilder was born in the town of Sucha, south of Kraków. Wilder and Charles Brackett, the co-authors of the screenplay, give the emperor a touching speech about the obsolescence of the elite. Franz-Josef compares the falling aristocracy to snails: "They are majestic creatures with small coroneted heads that peer very proudly from their tiny castles. They move with dignity. I imagine they have a great sense of their own importance, but you take them from their shells, and they die. That is us."

Ten years after these fictional events, on 21 November 1916, the real Franz-Josef did die. Ten-year-old Billy Wilder watched the emperor's funeral procession from atop a marble table at the Café Edison on the Ringstrasse in Vienna. At birth, the boy had been named Samuel, but his mother had nicknamed him 'Billie' because she still cherished her earlier visit to America and in particular had enjoyed Buffalo Bill's Wild West show. Billy Wilder's family – his father Max, his mother Genia, and his older brother Wilhelm – had recently moved to Vienna partly to continue Max's hopeful business ventures. Max Wilder seems to have been at times a headwaiter, a manager of a chain of railway cafés, an importer of Swiss clocks, the owner of a trout farm and the part owner of a hotel-restaurant. The billiard room at this hotel provided an early education in human nature for Max's son Billy. He received another lesson in the difference between appearance and reality one day when going through the morning mail. He found an invitation for Max to attend a gathering at a boarding school for a third Wilder son, one that no one but Max was aware of. Young Billy Wilder apparently did not react with shock or denial. He confronted his father with the invitation, and the secret of the half-brother was evidently preserved in a father-son pact. Billy Wilder was learning about deception.

His worldly education continued with frequent movie-going, the imported recordings of American jazz, and, finally, a job as a crime reporter. (Some biographical accounts maintain that Wilder briefly studied law at the University of Vienna; others question this.) His attempts to interview the Viennese elite met with mixed results. Sigmund Freud abruptly sent Wilder away, but he had better luck with Ferenc Molnár, Alfred Adler, Richard Strauss, and Arthur Schnitzler. Wilder's enthusiasm for jazz and his articles about bandleader Paul Whiteman's concert tour led to an invitation for Wilder to accompany the band to Berlin.

Wilder stayed in Berlin as a freelance reporter after the Whiteman band continued its tour. His most famous series of articles described his work as a gigolo at the Hotel Eden, although he later said that he merely provided his services as a dance partner for lonely old ladies. His title for the series ('Waiter, Bring Me a Dancer: The Life of a Gigolo') coyly hints at both possibilities. (In one of the cabaret scenes in *A Foreign Affair* (1948), one can glimpse a drum with 'Hotel Eden' written on it in a directorial allusion to his youthful days as a Berlin reporter.) At the Romanisches Café on the Kurfürstendamm, Wilder associated with writers, artists and musicians, and observed the decadence of the most noto-

Still from 'The Emperor Waltz' (1948)
Virgil Smith (Bing Crosby, left) tells Emperor Franz-Josef (Richard Haydn, right) that he should not kill puppies simply because they are mongrels. The Baron (Roland Culver) and Countess Johanna (Joan Fontaine) look on.

On the set of 'Irma la Douce' (1963)
Billy Wilder shows Jack Lemmon some of the
tricks he learned in his youth.

rious city in Europe. Berlin at the time was filled with characters like Thomas Mann, Kurt Weill, Bertolt Brecht, Friedrich Hollander, Fritz Lang, Erich Maria Remarque and George Grosz. From his contacts at the café, Wilder began ghostwriting in the German film industry.

His transition to credited writer supposedly came about in the middle of the night in an unlikely encounter at a rooming house. Pounding on Wilder's door was a film producer still climbing into his clothes as he fled the jealous boyfriend of the girl he had been with in the next room. Wilder provided him with a place to hide and catch his breath. He also took advantage of the opportunity to sell the producer a script sight unseen. The story may have been embroidered slightly with time, but Wilder's career in Germany soon began to thrive. The high points came with *People on Sunday* (1929), an example of slice-of-life realism that follows two couples on a leisurely week-end, and *Emil and the Detectives* (1931), about a boy who organises the youth of Berlin to catch a thief. From one of his fellow writers, Wilder picked up the habit of beginning each script with the words *Cum Deo* ('With God'), a practice he would maintain for the rest of his life. In all, Wilder received screen credits for his work on thirteen films in Berlin from 1929 to 1933.

Two traumatic milestones also marked Wilder's life in Berlin. In the fall of 1928, Max Wilder came to see his son for an extended visit. One day in November, Max was stricken with stomach pains and died of an abdominal rupture in the ambulance on the way to the hospital. Sources vary as to whether his wife Genia was with him on the visit; perhaps the parents were travelling to visit Wilhelm, the son who had settled in Long Island. Billy Wilder put together enough money to have his father buried in a Jewish cemetery in Berlin. More turmoil came with the Nazis in 1933 and the growing public violence toward Jews. After the burning of the Reichstag, Wilder fled to Paris.

He roomed at the Ansonia Hotel and worked on script ideas with other exiles like Walter Reisch, Friedrich Hollander, Franz Waxman and Peter Lorre. Wilder also co-wrote and co-directed (with Alexander Esway) a film called *Mauvaise Graine* (1934), the story of a teenage girl (Danielle Darrieux) who gets involved with a gang of car thieves. It was his first directing credit, but he usually spoke unfavourably of the experience. His goal was to follow his brother to America. When he sold a script to Joe May, a former German producer now at Columbia, Wilder had a ticket on the *Aquitania* and the promise of steady work in Hollywood.

The problem was that the man who had been hired to write movies in Hollywood did not speak much English. During his first year or two in America, Wilder struggled to learn the language and to keep working. He went from Columbia to Fox to Paramount. When his first visa expired a few months after the Columbia job had fizzled, Wilder found himself without proper credentials and at the mercy of a border official in Mexicali, Mexico. He was, however, granted a new visa after he told a film-loving consul that he wrote movies. "Write some good ones," was the official's comment as he stamped the papers. Shortly after Wilder eventually settled at Paramount Pictures, he started doing so.

As Louis Giannetti says in *Understanding Movies*, about 90% of the films released in America and roughly 80% of those distributed in the world between

ABOVE
On the set of 'The Seven Year Itch' (1955)
Billy Wilder and Marilyn Monroe. Monroe was often late on the set and messed up lines causing many retakes but "Whenever I saw her, I always forgave her," Wilder said.

OPPOSITE
On the set of 'One, Two, Three' (1961)
Billy Wilder accepts a light from Lilo Pulver.

the wars were produced by five studios: MGM, Paramount, Warner Brothers, Fox and RKO. In retrospect, it is easy to assign each studio a particular style or speciality. In truth, all five major studios released films each year in a number of genres and styles. When a hit came along and the studio had a property it could replicate, a signature look seemed to exist if only in the mind of the audience. When RKO began their successful string of Fred Astaire-Ginger Rogers musicals, for example, the studio was in receivership. As this profitable series continued, with its memorable Art Deco sets by designer Van Nest Polglase, RKO was back in the black. However, Polglase also supervised the design of darker RKO films like *King Kong* (1933) and John Ford's *The Informer* (1935) at roughly the same time. Set designer Anton Grot is similarly credited with giving the Warner Brothers gangster film its distinctive look of gritty realism, and Cedric Gibbons is often mentioned as the visual guide behind the high-keyed lighting and opulent optimism of MGM's family films.

At Paramount, a European flavour seasoned the product. The art department was headed by Hans Dreier, who had worked at the respected UFA studios in Germany. His tenure at Paramount lasted from 1927 until 1951, and he helped to create the distinguishing look that writer Bernard F. Dick has described as the studio's 'white look': "Bedrooms looked like shrines; walls and staircases gleamed like burnished ivory. The studio seemed to revel in whiteness, from satin sheets to that indisputable touch of class, the white telephone." Ernst Lubitsch, another transplanted European, was head of production at Paramount from 1934 to 1935, the only time in Hollywood history that a major director held such a powerful position. From 17 July 1936 onwards, Billy Wilder was teamed at Paramount with writer Charles Brackett. In December of that year Wilder married Judith Iribe, a sophisticated woman who had lived for a while in France. Wilder had first met her on a blind date.

The 104 screenwriters in the Paramount bullpen may or may not have been much like Pat Hobby, F. Scott Fitzgerald's fictional screenwriter, or like the screenwriting hero of John O'Hara's novella *Hope of Heaven*. Biographer Maurice Zolotow asked Wilder about his brief acquaintance with Fitzgerald as a fellow writer on the Paramount assembly line. Wilder compared him to a great sculptor hired for a plumbing job. Fitzgerald could handle the finesse of writing memorable dialogue but was all thumbs when it came to organising a scenario. Good construction and good conversation were both essential ingredients for the successful Hollywood script in the 1930s. "Most people do not say clever or interesting things," Wilder told Zolotow. "That is why they have to pay clever screenwriters so much money to make up these clever things."

On the set of 'One, Two, Three' (1961)
Billy Wilder walks James Cagney through a scene.

On the set of 'Irma la Douce' (1963)
Jack Lemmon apes Billy Wilder's exact movements. The precise visual movement and rhythm of a scene were as important to Wilder as the verbal.

"My mother never saw me successful. My father, of course, never saw me successful, because he died in 1928… I regret that very much because they would have been proud of me. I never saw her after 1935."

Billy Wilder[3]

Writer
1936–1941

The most representative scene in all of Billy Wilder's movies may be the night-time writing sessions between Joe Gillis (William Holden) and Betty Shaefer (Nancy Olson) in *Sunset Boulevard* (1950). They meet in Betty's cubbyhole of an office in the reader's department at Paramount – two lonely people who have to sneak away from their daytime lives in order to try to write a movie. The darkened, deserted studio around them serves to intensify the personal warmth they have created in their homey, well-lit space.

Joe and Betty are trying to reshape one of his earlier, unfinished scripts that she salvaged from the archives. Eventually they give it the apt designation, 'Untitled Love Story.' She is too inexperienced to do the rewrite job by herself; he has grown too jaded by continual rejection at the studios to see the merits of his own earlier work. Their collaboration thus begins on the common ground of mutual need. In a wonderful touch, screenwriters Charles Brackett and Billy Wilder in their last work together reveal a good deal about the interdependency of collaboration and the nature of Hollywood artifice when they have Joe provide Betty with a suggestion for new possibilities in plotting. "Don't make it too dreary," he says. "How about this for a situation: she teaches daytimes, he teaches at night. Right? They don't even know each other, but they share the same room. It's cheaper that way. As a matter of fact, they sleep in the same bed – in shifts, of course." A cut follows to a close shot of Betty and her half-smiling, nonplussed expression. "Are you kidding?" she says after a moment. "Because I think it's good."

Betty's response also fits many of the scripts Wilder co-authored in the 1930s. The pleasant artifice of careful plotting overrules the realism of the everyday. To apply a Hitchcock distinction, the films are pieces of cake more than slices of life. The feathery touch of Ernst Lubitsch, the mistaken identities from old-world operetta, the withheld secrets of the well-made play tradition, and some of the elements of screwball comedy all blended to influence the Paramount version of sophisticated screen comedy and drama.

Wilder began writing in a studio system that operated like a factory with movies rolling off the assembly line like Buicks. The films were shot on sound stages or on back lots that the studio owned. When Joe Gillis and Betty Shaefer

Billy Wilder and Charles Brackett (1944)
Billy Wilder walks and talks whilst brandishing his trademark cane. His scripting partner, Charles Brackett, who also produced their films, takes notes.

"I was under contract to Paramount. In those days, Paramount had a hundred and four writers under contract. There was a writers' building, and a writers' annex, and a writers' annex annex."

Billy Wilder [2]

get stuck with their script in *Sunset Boulevard*, they stroll around the studio back lot for inspiration. Betty is a third-generation Hollywood kid, and it is easy to hear in her simple words to Joe Billy Wilder's own love for the system he came to know so well: "Look at this street. All cardboard, all hollow, all phoney. All done with mirrors. I like it better than any street in the world." In the studio system, the personnel were all under exclusive, long-term contract to a particular studio. James Cagney and Humphrey Bogart worked at Warner Brothers. W. C. Fields and Mae West worked at Paramount. Clark Gable worked at MGM. To some performers who were content to toil in mediocrity and enjoy a lucrative weekly paycheque, the paternalistic restrictions of the studio system meant security and comfort, but to others who wanted to accomplish something original and worthwhile, the limits could become confining. Billy Wilder was one of these.

Among the 104 writers at Paramount, it would be difficult to find two more different than Charles Brackett and Billy Wilder. Maurice Zolotow makes an apt comparison when he likens the creative tension between Brackett and Wilder to that between Gilbert and Sullivan. Charles Brackett knew F. Scott Fitzgerald too but from the comparatively equal standing of fellow novelist. Brackett, who was fourteen years older than Wilder, had written the satirical *Entirely Surrounded*, a novel about the famed Algonquin Round Table. His novel *Week-End* had also received favourable notices. He was the first drama critic for *The New Yorker* magazine, and the conservative Brackett socialised with the gentry at Saratoga Springs, New York. Today, the Charles Brackett novels, long out of print, are difficult to obtain even in libraries. Many of his scripts with Billy Wilder, however, which like the plays of Shakespeare were written to be performed rather than printed, can still be found in bookstores.

Manny Wolfe, one of the producers at Paramount, deserves the credit for teaming the two opposites who became the most famous screenwriters in the movies. The first collaboration of Brackett and Wilder was their script for an Ernst Lubitsch film, *Bluebeard's Eighth Wife* (1938). It begins with perhaps the best example from classical-era Hollywood of the meet-cute. In Hollywood parlance then and now, film-makers tried to avoid 'on the nose' or predictable touches. Staying ahead of the audience with unexpected twists in plotting was one way to keep the audience interested. Especially in romantic comedy, the rule of thumb was that the hero and heroine should not meet in an ordinary way. Ed Sikov writes that Wilder even claimed to have kept a notebook with ideas for clever ways for characters to meet. In *Bluebeard's Eighth Wife*, Gary Cooper plays an American millionaire. When he shops for pyjamas at a department store on the French Riviera, he declares that he wants to pay for only the tops, which is all he sleeps in. He did not become rich by throwing money around carelessly, he reasons. This unusual request causes some consternation among the store personnel. Eventually the request reaches the owner, who is awakened by a phone call from the nervous manager. The owner refuses to permit Cooper's request, even though, as we see, he himself only uses the tops of his pyjamas. Claudette Colbert, observing the squabble at the clothing counter, agrees to split the cost with Cooper since she herself only uses the bottoms. The mix of improbability and cleverness hooks the viewer. As Betty Shaefer said: "Are you kidding? Because I think it's good."

TOP
On the set of 'Bluebeard's Eighth Wife' (1938)
Director Ernst Lubitsch (left) takes Gary Cooper and Claudette Colbert for a ride. Lubitsch was constantly in search of the superjoke that would top all the other jokes – Wilder's definition of 'the Lubitsch touch.'

BOTTOM
Still from 'Bluebeard's Eighth Wife' (1938)
The screwball comedies of the 1930s expressed the anger, rage and frustration that is all part of the battle of the sexes.

Such an unconventional meeting also signals a significant future for the couple. Before the meet-cute is dismissed as a relic from a bygone era, consider the example of the contemporary film *True Colors* (1991) with James Spader and John Cusack. This serious drama, the story of two initially idealistic law students at the University of Virginia who enter the corrupting world of American politics, opens with the protagonists meeting as first-day college freshman. They smash fenders trying to get the last parking space in front of the dormitory. Later, they learn that they have been assigned to share the same room. The unfolding movie tells how their lives continue to intersect for years. Just as the withheld secret from the well-made play convention insinuated itself into the structure of much of twentieth-century drama, so the meet-cute became a trusted tool of the screenwriting trade.

The pyjama idea for *Bluebeard* was Wilder's. Both Lubitsch and Brackett liked it. Encouraged by her debt-ridden father, Colbert succeeds with her scheme to marry Cooper, who has already wed seven women, got bored with each of them, and paid them off in generous divorce settlements. Colbert refuses to sleep with him in order to speed up the financial payoff. The new collaborators hammered away at the construction of the story and its comic possibilities, but the finished film reveals the rough edges that new craftsmen often leave behind. Some scenes belabour their points, as when Colbert bites into an onion before she lets Cooper kiss her, a joke that is too slim to sustain the longish scene it appears in.

A good example of the film-makers' struggles turns up in an anecdote told by Maurice Zolotow. Lubitsch wanted the writers to give him the perfect word for Colbert to shout at Cooper when she jumps into water and swims away. It was to be something flirtatious and taunting that would intrigue Cooper and get him to pursue her, something that could function like a catchphrase. Lubitsch pantomimed Colbert looking coyly at Cooper as she prepares to plunge into the Mediterranean. He hoped to spark a flash of inspiration in his writers for the perfect verbal stimulus to set up the subsequent scenes of their story. He never did. The near-miss of *Bluebeard's Eighth Wife* is probably as revealing of the slippery nature of good scriptwriting as the times when Brackett and Wilder 'rang the bell,' as Lubitsch described it.

Their second collaboration has nothing forced about it. Brackett and Wilder took a story by Edwin Justus Mayer and Franz Schultz based on the Cinderella myth and created one of the great romantic comedies of the 1930s. Both the construction and the conversation are more polished in *Midnight* (1939), which also stars Claudette Colbert, appearing this time opposite Don Ameche. Colbert plays a gold-digging chorus girl from Kokomo, Indiana, who rolls into Paris on a train from Monte Carlo having just had her system at the gaming tables fail her. Now she must navigate her way through a rainy night in Paris with no resources but the gold lamé dress she wears, a pawn ticket, one last centime and her wits.

What screenwriters devote time and pages to and what they rush through in developing a story usually reveals what attracts them most to the material. In *Midnight,* Ameche plays a cabdriver who drives Colbert to all the Parisian nightclubs in a vain search for a singing job. Writers interested in exploiting the comedy of her limited performing talent would have expanded this part of the story. Such a tack would have produced satire and the low comedy of laughing at a

ABOVE
Still from 'Bluebeard's Eighth Wife' (1938)
Multimillionaire Michael Brandon (Gary Cooper) gets to grips with impoverished French heiress Nicole de Loiselle (Claudette Colbert) in a film director Ernst Lubitsch called a 'mental slapstick.'

OPPOSITE
On the set of 'Bluebeard's Eighth Wife' (1938)
Director Ernst Lubitsch (right) with Gary Cooper and Claudette Colbert. Lubitsch sought visual and verbal ways of avoiding the clichés of romantic comedy – Wilder recognised such finesse as an essential ingredient of 'the Lubitsch touch.'

character. Brackett and Wilder, in keeping with the customary emphasis at Paramount, aimed for the higher comedy of laughing with a character. Consequently, Colbert's nightclub auditions rush by in a ten-second montage of flashing neon signs superimposed over night shots of Paris. When Ameche takes Colbert to a workers' café afterwards for a meal, the writers slow the pace for a longer scene in which these two characters get to know each other.

This restaurant scene sets up the rest of the film. In a sense, it is the dramatic equivalent of the elusive word that Lubitsch hoped Brackett and Wilder would find for *Bluebeard's Eighth Wife*. In *Midnight*, the puzzle piece fits. On the screen two near-strangers chat as they share a frugal meal, but what is really happening is that the audience is being brought in to the story by two gifted screenwriters reaching their considerable proficiency for the first time. Ameche proudly declares to Colbert his plebeian philosophy. Like all good dramatic writing, his words reflect the perfect idiom for his personality. The simple, blunt sentences match his straightforward, unapologetic views: "I'm a rich man… I need forty francs a day, and I earn forty francs a day. No bank account. No real estate. No possessions. Three handkerchiefs. Two shirts. One tie. No worries… Listen, if you want peace of mind, get yourself a cab."

His last word provides a natural tool for further character development as Colbert reveals her longing for a limousine. "It doesn't ride any better," Ameche scolds her. Now the scene effortlessly slips in the background to Colbert's character – how she and other chorines latched on to a group of British peers, how the mother of one of them offered Colbert money to leave her son alone. Her amused and matter-of-fact tone offends and irritates Ameche as much as her story of gold-digging girls. "I hope you threw her out!" he says indignantly. Once again, the writers find the right voice for their character: "How could I," Colbert blithely replies, "with my hands full of money?" She went straight to Monte Carlo and lost it all. "Serves you right! Trying to get something for nothing," gloats Ameche. The humour in the scene consistently comes from recognising and smiling at the humanity of these people. Ameche's haughtiness seems to result, as perhaps it often does, from less life experience. It is easy to condemn what you don't know.

Though he was not working for Lubitsch on this film, Wilder had learned some useful screenwriting lessons, such as how Lubitsch would reveal to the audience information and let them come to conclusions themselves. They would see a 'two' and over here another 'two,' but Lubitsch would let them do the cinematic arithmetic of drawing the line and adding it up. Speaking to Chris Columbus in an interview for *American Film* magazine, Wilder explained this Lubitsch refinement of high comedy: "The audience is the co-writer. And that's where the laugh comes in… His technique is clear to the last village idiot. But he makes him feel that he is very smart."

At some level an audience watching *Midnight* now adds up that what these two people in the café really need, paradoxically, is each other. Ameche is too comically proud in his Puritanism. His stiffness dehumanises him. Colbert is too flighty in her gadding about through life. Just as she needs a dose of his seriousness, he could do with some of her mirth. In one scene of less than two minutes, the screenwriters have subtly stamped their characters, established their needs, slipped in background information, and created curiosity in the audience. The

ABOVE
Still from 'Midnight' (1939)
Eve Peabody (Claudette Colbert) leads the dance and George Flammarion (John Barrymore, right) is happy to follow.

OPPOSITE
Publicity from 'Midnight' (1939)
Claudette Colbert plays Eve Peabody, a woman with only an evening dress to her name and her eyes set on marrying a millionaire.

viewers want to see how this Cinderella and her unlikely prince eventually get together. Comic suspense comes from delaying her inevitable exposure. One searches in vain for an indifferently planned scene or a purposeless passage of dialogue in *Midnight*. John Douglas Eames calls the film "quintessential Paramount: verbal sparring and elegant adultery among *le beau monde*."

One might think that after producing a work of such charm, Brackett and Wilder would have some command over their story choices. If so, they probably would not have selected for their next assignment *What a Life* (1939), the first in a series of teen comedies that Paramount came up with to rival the popular Andy Hardy series at MGM. The writers' project after this, teamed with Lubitsch at MGM for a comedy with Greta Garbo, taught them even more about the art of good screenwriting. It also provided one of their most pleasant working experiences.

Some of the plotting for *Ninotchka* (1939) had already been worked out when Brackett and Wilder joined this project about a proud Marxist woman who comes to Paris from Moscow in pursuit of Tzarist treasures and who becomes humbled by capitalism and romance. Nearly all of Wilder's films show a deftness at using objects for dramatic purposes, to reveal a character's personality, to illustrate an idea and to motivate the action. It may be that the writing sessions with Lubitsch on *Ninotchka* refined for him some of the possibilities for dramatic economy and subtlety in the suggestive use of objects. To show, for example, that the three members of the Russian board of trade who come in Paris have abandoned their Marxist ideals and yielded to capitalistic charms, Lubitsch simply dissolves from a hat rack with their wintry, functional headgear to one with three elegant top hats. Wilder was also impressed with the way Lubitsch used a hat to indicate pictorially the softening and change of outlook in Ninotchka. In an early scene, she scorns a silly hat she sees in a shop window; later, alone in her hotel room, she carefully removes this same hat from a drawer. We see her self-consciousness and shyness in the way she tentatively regards it.

Henri Bergson's famous observation that comedy is the mechanical encrusted on the living can hardly find a better illustration than in Garbo's super-serious envoy Ninotchka. The romantic premise of opposites eventually attracting is so rich and the dialogue of the early scenes so natural sounding that the script seems nearly to have written itself, usually a sign of considerable labour on the part of the screenwriters. Melvyn Douglas, an idle playboy, meets Garbo on a traffic island when she asks for directions to the Eiffel Tower. He guides her finger to the correct spot on her map and gives it a squeeze. "Must you flirt?" Garbo drones in her lugubrious voice and then in a corrective tone tells him: "Suppress it!" Fascinated, he follows her even though she describes him as "the unfortunate product of a doomed culture." He shows her the City of Lights from the top of the Eiffel Tower. "I do not deny its beauty," she says with a real sadness, "but it is a waste of electricity." Douglas happily discovers that she is perfectly willing to go to his apartment with him. She regards him as an interesting specimen for study. He resumes his florid seduction attempt ("It's midnight. One half of Paris is making love to the other half. Look at the clock. One hand has met the other hand. They kiss. Isn't that wonderful?"), but her literalness once again deflates him: "That's the way a clock works. There's nothing wonderful about it."

ABOVE
Still from 'Ninotchka' (1939)
Stern, impassive Ninotchka (Greta Garbo) is sent to Paris to check on the bungling trade representatives, Buljanoff, Iranoff and Kopalski. She eventually opens herself up to the comradeship of others and becomes a human being.

OPPOSITE
Still from 'Ninotchka' (1939)
Ninotchka is slowly seduced by European decadence and Count Leon d'Algout (Melvyn Douglas).

The writers subtly unify the scene at the apartment with references to a Polish lancer. Garbo tells Douglas about wanting to fight on the barricades rather than work the family farm. She shows him the scar (on her neck) courtesy of a Polish lancer, and when he fawns over her hurt, her blunt honesty again disrupts him: "Don't pity me. Pity the Polish lancer. After all, I'm still alive." The surprise comes at the end of the scene after a phone call reveals to Garbo that Douglas was the one who corrupted her associates with the hedonism of Paris. She suddenly prepares to go. He tries to stall her. Finally, when she is at the door, he reminds her that before the phone rang she had kissed him. The timing is now perfect to show the audience the undernourished, feeling person inside Ninotchka, the one who will later buy the hat: "I kissed the Polish lancer too – right before he died." It is a great exit line.

Ninotchka's director Ernst Lubitsch earned Wilder's affection and respect as much as Mitchell Leisen, the director of *Midnight*, drew his wrath. Evidently Leisen regarded a Brackett-and-Wilder script as a suggested blueprint for a film rather than the masterplan the writers had intended. Leisen deferred to actors who wished to have dialogue or scenes changed or dropped. Wilder fought with Leisen constantly, and he maintained that even reserved, patient Charles Brackett came to detest the director. There may be something in the writers' insistence that a good script should be shot as written since today Leisen is mostly remembered for the films he directed from scripts by noted writers – by Brackett and Wilder, by Maxwell Anderson (*Death Takes a Holiday*, 1934), and by Preston Sturges (*Easy Living*, 1937).

Brackett and Wilder's two other screenplays for Leisen fall below the level set by *Midnight*, but they are often interesting and sometimes inspired. The script for *Arise, My Love* (1940) reached them after other writers had already worked on it. It also stars Claudette Colbert, playing a character seemingly based on Martha Gellhorn, the famous war correspondent and the third wife of Ernest Hemingway. The three-act structure of the classical Hollywood screenplay can be recognised more clearly in *Arise, My Love* than in any other Brackett-and-Wilder script because the acts vary so much in tone. The film almost seems more like an anthology of three loosely connected but different stories. Act One emphasises action and adventure. Colbert, in Spain during the Civil War, manages to rescue from a Spanish prison a soldier of fortune played by Ray Milland. Two fast-paced chases add energy to this part of the film. Act Two is a romance set in Paris. Milland declares his affection for Colbert while she tries to concentrate on her job as a journalist. Act Three, reminiscent of the end of Hitchcock's *Foreign Correspondent* (1940), turns its attention to the conflict in Europe and concludes in the fashion of a propaganda piece. Planning to marry, Colbert and Milland are travelling on the *Athenia* when it is sunk on 3 September 1939. They postpone their wedding and decide to work separately for the war effort. Emotional honesty and intelligence were becoming trademarks for Brackett-and-Wilder scripts even in genres as constricting as those described here. At an inn where Colbert and Milland retreat for a romantic idyll, for example, a maid pauses after seeing a luggage sticker for the American line. She recalls her sister in America and reflects painfully on the prospect of another war.

The rift with Mitchell Leisen over changes to the script for *Hold Back the Dawn* (1941) sharpened Wilder's desire to direct as a way to protect his scripts.

Still from 'Arise, My Love' (1940)
Successful reporter Augusta Nash (Claudette Colbert) and mercenary Tom Martin (Ray Milland) are caught up in the events of World War Two. Colbert later commented that the 'Gusto' Nash role had been her favourite.

Still from 'Arise, My Love' (1940)
Gusto and Tom hijack a plane so that they can escape the dictatorship in Spain.

The movie concerns stranded refugees waiting in a Mexican border town for
their quota numbers to enter the United States. Charles Boyer plays an opportunist who sees in a lonely young schoolteacher a chance for marriage and an
easy entry into America. In one scene the writers give Boyer a speech to a cockroach in which he imagines himself the border official delaying the bug's passage
across the wall of his hotel room. Boyer thought the whole idea was silly, and
he went to Leisen to get the scene dropped. Leisen supported his star. What
was worse, Boyer later spoke abruptly to Wilder when he dared to interrupt
the star's lunch to discuss the matter.

Perhaps the dismissive lunchtime behaviour mattered more to Wilder than
Boyer's failure to understand the cockroach scene. For all the intelligence
required of scriptwriters in classical-era Hollywood – the intelligence of poise
and versatility and patience with the system as well as the intelligence of putting
words on paper effectively – the writer's position in the studio system was not
a respected one. They formed the sentences that became the memorable dialogue and the beautifully dovetailed plots, but they were regarded as inter-
changeable parts. When Brackett and Wilder turned over their wonderfully
written script for *Midnight* to producer Arthur Hornblow, for example, he automatically handed it to writer Ken Englund for a polish job. Hornblow was operating on the producer's superstition that, good or bad, a script could always
be sent through one more typewriter. After Englund made his changes, Hornblow returned the script to Brackett and Wilder for more work. They then
resubmitted their original version with a few cosmetic changes, which the producer decided he liked. (All the Wilder biographers as well as a *Life* magazine
article from 1944 report this apocryphal-sounding story; Ed Sikov confirmed it
by checking the studio production records.) It had to be galling, knowing that
administrators with money and power but limited verbal and intellectual skills
were routinely passing uninformed judgements on your hard work. Speaking no
doubt for many disaffected writers, Wilder said what he really thought to Michel

*"It's not necessary for a director to know how to
write; however, it helps if he knows how to read."*

Billy Wilder [4]

Ciment for a series of articles in *Positif*: "What we wrote was a bit of toilet paper that they either used or they didn't."

The Boyer incident was the last straw, evidently for calm and collected Brackett as well as for brash Billy Wilder. Their mutual animosity united them in rewriting the final third of the movie and giving most of Boyer's lines to Olivia de Havilland, who plays the schoolteacher and who was thrilled to be the beneficiary of Boyer's stupidity and arrogance. (The writers must have still been fuming over a year later when they wrote *The Major and the Minor*, since the train-station scene features a little girl who pulls her mother over to a newsstand and points out a magazine article called 'Why I Hate Women' by Charles Boyer.)

All of the weaknesses in *Hold Back the Dawn* turn up in the final third, so perhaps the hasty rewrite took a toll on unity. The movie rushes through a number of key scenes (a chase, a bedside hospital vigil and a tearful reunion) in the final few minutes. Boyer's limited range makes his later crisis of conscience and regeneration unconvincing, but the spinsterish schoolteacher emerges as a real person. Brackett and Wilder again find the right personalising details. Perhaps in an effort of keeping the sentimentality in their story from becoming mawkish, they often use objects rather than dialogue to convey de Havilland's hunger for love. Driving with Boyer in a rainstorm, she happily interprets the rhythm of the car wipers to be saying "together, together, together." In some ways, this character is a sister to Phoebe Frost, the emotionally starved congresswoman played by Jean Arthur in *A Foreign Affair* (1948).

Samuel Goldwyn offered Brackett and Wilder their next writing job. In negotiating the deal, Wilder made sure that he would have permission to be on the set to watch Howard Hawks direct their script. He had been encouraged by the examples of John Huston at Warner Brothers and Preston Sturges, fellow writers who were getting the chance to direct. Huston was ready to direct *The Maltese Falcon* with Humphrey Bogart, and Sturges, a fellow Paramount hand, had written and directed two trial runs in 1940: *The Great McGinty* and a sixty-seven

ABOVE
Still from 'Ball of Fire' (1941)
Sugarpuss O'Shea (Barbara Stanwyck, sitting) helps out Bertram Potts (Gary Cooper), professor of linguistics, in his pursuit of her slang words. "This is the first time anybody moved in on my brain," she says.

LEFT
Still from 'Ball of Fire' (1941)
Sugarpuss O'Shea and the professors of the Daniel S. Totten Foundation dance in a lexical remake of 'Snow White and the Seven Dwarfs.'

minute B-picture called *Christmas in July*. Both had been commercial enough for the studio to let him continue in the director's chair.

Billy Wilder also chose a promising commercial property for the Samuel Goldwyn/Howard Hawks movie, a modernised retelling of *Snow White and the Seven Dwarfs*. He and Charles Brackett would set their version among a group of eccentric and cherubic college professors busy writing an encyclopaedia. Gary Cooper plays the professor assigned the essay on slang. He realises that his sheltered life has left him ignorant of his subject, so he ventures into the city to discover first-hand how real people talk. Barbara Stanwyck plays a nightclub singer who speaks little else but slang. On the run from her gangster boyfriend, she also needs a place to stay. The film, *Ball of Fire* (1941), is one of the lightest and freshest and most pleasantly artificial that Brackett and Wilder ever wrote.

Watching Hawks direct, Wilder observed an austere film-maker at work, one who avoided displays of style for their own sake. Like many directors from classical-era Hollywood, Hawks favoured a no-frills visual approach, one that ranked the content, the acting, and the writing higher in importance than the camerawork. Wilder always claimed something of the same for himself – elegance in shooting the story but nothing too fancy. Whenever film direction called attention to itself, Wilder questioned the needless showmanship. "Helicopter shots I don't mind, but not in the living room, please," he said to Axel Madsen. "There is a disregard for neatness in directing." To Chris Columbus, Wilder elaborated: "There's never, never a phoney shot in any of my pictures. Never one of those astonishing 'living room seen through the burning fireplace from the point of view of the roofer on top.' … It's all logical and you don't know where the cut is. I don't shoot it like a hack. I shoot it elegantly." The colourful nature of these quotes reminds us that the flamboyance in a Billy Wilder film usually comes from verbal rather than visual fireworks. But *usually* is a good qualifier. As Stephen Farber points out, visual exaggeration turns up too, and when such overt touches of style appear more rarely, they can be more memorable: "It is Wilder's delight in the outrageous that is the most distinguishing visual characteristic of his films. In spite of Wilder's cynicism, there is a rather astonishing exuberance in the imagery of his films, an exuberance in the power of art that his films so often celebrate."

In the work of writer-director Billy Wilder, both types of flamboyance – the verbal and the visual – are worth looking for.

Billy Wilder and Charles Brackett (1944)
In their office at Paramount studios.

"I worked with two people and they were ideal: Diamond, of course, and Brackett, with whom I had lots of fights, but they were difficult, constructive fights."

Billy Wilder [3]

Writer-Director
1942–1950

The first two films that Billy Wilder directed conform to rather than challenge the conventions of their genres. Knowing that the risk of failure was high for his first directing efforts, he intentionally chose properties likely to satisfy audiences. Both did. The first is a comedy called *The Major and the Minor* (1942). It was based on a magazine story (and later a play) about a woman who fails to establish herself in the big city and who has to return home by buying a child's train ticket (since the price of fares has risen). This comic premise of mistaken identity is sustained throughout most of the film.

Disguises and their various comic and dramatic complications were by now a recurrent motif in Brackett-and-Wilder scripts. The Wilder films often exploit in light and dark shades the wit it takes on the part of the protagonist to carry off a disguise. The film-makers obviously respect the Claudette Colbert character in *Midnight* because, though penniless, she has the guts and the brains to pull off her masquerade as a Cinderella who belongs in the higher social set. The film implies that this kind of cleverness enriches her much more than all their money benefits the vapid sophisticates. A psychological rather than a physical disguise in Wilder films, however, often confines rather than liberates. The plot of *Ninotchka* is calculated to get the Russian envoy to see that her outer demeanour of sternness is, after all, merely a comfortable role she has unknowingly slipped into, and that the real Ninotchka is the inner woman who can laugh in the famous restaurant scene. Melvyn Douglas recognises this inner person and uses love and laughter to free Ninotchka from her ideological corset. In *Hold Back the Dawn*, the Charles Boyer character becomes uncomfortable in his own skin for different reasons. He comes to feel that the manipulating gigolo who has married Olivia de Havilland just to gain entry into America is a role that is unworthy of him. A reformation is called for.

A plot in which physical or psychological disguise plays an important part can also engage its audience through the time-tested technique of discrepant levels of awareness. In other words, when the audience knows more about what is going on than at least one of the characters in a scene, they feel smarter, attend more closely, and pick up subtleties. Comic and dramatic ironies can occur. When a greater discrepancy exists between the understanding of the audience and more

Still from 'Sunset Boulevard' (1950)
Has-been silent movie star Norma Desmond (Gloria Swanson) shows her disgust for her ghostwriter/gigolo Joe Gillis (William Holden).

"...if a disguise, or if anything of that sort, is helpful for the development of a picture, then I will do it. I will stoop to nothing but to excellence."

Billy Wilder [3]

than one character in a scene, the dramatic possibilities multiply. A graphic break-down of such a screen situation might look like this:

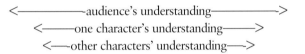

One could even say that this reliable dramatic strategy is to the cinema of Billy Wilder what the three-shot pattern of editing is to the movies of Alfred Hitchcock. In interviews throughout his career, Hitchcock delighted in explaining how the early Soviet film theorists conducted experiments with audiences. They would show them a shot of a character looking, a shot of what the character sees, and a shot of the character's mostly neutral reaction. When they then changed only the middle shot (from, say, a bowl of soup to a person in a coffin) the audience would say that the reaction changed, too (from hunger to grief). Hitchcock savoured such stories for a number of reasons. They suggested in a sense that a film-maker could photograph thought, something possible in no other art form. They also suggested that a film-maker could construct a performance at the editing bench, that actors were really just another prop in the making of a film, like lights and cameras. Hitchcock's *Rear Window* (1954) is built upon such three-shot editing patterns. Hitchcock told Peter Bogdanovich in an interview that the possibilities of such editing were "limitless."

Similarly, Wilder was a virtuoso at working out the permutations of discrepant levels of awareness. This tactic gives the audience a higher, privileged position from which to experience the developing story. *The Apartment* (1960), for example, is built upon on such discrepancies. The audience sees, first, that Jack Lemmon is lending his apartment key to philandering executives at work as a place to shack up with their girlfriends. They also notice, second, that Lemmon

has a shy affection for Shirley MacLaine, the elevator operator at work. Third, they observe that when Lemmon is called in by Fred MacMurray, the boss, to be reprimanded for his pimping, Lemmon is surprised to have his married boss ask to borrow the apartment key for himself. Having, like Lemmon, been caught off guard by this twist, the audience is less ready for, fourth, the scene in which MacMurray later meets up with his girlfriend, who turns out to be MacLaine. As they head off to Lemmon's apartment and the film cuts back to a shot of Lemmon all alone in front of a theatre where he had planned to meet MacLaine, the careful dramatic construction and the greater knowledge of the audience create poignancy rather than sentimentality. Wilder could exploit the possibilities of the comic and dramatic discrepancies of a plot as neatly as Hitchcock could develop his beloved editing strategy in moving and complex ways. No one in the history of the movies orchestrated the possibilities of plotting better than Billy Wilder.

In *The Major and the Minor,* Ginger Rogers plays a woman who has tried twenty-four different jobs during her year in New York. She has quit the last one – demonstrating scalp treatments in the home – when customer Robert Benchley decides that rather than hair care he would like her to "slip out of that wet coat and into a dry martini." She leaves. In desperation to return home, Ginger adapts the contents of her suitcase into the disguise of a twelve-year old girl and buys a half-fare ticket. The screenwriters stumble a bit in their early attempts to exploit the audience's greater knowledge that Ginger really is an adult, perhaps because two suspicious train conductors are all but certain that she is not a child at all.

When Ginger ducks into a private stateroom belonging to Ray Milland, who plays a teacher at a cadet academy, the film shifts smoothly into a higher gear. It is the first of two memorable train-compartment scenes in the cinema of Billy Wilder (the other, also built around a disguise, appears in *Some Like It Hot* with

"I would just like to write good parts, to make pictures where, after the people leave the theatre, they can go to the drugstore and talk about it for fifteen minutes. I'm very happy if there is something worth discussing."

Billy Wilder [2]

Jack Lemmon and Marilyn Monroe). Seeing a person dressed as a child, Milland unthinkingly slips into the avuncular persona he adopts around children at school (which, we later see, is something of his own psychological disguise). The following conversation in his train compartment plays on two levels, his innocent-seeming small talk being taken by Sue-Sue (as he calls Ginger) and the audience in a more adult way. As Milland goes off to the bathroom to get ready for bed, for example, he tells Ginger to call out if she needs any help with her buttons. Out of the innocent-looking twelve-year old Sue-Sue comes the wary voice of the woman who has just escaped the libidinous clutches of Robert Benchley: "Oh, I haven't had any button trouble for a long time, Uncle Philip." The audience, superior in knowing more about who is who, enjoys the moment.

Later in the film, Wilder and Brackett achieve some effective moments by having a character display unexpected discernment. This surprise comes when the adolescent sister of Milland's fiancée is finally alone with Sue-Sue: "Oh, cut the baby talk. You're not twelve just because you talk like you're six. How old are you? Twenty? Twenty-five? Or *what*?" The tone of the "or what" suggests appalling middle-aged possibilities. Diana Lynn plays Lucy, this street-smart teen. Like John Barrymore in *Midnight*, Lucy functions essentially as a choric character who stage-manages the developing plot. She is the embodiment of Brackett and Wilder on the screen. Her realistic voice adds some fresh air, and the irony of the least-likely person seeing through Ginger's disguise is a smart, effective touch. Lucy keeps Sue-Sue in cigarettes and teaches her the twenty-three musts and the twenty-four must-nots of life at the academy. Wilder and Brackett know what can be gained in honesty when a character takes off the mask. An effective, unguarded moment occurs when this canny teenager lets the tough demeanour slip long enough to admit to Ginger that she feels closer to her than she ever did to her own real sister.

The visual and verbal exaggeration is applied to comic purposes. When a cadet finally gets alone with Ginger, he seemingly recites his lesson about military tactics involving the Maginot Line. It's really a convoluted spiel calculated to permit him to get her in a clinch and kiss her. Visually, the perspective of cadets turning to watch Ginger enter the mess hall registers the considerable impact on these adolescent boys of a girl on campus. At the dance scene with the girls from Miss Shackleford's school, a witty perspective shot of a line of girls shows them all with the peekaboo hairstyle of Veronica Lake.

On the set of 'The Major and the Minor' (1942)
Billy Wilder (right) with Rita Johnson, Ray Milland and Ginger Rogers. About directing, Wilder once said, "A director must be a policeman, a midwife, a psychoanalyst, a sycophant and a bastard."

ABOVE
Still from 'The Major and the Minor' (1942)
Susan Applegate makes a big impression in the boys-only academy. Although the film seemed innocuous on paper, on the screen it flirted with paedophilia.

LEFT
Still from 'The Major and the Minor' (1942)
Lucy Hill (Diana Lynn) sees through Susan's disguise immediately. Lucy is a true friend and her sharp mind gives an edge to an otherwise saccharine film.

PAGES 38/39
Still from 'Five Graves to Cairo' (1943)
British soldiers march across Indio, California, which stood in for North Africa. The photography is by John F. Seitz, who also filmed 'Double Indemnity', 'The Lost Weekend' and 'Sunset Boulevard'.

ABOVE
Publicity still from 'Five Graves to Cairo' (1943)
Erich von Stroheim and Anne Baxter.

RIGHT
Still from 'Five Graves to Cairo' (1943)
John J. Bramble (Franchot Tone, second left) is
a lost British soldier who disguises himself as a
dead waiter when the Germans arrive. He is
about to find out that the waiter was spying for
Rommel (Erich von Stroheim, centre).

Wilder's second directing effort, *Five Graves to Cairo* (1943), uses the genre of the wartime melodrama to present an updated version of *Hotel Imperial*, a play by Lajos Biró which was also the first film that Charles Brackett produced. This time the tools of disguise and mistaken identity in the Brackett-and-Wilder script are applied to drama rather than comedy. Franchot Tone plays the sole British survivor from a tank attack in North Africa. He just makes it to a hotel ahead of the advance troops of Field Marshal Rommel (Erich von Stroheim) and his German tank corps who have routed the British Eighth Army at Tobruk. To protect himself, Tone adopts the identity of a hotel waiter who was killed in an air attack. He discovers after Rommel arrives, however, that the waiter was really an advance agent-in-place for the Germans. Tone must now maintain this identity for protection and also try to discover the secret desert location of Rommel's supply depots. The crafty reputation of Rommel (along with a kingly performance by Stroheim) makes the scenes in which Tone wins Rommel's trust some of the most effective in the film. Tone treads a shaky verbal tightrope. He must answer Rommel's questions about his supposed work as a spy in a satisfactory manner while also attempting to gain useful military information from the cunning Desert Fox. The film becomes a series of mental moves and countermoves.

The verbal flair that Wilder favours is thus applied to these two military chessmen. Tone flamboyantly describes himself as a spy as "the vulture who flies ahead of the Stukkas." Rommel applauds the colourful metaphor: "Rather well said." Later, the field marshal himself does a bit of boasting about his plans for capturing Churchill. Tone now repays the compliment by quoting Rommel to Rommel: "Rather well said." In such slight and incremental ways, Tone wins Rommel's trust.

A group of British officers are brought as prisoners into the hotel, and Rommel becomes the expansive host who cannot resist gloating about the ingenuity of his hidden desert supplies. Wilder uses the omniscient camera as a visual means for further exploiting the discrepant levels of awareness that organise the plotting. The introduction of Franchot Tone's character had earlier involved a striking shot in which John Seitz's camera had pushed in closer and closer on the unconscious, heat-fatigued soldier until it focused on the name (J.J. Bramble) on his dogtags. Now, with Tone rushing about as the waiter serving Rommel and the British prisoners, the camera begins another extreme push in. It stops on the whiskey decanter that Tone has just placed in front of the British, around which he has wrapped, nearly imperceptibly, the same dogtags identifying himself. Without the help of dialogue, Wilder's camera elevates the knowledge of the audience and comments on the disguise and deception at work in the scene.

ABOVE
On the set of 'Five Graves to Cairo' (1943)
Erich von Stroheim was a strong directorial influence on Wilder. When they first met, Wilder complimented von Stroheim by saying that he was ten years ahead of his time. "Twenty," corrected von Stroheim.

PAGES 42/43
Screenwriters playing a word game at the Paramount commissary (1944)
Clockwise from the foreground: Charles Brackett, Walter DeLeon, Frank Waldman, Dwight Mitchell Wiley, Billy Wilder and Frank Partos.

*"When I did Double Indemnity, I tried every
leading man in town. I went about as low as
George Raft, that's pretty low."*

Billy Wilder[3]

Just as his first two directing efforts conformed to their genres, Wilder's
next two projects challenged cinematic conventions. As would be expected,
both were controversial. *Double Indemnity* (1944), his next film, was based on
a crime novel by James M. Cain. The subject matter of an insurance salesman
and a lonely housewife who plan to insure and then kill her husband was too
sordid for Charles Brackett. After reading *The Big Sleep*, Wilder brought in
detective novelist Raymond Chandler as a collaborator. He had in mind for
the film a stylised realism with one of Hollywood's first anti-heroes as the protagonist. John Seitz would shoot the film with low-key lighting and use everyday settings like local supermarkets, bowling alleys and burger joints to add
seediness.

The language is just as gritty as the locales. Fred MacMurray plays Walter
Neff, whose speech reveals a streetwise cockiness. He mentions a "crown
block" falling on a victim, a "monoxide job," "a morgue job," his urge to
"crook the house," "hitting it to the limit," going "straight down the line"
and a "three-to-ten stretch in Tehachapi." The snap and crackle of idiomatic

LEFT
On the set of 'Double Indemnity' (1944)
Billy Wilder instructs Barbara Stanwyck on how to make *femme fatale* Phyllis Dietrichson as sleazy as possible.

ABOVE
On the set of 'Double Indemnity' (1944)
Billy Wilder encourages Barbara Stanwyck, whilst Fred MacMurray looks on.

train. And do you know how fast that train was going at the point where the body was found? Fifteen miles an hour. Now how can anybody jump off a slow-moving train like that with any kind of expectation that he would kill himself? No, no soap, Mr Norton. We're sunk and we'll have to pay through the nose. And you know it."

The last four words are the *coup de grâce*. In addition to the satisfaction of verbally dressing down the boss, Robinson reveals his character. He hates the officialdom and formality that often covers incompetence, and he enjoys cutting straight to the bone. In that regard, he is like MacMurray's character. He also seems to be married to his job. He apparently pores over actuarial tables the way some people, like Walter Neff perhaps, read pulp fiction. His commitment to integrity, other scenes suggest, has made him lonely. Roger Ebert, in his book *The Great Movies,* suggests that *Double Indemnity* shows the dangers inherent in abandoning structure and rules, as illustrated by MacMurray and Stanwyck, but also the dangers of adhering too closely to the rules, as illustrated by Robinson. In one scene Robinson asks MacMurray to quit selling insurance and become his assistant. Wilder and Chandler give him another colourful speech in which he compares the desk of the insurance investigator to a surgical table. He sees his pencils not as pencils but as scalpels and bone chisels. It is a proposal of sorts – one lonely man reaching out to another and shielding his feelings and the chance of rejection with an exaggerated language. This is the unconscious disguise of Barton Keyes. He lets the mask slip only at the very end, when a dying MacMurray tells him that Robinson missed nabbing the killer because he was too close to him – just across the desk. "Closer than that," Robinson softly admits, and MacMurray responds with the film's last words: "I love you, too."

Wilder and Chandler unify the film with the running business of Robinson never having a match for his cigar and MacMurray always having to strike one for him. The mutuality of the gesture suggests a deeper tie between the men. In another scene a worried MacMurray sneaks into Robinson's office and listens to Dictaphone cylinders to see if Robinson suspects him. He hears Robinson personally vouch for him. Wilder keeps the camera on MacMurray as he listens uneasily to his friend praise him. MacMurray's betrayal of Robinson rivals his other crimes in emotional severity.

Part of the dark pleasure of *Double Indemnity* comes from watching Mac-Murray create what he and Stanwyck think will be a great deception. Another part of the pleasure comes in watching their attempt to "crook the house" crumble before them. Wilder and Chandler exploit the audience's shared knowledge with MacMurray of how the crime was carried out so that viewers often find themselves rooting for the killer. When Robinson later tells Mac-Murray his theory of what really happened – that the husband was killed first and then thrown on the train tracks – we sweat along with the nervous Mac-Murray over whether he will be found out. Robinson correctly spells it all out with references to a "somebody else" who was really on the train, not knowing that he is looking at that "somebody else." A chill seems to pass through MacMurray and perhaps the audience when Robinson even unconsciously uses the same trolley metaphor ("straight down the line") that MacMurray and Stanwyck have used for mutual encouragement. To them, the metaphor

On the set of 'Double Indemnity' (1944)
Wartime food shortages meant that security
guards were posted to protect the real cans of
food on the grocery store set. Despite this, a can
of peaches and four bars of soap went missing.

suggests their intensity of commitment to each other. To Robinson, it suggests
the culprits' inability to escape punishment, to get off the trolley until the end
of the ride.

The stylised realism of the film is further established by the narration. The
movie begins with MacMurray, shot in the shoulder, staggering into his office
late at night to dictate his confession to Robinson. Wilder returns to shots of
MacMurray at his Dictaphone, the sweat standing out on his face, the stain on
his jacket shoulder spreading. His narration serves as transitions between many
scenes, the first time in Wilder's career that he used voice-over narration, other
than the framing device and a few subsequent voice-overs in *Hold Back the
Dawn*. Since such narration can emphasise irony and the gap between a character's understanding and what has really happened, Wilder found it useful and
returned to the device often, most famously in *Sunset Boulevard* (1950), a film
narrated by a dead man. A good deal of MacMurray's humanity and some of
the film's unique poetry also emerge in these voice-over monologues: "It was a
hot afternoon, and I can still remember the smell of honeysuckle all along the

Still from 'Double Indemnity' (1944)
An alternative ending, where Barton Keyes
witnesses the execution of Walter Neff (in gas
chamber), was filmed but not used.

street. How could I have known that murder can sometimes smell like honeysuckle?" Sometimes, the narration is just plain coy. On Stanwyck's first visit to
MacMurray's apartment, they kiss and plan murder and when the obligatory
dissolve comes, MacMurray's voice-over says, "So we just sat there." When
we dissolve back, however, we see MacMurray reclined on the sofa smoking
and Stanwyck silently staring off in what may be a 1944 non-censorable image
of post-coital lassitude.

ABOVE
Still from 'The Lost Weekend' (1945)
Don Birnam (Ray Milland) is an alcoholic writer who pawns his typewriter for a drink.

RIGHT
Still from 'The Lost Weekend' (1945)
Ray Milland was so convincing that he got picked up by a cop whilst filming on location.

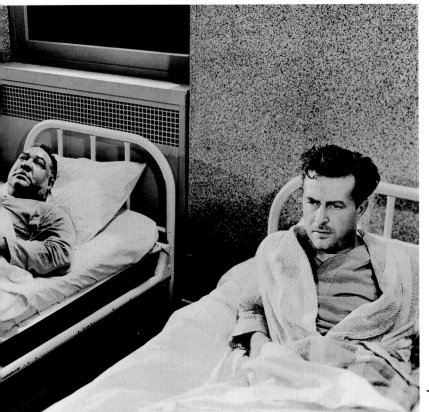

Still from 'The Lost Weekend' (1945)
The brutally realistic portrayal of Don Birnam is still shocking today. The film went on to win four Oscars from seven nominations.

Still from 'The Lost Weekend' (1945)
Don Birnam wakes up in Bellevue Hospital where he meets a gay nurse. The subtext of the novel is that Birnam drinks because he cannot acknowledge his homosexuality. This subtext was not allowed to be mentioned in the film.

TO31046

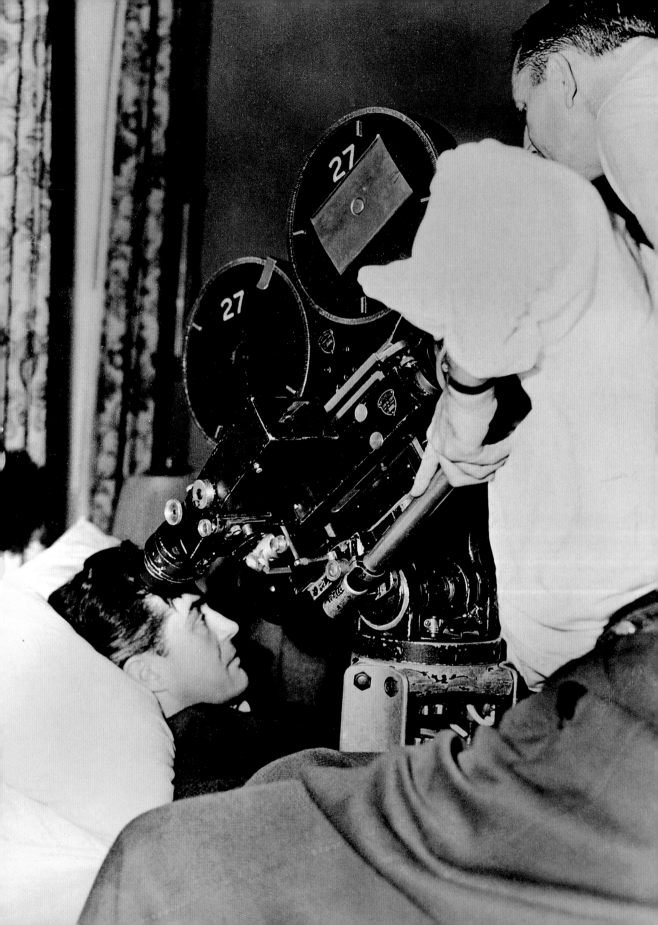

The Lost Weekend (1945), Wilder's next film, is a foray into social realism and Hollywood's first serious look at alcoholism. The style effectively mixes documentary-like shots of New York (Bellevue Hospital, Third Avenue) with expressionistic distortions. Wilder was back collaborating with Charles Brackett after reading Charles Jackson's novel on a train trip and deciding that it would make a good film.

Ray Milland plays Don Birnam, a would-be novelist whose drinking seems to give him the illusion of greater literary creativity. "Pour it softly, pour it gently, and pour it to the brim," Milland says to Nat (Howard da Silva), his bartender. The feeling he puts into these words, however, suggests additional reasons for his drinking, which the film indirectly explores. One of them is Milland's softness or perhaps even self-disgust. In the opening scene, for example, Milland channels his novelistic plotting skills not into the new book he intends to start but into ploys for smuggling two bottles of liquor into the country cottage he and his brother have reserved for the weekend. Milland proudly tells Nat his plan for his brother to find one of the bottles, which will then free him to drink the other at his leisure.

Like Billy Wilder, the Milland character loves forming florid sentences and, emboldened by drink, he soliloquises grandly. His colourful prose may also signal a wallowing in his condition: "Another drink, another binge, another bender, another spree." Nat later scolds Milland for his indifference to the feelings of others: "You're drunk and you're just making with the mouth." Making with the mouth – that is, drinking and forming sentences – is what this character does best. The concentric shot-glass rings on the bar top are his "little vicious circles." Much of the realism of the film comes not from clinical information about alcoholism (though there is a chilling scene in the alcoholic ward at Bellevue) but from the sheer cravenness of Milland's character and the self-abasement he will endure for the next drink. This human element has made the film endure. In one of his comments to Nat, Milland suggests something of the tangled motives of the long-term drinker: "There was despair, and a drink to counterbalance the despair, and then one to counterbalance the counterbalance." He senses the labyrinthine tangle of his own desires.

Wilder's visual style in *The Lost Weekend* uses *mise en scène* and depth of space in forceful ways. He often foregrounds objects that comment tellingly on Milland's plight. When Milland first visits a liquor store, for example, the camera shoots behind a shelf of bottles that partially blocks our view. After the clerk takes down the two bottles Milland requests, we see him more clearly. Later, he ransacks his apartment when he forgets where one of these bottles is hidden. Wilder shows him at the back of a shot with an upturned lamp, an image of his desperation, filling most of the foreground and dominating the frame. In another example, an insistently ringing telephone (a call from his worried girlfriend) appears in the foreground while Milland ignores it. Toward the end, he again enters a shot in the background, sneaks into the living room past his sleeping girlfriend and picks up her leopard coat from a chair near the camera. He moves to the coat, which he will exchange at a pawn shop for a revolver, as if it draws him like a magnet. In a nice spatial contrast, Wilder at one point films Milland from inside a liquor store that has not yet opened. We see him cross the street, recede into the distance and stand before a church to wait. It is clear from his tor-

"Voice-over is good as long as you're not describing what the audience is already seeing… Show, don't tell."

Billy Wilder[3]

On the set of 'The Lost Weekend' (1945)
Extreme close-ups help emphasise the degradation of Don Birnam.

ment that the stock of the small liquor store holds his attention more forcefully than anything offered at the large cathedral. As a further visual comment, Wilder often positions Milland's typewriter in the background of shots, suggesting its reduced importance to this hopeful writer.

The unconventional subject of *The Lost Weekend* and some negative advance screenings made the front office at Paramount nervous. The studio shelved the movie temporarily. Wilder accepted an offer to work in the Psychological Warfare Division of the United States army to assist in the post-war reconstruction of German film and theatre, essentially to de-Nazify them. Biographers from Maurice Zolotow on have pointed out the further disillusioning effects these five months had on Billy Wilder. He left New York after VE Day and viewed the increasing devastation in London, in Paris and finally in Berlin. The Red Cross may have verified what he had dreaded and feared – that his mother and grandmother and stepfather had been killed at Auschwitz. Maurice Zolotow and Kevin Lally indicate this, but Ed Sikov gives a differing account of the Red Cross having no information at all – that Wilder's family was gone without a trace. Looking for the grave of his father in Berlin, Wilder found the cemetery in ruins as a result of a tank battle, and met a cadaverous-looking rabbi whose accounts of wartime horrors like the rape and murder of his own wife were so horrific that Wilder's tough young driver broke down in tears. The raw film footage of the concentration camps shot by the liberating armies had now been gathered and the director was asked by the Office of War Information to shorten and polish the first cut of a documentary. The revision was called *Death Mills.* When he returned to the U.S., Wilder heard that Paramount head Barney Balaban had come to the rescue of *The Lost Weekend* and that it would have its national release. It was a critical and commercial hit, and Wilder won his first two Oscars for co-writing and directing the film.

The next few years for Billy Wilder led to changes at home and at work. The two longest relationships of his life in America were in the process of breaking up. He and his wife Judith had changed since their marriage in late 1936. Maurice Zolotow describes her change as that of a "Ninotchka in reverse," meaning that, among other things, as her husband was becoming the famous accumulator and collector, especially of art, she was becoming less interested in such things. The marriage ended in 1947; in 1949, Wilder married Audrey Young, a former singer with the Tommy Dorsey orchestra. They celebrated their fiftieth anniversary in 1999.

The working partnership with Charles Brackett, always marked by arguments over differences of taste, was also in its last stages although they would complete three more scripts. Their first collaboration after the war was *The Emperor Waltz* (1948), a musical with Bing Crosby and Joan Fontaine set in the dying days of the Austro-Hungarian Empire. Wilder's first movie in Technicolor, this lightweight film employs the meet-cute of two people brought together by their dogs. The film is one of Wilder's weakest. The partners' final two collaborations were *A Foreign Affair* (1948) and *Sunset Boulevard* (1950), both of which Brackett objected to.

ABOVE
Still from 'The Emperor Waltz' (1948)
Countess Johanna (Joan Fontaine) and phonograph salesman Virgil Smith (Bing Crosby) enjoy themselves in the Austrian Tyrol.

OPPOSITE
Still from 'The Emperor Waltz' (1948)
This hugely expensive Technicolor film went over budget. Also, Wilder was not happy that star Bing Crosby brought his own writers to rewrite his lines from the Brackett-and-Wilder script.

"I would worship the ground you walk on if only you lived in a better neighbourhood."

**Billy Wilder to Audrey Young,
whom he later married**

ABOVE
Still from 'A Foreign Affair' (1948)
Ex-Nazi Erika von Schlüetow (Marlene Dietrich) is a cabaret singer.

LEFT
Still from 'A Foreign Affair' (1948)
Frigid Congresswoman Phoebe Frost (Jean Arthur, left) is on a factfinding mission to investigate the immoral behaviour of US soldiers in rubble-strewn Berlin. She vies with the overtly sexual Erika von Schlüetow for the affections of Johnny Pringle.

OPPOSITE
Still from 'A Foreign Affair' (1948)
In post-war Berlin, Johnny Pringle (John Lund), like a lot of soldiers, trades with the Berliners. When he tries to trade a mattress with Erika von Schlüetow she spits in his face.

A Foreign Affair takes place in the bombed-out, post-war Berlin setting that Wilder had recently seen first-hand. It explores the fraternisation of American servicemen and the women of Berlin, particularly the secret relationship between John Pringle (John Lund) and Erika von Schlüetow (Marlene Dietrich), a German believed by the army brass to be shielding a former Nazi. When a congressional committee arrives to investigate post-war reconstruction and the "moral malaria" rumoured to be occurring, tension rises for Pringle. One of the committee members, Phoebe Frost (Jean Arthur) comes from Pringle's home state and makes him her unofficial host in Berlin. He pretends an attraction to her as a way of keeping her from learning the truth about Erika. An unusual love triangle results.

Or is it so unusual? On the surface, this rivalry bears some resemblance to the situation in *Ninotchka*. Greta Garbo plays an emotionally dry woman brought to life by love (like Jean Arthur's character in *A Foreign Affair*); Melvyn Douglas plays the man with two women in his life, and Ina Claire in *Ninotchka*, playing the Grand Duchess Swana, is the selfish, materialistic, pleasure-seeking rival. But Swana is meant to be laughed at; Dietrich's character in *A Foreign Affair* is meant to be understood. The decade that separates these two scripts had turned Wilder into more of a realist, and he presents a more complex, darker picture of the three characters in the latter film. All three are more human, especially the Marlene Dietrich character. Wilder shows that much of her survivalist hardness is the legacy of the war and the attendant loss of illusions. She sings about it in one of the cabaret scenes.

Charles Brackett, whose genteel outlook regarded women as either good or bad, objected to the scene in which Dietrich spits toothpaste in the face of John Lund (and into the camera) when he brings a mattress to her in her crumbling building. Dietrich understands the need on both sides for trading. According to Zolotow, Wilder told Brackett that it was her way of showing affection. To Brackett, she was simply a whore. "It offends me beyond words, Billy," Brackett said, a comment that was evidently becoming a refrain in their collaboration. Brackett no doubt also noticed and was offended by the way each of the main characters represents a nation's state of mind. As Kevin Lally puts it, "Wilder's genius stroke is his shaping of a comic romantic triangle into a metaphor for the confrontation between a paternalistic, innocent America and a war-ravaged, unsentimental Germany."

Still from 'Sunset Boulevard' (1950)
The bravura opening scene is narrated by the dead Joe Gillis floating in Norma's pool.

Still from 'Sunset Boulevard' (1950)
Joe Gillis (William Holden) resents being pampered like a pet poodle by his lover, ex-film star Norma Desmond (Gloria Swanson).

RIGHT
Still from 'Sunset Boulevard' (1950)
Norma's butler Max von Mayerling (Erich von Stroheim) buries her pet monkey.

BELOW
Still from 'Sunset Boulevard' (1950)
Norma dances with her gigolo Joe.

OPPOSITE
Still from 'Sunset Boulevard' (1950)
When Joe decides to leave Norma, she goes mad and shoots him.

Sunset Boulevard had initially been Brackett's idea, but he saw the premise of a
faded silent-screen star's comeback vehicle as material for comedy. As it became
what writers Louis Giannetti and Scott Eyman have described as "a fable and
meditation on the nature of Hollywood that turns into authentic tragedy,"
Brackett objected but lost out. All of the staples of Wilder's cinema are applied
to the tragic outcome. It had looked as if *The Lost Weekend* would end tragic-
ally, but a new ending had saved Ray Milland at the last minute from using the
revolver. Previously, Wilder had shown people who recognise their demeaning
psychological disguises and who reject them. In *Sunset Boulevard*, however, as
William Holden's voice-over narration explains, the dream that Norma "had
clung to so desperately… enfold(s) her."

The various gaps in the knowledge among characters add drama and tragic
irony rather than comedy. The audience sees that for Joe to call his relationship
with Norma "ghostwriting" is uncomfortably closer to the truth than he knows.
They also see that Betty Shaefer and her life-affirming world of writing and
young people are healthier for Holden's Joe Gillis than Norma Desmond and life
in her lonely, decayed mansion. Joe's lighter moments with both women reveal
this contrast well. Norma remains the centre of attention as she entertains Joe
dressed as Chaplin and, ludicrously, as a bathing beauty. At the New Year's Eve
party, however, Joe and Betty escape the throng of people and retire to the bathroom ("the Rainbow Room") where in a contest of equals they jokingly try to
top each other at creating corny movie dialogue. In spite of his rapport with
Betty, however, Joe favours the gold cigarette cases, the vicuna coats and his status as kept man until it is too late. He and Norma feed each other's worst, self-
indulgent illusions about Hollywood and both become caught up in the tragic
outcome.

Wilder finds interesting ways to make the verbal and visual high points coin-
cide. When Norma and Joe screen some of her silent classics (actually, a clip
from *Queen Kelly* (1928), directed by Erich von Stroheim), she rises, announces
the sureness of her return to the spotlight and is caught by the projector beam
as she turns imperiously to Joe. In another example, Joe's laconic narration of
how he ended up dead in Norma's pool is highlighted with the famous shot
looking up at him from the bottom of the pool. We hear his explanation while
we see him floating face down, the reporters lined around the edge, their flash-
bulbs popping.

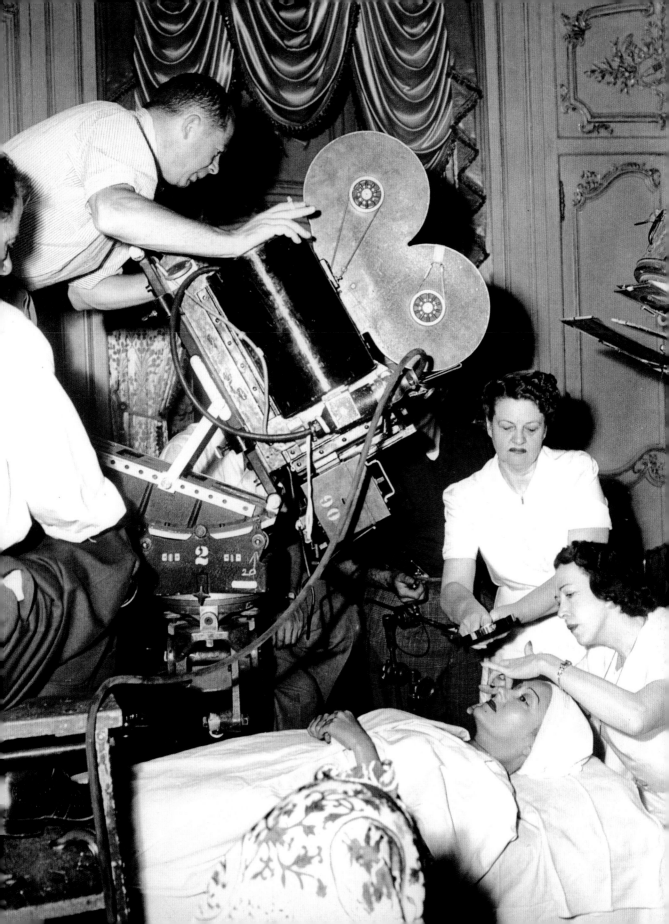

RIGHT
On the set of 'Sunset Boulevard' (1950)
Filming the final close-up. Erich von Stroheim
plays Max von Mayerling, Norma's butler and
one-time husband and director. Stroheim had
directed Swanson in the aborted 'Queen Kelly'.

PAGES 72/73
Still from 'Sunset Boulevard' (1950)
Norma: "I'm ready for my close-up Mr DeMille."

Writer-Director-Producer 1951–1957

Lacking Charles Brackett but having another Academy Award (his third) for co-writing *Sunset Boulevard*, Wilder now undertook the triple challenge of co-writing, directing and producing his films. During this period he worked with a different collaborator on each new script. His first project became the biggest failure so far in his career, though today it ranks high among his films. Wilder and writers Lesser Samuels and Walter Newman based their script on the 1925 mine disaster in which the nation followed the fate of a trapped worker named Floyd Collins. Wilder focused on the vulture-like climate the press can manufacture in such circumstances. In 1951, before sleazy talk shows and the proliferation of the tabloid press, he was decades ahead of his time.

Kirk Douglas plays a cynical reporter stranded in New Mexico who delays the rescue of Leo Minosa (Richard Benedict), the man trapped in an Indian burial mound. Douglas seeks to exploit the incident with the wire services, make a name for himself and reclaim his lost job at a big city newspaper. He trades upon the venality of the local sheriff (Ray Teal, whose defining image is his pet rattlesnake) by promising more votes if Leo is rescued in days rather than hours. He also starts an affair with Leo's bored wife (Jan Sterling). As the spectacle around the burial site grows to include vacationers arriving by the trainload and even circus rides to entertain them, Douglas' loathing of himself finally takes over and he orders the thrill-seekers to disperse.

In *Ace in the Hole,* Wilder indulges his misanthropy as never before. It appears in the language of Kirk Douglas, especially in his gloating words to his press rivals. In one scene, he arrives at the tent near the mountain and stares back at the colleagues who have always looked down on him. "Now I'm in the boat," he sneers, "and you're in the water. Let's see you swim." It appears in the striking visual touches, as when Douglas issues orders to the construction crew from atop the mountain and surveys the spread of cars and onlookers below like a monarch above his kingdom. It appears in the stunning final shot of the film. Stabbed by Leo's wife, Douglas hobbles back to the newspaper office and to the editor whose simple integrity Douglas had scoffed at. He reintroduces himself with words similar to those he used in their first meeting, pitches forward suddenly and lands dead at the editor's feet, his face staring straight into the floor-

"I have ten commandments. The first nine are, thou shalt not bore. The tenth is, thou shalt have right of final cut."

Billy Wilder[1]

Still from 'Ace in the Hole' (1951)
Chuck Tatum (Kirk Douglas) is the cynical reporter who delays Leo Minosa's rescue from a cave so that he can become well-known and get a better job.

level camera. Critics and audiences rejected the film and its corrosiveness. Paramount even retitled it *The Big Carnival* in an effort to soften the bluntness of the cynicism but had no better luck at getting people to see it. Wilder turned to the relative safety of popular Broadway plays for his next two movies.

Stalag 17, the first Hollywood treatment of life in a prisoner-of-war camp, begins like slice-of-life realism, which was quite uncharacteristic for Wilder. For the first time since *People on Sunday*, Wilder (this time working with co-writer Edward Blum) uses vignettes and loose plotting to create the flavour of prison camp life. The men bet cigarettes on their 'horse races' (running mice in mazes) and pay cigarettes to peek through a homemade telescope at women in the Russian compound. Realism colours attitudes as well as actions in the film. Dramatising discord within the barracks among the Americans (rather than simply between the Americans and Germans) is the smartest, freshest element of

Still from 'Ace in the Hole' (1951)
When the media report that Leo Minosa is
trapped in a cave, people from all over come
to witness the grisly spectacle.

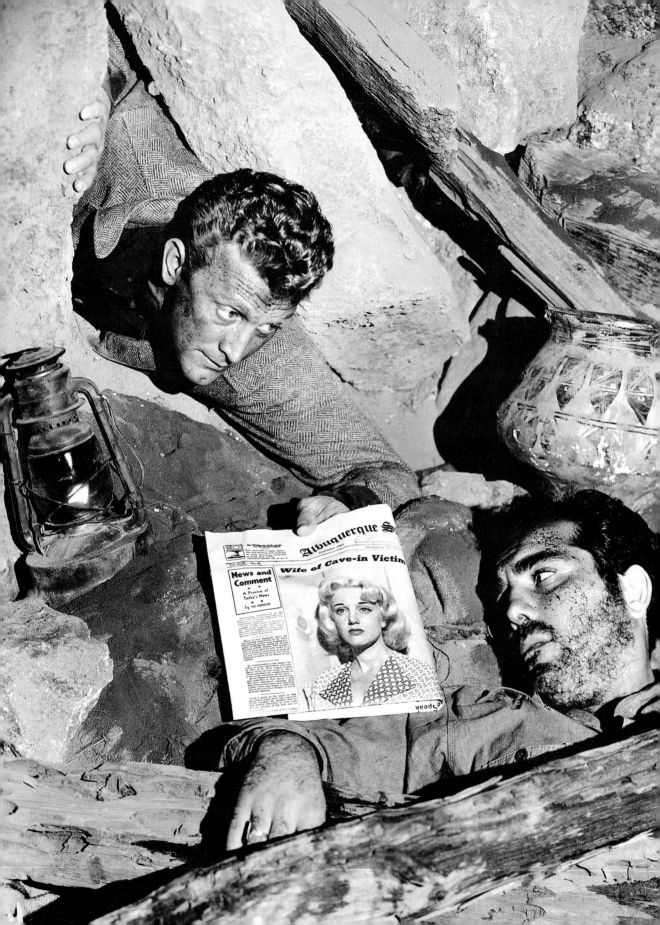

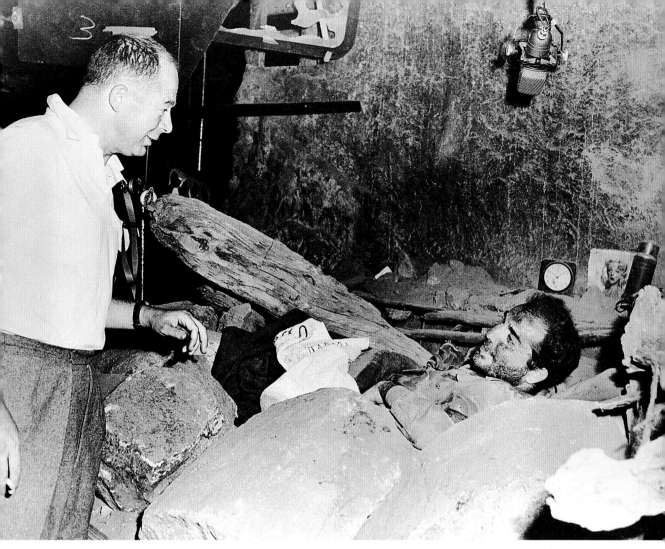

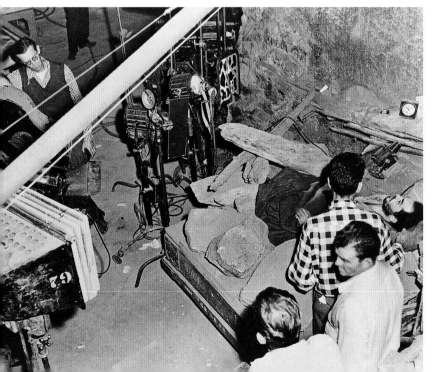

ABOVE
On the set of 'Ace in the Hole' (1951)
Billy Wilder checks to make sure that Richard Benedict is comfortable.

LEFT
On the set of 'Ace in the Hole' (1951)
This picture shows how little space is needed to create the illusion of a cave-in.

OPPOSITE
Still from 'Ace in the Hole' (1951)
Chuck Tatum plays the hero and pretends to be acting in Leo's (Richard Benedict) best interests.

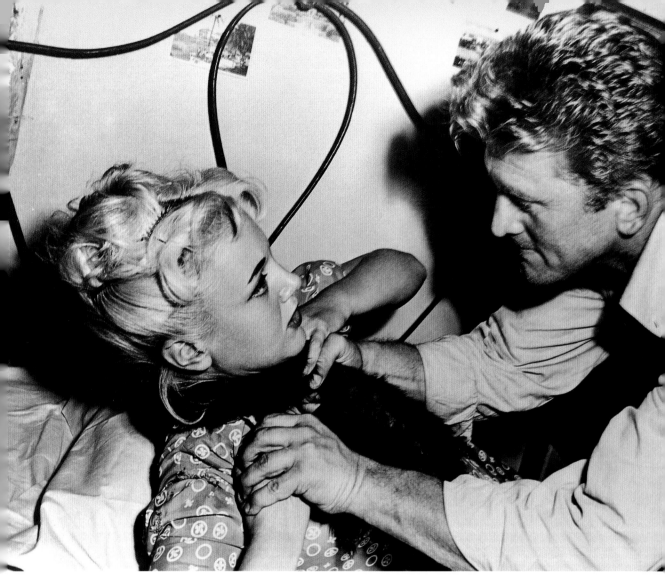

RIGHT
Still from 'Ace in the Hole' (1951)
Leo's wife Lorraine (Jan Sterling) makes lots
of money at the restaurant and makes a pass
at Chuck.

ABOVE
Still from 'Ace in the Hole' (1951)
When Chuck realises that Leo will die, he
quarrels with Lorraine, who fatally stabs him.

Wilder's approach. Though some of the attempts at comedy have aged the film, the depiction of the cynicism of barracks life and of the Americans' quick descent to scapegoating and vigilantism has kept the film honest and alive.

The object of the men's suspicions is Sefton, played by William Holden in a performance that *The Virgin Film Guide* aptly says 'made him Bogie's successor to American Cynicism.' Holden trades with the Germans and even bets against the chances of his own barrack mates getting out of the forest on their escape attempt. He wins. Failed escapes like this have made the POWs suspect an informer is among them. The men blame Holden partly because he has accumulated a footlocker full of loot at their expense. He is the nonconformist. Therefore, he must be guilty.

In the final hour of the film, Wilder lets the audience learn slightly before Holden does that the traitor is really the true-blue-seeming security chief Price (Peter Graves). This suspenseful delay pays off richly. The brief horseshoe-pitching scene occurs right after the audience sees Graves leave a note for the German guard in a hollowed-out chess piece. While playing horseshoes, Graves pumps one of the new camp arrivals to discover how a makeshift time bomb destroyed a German supply train. It is the first scene in the film in which the audience's superior knowledge of Graves as the informer allows them to savour the seemingly casual subtext of their conversation. Wilder is now back in his element of orchestrating various levels of awareness for dramatic effectiveness. He cannot resist the witty final shot to this scene: a close-up of Graves' horseshoe clanging on its stake with the off-camera voice commenting, seemingly about Graves, "A ringer!"

The audience now enjoys watching Holden rise to their level of understanding. He hides out in the barracks during an air-raid alert and observes Graves report his information about the bomb to a German guard. Graves, we now discover, is a German spy planted in the barracks. The second half of the film intensifies audience identification with Holden as he considers how to expose Graves. It is the only way to clear himself. Holden's outsider status has become his greatest asset in working out his plan. But his motivation would be sufficiently strong, anyway. In one of the most terse and telling lines in the script, Holden describes the gang beating his fellow POWs gave him. They all piled on, "only he beat the hardest," he says of the spy. *Stalag 17* turned out to be Billy Wilder's biggest hit at Paramount.

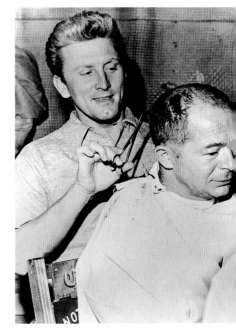

ABOVE
On the set of 'Ace in the Hole' (1951)
Kirk Douglas attends to Billy Wilder's follicles.

PAGE 82
Still from 'Stalag 17' (1953)
Animal (Robert Strauss) and Shapiro (Harvey Lembeck) are comedy characters who follow their desires. In this case, a female prisoner of war.

PAGE 83
Still from 'Stalag 17' (1953)
Shapiro dresses as Betty Grable, much to Animal's delight. Both actors were in the original smash-hit play and their roles were expanded by Wilder for the film.

ABOVE
Still from 'Stalag 17' (1953)
The camp commandant von Scherbach
(Otto Preminger) examines a dead prisoner.

RIGHT
Still from 'Stalag 17' (1953)
Sefton (William Holden), the despised profiteer,
confronts Price (Peter Graves), the righteous
security officer.

On the set of 'Stalag 17' (1953)
Billy Wilder directs famed director Otto
Preminger, who plays von Scherbach.

Still from 'Stalag 17' (1953)
Sefton attempts to escape with Dunbar
(Don Taylor).

His next project (co-written with Ernest Lehman) was *Sabrina* (1954), a return to the world of sophisticated romantic comedy suggestive of Ernst Lubitsch and of Wilder's early days at Paramount. Audrey Hepburn, who had just captivated the movie world in *Roman Holiday* (1953), plays the title character, a chauffeur's daughter on a palatial Long Island estate. Audrey has a crush on the family's playboy younger son (William Holden) but ends up choosing the stuffy, older brother (Humphrey Bogart). Wilder wanted to augment an aspect mentioned but not much developed in Samuel Taylor's play – the idea that Bogart uses himself to break up the girl's crush on his brother so that Holden can marry the daughter of a sugar-cane tycoon and guarantee a lucrative business merger for the family.

By focusing on the Bogart character, Wilder was making him into a sort of male Ninotchka, a life-denying figure whose dull, glum attitude results from being married to his job. Most of the memorable visual touches reveal Bogart's business-first approach to life. He calls in a dozen middle-aged secretaries to prove the resilience of a sheet of plastic by bouncing on it with an embarrassed William Holden. The loose framing of Bogart striding about in his cavernous office emphasises his successful but lonely life. When he resigns to pursue Hepburn on her voyage to Europe, Wilder films him jogging through a long perspective of opening doors, the end to his empty life as an executive.

Bogart undertakes the deception of replacing Holden with himself in the company of Hepburn for selfish business reasons, but once he gets to know her he experiences the same guilt that Charles Boyer does in *Hold Back the Dawn*, coupled with a Ninotchka-like recognition of his need for love. These insights emerge with exceptional finesse on the part of Wilder and Lehman. In one scene Bogart dances with Hepburn, ostensibly getting from her a French lesson for his upcoming trip to Paris. "How do you say, 'My sister has a yellow pencil?'" he asks her. She tells him. "How do you say, 'My brother has a lovely girl?'" After her translation and a slight pause, he asks, "And how do you say, 'I wish I were my brother.'" The sentences form a sort of syllogism for stylish comedy in which affection is revealed indirectly. It is akin to the cinematic arithmetic that Ernst Lubitsch practised with his theory of giving the audience information but letting them add it up. As Bogart turns Hepburn on the dance floor and we see her pensive expression, we realise that she, like us, has been paying attention.

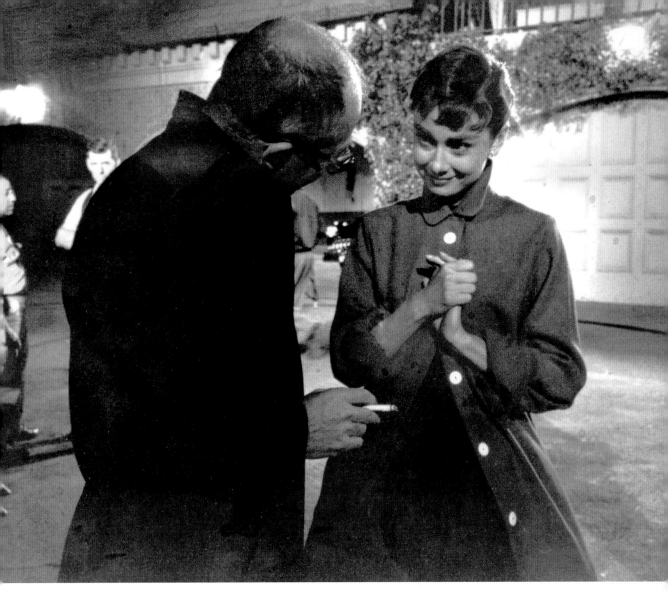

ABOVE
On the set of 'Sabrina' (1954)
Wilder said that there was something "absolutely adorable" about Audrey Hepburn. The production was difficult because of the actors' conflicting schedules and the constant rewrites. One Friday Wilder only had a page and a half to direct so Audrey delayed filming by feigning headaches and fumbling her lines. This enabled Wilder to do the necessary writing over the weekend.

OPPOSITE
On the set of 'Sabrina' (1954)
Audrey Hepburn on Wall Street between takes.

Still from 'The Seven Year Itch' (1955)
Richard Sherman (Tom Ewell) is a sexually repressed book editor. He dreams of seducing the girl upstairs, played by Marilyn Monroe.

OPPOSITE
On the set of 'The Seven Year Itch' (1955)
Marilyn Monroe shot this scene on location in New York. Her husband, Joe DiMaggio was disgusted by the whole thing and their marriage broke up. The footage was unusable and reshot on a set.

The era of the studio system was now ending. The United States Supreme Court had ruled against vertical integration, declaring that by also owning the theatre chains into which they released their films, the major studios were guilty of monopolistic business practices. It was a severe financial blow. With the rise of television occurring at roughly the same time, Hollywood was drastically changing. Billy Wilder owed Paramount Pictures three movies after his success with *Sunset Boulevard*. However, he left the studio after the third film (*Sabrina*) because of a clash with the front office. *Stalag 17* was being released in Germany and the studio wanted in the dubbing to make the German spy a Pole so as not to give offence. Wilder told Richard Brown in 1993 and Kevin Lally in 1994 that he objected and demanded an apology, which he never got. The film was released without the change of nationality, however.

His first two films after Paramount contain interesting moments, but neither reveals his distinctive stamp. *The Seven Year Itch* (1955), which he produced at Twentieth-Century Fox and co-wrote with George Axelrod (based on Axelrod's play), elaborates on the premise of the first scene in *The Major and the Minor*. Tom Ewell plays the summer bachelor with adulterous thoughts, and Marilyn Monroe is his neighbour subletting the hot apartment upstairs. Ewell uses his air conditioning to set up a seduction ploy. He has more of a conscience than Robert Benchley in the earlier movie and also more of an imagination. The film reveals how he alternates between mental images of gratification and exposure. Most viewers of the movie are disappointed to discover that the famous image of Marilyn in her billowing dress standing on the subway grating was initially in the film but was removed by a studio nervous over the sexual subject matter. The image was used in publicity for the film.

Still from 'The Seven Year Itch' (1955)
Richard and the girl get comfortable at the piano.

Still from 'The Seven Year Itch' (1955)
Richard's every move ends in disaster.

"[Marilyn Monroe] was never on time, not once.
Not once. Of course, I have an old aunt in Vienna
who was always on time to everything, but who
would want to see her in a movie?"

Billy Wilder

Still from 'The Seven Year Itch' (1955)
The film owes more to Marilyn Monroe's sweet
sexuality than to Billy Wilder's writing and
directing skills.

Still from 'The Seven Year Itch' (1955)
If Richard gives in to his adulterous fantasies he will lose his integrity and betray the trust of his wife and son.

Still from 'The Seven Year Itch' (1955)
The girl is just too hot!

Similarly, *The Spirit of St. Louis* (1957), produced at Warner Brothers and co-written with Wendell Mayes, has parts better than the whole. The take-off from Roosevelt Field and the landing in Paris are virtuoso set-pieces beautifully edited (by Arthur P. Schmidt) and scored (by Franz Waxman). However, this biographical film about Charles Lindbergh and his transatlantic flight suffers from never cracking the shell of the Lindbergh persona. Lindbergh's autobiography, on which the film is based, and the man himself, with whom Wilder often associated during the filming, were simply too enigmatic. If Lindbergh, a national hero at a young age, had become accustomed to the role of the great man, by 1957 the mask had grown to fit the face. Wilder was better able to bring fictional figures to life than this real person.

"I like [critic] Pauline Kael. She never had a good word to say about my pictures... But then again, if she had not written it at all, that would not have been better for me. It was better for me that she wrote it."

Billy Wilder [3]

On the set of 'The Spirit of St. Louis' (1957)
Billy Wilder watches 'The Spirit of St. Louis' land.

On the Fringe

When Joe Gillis pitches a movie idea to a Paramount producer in *Sunset Boulevard*, he tries to interest him in *Bases Loaded*, a baseball script. Gillis becomes enthusiastic as he talks about his writing project, one of the few times in the movie he reveals a genuine eagerness: "And there's a great little part for Bill Demarest. One of the trainers, an old-time player who got beaned and goes out of his head sometimes." The nooks and crannies of Billy Wilder's films are peopled with a number of such colourful and memorable minor characters. Here is a sampling.

Minor characters sparkle in *Midnight*. Rex O'Malley, for example, plays a fey hanger-on at the fringes of the John Barrymore social set. When Claudette Colbert meets these people, she is invited to join them at bridge. O'Malley introduces himself as a "telephone worshipper." He explains: "Whenever a day comes without an invitation, I pray to my telephone as though it were a little black god. I beg it to speak to me, to ask me out somewhere, anywhere there is caviar and champagne." In a later scene he announces matter-of-factly: "When I was a child I used to swallow things. They didn't dare leave me alone in a room with an armchair."

Ninotchka's brief conversation in Moscow with her friend Anna is a wonderfully human vignette. Anna plays the cello in the Moscow Opera. She was barred from the May Day parade because of one wrong note she played during a performance of *Carmen*. Anna doesn't mind. In some lines from the published script, we hear her life-affirming nature: "My heart is sad, but my feet are happy. When all the tanks and guns were roaring over the Red Square, I sat here all by myself and played a Beethoven sonata." Anna adds life to the darker Moscow scenes. We can easily see why Ninotchka likes her. A sour-faced man suddenly interrupts their conversation simply by walking sternly through the common room. Anna has learned that in Moscow, as Samuel Goldwyn once advised Billy Wilder about life, you have to take the bitter with the sour: "That Gurganov," she philosophises, "you never know whether he's on his way to the washroom or the secret police." Anna also warns Ninotchka about the subversive danger of hanging her silk slip from Paris on a Moscow clothesline for all to see. This leads to talk about clothes, and Ninotchka confides to Anna that she brought back with her the silly Paris hat. She admits that she would be ashamed to wear

it in Russia. Anna's quick mind catches her meaning. "As beautiful as that!" she says. Finally, Ninotchka makes a wedding present to her friend of the slip. Anna cannot believe her good fortune. As she heads for the opera, she says, "Am I going to play that cadenza tonight!"

In the opening scene of *The Major and the Minor*, Ginger Rogers arrives at a high-rise apartment to demonstrate a scalp massage contraption on Robert Benchley. The smart aleck elevator operator looks at the attractive girl and the equipment she carries and listens cynically to her explanation. He also evidently knows something about the Benchley character. As Ginger leaves the elevator, he says with meaningful deliberation, "Ain't it awful the way a fellow's scalp dries out this time of year?"

Bim, the night nurse in the alcoholic ward in *The Lost Weekend*, is another character whose brief appearance is hard to forget. "Hello, Mary Sunshine," he oozes when Ray Milland wakes up. Milland wants to know why he is in the alcoholic ward. "Are you kidding?" says Bim with relish. "We took a peek at your blood – pure applejack." Bim seems also to be a sadist and something of a predatory gay, not a happy combination for someone working among weak and dependent men. He savours describing the *delirium tremens* to Milland. In contrast, Gloria, the prostitute who drops in at Milland's favourite bar, adds humour and humanity. She is a hard-shell character who is vulnerable inside. She enlivens the film with her special sort of slang ("Natch! Don't be ridick!"), and when Milland shows up a day after their planned date having gotten drunk instead she initially scolds him but then after he kisses her, she whispers girlishly, "I waited half the night like it was the first date I ever had."

Erich von Stroheim appeared in his second Wilder film as Max the butler in *Sunset Boulevard*. Max dwells in seeming comfort in his psychological disguise of the loyal keeper of Norma's celebrity flame. He writes her the weekly fan letters, discreetly tells her when her eye shadow is unbalanced, and generally feeds her illusions. Stroheim suggested a shot to Wilder of Max deriving erotic gratification from washing Norma's underwear, but the director politely rejected the idea. The moment toward the end when Max is revealed as one of Norma's ex-husbands is perfectly timed.

ABOVE
Still from 'Sunset Boulevard' (1950)
Max (Erich von Stroheim, left) directs Norma Desmond (Gloria Swanson) in her last scene.

OPPOSITE TOP
Still from 'The Major and the Minor' (1942)
Susan Applegate (Ginger Rogers) gives a scalp massage to Mr Osborne (Robert Benchley).

OPPOSITE BOTTOM
Still from 'The Lost Weekend' (1945)
Don Birnam (Ray Milland, left) and Gloria (Doris Dowling) at Nat's (Howard Da Silva) bar.

A New Collaborator
1957–1963

Billy Wilder's writing career can be viewed as primarily a tale of two long-term collaborations. After his apprenticeship in Berlin and Paris, he learned the structure and genres of American movies in part by working with Charles Brackett. Fourteen years younger than his collaborator, Wilder began the partnership as the subordinate contributor. When he and Brackett became a producing-directing tandem in 1943, Wilder began to indulge his tendency toward realism. The verbal exaggeration and snap of his scripts disclosed a more stylised reality. The subject matter, however, featured the social realism of the artist examining unconventional topics – an anti-hero lustfully planning a murder, the torments of alcoholism, philandering American G.I.s in post-war Berlin, the rigors of the prison camp, the cynicism and heartlessness of the media. Like Bernard Shaw, Wilder had developed the realistic eye of the comic iconoclast. Charles Brackett preferred the light confections of romantic comedy.

During their collaboration Brackett and Wilder enjoyed the company and professionalism of Helen Hernandez, reputedly the best secretary at Paramount Pictures. At the time the partnership dissolved, the writers' roles appear to have reversed, with Brackett now having become the subordinate one. Interviewed by Maurice Zolotow in the 1970s, Hernandez described Brackett as "a clinging vine," yet she chose to continue with him when Wilder ended the collaboration after *Sunset Boulevard*.

Wilder was fourteen years older than I.A.L. Diamond, a writer whose work he had appreciated in magazine pieces and in skits at a screenwriters' banquet. Born Itek Dommnici in Romania, Diamond and his mother moved to Brooklyn when he was nine to join his father (who had changed the family name). Reportedly, Diamond adopted the triple initials when he was older to give himself the credibility of a more literary-sounding byline. One story maintains that they stand for the Interscholastic Algebra League, of which as a schoolboy Izzy Diamond was the tri-state champion in consecutive years. Ed Sikov quotes an essay by George Morris in *Film Comment* about the greater harmony existing in Wilder's partnership with Diamond: "The two men complement each other beautifully. Diamond's ready wit leaves Wilder free to tap his emotional resources more fully." Sikov concludes that on the whole Wilder became more introspec-

Billy Wilder and I.A.L. Diamond (1960)
Although there was the occasional heated discussion, their writing collaboration was harmonious. Diamond believed that screenwriters made the best directors and Wilder found that he agreed with him.

"Everything is possible if you've just got a certain amount of charm."

Billy Wilder[4]

ABOVE
Still from 'Love in the Afternoon' (1957)
Ariane (Audrey Hepburn) adores listening to her father's (Maurice Chevalier) stories about the people he investigates. She is particularly fascinated by the exploits of playboy Frank Flannagan.

RIGHT
Still from 'Love in the Afternoon' (1957)
Lovesick Frank Flannagan (Gary Cooper, right) seeks advice from Mr. X (John McGiver), whose wife Flannagan previously had an affair with. Flannagan is accompanied by a Gypsy band to help with his seductions.

OPPOSITE
On the set of 'Love in the Afternoon' (1957)
Billy Wilder gently moves Audrey Hepburn and Gary Cooper.

tive in his work with Diamond: "Wilder's movies continued to have a sour streak, sometimes even violently so. But in the scripts he composed with Diamond, Billy found himself able to develop themes of affection, even joy." The cynic and realist inside Wilder began to make room for the romantic, often in an autumnal mood.

The new partners' first collaboration, *Love in the Afternoon* (1957), resembles *Sabrina* in many ways, even in its regrettable absence of Cary Grant. Unable to secure Grant for the Bogart role in the earlier film, Wilder now missed him again for the male lead in this later project. Instead, Gary Cooper plays a part superficially similar to his role in *Bluebeard's Eighth Wife*, that of an American tycoon whose dinner-jacketed, wealthy life is essentially a series of empty love affairs. Audrey Hepburn plays the daughter of a French private detective (Maurice Chevalier). The father specialises in verifying adulteries for jealous spouses. Hepburn saves Cooper from a pistol-packing husband by pretending to be his companion for the evening.

The comedy of role reversal supplies the film's sweetness and light irony. An innocent, Hepburn enthrals Cooper with details she remembers from her father's cases to create for herself a sexually experienced, mysterious (and completely fictitious) past. The discrepancy between who she really is and what she claims to be gives the audience its higher perspective and comic awareness. Eventually, Cooper's frustrations drive him to hire the services of Hepburn's father to discover the real identity of this mystery woman. The logic of Wilder and Diamond's plotting merges beautifully with the growing emotions of the characters. "She is a little fish," the father poignantly confesses to Cooper after he recognises the details of his own detective cases. "Throw her back." The cynical rake, however, finds that his real emotions, which he has kept untouched through so many affairs, have been touched by this disarming girl. The film's appeal results from the elegant balance between the virginal Hepburn bravely creating her identity as the young reprobate and the seasoned playboy Cooper timidly revealing his virginal emotions.

Wilder's involvement in his next project, *Witness for the Prosecution* (1957), an adaptation of an Agatha Christie play, may have commenced before his first script with Diamond was completed, or perhaps Diamond was unavailable for work on the Christie screenplay. Either way, this courtroom thriller with Charles Laughton, Tyrone Power and Marlene Dietrich was Wilder's last work without his new partner. The popular Christie play was predictably strengthened in character and unexpectedly given a new twist at the end. Wilder and co-writer Harry Kurnitz added the comic character of Miss Plimsoll (Elsa Lanchester), a chirpy nurse who scolds barrister Laughton back into good health and tries to insulate him from the excitement of his new murder case. Like John Barrymore in *Midnight* and Lucy in *The Major and the Minor*, she is a comic chorus figure, a loveable nuisance who guides the reactions of the audience during the trial. The film is a polished, literate, well-acted and well-directed thriller. It explores Wilder's interest in role-playing in a light and entertaining way.

Laughton's barrister receives all the flamboyant verbal and visual touches. For example, his monocle is his visual lie detector. With it he catches and directs sunlight like the beam of an interrogation lamp. It permits him to verify the truth of his clients' answers. Laughton also has a virtuoso speech in which he exposes a lying witness on the stand. His grand part is written in larger-than-life dimensions, and he delivers wonderfully. Wilder always spoke glowingly of his friendship with Laughton and even intended him for a part in *Irma la Douce* (1963), but the actor's failing health prevented another collaboration. In spite of the effectiveness and success of the film (Christie herself reportedly praised the adaptation), it is nonetheless a safe, somewhat unambitious venture. Wilder had not undertaken a risky project since *Ace in the Hole* and *Stalag 17*. But all that was about to change.

Still from 'Witness for the Prosecution' (1957)
Charles Laughton and his wife Elsa Lanchester in discussion with Wilder. Laughton plays Leonard's barrister Sir Wilfrid Robarts.

ABOVE
Still from 'Witness for the Prosecution' (1957)
When Christine no longer gives Leonard an alibi for murder, she becomes the witness for the prosecution. Many shocking twists follow in this rewritten version of the Agatha Christie play.

PAGES 118 & 119
Stills from 'Some Like It Hot' (1959)
Sugar Kane (Marilyn Monroe, centre) sings 'Running Wild' with Joe/Josephine (Tony Curtis, left) and Jerry/Daphne (Jack Lemmon, 2nd left) as part of the band.

PAGES 120 & 121
Stills from 'Some Like It Hot' (1959)
Sugar and Daphne meet Shell Oil, an oil millionaire (aka Joe in disguise, with a Cary Grant accent). He is everything Sugar has dreamed of. This is not surprising because she described her dream man to Josephine/Joe.

Some Like It Hot (1959) reunited him with Izzy Diamond and raised eyebrows in the industry by mixing comedy with murder. Producer David O. Selznick warned Wilder that machine guns and cross-dressing would never work in the same movie. His advice was a measure of Selznick's old Hollywood outlook and his slipping familiarity with audiences. With Marilyn Monroe, Jack Lemmon, Tony Curtis, and the classic Wilder and Diamond script, the film has become a milestone of the movie-making art. The American Film Institute ranked it first in its millennial survey of the one hundred best screen comedies.

Previously, as in *The Major and the Minor,* a Wilder script had exploited for a single character the comic possibilities of a physical disguise (Ginger Rogers becoming Sue-Sue) or those of a psychological disguise (Ray Milland's role as teacher delaying his realization of love). In *Some Like It Hot*, however, Wilder and Diamond mix both types of disguises with dizzying, hilarious and insightful results. As in some of Shakespeare's comedies, a physical disguise actually liberates and enables psychological growth. Tony Curtis, for example, dresses as Josephine, the female sax player in an all-girl band, to flee Prohibition gangsters who pursue him as one of the witnesses of their St. Valentine's garage shootout. On the band's train ride to Florida, he meets Marilyn, the vocalist, who later pretends to be one of the social elite in order to trap a millionaire in marriage. Curtis then adopts the accent of Cary Grant and the disguise of a Shell Oil millionaire simply to seduce Marilyn. As Josephine, however, he hears from Marilyn for the first time how the other half feels – what it is like to be loved and left, to get "the fuzzy end of the lollipop." The two disguises of Josephine and Shell Oil embody the selfish and unselfish sides of his character. On the run again from the mob, Curtis later pauses while still dressed as Josephine to kiss a tearful Marilyn on the bandstand and to tell her that "no guy is worth it." The disguises have permitted Curtis to experience some emotional growing pains.

Just as high comedy results from the mix of Curtis' various identities, low comedy comes from Jack Lemmon's disguise as Daphne, the girl with the bull fiddle. Roger Ebert also discusses this in his chapter on the film in *The Great Movies*. Unexpectedly, Daphne has attracted "a *rich* millionaire," the much-married Joe E. Brown, who is hot to make her his wife *du jour*. Lemmon tangos the night away with Brown, ostensibly to keep him busy while Curtis as Shell Oil sneaks aboard Brown's yacht to wine and dine Marilyn. But disguise brings out the suggestible side of Lemmon, who seems to find as Daphne that security can compete in importance with gender in a relationship. In addition, for Marilyn, who has been hurt by a string of male sax players, love and a future finally become possible not when she is candid and straightforward about herself but when she adopts the role of the socialite. It is the film's biggest comic irony. Attempting a scam of her own, she is finally rewarded with true love. As Stephen Farber writes, 'Deception is, in some twisted way, the one truthful, respectable act in the Wilder universe.' This mix of unconventional elements in *Some Like It Hot* was followed by a movie even harder to pigeonhole.

ABOVE
Still from 'Some Like It Hot' (1959)
After meeting Shell Oil, Daphne suggests they run back to tell Josephine the good news.

OPPOSITE
Still from 'Some Like It Hot' (1959)
Daphne is wooed by Osgood Fielding (Joe E. Brown).

On the set of 'Some Like It Hot' (1959)
Marilyn seems to like Billy Wilder's suggestion.

*"We must think of the finished product and
forgive Marilyn for everything, you know."*

Billy Wilder [3]

ABOVE
Still from 'Some Like It Hot' (1959)
Sugar tells Josephine all about Shell Oil.

PAGE 126
On the set of 'Some Like It Hot' (1959)
Billy Wilder and crew watch Tony Curtis and Marilyn Monroe prepare to embark on a night of lovemaking.

PAGE 127
Still from 'Some Like It Hot' (1959)
Sugar tries to thaw the frigid Shell Oil, and succeeds.

As mapped out in chapter three, the deceptions in the plot unfold gradually in *The Apartment*, the next project for Wilder and Diamond. For the first half of the film only the viewers know that Shirley MacLaine, the woman Jack Lemmon loves, is really using his bed to sleep with Fred MacMurray, the boss who has swapped Lemmon's promotion at work for the use of Lemmon's apartment key. The premise for the film had come to Wilder from watching David Lean's *Brief Encounter* (1945). Wilder pitied the poor guy who lent his rooms to the lovers and then had to climb back into the warm bed. Lemmon's character, as Louis Giannetti points out, represents a basic conflict in Wilder's cinematic world: 'He's both a schnook and an opportunist, a victim and a victimiser. But in the end, he prefers being a *mensch* to being a swine. He's Wilder's portrait of the loser as a winner, with more class than he realises.'

The Apartment questions the many deceptions forced on us by a society and a workplace that thrive on ambition, money and status. Its soft centre, the sort of heart-related concerns that Wilder was now able to focus on more fully, insists that the elusive intangibles of life matter more, that self-esteem often escapes us until someone willingly accepts us knowing our faults and that our integrity is most appreciated once it is gone. Metaphorically, the film could be subtitled 'How to Regain Your Virginity.' Getting back our integrity, however soiled, is presented as something that elevates the individual in maturity, in self-confidence, in love. Jack Lemmon's progress in the movie is to become a *mensch*, a full human being. Though the sordid subject matter caused some offence, its essential life-affirming nature may be seen as, in reviewer Hollis Alpert's words, a 'fairy tale' albeit a 'dirty' one. The film won five Oscars in 1960 and Wilder doubled his own total of wins with three more for producing, directing, and co-writing.

ABOVE
Still from 'The Apartment' (1960)
When C. C. 'Bud' Baxter (Jack Lemmon, right) lends his apartment to his boss Sheldrake (Fred MacMurray) for some private time with his mistress, Bud gets promoted.

PAGES 130/131
Still from 'The Apartment' (1960)
Bud's life is hollow and lonely.

PAGE 132
On the set of 'The Apartment' (1960)
Shirley MacLaine plays peekaboo with Billy.

PAGES 133 & 134/135
Stills from 'The Apartment' (1960)
When Fran Kubelik (Shirley MacLaine) tries to commit suicide after she is dumped by Sheldrake, Bud saves her and restores her to full health. They play cards all the time.

A change of pace and a change of fortune followed. Wilder and Diamond's next project was an adaptation of a one-act farce by Ferenc Molnár. *One, Two, Three* (1961) is a comedy about capitalism and communism set in the offices of a Coca-Cola executive working in East Berlin, where James Cagney wants a promotion to London badly enough to whip up the illusion that the barefoot Marxist who has married the hedonistic teenage daughter of his boss is really a titled aristocrat. When the boss visits Berlin from Atlanta, Cagney discovers he has done such a good job in the masquerade that the son-in-law will now get the London job. The rapid pacing of the film recalls the auctioneer speed of some of the dialogue in *His Girl Friday* (1940). Using the politics of the sectored city as a pretext for farce gives the film a hard edge that is lacking in the first three Wilder-Diamond collaborations. The results are effective, but the film is something of an acquired taste. For perhaps the first time since *Ace in the Hole,* Wilder had directed a film whose lack of popularity might be linked in some way to directorial self-indulgence.

This self-indulgence may be even better documented in *Irma la Douce* (1963), a splashy colour production that once again teamed Jack Lemmon with Shirley MacLaine. The film concerns a Parisian policeman who falls in love with a prostitute, becomes her new pimp and then jealously dresses up as the mysterious and generous Lord X to keep her from other customers. The silliness of the human comedy grows out of the love triangle that develops among the woman and the man's two roles. This premise is stretched out to 147 minutes. The hardness of *Irma la Douce,* reminiscent of *One, Two, Three,* mostly supplants traces of the tenderness found in *The Apartment.* The scene in which Irma first takes the policeman home with her is touching and memorable, and the film became Wilder's most financially successful. However, the attempt to combine the tawdry and the tender would produce more interesting results in his next film.

On the set of 'One, Two, Three' (1961)
Wilder's ambitious capitalist satire, a reversal of
'Ninotchka,' exposes the politics of business and
the business of politics. Filming on location in
Berlin at the Brandenburg Gate proved difficult.
It became impossible when the Berlin Wall went
up. To solve the problem, Wilder had a duplicate
gate constructed on the backlot of the Munich
studios.

ABOVE
Still from 'One, Two, Three' (1961)
Otto Piffl (Horst Buchholz) is the communist
who disrupts the plans of Coca-Cola and
MacNamara.

PAGES 140/141
On the set of 'One, Two, Three' (1961)
A giant airport set was built in the Munich
studios when Tempelhof airport proved too
noisy. James Cagney stands patiently on the
tarmac, whilst Wilder is behind the assistant
with the megaphone.

Still from 'Irma la Douce' (1963)
Nestor (Jack Lemmon) is the new over-zealous
Parisian policeman who arrests all the prostitutes
in the Hotel Casanova. Since his inspector is a
regular customer, Nestor loses his job.

Still from 'Irma la Douce' (1963)
Moustache (Lou Jacobi) gives Nestor a soda shower.

Still from 'Irma la Douce' (1963)
Irma (Shirley MacLaine), the life and soul of the
party, is watched by her pimp Hippolyte (Bruce
Yarnell). She eventually falls in love with Nestor.

OPPOSITE
On the set of 'Irma la Douce' (1963)
Shirley MacLaine lines up her foot on Billy Wilder
during rehearsal. The film became Wilder's
biggest commercial hit.

Visual Style

Probably the biggest surprise for anyone encountering the films of such an accomplished writer-director is discovering how often the visual design of Wilder's films rewards close scrutiny. Though he wrote some of the most memorable dialogue in movie history, Wilder consistently reveals in his films a discerning eye for visual compositions. Often the visual element in a Wilder film speaks as clearly as the dialogue. Wilder once said, "There's never, never a phoney shot in any of my pictures... I don't shoot it like a hack. I shoot it elegantly." These examples from *The Apartment* are ample proof of that.

1. The widescreen frame here permits Wilder to provide the audience with multiple viewing options. It's an effective illustration of the often-cited remark by film theorist André Bazin that when the essence of a scene depends on the simultaneous presence of two or more elements, editing should be minimised or even ruled out. Here, Bud Baxter hides in the shadows of his own apartment steps as he defers once again to an office superior leaving after a late tryst. Wilder designs a shot with both action (the smarmy executive with his girlfriend in the foreground) and reaction (Bud's reduced appearance in the shadows). Bud looks as small and unimportant as his spinelessness no doubt makes him feel. Visually, he almost blends in with the garbage cans.

2. This picture of loneliness sums up Bud's life in the big city. The long perspective of park benches stretching into the distance combined with the loose framing illustrates Bud's isolation after yet another office executive has called up to use the apartment and literally thrown Bud out into the cold.

3. Wilder uses space in a similar way when Fran stands Bud up for their date to see *The Music Man*. We see Bud in a long shot all alone with his box of Kleenex on the wintry sidewalk after the throng of theatregoers has gone in to enjoy the show. Some of the most memorable shots in the film position Bud in big spaces like this (such as the opening shots at the insurance company with the long rows of desks) in order to call attention to his solitary status. Wilder pictorialises Bud's loneliness.

4. Sometimes an effective *mise en scène* does not result in an overly balanced or prettified design. This shot is one of Wilder's most effective. Sheldrake has just remembered that he has no Christmas present for Fran, so he crassly peels off a hundred-dollar bill from his wad of cash. Wilder de-personalises Sheldrake by shooting only his arm extending the money and using light to make the visual centre of the shot Fran's look of loathing. He towers above her and fills much of the frame in a suggestion of his power. She doesn't speak to convey her contempt for Sheldrake's offer. Thanks to the careful visual design, she doesn't have to. We are not surprised when the hundred-dollar bill later reappears in the envelope addressed to Sheldrake after Fran's suicide attempt.

Final Works
1964–1981

Directors with long careers often create some of their most intriguing works in their final decades. They do not, however, very often create their most perfect works. In writing about one of Billy Wilder's last fims, Andrew Sarris drew an analogy to the later works of masters like D. W. Griffith, Charlie Chaplin, Jean Renoir, Orson Welles and John Ford, and theorised that some films 'can be understood and appreciated only in the context of an entire career as a testament of twilight.' He is right. We would probably find the later Billy Wilder films less worth our attention if they had not been made by the same man who also co-wrote and directed *Double Indemnity*, *Sunset Boulevard*, *Some Like It Hot* and *The Apartment*.

After the great success of *Irma la Douce,* Wilder struggled to find another hit. He and Izzy Diamond followed that French farce with a hard-hitting comedy called *Kiss Me, Stupid* (1964), a film that critiqued and shocked middle-class morality. Peter Sellers was cast as a small-town Nevada piano teacher who writes songs with the local auto mechanic (Cliff Osmond) and dreams of success. When Dino (Dean Martin), the Las Vegas crooner, has to stop for auto repairs on his way to Hollywood, the boys try to prolong his visit and convince him to sing one of their songs on his upcoming television special. The lecherous Dino, however, demands some companionship for the night, and one way to gratify him and get a song on the air is to offer him the piano teacher's wife. By angering and sending off his wife (Felicia Farr) and by recruiting Polly the Pistol (Kim Novak), the local hooker, to take her place, the songwriters have seemingly got it all worked out.

Sellers filmed for four weeks before a series of heart attacks left him at death's door. Wilder and some of the cast spoke enthusiastically about the quality of the Sellers footage though the director and the star repeatedly clashed. Sellers' skillful improvisation provoked the director's desire to protect his script. The insecure Sellers also resented the clubby atmosphere that made him feel like an outsider. After his recovery he complained about the whole experience to an interviewer, which deepened the rift between hm and the director. Wilder replaced Sellers with Ray Walston, who had played one of the corporate bosses in *The Apartment*.

On the set of 'Buddy Buddy' (1981)
Billy Wilder (left) at the wrong end of Jack Lemmon's gun. Walter Matthau is relieved.

"Nobody talks about the picture, just about what kind of deal: Who presents? Whose picture is it? And all that totally idiotic crap! It's a world with ugly, ugly terrifying words like 'turnaround' and 'negative pickup.' (Although I think the two ugliest words in the world are 'root canal' – with the possible exception of 'Hawaiian music.')"

Billy Wilder[2]

149

ABOVE
On the set of 'Kiss Me, Stupid' (1964)
Billy Wilder walks Kim Novak through a scene.

TOP RIGHT
Still from 'Kiss Me, Stupid' (1964)
When Orville J. Spooner (Ray Walston) finds out
Dino is in town, he argues with his wife so that
she will not fall for Dino's charms. He then
persuades Polly the Pistol (Kim Novak, right) to
pretend to be his wife.

RIGHT
Still from 'Kiss Me, Stupid' (1964)
Something catches the eye of Dino (Dean Martin,
left), the oversexed, lecherous Las Vegas singer.

The tawdriness and tenderness that had been out of balance in *Irma la Douce* were better built into the structure of *Kiss Me, Stupid*. The first hour of the film stresses the sleaze as we see the wife-substitution plan take shape. The second hour stresses the tender. Novak adopts the role of housewife, and both she and Walston are transformed by the experience. Sweetness suddenly turns up in some unexpected moments. Novak carries candles to the dinner table like a worshipper approaching a shrine. A near-bride herself who was abandoned in Nevada, she quotes chapter and verse from women's magazines on the proper domesticity at dinner. Once again, the power of disguise to transform works its Billy Wilder wonders. Novak is no longer a thing to be bought but a person, if only for one night.

Meanwhile, wife Felicia Farr winds up drowning her anger at the local bar, where she is told to sleep it off in Novak's trailer out back. Unexpectedly, Dino walks in the trailer still looking for a woman. Walston, we discover, had become jealous and affectionate even toward his replacement wife and had chivalrously thrown Dino out. Just as the hooker benefited from her one night as a housewife, now the housewife adopts the masquerade of the hooker. The former president of a Dino fan club in high school, Farr cannot quite believe her situation, but she, too, finds it liberating. Wilder and Diamond include a scene in which the two women confer the morning after. Novak returns the husband's wedding ring she wore last night, and Farr hands over the $500 Dino gave her.

The film proved to be a worse critical and financial disaster than even *Ace in the Hole*. Only Bosley Crowther and Joan Didion offered kind words among reviewers. (Didion's review has itself become something of a classic: Wilder's Las Vegas, she wrote, is 'a town… where cocktail waitresses sleep in trailers surrounded by butane tanks. It is a place where time is told in television schedules, where no one is beautiful or gifted,… where the flesh is urgent because nothing else is.') The film was condemned by the Catholic Legion of Decency and United Artists released it through a subsidiary distributor, Lopert Pictures. The bandwagon of disapproval and scandal gained momentum until the movie became a complete embarrassment, as if a major director had turned out a stag film in 16 mm. Writer and Wilder friend John Gregory Dunne called the movie "the car wreck on Wilder's career highway."

The leering tone of the movie might have seemed less coarse with Sellers rather than Walston. As it is, the script pushes the limits of acceptability even at the verbal level. On his last night in Las Vegas, for example, Dino has chorus girls stashed throughout the hotel but he plans simply to drive off to Hollywood. Each additional joke in his explanation to the stage manager nudges the script further toward tastelessness: "If I start saying goodbye to all of them dames, you'll have to carry me out of here – what's left of me – in a cigar box – baby."

Nevertheless, an unorthodox morality eventually surfaces. The film's structure invites the audience to consider how much their notions of marital virtue are made up of simple conformity and how much of life-affirming, mutual love. Ed Sikov correctly observes that the tenderness of the movie comes as a result of its earlier tawdriness.

ABOVE
On the set of 'Kiss Me, Stupid' (1964)
Billy Wilder directs Felicia Farr, who plays Orville's wife.

PAGE 152
Publicity still for 'Kiss Me, Stupid' (1964)
Zelda Spooner (Felicia Farr) as Polly the Pistol.

PAGE 153
Still from 'Kiss Me, Stupid' (1964)
Polly the Pistol as Zelda Spooner.

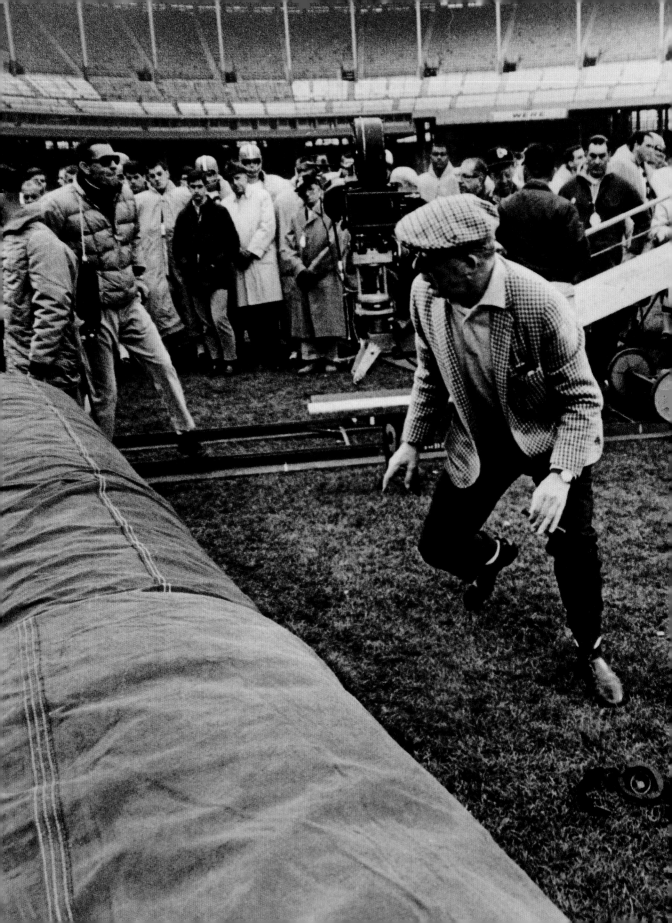

On the set of 'The Fortune Cookie' (1966)
Ron Rich (right) plays Boom Boom Jackson, who
accidentally knocks over TV cameraman Harry
Hinkle during a football game. Wilder (centre)
shows him how to do it.

155

ABOVE
Still from 'The Fortune Cookie' (1966)
Walter Matthau, who plays Willie Gingrich, stole the show in his first pairing with Lemmon.

TOP RIGHT
On the set of 'The Fortune Cookie' (1966)
After the game, Boom Boom feels guilty about the injuries and helps Harry convalesce. Here Wilder shows Ron Rich (right) what he wants him to do.

RIGHT
Still from 'The Fortune Cookie' (1966)
Harry Hinkle (Jack Lemmon) is persuaded by his brother-in-law Willie Gingrich to feign injury so that they can make lots of money from a lawsuit.

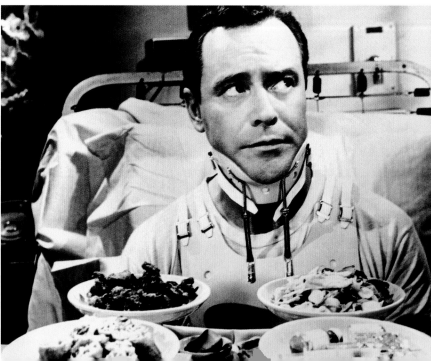

Wilder once quipped that after the furore over *Kiss Me, Stupid*, he and Diamond felt like the parents of a two-headed child who were reluctant to have intercourse again. Eventually, however, the two collaborators did overcome their creative celibacy, and the result was *The Fortune Cookie* (1966), a story about greed rather than sex. The film turned a small profit, mainly on the strength of the chemistry between Walter Matthau and Jack Lemmon in their first screen pairing. Lemmon plays a sideline cameraman at a football game who is injured by a player (Ron Rich) running out of bounds. Matthau is his brother-in-law, a lawyer who senses a chance to hustle some money. He concocts an insurance scam, but Lemmon's conscience slowly awakens. One of the most interesting aspects of the film is the opposition set up between the self-serving motives of Lemmon's ex-wife (Judi West) and the unselfishness of the football player who frets about Lemmon's recovery. Lemmon initially goes along with the scheme to get his wife back but he comes to see that, like Matthau, she was only interested in the money. He exposes the fraud and ends the film playing catch with the football player.

Still from 'The Private Life of Sherlock Holmes' (1970)
Sherlock Holmes (Robert Stephens) and Dr Watson (Colin Blakely) are welcomed home to 221B Baker Street by Mrs Hudson (Irene Handl).

It was four years before another Wilder film appeared. The trials that beset *The Private Life of Sherlock Holmes* (1970) reveal an older director struggling in a changing industry. Shot as a three-hour anthology film of Holmes' most sensitive and secret cases, the truncated two-hour movie that exists today is necessarily simpler in plot and emotion. Robert Stephens and Colin Blakely play Holmes and Watson assisting a beautiful woman (Genevieve Page) with amnesia who seeks her missing husband. The film was shortened by about seventy minutes at the suggestion of United Artists due to the failure of some recent extravaganzas like Robert Wise's *Star!* (1968). Wilder's film is a beautifully photographed movie (by Christopher Challis) with a wistfulness and affection that was to recur in some of his remaining films. It was not, however, a success.

"No one says, 'Boy I must see that film – I hear it came in under budget.'"

Billy Wilder [1]

158

ABOVE
Still from 'The Private Life of Sherlock Holmes' (1970)
Mrs Hudson averts her eyes as Holmes and Watson discuss a case.

PAGE 160 TOP
Still from 'The Private Life of Sherlock Holmes' (1970)
Gabrielle Valladon (Genevieve Page) is a lady in distress who comes to Holmes for help. He gives her his help, and more.

PAGE 160 BOTTOM
Still from 'The Private Life of Sherlock Holmes' (1970)
This flashback of Holmes at Oxford University was one of many sequences deleted from the three hour and twenty minute first cut. Wilder was forced to reduce it to two hours, which broke his heart.

PAGE 161
On the set of 'The Private Life of Sherlock Holmes' (1970)
Billy Wilder and friends.

PAGES 162/163
Still from 'The Private Life of Sherlock Holmes' (1970)
Face to face with the Loch Ness monster.

ABOVE
Still from 'Avanti!' (1972)
Pamela Piggott (Juliet Mills) and Wendell
Armbruster III (Jack Lemmon) enjoy an illicit
sojourn in the Mediterranean, just as their
parents had done.

OPPOSITE
Still from 'Avanti!' (1972)
Juliet Mills put on weight to play Pamela Piggott
by eating three big meals a day and drinking lots
of Guinness. Pamela is one of Wilder's most
loveable characters.

PAGES 166/167
On the set of 'Avanti!' (1972)
Billy Wilder, right of camera, filming Juliet Mills
and Jack Lemmon off the Italian coast.

The elegiac tone continued in *Avanti!* (1972), a film in which breaking the shell
of social conformity, as in *Kiss Me, Stupid*, turns out to be the emotionally honest
act. Jack Lemmon plays a business executive who travels to Ischia to claim the
body of his father. He discovers that his straight-laced, married father had for
years been spending his month-long foreign vacations in the company of another
woman. Juliet Mills plays the free-spirited daughter of the other woman. The
film simultaneously explores the past relationship between the living son and
his dead father and the new relationship between Lemmon and Mills. Like his
father, Lemmon comes out of the cocoon of conformity – for one month a year.
Bernard F. Dick correctly identifies the film's point of view as middle-aged. The
lovers 'give society eleven months of the year' and reserve one for each other.
Commercially, the film fared no better than its predecessor.

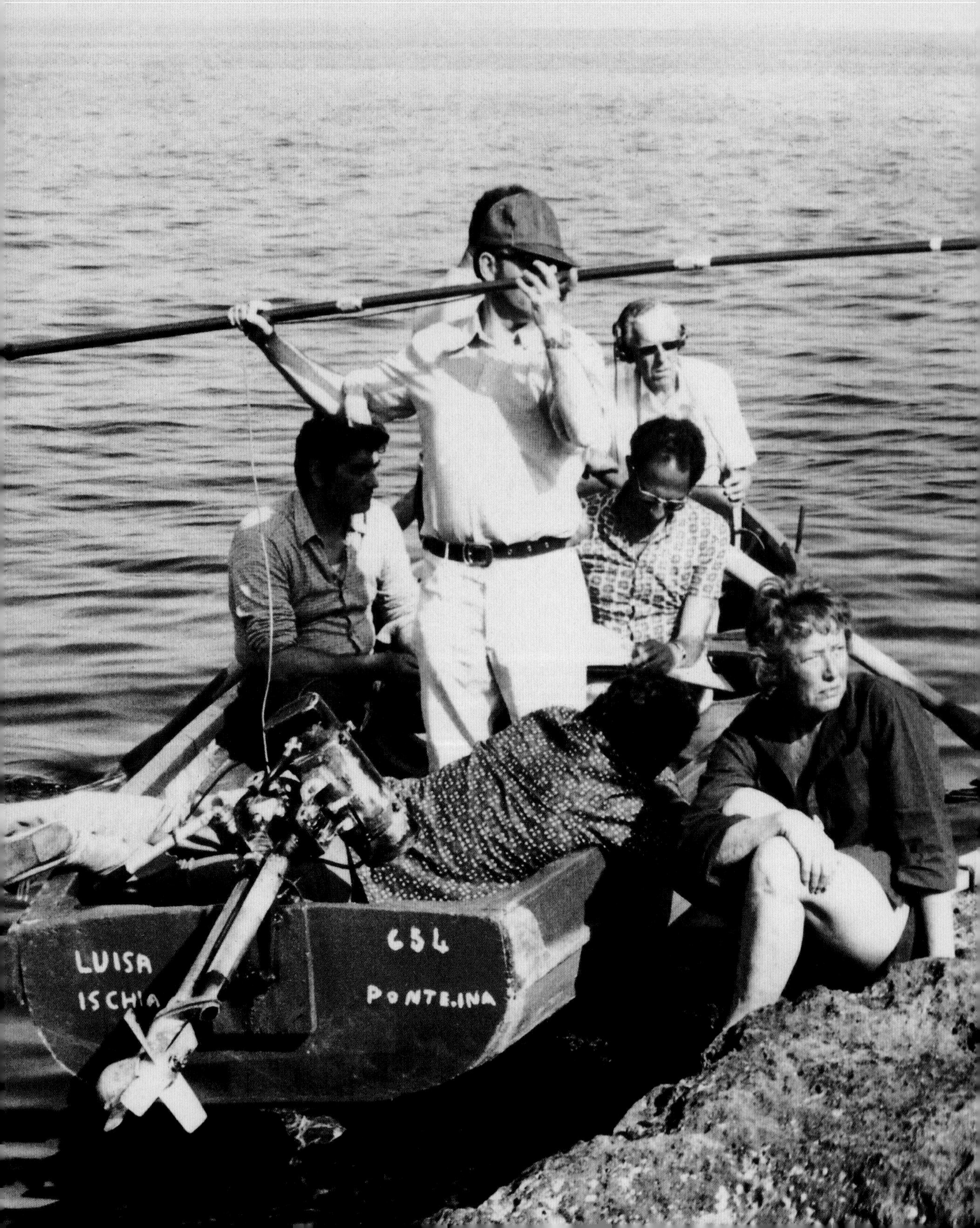
LUISA
ISCHIA

ABOVE
Still from 'The Front Page' (1974)
Mollie Malloy (Carol Burnett), the prostitute
with a heart of gold, holds off the reporters in
an attempt to shield escaped murderer Earl
Williams.

RIGHT
Still from 'The Front Page' (1974)
Editor Walter Burns (Walter Matthau) and
reporter Hildy Johnson (Jack Lemmon) argue
constantly. The father/son relationship in Wilder's
films can be traced back to Barton Keyes and
Walter Neff in 'Double Indemnity'.

On the set of 'The Front Page' (1974)
Billy Wilder explains precisely what he wants
from Vincent Gardinia (right).

Perhaps it was the urge for the security of a box-office hit that led Wilder and
Diamond to choose the reliable stage comedy *The Front Page* by Ben Hecht and
Charles MacArthur for their next project. Featuring Lemmon and Matthau again,
it is one of Wilder's least ambitious films, but it was a success, earning fifteen million dollars against a cost of four million. It also was the last Wilder film before
the '*Star-Wars* era,' that post-1977 period when blockbusters and marketing
began to dominate Hollywood thinking and when ambitious, edgy films often
depended on the backing of a growing independent film movement. When
Wilder was interviewed in 1986, writer Chris Columbus would correctly remark
that 'Wilder's iconoclastic film-making is a necessary antidote to the sequelmania
and cartoon realism of today's films.' But back in 1974–75, when *The Conversation*, *Nashville* and *The Godfather II* appeared in theatres, Wilder chose to film a
dialogue-heavy 1928 play about fast-talking Chicago newspaper men. Jack Lemmon told Wilder biographer Kevin Lally that he had wanted Wilder the director
to permit some of Wilder the writer's lines to be obscured through overlapping
the dialogue more naturalistically. But it was not allowed. The fidelity to the
script that had proved to be such a trusted recipe for decades resulted in a
respectable, if stodgy, hit.

*"If people don't go to see a picture, nobody can
stop them."*

Billy Wilder [4]

ABOVE
Still from 'Fedora' (1978)
Countess Sobryanski (Hildegard Knef) is really
the enigmatic actress Fedora. A treatment to
perserve her youthful beauty went horribly
wrong and disfigured her.

RIGHT
Still from 'Fedora' (1978)
Fedora's illegitimate daughter Antonia (Marthe
Keller) took on the role of Fedora, but it trapped
her. When she fell in love she could not reveal
her true identity and so lapsed into depression
and drug addiction.

The next Wilder project, *Fedora* (1978), concerned the mysterious past of a reclusive, Garbo-like film star approached in retirement by a desperate producer. In spite of the success of *The Front Page*, Universal exercised its right of first refusal on Wilder-and-Diamond's script. William Holden, in his last collaboration with his favourite director, would play the producer, and Michael York appeared in a small part. York, in a 2002 interview with *USA Today*, talked about Wilder and *Fedora*: "I know he had trouble getting the picture on. The studios were run by kids who had no regard for the laurels of someone's career." The film's backing came from Geria Films, a small German company. Wilder wanted so much to finish under budget that he reduced and often eliminated rehearsal time. According to Kevin Lally, William Holden excused his good friend by pointing out that in the past Wilder had always afforded the actors ample time to rehearse. The reviews were largely negative or mixed, but the limited release and publicity also hampered the film's chances for success.

Wilder's last film appeared in 1981, a comedy about a hit man prevented from doing his job by a despondent pest. *Buddy Buddy*, another vehicle for Lemmon and Matthau, is for the most part an uninspired effort.

On the set of 'Fedora' (1978)
William Holden (left) and Billy Wilder (right) discuss the funeral scene in a film which, like 'Sunset Boulevard', analyses the cult of celebrity. I. A. L. Diamond is behind Wilder with script in hand.

ABOVE
Still from 'Buddy Buddy' (1981)
Victor Clooney's (Jack Lemmon) suicide
attempt interferes with hitman Trabucco's
(Walter Matthau) assassination attempt.
A drugged Trabucco now has to let Victor
make the fatal shot.

RIGHT
Still from 'Buddy Buddy' (1981)
Trabucco tries to get rid of Victor in many
different ways, but Victor always returns out
of some misguided assumption that they are
friends.

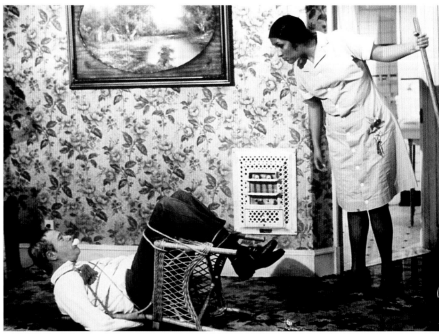

ABOVE
On the set of 'Buddy Buddy' (1981)
Matthau and Wilder discussing the scene where Trabucco finds out Victor has killed the right man. I. A. L. Diamond (right) is on hand to discuss any script changes.

LEFT
Still from 'Buddy Buddy' (1981)
No matter what Trabucco does, he is always haunted by Victor. In the final scene, Trabucco has escaped to paradise on a deserted atoll when Victor sails back into his life. It is the final black moment in Wilder's career.

Missing Scenes

Still from 'Midnight' (1939)
Eve (Claudette Colbert, left) objected to filming an indoor picnic so the scene was played with her leading a conga line instead.

Still from 'The Private Life of Sherlock Holmes' (1970)
Sherlock Holmes (Robert Stephens) examines a dead man in the upsidedown room. The episode was cut from the final version and only a soundtrack and stills exist.

Some of the most talked-about scenes in the movies of Billy Wilder are the ones that got away. The cockroach scene with Charles Boyer in *Hold Back the Dawn* is a famous example of a good scene excised against the writers' wishes (after the actor complained about it to director Mitchell Leisen). Ed Sikov, however, points out that a comparable moment seems to have occurred during the filming of *Midnight* two years earlier. By checking the Paramount archives, Sikov noticed that the scenes at the estate of the John Barrymore character should have culminated with the guests roasting hot dogs in the fireplace. Claudette Colbert, however, on the day the scene was to have been shot, refused to take part in the indoor picnic. The conga line dance replaces the lost material in the finished film. Sikov speculates reasonably that Wilder complained about Boyer's temper tantrum more than Colbert's because his status as a writer had risen by the time of the later film.

The two most famous lost scenes in Wilder's films are the original ending to *Double Indemnity* and the original opening to *Sunset Boulevard*. Wilder himself chose to delete them both.

Double Indemnity was to have concluded with a gritty depiction of Walter Neff's execution in the California gas chamber. The University of California edition of the published script includes this two-and-a-half-page scene. Barton Keyes (Edward G. Robinson) watches his friend as he is taken into the death chamber and readied for his execution. The only dialogue is a guard's words for Keyes to leave the ante-room. On the long walk out, Keyes takes out a cigar and looks for a match, which Neff had always given him. This is the moment when the death of his friend seems to register on Keyes. Another guard opens the outer door into a blaze of sunlight, and the script concludes: 'Keyes slowly walks out into the sunshine, stiffly, his head bent, a forlorn and lonely man.' Wilder removed this scene when he realised that the final conversation between Neff and Keyes at the Pacific building (ending with the words, "I love you, too") made for a simpler and, in its own way, more emotional ending.

Sunset Boulevard originally opened in a morgue as attendants toe-tag corpses. One by one in voice-over the corpses share stories of how they died. One of them is Joe Gillis (William Holden), who admits that he had always wanted a pool and that he finally got his wish because he was found shot in it. Preview audiences reacted to the scene with unexpected laughter, so Wilder abandoned the morgue idea but kept the premise of the movie being narrated by a dead man. Some interesting fragments of this

discarded opening have been found by Paramount archivists and used in their 2002 special edition DVD of *Sunset Boulevard*.

The hard copy published script for *Sunset Boulevard*, which unfortunately does not include the original opening, does reveal other cuts probably made out of the need to trim extraneous material. At the end of the scene in which Norma first shows Joe her *Salome* script, she calls for Max to take Joe to the bedroom over the garage. Before that happens, in material cut from the original script, the camera was to move slowly toward Norma and stop on a close-up of her eyes while we hear Joe's voice-over narration: "She sure could say a lot of things with those pale eyes of hers. They'd been her trademark. They'd made her the Number One Vamp of another era. I remember a rather florid description in an old fan magazine which said, 'Her eyes are like two moonlit waterholes, where strange animals come to drink.'" The writers probably came up

with that touch because they liked the baroque quality of the last sentence; the film is probably better off without it.

The Private Life of Sherlock Holmes lacks about seventy minutes of footage, some of which has also been found. To reduce the original running time to a length that would permit exhibitors more showings per day, two major scenes were cut along with a prologue and a transitional flashback scene. One of the longer scenes involves the comic attempts of Watson to solve a shipboard murder. The other presents Holmes with a bizarre crime scene in which all the furniture has been nailed to the ceiling. The 1994 laser disc of the film features some tantalising shreds of this missing material, the most complete fragments that have been found. It includes soundless video of the shipboard scene, and the soundtrack (without video) of the upside-down room mystery. The laser disc also includes the entire shooting script for the long version.

Still from 'Double Indemnity' (1944)
In one of two alternative endings written by Billy Wilder and Raymond Chandler, Barton Keyes (Edward G. Robinson, right) was to witness the execution of Walter Neff (Fred MacMurray, centre). It was not used.

Active Retirement
1982–2002

Following the low point of *Buddy Buddy,* Billy Wilder's gregariousness and con- sistently sharp wit enhanced his standing as a pungent observer of the Holly- wood scene. Some of his comments appeared in acceptance speeches since Wilder was receiving in steady succession the most prestigious awards available to a film-maker. In 1985, he accepted the D. W. Griffith Award for lifetime achievement from the Directors Guild. In 1986 the American Film Institute gave him their lifetime achievement award, which was followed by the Irving Thalberg lifetime award at the 1988 Oscar ceremony. The honours continued – from the Kennedy Center (1990), the European Film Academy (1992), the Berlin Film Festival (1993), the White House (1993), PEN (1994), the Los Angeles Film Critics (1995), the British Academy of Film (1996) and so on. In 1995 he fittingly received the first annual Billy Wilder Award for lifetime achievement given by the National Board of Review. Wilder remained in the news for other reasons as well. Sir Andrew Lloyd Webber's musical version of *Sunset Boulevard* opened in 1993 and, in a headline-making event at Christie's in 1989, Wilder received over thirty-two million dollars from the auction of ninety-four works from his collec- tion of art masterpieces. With the help of artists like Richard Saar and Bruce Houston, Wilder also realised various creative ideas of his own for pop sculp- tures, such as a piece called *Stallone's Typewriter,* an old Underwood in camou- flage colours adorned with shell casings and the American flag.

Books about him were appearing regularly. Maurice Zolotow interviewed Wilder for an informal biography published in 1987 as did Hellmuth Karasek for a German-language biography in 1992. Though the director spoke negatively about both books, it is easy for a reader to enjoy them and their picture of Wilder's crusty but open-hearted personality, his many warm friendships, and his marriage to Audrey, by all accounts one of the healthiest, happiest, longest and sanest in Hollywood history. In 1996, Keven Lally contributed another Wilder biography. Two years later, Ed Sikov's even longer biography was pub- lished, and a year after that the book *Conversations with Wilder* appeared, a fascinating series of talks about Wilder's films between the director and Cameron Crowe done mostly in the fashion of François Truffaut's seminal book on Alfred Hitchcock. Charlotte Chandler interviewed Wilder intermittently over many

Billy Wilder (1960)
In the midst of his famed art collection. Wilder had collected pieces since his time in Germany, and eventually sold 94 pieces for over $32 million.

"Neither am I a genius nor do I know how to define a genius... There is no such thing as a man making only good or only genius product... George Bernard Shaw wrote about fifty plays, of which there are seven or eight well known today, still being played in the repertory. But the other ones were just plays. And he was a genius."

Billy Wilder[3]

On the set of 'Irma la Douce' (1963)
Billy Wilder rehearses a scene with Jack Lemmon. Billy, of course, takes no pleasure from this.

years and published her own book, *Nobody's Perfect*, in 2002. Lest anyone should miss the allusion to the last line of *Some Like It Hot*, she clarified matters with her affectionate dedication: 'To Billy Wilder: Somebody's perfect.'

Ten days after Wilder's acceptance of the Thalberg Award at the 1988 Oscars, Izzy Diamond died. The likelihood of doing another film diminished without his long-time writing partner. One project that nevertheless appealed to Wilder as a valedictory movie was *Schindler's List*. In a sense, the story of the man who mis-led the Nazis and saved lives was perfect for the writer-director who had spent a career exploring the gap between who we are and who we pretend to be. Wilder saw the film as a way of honouring his mother and grandmother and stepfather, who had perished at Auschwitz. Universal had purchased the novel, and Steven Spielberg talked with Wilder about the project. Biographer Joseph McBride quotes Spielberg about Wilder: "He made me look very deeply inside myself when he was so passionate to do this. In a way, he tested my resolve." Wilder praised the finished film and wrote Spielberg a humble, congratulatory letter, one great film-maker saluting another: 'They couldn't have gotten a better man.'

Throughout his long retirement, the great director was respected and idolised in Hollywood and among those anywhere who loved and appreciated film. Three days before Billy Wilder died in March 2002, Tom Cruise walked onstage at the Academy Awards to commence the proceedings with, of course, a Billy Wilder quote. Being able to quote Billy Wilder in apposite ways had long been a necessary part of movie know-how for professional and amateur alike. Wilder had lived ninety-five years and had lately endured the multiple maladies that advanced age can bring. His death saddened millions who had never met him but who knew him through his films and interviews. Now many of these people would have to come up with a new answer to the question, "Who in the world would you most like to meet and converse with?"

On the set of 'Love in the Afternoon' (1957)
Gary Cooper and Billy Wilder share a moment together.

"An elderly man went to his doctor. The doctor said, 'What is the problem?' The man said, 'Doctor, I cannot pee.' The doctor said, 'How old are you?' The man said, 'I'm ninety.' The doctor said, 'You've peed enough.'"

Billy Wilder [7]

ABOVE
On the set of 'The Apartment' (1960)
Billy Wilder shows Shirley MacLaine how to play
cards. She requires this knowledge to play her
scenes with Jack Lemmon.

OPPOSITE
On the set of 'The Seven Year Itch' (1955)
Billy Wilder is smiling because he knows how
many men begged him to operate the fan
underneath Marilyn Monroe.

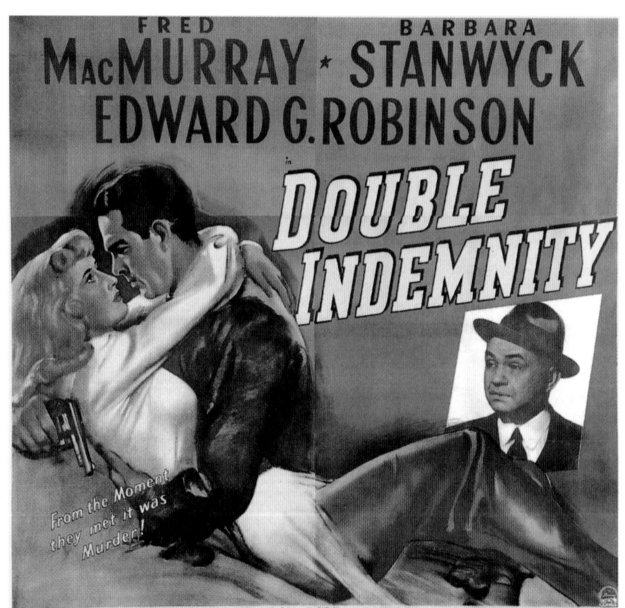

Filmography

Mauvaise Graine *(1934, Bad Seed)*
Crew: *Directors* Billy Wilder & Alexander Esway, *Producers* Edouard Corniglion-Molinier & Georges Bernier, *Writers* Billy Wilder, Max Kolpe, Hans G. Lustig & Claude-Andre Puget, B&W, 77 minutes.
Cast: Danielle Darrieux (Jeanette), Pierre Mingand (Henri).
Mauvaise Graine is a drama about an idle young man looking for fun who becomes a car thief to escape his father's threat of a desk job.

The Major and the Minor *(1942)*
Crew: *Director* Billy Wilder, *Producer* Arthur Hornblow, Jr., *Writers* Charles Brackett & Billy Wilder (screenplay), Edward Childs Carpenter & Fannie Kilbourne (story), B&W, 101 minutes.
Cast: Ginger Rogers (Susan Applegate), Ray Milland (Philip Kirby), Rita Johnson (Pamela), Diana Lynn (Lucy), Robert Benchley (Mr Osborne).
The Major and the Minor is a comedy of mistaken identity in which an out-of-work woman masquerades as a child to qualify for half-fare on a train; along the way she meets a captain from a boys' military school.

Five Graves to Cairo *(1943)*
Crew: *Director* Billy Wilder, *Producer* Charles Brackett, *Writers* Charles Brackett & Billy Wilder (screenplay), Lajos Biró (story), B&W, 97 minutes.
Cast: Franchot Tone (Bramble), Anne Baxter (Mouche), Erich von Stroheim (Rommel), Akim Tamiroff (Farid).
Five Graves to Cairo is spy story that updates the

play *Hotel Imperial* to the setting of North Africa during World War Two.

Double Indemnity *(1944)*
Crew: *Director* Billy Wilder, *Producer* Joseph Sistrom, *Writers* Billy Wilder & Raymond Chandler (screenplay), James M. Cain (story), B&W, 107 minutes.
Cast: Fred MacMurray (Walter Neff), Barbara Stanwyck (Phyllis Dietrichson), Edward G. Robinson (Barton Keyes).

Double Indemnity is a noir melodrama about an insurance man and his lover who conspire to kill her husband and defraud the insurance company.

The Lost Weekend *(1945)*
Crew: *Director* Billy Wilder, *Producer* Charles Brackett, *Writers* Charles Brackett & Billy Wilder (screenplay), Charles R. Jackson (story), B&W, 101 minutes.
Cast: Ray Milland (Don Birnam), Jane Wyman (Helen St James), Howard Da Silva (Nat).
The Lost Weekend is a realistic drama about a writer's struggle to stop drinking.

The Emperor Waltz *(1948)*
Crew: *Director* Billy Wilder, *Producer* Charles Brackett, *Writers* Charles Brackett & Billy Wilder, *Musical Score* Johnny Burke & Victor Young, 106 minutes.
Cast: Bing Crosby (Virgil Smith), Joan Fontaine (Countess Johanna), Richard Haydn (Emperor Franz-Josef), Roland Culver (Baron Holenia).
The Emperor Waltz is a musical comedy about an American phonograph salesman in 1906 Europe who falls in love with a countess.

A Foreign Affair *(1948)*
Crew: *Director* Billy Wilder, *Producer* Charles Brackett, *Writers* Charles Brackett, Billy Wilder & Richard L. Breen (screenplay), David and Irwin Shaw (story), B&W, 116 minutes.
Cast: Jean Arthur (Phoebe Frost), Marlene Dietrich

(Norma Desmond), Nancy Olson (Betty Shaefer), Erich von Stroheim (Max von Mayerling), Fred Clark (Sheldrake), Jack Webb (Artie), Cecil B. DeMille (himself), Buster Keaton (himself), Hedda Hopper (herself).

Sunset Boulevard is the tragic drama of a second-rate Hollywood scriptwriter's status as kept man for a faded silent film actress.

Ace in the Hole *(1951, The Big Carnival)*
Crew: *Director & Producer* Billy Wilder, **Writers** Walter Newman, Lesser Samuels & Billy Wilder, B&W, 111 minutes.
Cast: Kirk Douglas (Chuck Tatum), Jan Sterling (Lorraine), Porter Hall (Mr Boot), Bob Arthur (Herbie), Richard Benedict (Leo), Ray Teal (the sheriff).

Ace in the Hole is the tragic drama of a cynical news reporter's efforts to reap big headlines by delaying the rescue of a man trapped in a cave.

Stalag 17 *(1953)*
Crew: *Director & Producer* Billy Wilder, **Writers** Billy Wilder & Edward Blum (screenplay), Donald Bevan & Edmund Trzcinski (story), B&W, 120 minutes.
Cast: William Holden (Sefton), Don Taylor (Dunbar), Otto Preminger (von Scherbach), Peter Graves (Price), Sig Ruman (Schulz).

(Erika von Schlüetow), John Lund (Pringle), Millard Mitchell (Plummer).

A Foreign Affair dramatizes the visit of an American congresswoman to post-war Berlin where she falls in love with the American colonel who is shielding a German woman from official investigation.

Sunset Boulevard *(1950)*
Crew: *Director* Billy Wilder, *Producer* Charles Brackett, **Writers** Charles Brackett, Billy Wilder & D. M. Marshman, Jr., B&W, 110 minutes.
Cast: William Holden (Joe Gillis), Gloria Swanson

Stalag 17 is a World War Two prisoner-of-war drama about the tribulations of a man wrongly thought by his fellow American prisoners to be a German spy.

Sabrina *(1954, Sabrina Fair)*

Crew: *Director & Producer* Billy Wilder, *Writers* Billy Wilder & Ernest Lehman (screenplay), Samuel Taylor (story), B&W, 113 minutes.
Cast: Audrey Hepburn (Sabrina Fairchild), Humphrey Bogart (Linus Larrabee), William Holden (David Larrabee), John Williams (Fairchild), Marcel Dalio (the baron), Ellen Corby (Mrs McCardle).
Sabrina is a romantic comedy about a chauffeur's daughter and her shifting affections for two wealthy brothers.

The Seven Year Itch *(1955)*

Crew: *Director* Billy Wilder, *Producers* Charles K. Feldman & Billy Wilder, *Writers* Billy Wilder & George Axelrod (screenplay), George Axelrod (story), 105 minutes.
Cast: Marilyn Monroe (the girl), Tom Ewell (Richard Sherman), Evelyn Keyes (Helen Sherman).
The Seven Year Itch is a satiric comedy about a husband wrestling with his conscience over his attraction to an attractive neighbour during a hot New York summer.

The Spirit of St. Louis *(1957)*

Crew: *Director* Billy Wilder, *Producer* Leland Hayward, *Writers* Billy Wilder, Wendell Mayes & Charles Lederer (screenplay), Charles Lindbergh (story), 135 minutes.
Cast: James Stewart (Charles Lindbergh), Murray Hamilton (Bud Gurney), Marc Connelly (Father Hussman).
The Spirit of St. Louis is a biographical drama about Charles Lindbergh's transatlantic flight.

Love in the Afternoon (1957, Ariane)

Crew: *Director & Producer* Billy Wilder, *Writers* Billy Wilder & I. A. L. Diamond (screenplay), Claude Anet (story), B&W, 125 minutes.
Cast: Gary Cooper (Frank Flannagan), Audrey Hepburn (Ariane Chevasse), Maurice Chevalier (Claude Chevasse), John McGiver (Mr X).
Love in the Afternoon is a romantic comedy about a girl's fascination for an American playboy whose romantic exploits she first learns about from her detective father.

Witness for the Prosecution (1957)

Crew: *Director* Billy Wilder, *Producers* Arthur Hornblow, Jr. & Edward Small, *Writers* Billy Wilder, Harry Kurnitz & Larry Marcus (screenplay), Agatha Christie (story), B&W, 116 minutes.
Cast: Tyrone Power (Leonard Vole), Charles Laughton (Sir Wilfrid Robarts), Marlene Dietrich (Christine Vole), Elsa Lanchester (Miss Plimsoll).
Witness for the Prosecution is a courtroom who-

dunit about a man accused of murder whose wife unexpectedly testifies against him.

Some Like It Hot (1959)

Crew: *Director & Producer* Billy Wilder, *Writers* Billy Wilder & I. A. L. Diamond (screenplay), Robert Thoeren & M. Logan (story), B&W, 120 minutes.
Cast: Marilyn Monroe (Sugar Kane), Tony Curtis (Joe), Jack Lemmon (Jerry), George Raft (Spats Columbo), Joe E. Brown (Osgood Fielding), Pat O'Brien (Mulligan).
Some Like It Hot is a farce about two musicians in Prohibition Chicago who witness the St Valentine's Day Massacre, disguise themselves as women, and take jobs in an all-girl band travelling to Florida to elude the gangsters.

The Apartment *(1960)*

Crew: *Director & Producer* Billy Wilder,
Writers Billy Wilder & I. A. L. Diamond, B&W,
125 minutes.
Cast: Jack Lemmon (Bud Baxter), Shirley MacLaine
(Fran Kubelik), Fred MacMurray (J. D. Sheldrake),
Jack Kruschen (Dr Dreyfuss),
Ray Walston (Dobisch).
The Apartment is a bittersweet comedy-drama
about a corporate worker who lets his married
superiors use his apartment for their trysts and
who learns that the woman he loves is also his
boss' current girlfriend.

One, Two, Three *(1961)*

Crew: *Director & Producer* Billy Wilder,
Writers Billy Wilder & I. A. L. Diamond (screen-
play), Ferenc Molnár (story), B&W, 115 minutes.
Cast: James Cagney (MacNamara), Horst Buchholz
(Otto Piffl), Pamela Tiffin (Scarlett Hazeltine),
Arlene Francis (Phyllis MacNamara).
One, Two, Three is a fast-paced farce set in Cold
War Berlin about the frustrations of a Coca-Cola
executive who seeks a promotion to London.

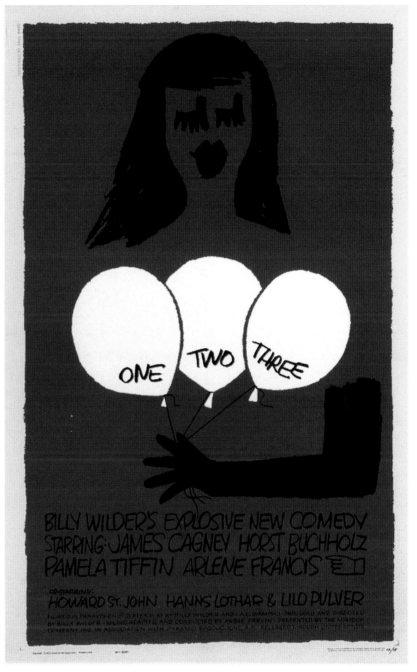

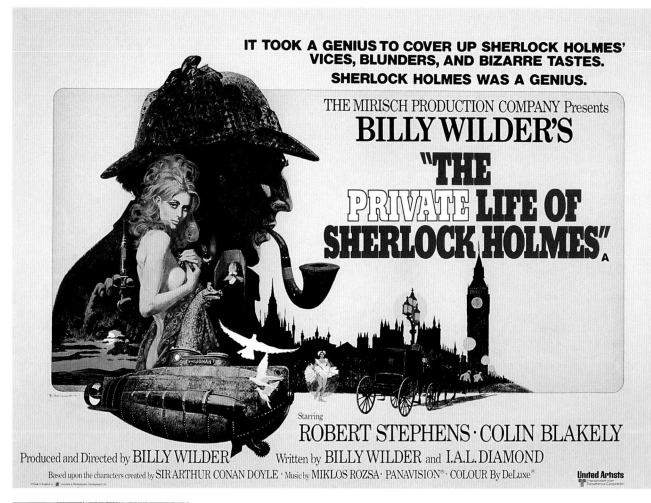

IT TOOK A GENIUS TO COVER UP SHERLOCK HOLMES' VICES, BLUNDERS, AND BIZARRE TASTES. SHERLOCK HOLMES WAS A GENIUS.

THE MIRISCH PRODUCTION COMPANY Presents

BILLY WILDER'S

"THE PRIVATE LIFE OF SHERLOCK HOLMES" A

Starring

ROBERT STEPHENS · COLIN BLAKELY

Produced and Directed by BILLY WILDER   Written by BILLY WILDER and I.A.L. DIAMOND

Based upon the characters created by SIR ARTHUR CONAN DOYLE · Music by MIKLOS ROZSA · PANAVISION® · COLOUR By DeLuxe®

United Artists

Irma la Douce (1963)

Crew: *Director & Producer* Billy Wilder, *Writers* Billy Wilder & I. A. L. Diamond (screenplay), Alexandre Breffort (story), 147 minutes. Cast: Jack Lemmon (Nestor), Shirley MacLaine (Irma), Lou Jacobi (Moustache), Bruce Yarnell (Hippolyte).

Irma la Douce is a comedy about a Parisian policeman and his prostitute lover, and the complications that result when he jealously disguises himself as customers to keep her from other men.

Kiss Me, Stupid (1964)

Crew: *Director & Producer* Billy Wilder, *Writers* Billy Wilder & I.A.L. Diamond (screenplay), Anna Bonacci (story), B&W, 124 minutes. Cast: Dean Martin (Dino), Kim Novak (Polly the Pistol), Ray Walston (Orville J. Spooner), Felicia Farr (Zelda), Cliff Osmond (Barney Millsap).

Kiss Me, Stupid is a dark comedy about two would-be songwriters who desperately try to interest a Las Vegas singer in their material – even if it means plying him with a woman for a night.

The Fortune Cookie (1966)

Crew: *Director & Producer* Billy Wilder, *Writers* Billy Wilder & I. A. L. Diamond, B&W, 126 minutes.

Cast: Jack Lemmon (Harry Hinkle), Walter Matthau (Willie Gingrich), Ron Rich (Boom Boom Jackson), Judi West (Sandy), Cliff Osmond (Purkey).

The Fortune Cookie satirizes the greed of a shyster lawyer who talks his brother-in-law into faking injuries to swindle an insurance company in the hope that the money will make him attractive to his ex-wife.

The Private Life of Sherlock Holmes (1970)

Crew: *Director & Producer* Billy Wilder, *Writers* Billy Wilder & I. A. L. Diamond, 125 minutes.

Cast: Robert Stephens (Sherlock Holmes), Colin Blakely (Dr Watson), Genevieve Page (Gabrielle Valladon), Christopher Lee (Mycroft Holmes).

The Private Life of Sherlock Holmes concerns the cases of the great detective initially suppressed by Dr Watson to avoid scandal.

Avanti! (1972)

Crew: *Director & Producer* Billy Wilder, *Writers* Billy Wilder & I. A. L. Diamond (screenplay), Samuel Taylor (story), 145 minutes.

Cast: Jack Lemmon (Wendell Armbruster III), Juliet Mills (Pamela Piggott), Clive Revill (Carlo Carlucci).

Avanti! is a comedy-drama about a man and a woman who meet in Ischia to claim the bodies of their parents, who were secret lovers.

The Front Page (1974)

Crew: *Director* Billy Wilder, *Producers* Jennings Lang & Paul Monash, *Writers* Billy Wilder &

I. A. L. Diamond (screenplay), Ben Hecht & Charles MacArthur (story), 105 minutes.

Cast: Jack Lemmon (Hildy Johnson), Walter Matthau (Walter Burns), Susan Sarandon (Peggy Grant), Carol Burnett (Mollie Malloy).

The Front Page is a fast-paced comedy set in 1929 Chicago about a ruthless newspaper editor who schemes to keep his best reporter from marrying and leaving the paper – especially on the eve of a sensational hanging.

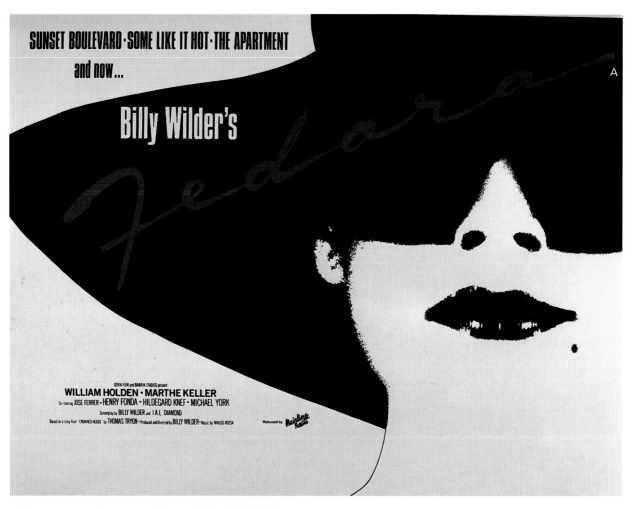

SUNSET BOULEVARD·SOME LIKE IT HOT·THE APARTMENT

and now...

Billy Wilder's

Fedora

GERIA FILM and BAVARIA STUDIOS present

WILLIAM HOLDEN · MARTHE KELLER

Co-starring JOSE FERRER · HENRY FONDA · HILDEGARD KNEF · MICHAEL YORK

Screenplay by BILLY WILDER and I.A.L. DIAMOND

Based on a story from "CROWNED HEADS" by THOMAS TRYON · Produced and Directed by BILLY WILDER · Music by MIKLOS ROZSA

Released by Mainline Pictures

A

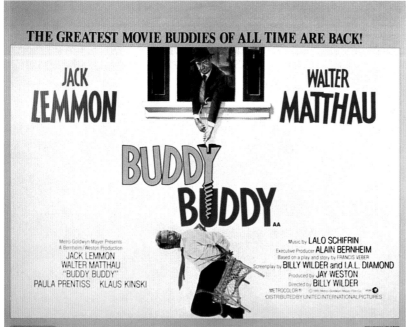

THE GREATEST MOVIE BUDDIES OF ALL TIME ARE BACK!

Fedora *(1978)*

Crew: *Director & Producer* Billy Wilder,
Writers Billy Wilder & I.A.L. Diamond (screenplay), Tom Tryon (story), 113 minutes.
Cast: William Holden (Barry Detweiler), Marthe
Keller (Fedora), Hildegard Knef (Countess Sobryanski), Jose Ferrer (Dr Vando), Henry Fonda (president
of the Academy), Michael York (himself).
Fedora is a wistful drama that explains in many
flashbacks the background and mysterious death of
a Garboesque film star.

Buddy Buddy *(1981)*

Crew: *Director* Billy Wilder, *Producer* Jay Weston,
Writers Billy Wilder & I.A.L. Diamond (screenplay), Francis Veber (story), 96 minutes.
Cast: Walter Matthau (Trabucco), Jack Lemmon
(Victor Clooney), Paula Prentiss (Celia Clooney),
Klaus Kinski (Dr Zuckerbrot).
Buddy Buddy is a black comedy about a hit man
lining up a kill shot from a hotel window who is
plagued by the intrusions of the man in the next
room, a suicidal television censor whose wife has
left him.

Bibliography

Billy Wilder and His Films

— Armstrong, Richard: *Billy Wilder, American Film Realist.* North Carolina 2000
— Barnett, Lincoln: 'The Happiest Couple in Hollywood: Brackett and Wilder.' *Life* 11 December 1944
— Brackett, Charles, Billy Wilder, and Walter Reisch: *Ninotchka.* New York 1972
— Castle, Alison, (ed.): *Billy Wilder's Some Like It Hot.* Cologne 2001
— Chandler, Charlotte: *Nobody's Perfect.* New York 2002
— Ciment, Michel: 'Entretien avec Billy Wilder.' *Positif* July/August 1983
— Columbus, Chris: 'Wilder Times.' *American Film* March 1986
— Crowe, Cameron: *Conversations with Wilder.* New York 1999
— Dick, Bernard F.: *Billy Wilder.* New York 1996
— Didion, Joan: 'Kiss Me, Stupid: A Minority Report.' *Vogue* 1 March 1965
— Dunne, John Gregory: 'The Old Pornographer.' *The New Yorker* 8 November 1999
— Farber, Stephen: 'The Films of Billy Wilder.' *Film Comment* Winter 1971
— Hopp, Glenn: *Billy Wilder.* Harpenden 2001
— Karasek, Hellmuth: *Billy Wilder: eine Nahaufnahme.* Hamburg 1992
— Lally, Kevin: *Wilder Times. The Life of Billy Wilder.* New York 1996
— Madsen, Axel: *Billy Wilder.* Indiana 1969
— Meyers, Jeffrey, (ed.): *Double Indemnity.* Univ. of California 2000
— Meyers, Jeffrey, (ed.): *The Lost Weekend.* Univ. of California 2000
— Meyers, Jeffrey, (ed.): *Stalag 17.* Univ. of California 1999
— Meyers, Jeffrey, (ed.): *Sunset Boulevard.* Univ. of California 1999
— Morris, George: 'The Private Films of Billy Wilder.' *Film Comment* January/February 1979
— Poague, Leland: *The Hollywood Professionals. Wilder and McCarey.* London 1980
— Sarris, Andrew: 'Some Like It Not.' *Village Voice* 16 April 1979
— Sarris, Andrew: 'Why Billy Wilder Belongs in the Pantheon.' *Film Comment* July/August 1991
— Schickel, Richard: *Double Indemnity.* London 1992
— Seidman, Steve: *The Film Career of Billy Wilder.* New York 1977
— Sikov, Ed: *On Sunset Boulevard. The Life and Times of Billy Wilder.* New York 1998
— Sinyard, Neil & Turner, Adrian: *Journey Down Sunset Boulevard. The Films of Billy Wilder.* Isle of Wight 1979
— Wilder, Billy & Diamond, I. A. L.: *Two Screenplays. The Apartment and The Fortune Cookie.* New York 1971
— Zolotow, Maurice: *Billy Wilder in Hollywood.* New York 1987

Paramount, Hollywood and the Movies

— Bogdanovich, Peter: *Who the Devil Made It?* New York 1997
— Chierichetti, David: *Hollywood Director. The Career of Mitchell Leisen.* New York 1973
— Dick, Bernard F.: *Engulfed. The Death of Paramount Pictures and the Birth of Corporate Hollywood.* Kentucky 2001
— Eames, John Douglas: *The Paramount Story.* New York 1985
— Ebert, Roger: *The Great Movies.* New York 2002
— Eyman, Scott: *Ernst Lubitsch. Laughter in Paradise.* New York 1993
— Friedrich, Otto: *City of Nets. A Portrait of Hollywood in the 1940s.* New York 1986
— Fox, Ken & the editors at CineBooks: *The Virgin Film Guide.* London 1998
— Giannetti, Louis: 'Hustling: The Cinema of Billy Wilder.' *Masters of the American Cinema.* New Jersey 1981
— Giannetti, Louis: *Understanding Movies.* New Jersey 2001
— Giannetti, Louis & Eyman, Scott: *Flashback. A Brief History of Film.* New Jersey 1996
— Harvey, James: *Romantic Comedy. From Lubitsch to Sturges.* New York 1987
— Kendall, Elizabeth: *The Runaway Bride. Hollywood Romantic Comedy of the 1930s.* New York 1990
— Leff, Leonard & Simmons, Jerold L.: *The Dame in the Kimono. Hollywood, Censorship and the Production Code from the 1920s to the 1960s.* London 1990
— Lennig, Arthur: *Stroheim.* Kentucky 2000
— McBride Joseph: *Steven Spielberg. A Biography.* New York 1997
— Paul, William: *Ernst Lubitsch's American Comedy.* New York 1983
— Schatz, Thomas: *The Genius of the System. Hollywood Filmmaking in the Studio Era.* New York 1988
— Schickel, Richard: *The Men Who Made the Movies.* New York 1975
— Sikov, Ed: *Laughing Hysterically. American Screen Comedy of the 1950s.* New York 1994
— Sikov, Ed: *Screwball. Hollywood's Madcap Romantic Comedies.* New York 1989
— Svetkey, Benjamin: 'Who Killed the Hollywood Screenplay?' *Entertainment Weekly* 4 October 1996

Notes

1. *Halliwell's Filmgoer's Companion*
2. Columbus, Chris: 'Wilder Times.' *American Film,* March 1986
3. Crowe, Cameron: *Conversations with Wilder.* New York 1999
4. Stuart, Mel, director: *Billy Wilder: The Human Comedy.* 1998
5. *American Masters*
6. Freeman, David: 'Sunset Boulevard Revisited.' *The New Yorker,* 21 June 1993
7. *Speech, Producers Guild of America,* 1997

PAGE 192
Audrey and Billy Wilder (1985)
Photo by Helmut Newton for 'Vanity Fair'.